V. F. PERKINS ON MOVIES

Contemporary Film and Media Series

Series Editor

Barry Keith Grant
Brock University

A complete listing of the advisory editors and the books in this series can be found online at wsupress.wayne.edu.

Praise for *V. F. Perkins on Movies*

"Victor Perkins carved a unique path as a film critic. He was neither a reviewer nor a reporter; neither a polemical iconoclast nor a follower of academic fashion. His aim was clear, true, and steadfastly maintained: to understand the art of film, and the work of its finest artists, better."

—Adrian Martin, film critic

"The idea of gathering all of Perkins's shorter pieces into one volume is excellent. In my judgment, he is one of the absolutely indispensable critics of film. He was a legendary teacher, and all his criticism has the capacity to educate even sophisticated filmgoers in how to think more cogently about movie art as moral and emotional experience, and how to read films with greater precision and discrimination. Douglas Pye has provided a valuable overview of the phases of Perkins's career and offers a first-rate assessment of his major preoccupations and strengths."

—George Toles, University of Manitoba

"Since film studies became an academic field, no one has attended to movies with more care and insight than Victor Perkins, and no one has so inspiringly and effectively taught several generations of students and readers to attempt the same. The full range of his achievement is on view in *V. F. Perkins on Movies*, from his theoretical work to his critical studies. Anyone with any sort of interest in film owes a great debt of gratitude to Douglas Pye for making these powerful essays accessible."

—Robert B. Pippin, The University of Chicago

"Douglas Pye has performed a great service by putting together this indispensable collection of V. F. Perkins's writings and introducing it so eloquently. The tyrannical reign of theoretical systematizing, which for decades led academic film studies to subordinate criticism to what the field called 'theory,' has ended. But to move forward, the field must now visit its origins and history. Victor Perkins, perhaps the most brilliant, the most rigorous and perceptive writer of film criticism we have ever had, trusted the films he loved to teach him how to think about them, without letting some theory or other blind him to his own experience. He took the best popular movies to be exemplary of the art of film and stuck to his guns when academic film studies embraced a theoretical orthodoxy and it became dogma that the kind of movies Perkins wrote about were pernicious ideological constructs, not works of art to be valued. And he kept faith with his conviction that the study of film cannot be a worthwhile human enterprise if it isolates itself from the kind of criticism that seeks to articulate a work's idea—not a thought lying behind the work, but a thought the work expresses, in its own way, in its own medium—the kind of criticism Perkins never stopped writing—the kind of criticism whose value it is now more than ever incumbent upon the field to acknowledge."

—William Rothman, professor of cinematic arts at the University of Miami

V. F. PERKINS ON MOVIES

COLLECTED SHORTER FILM CRITICISM

EDITED BY
DOUGLAS PYE
Assistant Editor: Edward Lamberti

EDITORIAL ADVISORY GROUP
Edward Gallafent
John Gibbs
Andrew Klevan
James MacDowell
Polly Perkins

© 2020 by Wayne State University Press, Detroit, Michigan 48201. All rights reserved. No part of this book may be reproduced without formal permission.

ISBN 978-0-8143-4643-3 (paperback)
ISBN 978-0-8143-4642-6 (hardback)
ISBN 978-0-8143-4644-0 (ebook)

Library of Congress Control Number: 2020943886

All texts from *Movie* (1962–2000), *The Movie Book of Film Noir* (1992), and *The Movie Book of the Western* (1996) © Cameron & Hollis, www.cameronandhollis.uk.

Wayne State University Press
Leonard N. Simons Building
4809 Woodward Avenue
Detroit, Michigan 48201-1309

Visit us online at wsupress.wayne.edu

CONTENTS

Foreword by George M. Wilson   ix
Acknowledgments   xi

Introduction by Douglas Pye   1

1: 1960–1972—*Oxford Opinion* and *Movie*: The Battle for a New Criticism

The British Cinema and British Film Criticism

Fifty Famous Films 1915–45 (1960)	25
The British Cinema (On Behalf of the Editorial Board) (1962)	34
Clive Donner and *Some People* (1962)	51
Censorship (1963)	61
Forced to Be Free or Doing Business in a Great Art (1968)	64
Supporting the British Cinema (1969)	74

Developing a Detailed Criticism

Nicholas Ray (1960)	87
Charm and Blood (1960)	96
Words and Music: Two Recent Cukor Films (1960)	102

King of Kings (1962)	107
Why Preminger? (1962)	112
The Man with the Golden Arm (1962)	114
River of No Return (1962)	116
Merrill's Marauders (1962)	122
An Important Re-Release: George Stevens' *Giant* (1962)	126
Un-American Activities (1962)	130
Hawks Comedies (1962)	139
Hatari! (1962)	145
Rope (1963)	151
The Cinema of Nicholas Ray (1963)	162
55 Days at Peking (1963)	178
Cheyenne Autumn (1965)	184
Vivre sa vie (1967)	189
America America (1972)	197

2: 1981–2016

Film Criticism: Principles and Practice

Moments of Choice (1981)	209
Film Authorship: The Premature Burial (1990)	220
Must We Say What They Mean?: Film Criticism and Interpretation (1990)	240
The Atlantic Divide (1992)	257
Where Is the World?: The Horizon of Events in Movie Fiction (2005)	270
Acting on Objects (2013)	301

Directors and Movies

Letter from an Unknown Woman (On the Linz Sequence) (1982)	311
In a Lonely Place (1992)	334
Johnny Guitar (1996)	350
I Confess: Photographs of People Speaking (2000)	365
Ophuls contra Wagner and Others (2000)	392
"Same Tune Again!": Repetition and Framing in *Letter from an Unknown Woman* (2000)	408
Le Plaisir: "The Mask" and "The Model" (2009)	429
Le Plaisir: "La Maison Tellier" (2009)	442
Scarlet, No Empress (2011)	451
You Only Live Once (2012)	459
Omission and Oversight in Close Reading: The Final Moments of Frederick Wiseman's *High School* (2017)	477
Index	495

FOREWORD

George M. Wilson

No one writing on film since I became interested in the area has had the impact on me and on my work that Victor Perkins has had. No one has been even close in the extent of their influence and inspiration.

When I first read Victor's *Film as Film*, its effect on me was enormous. I was fascinated by what he had to say in the various chapters of the book but I was also captivated by the fact that the author of this terrific book wrote with perfect clarity, grace, and rhetorical force. I was much struck that someone could write in an utterly intelligible way on questions of the most probing and systematic aesthetic interest. I had read a number of the notable French critics of the period, and I was quite taken by much of their work. However, none of them—and no one else at that time or later—wrote with the exemplary depth and lucidity that I found in Victor's writing. I went on from *Film as Film* to read a range of Victor's film criticism, and I was also led to read a lot of the essays by the best contributors to *Movie*. These authors, and Victor especially, constituted the models I adopted as I began to write and teach in film.

Several years later, I published my first film book, *Narration in Light* (1986). The book did not sell a lot of copies, and, during the period in question, I think I never even saw it in a bookstore. Then I received a letter from Victor, and it explained at gracious length why he liked my book a lot. I had never received a commentary on any of my work that pleased me so much and that I valued as highly as this unexpected letter, and in all the time since it arrived, I have never been more pleased than I was by his generous remarks. I believe that it is pretty rare to get a strongly supportive letter from someone you have never met, but who has from long distance crucially shaped your own thinking about the fundamental area of research in question. I was simply thrilled, and it was his support at this juncture, more than anything else, that encouraged me to continue writing on film.

A few years later, we finally did meet in person, and our friendship was deepened by the personal contact. Meeting him several times in Britain and the United States, I came to learn that he was one of the kindest and most generous people I had ever met. He was also one of the wittiest and funniest. Over the years, we searched for lost film sites in San Francisco, following in the footsteps of Alfred Hitchcock, spotted swans in Stratford, admired Warwick Castle by moonlight, explored the ruins of Coventry Cathedral and, most recently, wandered the shores of Lake Windermere, all the time with Victor attired in his usual coat, tie, and V-neck sweater. We miss him.

I warmly welcome this collection of Victor's shorter writing. The volume is in itself a fitting tribute and a rich addition to the literature of film. Taking its place alongside his monographs, its publication also enables readers to access the whole of Victor's film criticism in book form for the first time and more readily to appreciate his remarkable achievements. It is an indispensable body of work for anyone with a serious interest in film.

ACKNOWLEDGMENTS

When Polly Perkins, Victor's daughter and literary executor, convened a group of friends and colleagues to consider his legacy, a volume of his uncollected film criticism became a major objective, and Wayne State University Press, publishers of *Britton on Film* and new editions of Robin Wood's work, was the logical publisher to approach. Barry K. Grant, editor of their series Contemporary Approaches to Film and Media, was immediately enthusiastic and has been the source of invaluable support and guidance throughout the book's evolution. Annie Martin, acquisitions editor at the press when the project began, and her successor, Marie Sweetman, have been unfailingly encouraging and helpful. I am also grateful for the advice of their colleague Ceylan Akturk. It has been a pleasure to work closely with Ed Lamberti, who crucially kept track of the various stages of the book's development and assembled the contents, as well as sharing many of the detailed editorial tasks; his meticulous work has been indispensable. The Editorial Advisory Group guided the decisions about the shape of the volume and have been the guardian angels of the project as it developed, contributing advice and help whenever it was needed. Polly's total commitment, on behalf of Victor's estate, has been an inspiration throughout.

The book would not have been possible without the generous permission of the publishers of journals and books in which the articles and chapters first appeared. We owe special thanks to Cameron and Hollis, publishers of *Movie* and the *Movie* books for which Victor wrote most of his work.

CineAction

"Film Authorship: The Premature Burial," *CineAction!*, nos. 20–21 (Summer/Fall 1990): 57–64.
"*I Confess*: Photographs of People Speaking," *CineAction*, no. 52 (June 2000): 28–39.
"'Same Tune Again!': Repetition and Framing in *Letter from an Unknown Woman*," *CineAction*, no. 52 (June 2000): 40–48.

The Cine-Files

"Acting on Objects," *The Cine-Files: A Scholarly Journal of Cinema Studies*, no. 4 (Spring 2013): http://www.thecine-files.com/current-issue-2/guest-scholars/v-f-perkins/ (accessed June 1, 2020).

Film Quarterly

"*Le Plaisir*: 'The Mask' and 'The Model,'" *Film Quarterly* 63, no. 1 (2009): 15–22. © 2009 by the Regents of the University of California. Published by the University of California Press.
"*Le Plaisir*: 'La Maison Tellier,'" *Film Quarterly* 63, no. 2 (2009): 66–71. © 2009 by the Regents of the University of California. Published by the University of California Press.
"Scarlet, No Empress," *Film Quarterly* 65, no. 2 (2011): 28–31. © 2011 by the Regents of the University of California. Published by the University of California Press.

Manchester University Press

"Where Is the World?: The Horizon of Events in Movie Fiction," in *Style and Meaning: Studies in the Detailed Analysis of Film*, edited by John Gibbs and Douglas Pye, 16–41. Manchester: Manchester University Press, 2005.

Movie

"The British Cinema (On Behalf of the Editorial Board)," *Movie*, no. 1 (June 1962): 2–7.
"Clive Donner and *Some People*," *Movie*, no. 3 (October 1962): 22–25.
"Censorship," *Movie*, no. 6 (January 1963): 16.
"Forced to be Free or Doing Business in a Great Art," *Movie*, no. 15 (Spring 1968): 17–19.

"Supporting the British Cinema," *Movie*, no. 16 (Winter 1968–69): 13–15.
"*King of Kings*," *Movie*, no. 1 (June 1962): 29–30.
"Why Preminger?," *Movie*, no. 2 (September 1962): 11.
"*The Man with the Golden Arm*," *Movie*, no. 2 (September 1962): 20.
"*River of No Return*," *Movie*, no. 2 (September 1962): 18–19.
"*Merrill's Marauders*," *Movie*, no. 2 (September 1962): 32.
"An Important Re-Release: George Stevens' *Giant*," *Movie*, no. 4 (November 1962): 33.
"Un-American Activities," *Movie*, no. 5 (December 1962): 3–6.
"Hawks Comedies," *Movie*, no. 5 (December 1962): 21–22.
"*Hatari!*," *Movie*, no. 5 (December 1962): 28–30.
"*Rope*," *Movie*, no. 7 (February 1963): 11–13.
"The Cinema of Nicholas Ray," *Movie*, no. 9 (May 1963): 4–10.
"*55 Days at Peking*," *Movie*, no. 11 (July/August 1963): 4–6.
"*Cheyenne Autumn*," *Movie*, no. 12 (Spring 1965): 36–37.
"*America America*," *Movie*, no. 19 (Winter 1971–72): 35–38.
"*Letter from an Unknown Woman* (On the Linz Sequence)," *Movie*, nos. 29–30 (Summer 1982): 61–72.
"Must We Say What They Mean?: Film Criticism and Interpretation," *Movie*, nos. 34–35 (Winter 1990): 1–6.
"Ophuls contra Wagner and Others," *Movie*, no. 36 (January 2000): 73–79.

Movie Books

"*Vivre sa vie*," in *The Films of Jean-Luc Godard*, rev. ed., edited by Ian Cameron, 32–39. London: Studio Vista, [1967] 1969.
"*In a Lonely Place*," in *The Movie Book of Film Noir*, edited by Ian Cameron, 222–31. London: Studio Vista, 1992.
"*Johnny Guitar*," in *The Movie Book of the Western*, edited by Ian Cameron and Douglas Pye, 221–28. London: Studio Vista, 1996.

Movie: A Journal of Film Criticism

"*You Only Live Once*," *Movie: A Journal of Film Criticism*, no. 3 (January 2012): 12–21. https://warwick.ac.uk/fac/arts/film/movie/contents/you_only_live_once_final_3.pdf (accessed June 1, 2020).

The Movie

"Moments of Choice," *The Movie*, no. 58 (1981): 1141–45.

Oxford Opinion

"Fifty Famous Films 1915–45," *Oxford Opinion*, April 30, 1960, 36–37.
"Nicholas Ray," *Oxford Opinion*, June 14, 1960, 31–34.
"Charm and Blood," *Oxford Opinion*, October 25, 1960, 34–35.
"Words and Music: Two Recent Cukor Films," *Oxford Opinion*, November 1960, 26–27.

Routledge

"The Atlantic Divide," in *Popular European Cinema*, edited by Richard Dyer and Ginette Vincendeau, 194–205. New York: Routledge, 1992.

Rowman & Littlefield

"Omission and Oversight in Close Reading: The Final Moments of Frederick Wiseman's *High School*," in *The Philosophy of Documentary Film*, edited by David LaRocca, 381–94. Lanham, MD: Rowman & Littlefield, 2017.

INTRODUCTION

Douglas Pye

This volume brings together the shorter criticism of one of the most brilliant of English-language film critics. Victor Perkins (1936–2016) was a foundational figure for the study of film both as a writer and as an educationalist and teacher who played a key role in establishing film within British higher education. Best known for his remarkable 1972 book *Film as Film*, Perkins has a worldwide reputation as a critic and theorist, a reputation which has been enhanced in recent years by a renewed interest among emerging scholars in the practices of detailed film criticism. Much of his shorter writing, spanning a career of almost sixty years, is less well known, despite its importance and quality, partly because it was published in small magazines with limited distribution. In particular, his early articles have long been largely unavailable to all those without access to the most specialist libraries. Making the uncollected criticism fully accessible for the first time makes it possible to see Perkins's books and essays as a coherent body of work and to appreciate both its historical significance and its contemporary relevance. This collection gives unimpeded access to one of the most distinctive and distinguished of critical voices.

Perkins was one of the small group of British writers who argued for a detailed and systematic film criticism and pioneered serious engagement with the achievements of Hollywood filmmakers. Beginning at the University of Oxford in the pages of *Oxford Opinion*, and then in *Movie*, the journal they established in 1962, they mounted a critique of prevailing taste and method as represented by the journal *Sight and Sound* and other publications of the British Film Institute (BFI), as well as of contemporary British cinema, which they compared unfavorably to the achievements of Hollywood.[1] Perkins and his colleagues played a crucial role in changing cultural attitudes to popular cinema in the 1960s and beyond.[2]

The early articles in part 1 of this volume, which covers the years 1960–72, are highly polemical, but they begin to articulate ways of thinking about criticism and movies that remained with Perkins throughout his career. In the first of his contributions to the film section of *Oxford Opinion*, a response to a BFI publication, *Fifty Famous Films, 1915–1945*, he writes: "Nowhere is there the slightest sign of the detailed, academic criticism which one might reasonably expect to find in a publication of this sort and from this source. If films are not to be subjected to close and intelligent study in the [BFI] National Film Archive, then there is little hope that they will be so anywhere else." A criticism rooted in the detailed decisions that make up the complex texture of a film became the central aim of *Movie* and remained fundamental to Perkins's work.[3] Instead of this careful, detailed analysis, Perkins argues, in *Fifty Famous Films* we are offered in most cases "a plot synopsis, a short account of the careers of people connected with the making of the film, details of production costs and hazards . . . and pious liberal sentiments." For Perkins and the other writers in *Oxford Opinion* and *Movie*, a criticism responsive to film style—not only to liberal sentiments, plot, or subject matter—was crucial to creating a climate of opinion that would recognize and praise genuine cinematic achievement—"talent" in the word that rings through Perkins's early writing.

In "The British Cinema," the sustained critique that Perkins wrote on behalf of the editorial board in the first issue of *Movie*, it was talent that was found conspicuously lacking. Of the British New Wave in the late 1950s and early 1960s, he writes:

> All we can see is a change of attitude, which disguises the fact that the British cinema is as dead as before. Perhaps it was never alive. Our films have improved, if at all, only in their intentions.

> We are still unable to find evidence of artistic sensibilities in working order. There is as much genuine personality in *Room at the Top* (1959), method in *A Kind of Loving* (1962) and style in *A Taste of Honey* (1961) as there is wit in *An Alligator Named Daisy* (1955), intelligence in *Above Us the Waves* (1955) and ambition in *Ramsbottom Rides Again* (1956).

A good deal of evidence is marshaled in support of this assault on films and directors that had in some cases been extensively praised elsewhere. Notably, it is through indicative detail that Perkins locates the "ambitious clumsiness of style," tendency to "sacrifice . . . everything to impact," and inability to integrate character with place that are among what he identifies as the films' crippling weaknesses. The targets here are filmmakers, but the criteria closely parallel those used in the response to *Fifty Famous Films*: a failure to engage with film style on the part of the writers; a failure of film style in the work of the directors; a preoccupation with liberal values and "positive affirmations of life" in the booklet; preconceptions about what a filmmaker *ought* to do governing the films. Perkins writes: "It is at this point that the beliefs behind the old and the new British films meet. Each is based on a preconception of the sort of film that ought to be made, whether it's a 'good story well told' or 'a long, hard look at the well-springs of the human condition as it displays itself in the grind of living.'" As against this, he sets examples of Hollywood directors who had also worked in British conditions—he cites Robert Aldrich's *The Angry Hills* (1959), Leo McCarey's *The Devil Never Sleeps* (1962), Howard Hawks's *Land of the Pharaohs* (1955), Nicholas Ray's *The Savage Innocents* (1960), Hugo Fregonese's *Harry Black* (1958), and Jacques Tourneur's *Night of the Demon* (1957). Of the latter, Perkins writes, "On a limited budget, with a script little better than that of the average horror picture, and in spite of some awful effects work, a director of no prestige but enormous talent made one of the finest 'occult' movies we have ever seen."

A few British directors are also singled out as exceptions: Alexander Mackendrick and Robert Hamer, although neither was currently very active; and Seth Holt, whose film *Taste of Fear* (US title: *Scream of Fear*, 1961), although suffering from an "untranscendable" script, nevertheless "reveals time and again a director who can create cinematically, where other directors are content with illustrating their scripts." Most striking is the article "Clive Donner and *Some People*," Perkins's celebration of a movie that initially received limited distribution and which was ignored or dismissed by reviewers: "*Some People* (1962) is the most intelligent, honest and enjoyable picture from a British director since Seth Holt's *Nowhere to Go* (1958). But it is not simply a triumph in the context of British film-making, which would not be difficult to achieve; it is, by any standards, a very good movie. It has a less self-conscious, and therefore more genuine, freedom than any of the films of the so-called British New Wave." Such views were—and were in part intended to be—a provocation in their rejection of prevailing film criticism and widely praised contemporary films. More important, though, the appreciation of Donner's achievement in *Some People* is one significant example of what was involved in seeking out filmmakers who could "create cinematically"— looking beyond story, overt subject matter, production circumstances, and cultural status to how the film's dramatic material was given life through the material processes of film production. To invoke an old dichotomy, which became the focus of intense debate and controversy in response to *Oxford Opinion* and *Movie*, "form" could not be separated from "content": film form embodies and therefore shapes and gives significance to "content"—or, to cite the title of a chapter from *Film as Film*, "How Is What."[4]

The attack on British cinema could not have been much fiercer, but in addition to the aesthetic weaknesses and failures that were identified, there was also a recognition that the structures and institutions of the British film industry were not conducive to the cultivation of talent. Perkins wrote two lengthy articles on the industry—"Forced to be Free or Doing Business in a Great Art" and "Supporting the British Cinema"—and a shorter one on censorship; although these are not film criticism, we include them in this book to flesh out the contemporary context and to illustrate the concern of Perkins and *Movie* with the crucial relationship between the conditions of production and the films produced. Perkins's article "Censorship," on the British Board of Film Classification (BBFC) in the John Trevelyan era, provocatively worded as it is, also manages, through its plea for "a classifying, but not mutilating system of film censorship," to anticipate the direction in which the BBFC was indeed to move in the decades that followed, from a focus on censorship to one on classification, providing information to put viewers in the best position to decide what to watch. In "Forced to Be Free or Doing Business in a Great Art" and "Supporting the British Cinema," Perkins turned to broader though no less focused considerations of the tensions in the British film industry between filmmaking and commerce, between artistic ambition and funding decisions. His analyses demonstrated his acute awareness of the ways in which what audiences get to see is determined by a range of industrial factors.

From a position almost sixty years on, with film long established as an academic discipline and with ever-increasing levels of publication in film history, theory, and criticism, it can be very difficult to enter imaginatively into a context before any of that came about, and in which entrenched cultural attitudes in the English-speaking world decreed that mass culture ("Hollywood" was a prime example) was an industrial product that, with a few notable exceptions, could not achieve the status of art. A central objective of Perkins and the other *Oxford Opinion* and *Movie* writers was to challenge the art vs. commerce dichotomy. One of their great achievements was to view popular movies in ways apparently unimpeded by the prevailing cultural blinkers and to recognize aesthetic value in what had been overlooked or dismissed. A significant aspect of Perkins's own motivation in this respect, underpinned by his working-class background, related to class; in an interview with John Gibbs he recalled, "I understand that as relating to a desire (certainly on my part, I don't know how widely this understanding would be shared) to escape from class-based notions of taste, where understanding is related to the person rather than to the process" (Gibbs 2019).

This was also a period long before VHS, DVD, and the other technologies that have transformed access to the minutiae of decision-making in movies by allowing us to stop and start at will.[5] Even to aim at a detailed criticism when films could only be seen in theaters was hugely ambitious; to achieve the accuracy and perceptiveness that characterizes their work was extraordinary.[6]

In Perkins's writing, these qualities are most evident in the articles on Hollywood films and directors that make up the majority of his contributions to *Oxford Opinion* and *Movie* from 1960 to 1972. His discussions of directors such as Sam Fuller, Howard Hawks, Alfred Hitchcock (including the first serious appreciation of *Psycho* in English), Nicholas Ray, and Otto Preminger form a central part of the body of critical writing in these journals that introduced ways of thinking about their films that have influenced much subsequent work.[7] (In a later article Perkins made clear what he saw as decisive differences between his director-centered criticism and some influential "auteurist" approaches to Hollywood cinema. Readers who would find it useful to begin with a sense of these distinctions are encouraged to read "Film Authorship: The Premature Burial" in part 2 of this book before reading Perkins's early essays.)[8]

From very early on, Nicholas Ray's movies had particular significance for Perkins, a commitment which remained constant throughout his life. One of Perkins's many grounds for objecting to *Sight and Sound* was that, although they had admired Ray's first film, *They Live by Night* (1948), they failed to find value in most of his later work: "I was affronted to my core by the way they received *The Savage Innocents* (1960), which is still one of my favorite films, and which was given such a disgusting dismissal at the back of *Sight and Sound*" (Gibbs 2019). The two overviews of Ray's films—in 1960 for *Oxford Opinion* and in 1963 for *Movie*—are clearly motivated by the anger he felt at Ray's treatment; they also remain the best succinct guides to the distinctive qualities of his cinema.

In the first article, Perkins writes of the reasons for Ray's critical neglect:

> He is . . . in English-speaking countries the most under-rated of all contemporary directors. The reasons for this are obvious enough: the majority of his films have been assignments—of the seventeen Ray pictures so far seen in England only three have been overtly serious in intention. Moreover they are melodramas whose importance derives not from what their characters do and say but from the way in which they do and say it, the way in which they move, talk and look at one another. Thus the quality of his films is not literary since it owes little to the original script, but cinematic; it results from

the subjection of a frequently banal narrative to an idiosyncratic mise-en-scène.

It is one of his clearest statements of the combination of prejudice and blindness to genuine cinematic achievement that seemed to him to characterize contemporary film criticism, *and* of where that achievement should be looked for.

Both articles eloquently combine finely observed and described detail with broader observations on Ray's preoccupations and methods, detail and comment complementing each other so that we never lose sight of how effect and meaning are produced in the interwoven processes of Ray's direction. Perkins had a wonderful ability to enter imaginatively into the director's world, to recognize the decisions that had been taken, and to understand the import of what he saw and heard. He repeatedly—here in brief, telling detail—takes the reader into the heart of the film:

> [55 Days at] Peking (1963), like any other Ray movie, is full of moments at which characters, attitudes or emotions are concentrated into their most direct visual form. Thus the years of rejection and uncertainty which have marked the childhood of Teresa (Lynne Sue Moon), the orphaned daughter of a Chinese woman and an American soldier, are summarized in one characteristic gesture—the arm tentatively outstretched towards any possible source of acceptance and security. Or again, Matt Lewis's (Charlton Heston) quick glance at Natalie's (Ava Gardner) extravagant dress is enough to contradict, for us, her claim that she is "not in uniform" and to change the significance of Matt's reply: "I like things fine the way they are" is now carried beyond the immediate context of polite flirtation to become a statement of Matt's refusal to risk emotional involvement.

The lucidity of Perkins's writing, achieved here and in all his work in ordinary language uncluttered by jargon, can make such insights seem straightforward, easily accomplished. It was part of his gift, from the earliest stages of his career, to make this seem so, although, even with his rare ability to grasp salient details and to extrapolate them into argument, the clarity of his prose was hard won. He was never content with an approximation and, as he often ruefully acknowledged, that frequently meant a long struggle to find the words that satisfied him.

The final article in part 1, on Elia Kazan's *America America* (1963), appeared in *Movie* 19 (Winter 1971–72). *Film as Film* was published in 1972, and in the same year the *Times Higher Education Supplement* announced: "A breakthrough in the progress of film as an academic discipline has occurred at the Berkshire College of Education, where the subject has been added to the range of Bachelor of Education degree courses. . . . The college is the first in Britain to establish the critical study of film as a main component of a first degree course" ("B.Ed. in Film" 1972). Perkins had been appointed by the college in 1968 and became one of the first full-time film academics in Britain.[9] Over the next twenty years, his work was decisive in creating two of Britain's leading film departments. At Bulmershe, following the introduction of the 1972 B.Ed. with its specialism in film, he played a central part in the development of innovative undergraduate programs in Film & Drama; the current Department of Film, Theatre, and Television at the University of Reading is the direct descendant of Film & Drama at Bulmershe. In 1978 he was appointed by the University of Warwick with the brief of developing a degree in film studies. At Warwick, where he spent the rest of his career, the department he founded and initially led has grown and prospered.[10]

Perkins's pioneering leadership within film education and his influence as a teacher are vital dimensions of his career and of his legacy. Establishing film within higher education was for him a key further stage in the battle to gain recognition for the subject as worthy of the same serious, detailed study as the other arts. He devoted much of his time and energy in these years to the often frustrating business of developing proposals and negotiating their passage through the institutional maze of committees, boards, and validating panels, sometimes against objections to the very idea of film as a potential academic subject.[11] He was also passionately committed to finding ways of effectively teaching film—in his early years, a subject with a very limited critical literature, no established pedagogy, and involving the formidable difficulty of detailed study when films (on celluloid) could be hired only for a few days at a time. These are further aspects of the film-studies past that can seem barely comprehensible from the perspective of today.

In the 1960s, *Movie* was at the forefront of new thinking about film: its writers and the debates they provoked on both sides of the Atlantic began to shift the paradigm for thinking about the arts and cultural value.[12] In the early 1970s, notably in the journal *Screen*, new forms of film theory that had little time for—or were actively hostile to—*Movie*'s work entered the emergent field of academic film studies. In Robert Ray's words: "*Film as Film* appeared in 1972, just as *Screen* was taking off, after its 1971 translation and adoption of *Cahiers du Cinéma*'s 1969 manifesto 'Cinema/Ideology/Criticism,' whose opening sentence dictated the new terms: 'Scientific criticism has an obligation to define its field and methods.' Armed with the new tools of semiotics, structuralism, Lacanian psychoanalysis, and Althusserian Marxism, the *Screen* approach rapidly displaced *Movie*'s commitment to aesthetic evaluation, now denounced as quaintly reactionary" (2018).

Movie and *Film as Film* were the subjects of a hostile review in *Screen* (Rohdie 1972). Perkins wrote a cogent and reasoned reply, but the conditions for a dialogue had already disappeared. As higher education programs spread during the 1970s and 1980s, they were often dominated by *Screen* theory, and the kind of detailed, evaluative criticism practiced by Perkins and other *Movie* writers became increasingly marginalized within academic film studies.

The work Perkins published in the 1980s and beyond, which makes up part 2 of this volume, was resolute in maintaining his critical commitments and, often in longer form (early *Movie* articles tended to be quite short), both elaborated his critical approach in studies of individual movies and their makers and reflected on major critical and conceptual issues. The first section of part 2 groups six articles published between 1981 and 2013 that engage with the principles and practice of film criticism—articles which are issue-driven rather than focused, like all of the pieces that follow, on individual films.

In all six, however, the insistence on an appreciation of the specific remains the touchstone of his approach. The first and last of the group, "Moments of Choice" (1981) and "Acting on Objects" (2013), are concerned throughout with particular moments in movies. The former—published in a partwork on cinema that appeared in weekly installments—makes no reference to the contemporary film studies context, but for anyone familiar with those developments it offers in its modest way a wonderful rebuke to influential work within the discipline that chose to ignore the moments of which movies are made and experienced.[13] Written for the general reader, it is a fine introduction to what a film director does and to what skilled direction can achieve beyond the already difficult job of bringing the story and characters to life. Many Hollywood directors, he writes, "seem to have lived quite happily within studio prescriptions, being ready to exert their skills within a range of genres to achieve effective versions of the accepted manner. The limitation of such adaptable know-how was that it would seldom carry a film beyond the qualities of the package originally handed down by the studio." But, he goes on, "more is possible. The films of Ophuls, Ray and Sirk, among others, are there to demonstrate how, with no sacrifice of movie-craft, the director can bind the movie together in a design that offers a more personal and detailed conception of the story's significance, embodying an experience of the world and a viewpoint both considered and felt."

The other articles in this section show Perkins's analytical intelligence applied to more overtly conceptual and philosophical matters. Two of them ("Film Authorship: The Premature Burial" and "Must We Say What They Mean?: Film Criticism and Interpretation") mount refined but pointed critiques of very influential film theorists. There have been no more rigorous and effective accounts either of the shortcomings of auteurism, notably in Peter Wollen's influential version, or of the severe limitations of David Bordwell's account of interpretive criticism.

In each case, as always with Perkins, a decisive test is the ability of any approach to recognize and account for the specific achievements of filmmakers. This is one basis of the distinction he makes between director-centered criticism and auteurism, and of his objection to being labeled an auteurist:

> I do not call myself an auteurist and I can be tetchy when others do. I think it is necessary to observe a distinction between *auteurism* and other practices of director-centered criticism. Auteurism and auteur theories declare their descent from the great polemic initiative of Andrew Sarris and his transformation of the "*politique des auteurs*" from *Cahiers du Cinéma*. To my mind auteurisms are defined by a common feature which is also a crucial error: their exaggerated concern with the continuities and coherence across the body of a director's work. . . . Auteurism does not just observe or welcome continuity from film to film; it insists on continuity.

At almost every stage, Perkins brings particularities to challenge the exclusive emphasis on continuities: "What a director does well is at least as important as what he does often. That is a matter of skill, certainly, but one that goes beyond skill to embrace such values as eloquence, subtlety, vividness and intensity. Adequately to describe a director's authorship involves an exposition of these and other qualities."[14] The same is true of "Must We Say What They Mean?" Here Perkins begins with extended discussion of two movie moments: an appreciation of the rich implications embodied in a few seconds from Max Ophuls's *Caught* (1949) and a withering refutation of Bordwell's claim in *Making Meaning* (1989) that the "point" of *The Wizard of Oz* (1939) might be found to be explicit in its last line of dialogue ("There's no place like home"). These moments and their contexts play central roles in an article that exposes the inadequacies of Bordwell's view of interpretation, while at the same time providing an explication and demonstration of what Perkins takes interpretive criticism to be:

"The demand that interpretation follow formal rules of inference results from understanding the critical process as extracting from the movie statements which are hidden but which otherwise resemble messages such as 'There's no place like home.' Most often, the interesting meanings of films are not like this at all. They consist rather in attitudes, assessments, viewpoints—balances of judgment on the facts and behavior portrayed." In a key sentence, Perkins writes that, rather than exposing hidden meanings, "I suggest that a prime task of interpretation is to articulate in the medium of prose some aspects of what artists have made perfectly and precisely clear in the medium of film."

Reflecting further on the role of criticism at the end of the article, he insists on the relationship between interpretive criticism and the reader's future experience of the film: "Insofar as [an interpretation] hopes to illuminate a whole film or body of work by drawing attention to overall patterns and representatively eloquent detail, an important test of its validity and usefulness will be the degree to which we can internalize it and use it to enrich our contact with the film. That is one reason why response is of critical rather than merely sentimental importance." Against the attempt to put film study onto a more systematic, even scientific basis (Perkins quotes the wonderful phrase "physics envy"), he writes earlier in the piece that in his account of *Caught* "judgments are made for which one could offer *support but not proof*" (emphasis mine). In his last paragraph he asserts the reader's enriched experience of the film as a test of criticism's validity and the place of feeling in the process that leads to interpretive criticism.

"Where Is the World?: The Horizon of Events in Movie Fiction," the third of the explicitly theoretical articles in this section, is perhaps Perkins's most significant contribution to the theory of criticism outside *Film as Film*. Beginning with a tour de force of sequence analysis—the most penetrating account of *Citizen Kane*'s ending in the extensive literature on that film—he elaborates the familiar but little-explored concept of the fictional world, to claim its fundamental place in criticism: "Film studies has in the main ignored the fictional world, at best taken it for granted. Lack of attention to the fictional world—what makes it a world rather than what makes it fictional—may be one product of the field's recoil from all that smells of realism. A new engagement with worldhood should be of value, not least in developing our grasp of styles and meanings. An immediate benefit could be to enrich our appreciation of film artistry both in the treatment of space and in the shaping of narrative." Central to this is a rejection of cause-and-effect models of narrative for a much more inclusive view of film drama and the complex web of cultural understandings that make creation and communication possible. "Worldhood" draws our attention to all that we take for granted about our own world and that forms a functioning background in any fiction, there for filmmakers to rely on but available to be woven into the film's significant patterns. A fictional world extends off-screen in time and space—characters have histories, space exists beyond the confines of the frame. In *You Only Live Once* (1937), we accept that in the film's world a car has driven off, although we only hear it and watch two men looking off-screen. In a film in which much will turn on issues of perception and prejudice, "here Lang offers an innocent example of our being led to understand more than we have seen," by drawing on what we habitually assume about the world. In a moment from *All I Desire* (1953), Perkins draws out the range of understandings, based on our common cultural experience, that Douglas Sirk activates in filming the simple action of a woman—returning after many years to her family home—reaching for and then returning a house key that she knows is concealed in a flower basket.

This is one of the very rare articles in which Perkins focuses directly on a critical concept and, in a film studies context dominated by concept and theory, his conclusion is striking. Summarizing the case he has made, he writes: "My examples demonstrate, to my mind, that understanding the events of a movie as taking place in a world is a prerequisite of the intelligibility not only of plot but also of tone, viewpoint, rhetoric, style and meaning. If I am right it should be a priority in thinking about cinema." But he goes on: "A priority but not an obsession. As a narrowly theoretical pursuit the fictional world is hardly preferable to any other. I would see no benefit in having worlds replace cause/effect, enigma resolution, or order/disruption/resolution as a formalist distraction." Worldhood, then, is not offered as a method or as a conceptual key; rather, it opens to view and significance what so much of film studies methodology had ignored. The conclusion articulates what the whole of Perkins's work demonstrates: a refusal to overvalue terms, concepts, or theories. What he deplores is their tendency to "distract"—to draw attention away from all that he passionately believes is of value in movies.

The essays in the final section of this book are among the most impressive evaluative studies of individual films in English. Published between 1982 and 2017, eight of the eleven are about directors to whom Perkins was devoted throughout his career: Nicholas Ray and Max Ophuls.[15] The pieces on *In a Lonely Place* (1950) and *Johnny Guitar* (1954) are Perkins's most developed appreciations of individual Nicholas Ray movies. The six essays on films directed by Ophuls constitute perhaps the most insightful body of work on this celebrated director. Three of them form interrelated stages in Perkins's extended exploration of *Letter from an Unknown Woman*, the clearest example of the ever-deeper understanding achieved by his almost continuous dialogue with the movies he most admired.

The argument of each essay is intricate—it invites and rewards attentive reading—but *clear*, both in its precise use of ordinary language and in its meticulous structure of thought from phase to phase. They exemplify what Deborah Thomas eloquently evoked in her tribute to Perkins: "In Victor's writing, language mirrored its object so aptly that it is scarcely possible to paraphrase him without losing the delicate intelligence of his insights, as well as his affinity with the seemingly ineffable filmic moments he somehow caught—texture and all—in the words he wove" (2016).

It is also characteristic of Perkins that the essays are very varied, and sometimes surprising, in their ways of coming at the films. He begins his exploration of *Letter from an Unknown Woman* by focusing on the Linz sequence, "partly because it enters very little into the already published discussion," and because "it seemed also to be characteristic and highly effective without being astonishing." And he chooses to extend that discussion in the second article by further probing what might have motivated Ophuls to replace the Innsbruck of the original story with Linz. That Hitler chose Linz for the declaration of the Anschluss in 1938 becomes the starting point for a strikingly original view of what Ophuls intended: "*Letter from an Unknown Woman* picks up scathingly on two aspects of Hitler's attachment to Linz: his partisanship in its imagined rivalry with Vienna, and his ambitions for the vindication of Linz in the sphere of culture." Central to this opposition between Vienna and Linz in the film is that between the music of Mozart and of Wagner. The military band in Linz plays Wagner, and "there was in 1947 no more certain way of affirming the identity of Linz as Hitler's town than by associating it simultaneously with a grotesque version of military pomp and with Wagner. Hitler consistently proclaimed his worship of Wagner; he named the composer, a vicious and noisy anti-Semite, as his only forerunner."

From seemingly left-field starting points, Perkins develops analyses that bring to light previously unexplored dimensions of what Ophuls accomplished.

Apparently even more marginal is the tiny decision that Perkins makes central to his essay on *High School* (1968). Frederick Wiseman chose to drop the sound as the principal's speech that concludes the film comes to an end, with a consequent focus solely on Dr. Haller's face and demeanor just before the image fades to black. That the detail had gone unnoticed in previous discussions of the film becomes part of the essay's profound meditation on movies and on film criticism. Of selecting such a tiny, unremarked decision, Perkins writes: "Examining moments of eloquence in film, however minute, can be a way of illuminating structure by relating part and whole. The practice can be motivated by simple curiosity, sometimes by hostility, but its larger justification lies in the way that it relates the achievements of a movie and its maker to a discovery of the medium and its possibilities." This is exactly the process of the *High School* essay. Rooted in the juxtaposition of this editorial decision with discussion of details in the documentary world over which the filmmaker had no control, Perkins reflects both on Wiseman's skill and on the "constant challenge [that film-makers face] to arrive at stresses that enrich our understanding, and achieve a weight of expression appropriate to the weight of significance that a moment can bear." The filmmaker's subtle grading of effects and qualification of what is "plainly shown . . . by what is delicately suggested" are possibilities inherent in the medium. One role of close reading in criticism is to acknowledge and appreciate such achievements as against the "possibilities of dishonesty, falsification, bad faith" that are also possibilities of the medium of film.

Of Wiseman's decision to drop the sound at the end of *High School*, Perkins records that in his own notes on the film, spanning many years, he first observed it at a time when he had had access to an analyzing projector or editing table. He hadn't previously registered a decision that was clearly designed to have an effect yet not to be consciously noticed. In the last section of the *High School* essay this leads him to consider the implications for criticism of the stop-start analysis that technology has now made so readily available: "It makes for an experience distinct from that of any ordinary viewing when one acquires the ability to pause, start, freeze, skip forward, or back. We should ask what safeguards should be put on our close readings when the control of time has been stolen from the artist in the interests of study. The temptations are many, and not the least of them is the temptation of cleverness. Distortion threatens when an aspect is isolated from its context to take on perhaps disproportionate weight or implausible significance." How, then are these temptations and threats to be avoided? Perkins's final words in the essay, which became his last published work, echo the last paragraph of "Must We Say What They Mean?," but here he directly addresses the responsibilities of film criticism. It is a passage profoundly characteristic of a great film critic.

> When analysis serves a critical purpose—one that goes beyond cataloging to touch on the significance of a work or the achievement of its makers—it must be held answerable to a true experience of the movie. The analyst must ask what case can be advanced with sincerity and conviction. Readiness for conversation and correction is a vital discipline. Still we cannot say that the reference point must always be past viewings, or the memory of them, as that would contradict a large part of the motivation for close work (either by scholars or by enthusiasts). It would rule out new discoveries and fresh realizations. When accurate analysis opens our eyes to new possibilities, or to new data that challenges our understanding, it is a future, better informed encounter with the movie that we have in prospect. Quite often a further viewing will be both possible and enriching. We may then see an offered reading as convincing, revelatory, merely credible or not even that. The question will need to be addressed through lively interrogation of our renewed experience. In this process of introspection we shall, at our best, be alert for what we can truthfully say and mean.
>
> Sincerity and introspection have not been terms privileged in the philosophy of film, but close reading cannot prosper without them.

With thanks to Edward Lamberti and the members of the Editorial Advisory Group.

Notes on the Text

Non-English film titles, release dates, and references for quotations were rarely given in the early issues of *Movie*, and these have been added wherever possible; if no reference is given for a quotation the source could not be traced. Actors' names have also been introduced to provide additional context. In some cases the most readily available location of a quotation has been given rather than the original.

Editorial endnotes have been introduced to provide additional information and context—plus, in one case, translations where quotations were given only in the original language. Notes from the editor are marked with the abbreviation "Ed."

For ease of reference, original publication details are provided at the beginning of each article.

Works Cited

"B.Ed. in Film Studies Course Approved for Berkshire." *Times Higher Education Supplement*, March 3, 1972, n.p.

Bowen, Peter. V. F. Perkins tribute, University of Warwick, 2016, https://warwick.ac.uk/fac/arts/film/archive/vfp/peterbowen (accessed June 1, 2020).

Cameron, Ian A., Mark Shivas, Paul Mayersberg, and V. F. Perkins. "*Movie* vs. Kael." *Film Quarterly* 17, no. 1 (1963): 57–62.

Gibbs, John. "Interview with Ian Cameron." *Movie: A Journal of Film Criticism*, no. 8 (2019): 39–44. https://warwick.ac.uk/fac/arts/film/movie/8_ian_cameron.pdf (accessed June 1, 2020).

———. "Interview with V. F. Perkins." *Movie: A Journal of Film Criticism*, no. 8 (2019): 45–52. https://warwick.ac.uk/fac/arts/film/movie/8_v.f_perkins.pdf (accessed June 1, 2020).

———. *The Life of Mise-en-Scène: Visual Style and British Film Criticism, 1946–78*. Manchester: Manchester University Press, 2013.

Kael, Pauline. "Circles and Squares." *Film Quarterly* 16, no. 3 (1963): 12–26.

———. "Criticism and Kids' Games." *Film Quarterly* 17, no. 1 (1963): 62–64.

Martin, Adrian. "What to Look for in a Film? (And How to Know When You've Found It?)" Unpublished keynote address, *Film as Film* Today: On the

Criticism and Theory of V. F. Perkins symposium, University of Warwick, September 4–5, 2018.

Perkins, V. F. *Film as Film: Understanding and Judging Movies*. Harmondsworth: Penguin, 1972.

———. "Ian Cameron: A Tribute." *Movie: A Journal of Film Criticism*, no. 1 (August 2010): 1–2. https://warwick.ac.uk/fac/arts/film/movie/contents/ian_cameron_-_a_tribute.pdf (accessed June 1, 2020).

———. "A Reply to Sam Rohdie." *Screen* 13, no. 4 (1972): 146–51.

Ray, Robert B. "*Film as Film*, the *Screen/Movie* Debate, and Wittgenstein's Case-by-Case Method." Unpublished paper, *Film as Film* Today: On the Criticism and Theory of V. F. Perkins symposium, University of Warwick, September 4–5, 2018.

———. "*Screen* vs. *Movie*: The Great Divide in Film Studies." In *The Structure of Complex Images*, 17–55. London: Palgrave Macmillan, 2020.

Rohdie, Sam. "Review: *Movie Reader* and *Film as Film*." *Screen* 13, no. 4 (1972): 135–45.

Thomas, Deborah. V. F. Perkins tribute, University of Warwick, 2016, https://warwick.ac.uk/fac/arts/film/archive/vfp/deborahthomas (accessed June 1, 2020).

Wollen, Peter. *Signs and Meaning in the Cinema*. 3rd ed. London: Secker & Warburg, [1969] 1972.

Filmography

All I Desire. Directed by Douglas Sirk. Universal Pictures, 1953.

America, America (UK title: *The Anatolian Smile*). Directed by Elia Kazan. Warner Bros., 1963.

The Angry Hills. Directed by Robert Aldrich. MGM, 1959.

Caught. Directed by Max Ophuls. MGM, 1949.

The Devil Never Sleeps. Directed by Leo McCarey. Twentieth Century Fox, 1962.

Harry Black. Directed by Hugo Fregonese. Twentieth Century Fox, 1958.

High School. Directed by Frederick Wiseman. Osti Productions, 1968.

In a Lonely Place. Directed by Nicholas Ray. Columbia Pictures, 1950.

Johnny Guitar. Directed by Nicholas Ray. Republic Pictures, 1954.

Land of the Pharaohs. Directed by Howard Hawks. Warner Bros., 1955.

Letter from an Unknown Woman. Directed by Max Ophuls. Universal-International, 1948.

Night of the Demon. Directed by Jacques Tourneur. Columbia Pictures, 1957.

Psycho. Directed by Alfred Hitchcock. Paramount Pictures, 1960.

The Savage Innocents. Directed by Nicholas Ray. Rank, 1960.

Some People. Directed by Clive Donner. Anglo-Amalgamated, 1962.

Taste of Fear (US title: *Scream of Fear*). Directed by Seth Holt. Columbia Pictures, 1961.

They Live by Night. Directed by Nicholas Ray. RKO Radio Pictures, 1948.
You Only Live Once. Directed by Fritz Lang. United Artists, 1937.

Notes

1. In addition to Perkins, the original editorial team of *Movie* consisted of Ian Cameron (editor and designer), Mark Shivas, and Paul Mayersberg.

2. John Gibbs provides a detailed and authoritative account of the role played by visual style in British film criticism in the decades after World War II, including extensive discussion of *Oxford Opinion* and *Movie* (2013). His book is an indispensable resource for anyone interested in the evolution of film criticism, as it has been in the writing of this introduction. Perkins's eloquent tribute to Ian Cameron, publisher and designer of *Movie* and the prime mover in the *Oxford Opinion* group, begins with memories of these early years (2010, 1–2).

3. In his 1997 interview with John Gibbs, Perkins says, "The inaccuracy of most reviewing and of most aspiring criticism in the pre-Film-Studies era is very impressive. Part of my understanding of where the motivation for *Movie* came from was a desire to make statements about film that *were* accurate in relation to the text (though at that time the habit of talking about films as texts was not in place), where there was some basis in observation for the things one wanted to say about the film. And part of that involved the discipline of checking what you had in mind to write against a further viewing" (2019, 45).

4. "The Battle of Form and Content, Circa 1960" is the subtitle of the chapter in which John Gibbs details these controversies, which involved *Sight and Sound* and writers in a number of other British journals (see Gibbs 2013, 95–125).

5. Perkins considers the implications of these technologies for film criticism in his last published essay, "Omission and Oversight in Close Reading: The Final Moments of Frederick Wiseman's *High School*" (2017), the concluding essay of this book.

6. See John Gibbs's interviews with Ian Cameron and V. F. Perkins in *Movie: A Journal of Film Criticism*, no. 8 (2019): 38–52.

7. In the Gibbs interview Perkins also talks of the impact on *Movie* of encountering *Cahiers du Cinéma*, and especially its interviews with Hollywood directors. He cites as a particular inspiration the level of serious discussion that Orson Welles's *Touch of Evil* received (2019).

8. In the interview with Ian Cameron these issues are discussed in relation to early *Movie* (Gibbs 2019).

9   Then known as Bulmershe College, the name that was later readopted when it became Bulmershe College of Higher Education.

10 A range of tributes from colleagues and former students at Warwick can be found at https://warwick.ac.uk/fac/arts/film/archive/vfp (accessed June 1, 2020).

11 In his tribute to Perkins, his friend and colleague Peter Bowen recalls the early years of film at Warwick (2016).

12 *Movie*'s writing on Hollywood cinema was attacked by Pauline Kael in *Film Quarterly* (1963, 12–26); the *Movie* editorial board's response and Kael's rejoinder were published in the Fall 1963 issue (Cameron et al. 1963, 57–62).

13 Robert Ray is illuminating on how this emphasis on specific detail figures in what he calls "the *Movie/Screen* contrast":

> A good way to think about the *Movie/Screen* contrast lies in a remark Wittgenstein once made to a friend: "Hegel seems to me to be always saying that things which look different are really the same. Whereas my interest is in showing that things which look the same are really different." *Screen* was Hegelian, often explicitly so (Alexandre Kojève's 1930s lectures on Hegel, translated into English in 1969, regularly turned up in *Screen* bibliographies). Its writers, eager to show that things which look different are really the same, were willing to ignore particulars. In one of *Screen*'s most influential articles, 1974's "Realism and the Cinema: Notes on Some Brechtian Theses," Colin MacCabe was candid about neglecting individual cases. . . . *Movie*, on the other hand, had always attended precisely to the kinds of cinematic details that MacCabe considered unimportant. In fact, the journal could have adopted Wittgenstein's ideal motto for his own *Philosophical Investigations*: "I'll teach you differences." (2018, n.p.)

14 I borrow the use of the term "particularity" from Adrian Martin's excellent keynote address, "What to Look for in a Film? (And How to Know When You've Found It?)" (2018).

15 In his profile on the website of the Department of Film and Television Studies at the University of Warwick, Perkins writes: "My main academic aim is to develop a deeper and more clearly articulated appreciation of the work of some great film artists. I have a continuing engagement with films by, for instance, Alfred Hitchcock, Fritz Lang, Max Ophuls, Yasujirō Ozu, Nicholas Ray, Jean Renoir and Orson Welles." https://warwick.ac.uk/fac/arts/film/staff/perkins/ (accessed June 1, 2020). Although Ophuls does not figure in his work before "Moments of Choice" in 1981 and the first of his articles dedicated to Ophuls was published in 1982, *Letter from an Unknown Woman* was one of the films he chose to discuss in the series he scripted for BBC Schools Television in 1968, and he taught Ophuls's movies throughout his career.

PART 1
1960–1972

Oxford Opinion and *Movie*:
The Battle for a New Criticism

THE BRITISH CINEMA
AND
BRITISH FILM CRITICISM

FIFTY FAMOUS FILMS 1915–45

First published in Oxford Opinion, *April 30, 1960, 36–37.*

Introductory note: Perkins's article was published in the "Film" section of the student journal Oxford Opinion *in March 1960. It was preceded by Ian Cameron's editorial, which we include here to indicate a little more of the context within which Perkins and his colleagues were beginning to engage with contemporary British film culture.*

Film criticism in Britain is dead. Hardly a single piece of perceptive criticism has been written here in the last few years. Indeed, it is sometimes difficult to believe that British criticism has ever been alive. Perhaps in the good old days of "*Sequence*" . . .[1]

    A first reaction to the latest *Sight and Sound* with its pale blue cover and pale pink contents was to scrap everything on films planned for this number of *Oxford Opinion* and to devote all our space to a dissection of that distressing journal. But it is only a pretty typical product of an approach to films that is fundamentally perverted and will continue to throw up muck until it begins to be flung back in the faces of its authors. At the moment there is hardly any sign of dissatisfaction with the current product. Therefore we are devoting the two main articles in this section to attacking two aspects of film criticism in Britain: the pallid philanthropy that has always provided its criteria for evaluation, and the falseness of the implicitly accepted distinction between art and commerce. How strange that a criticism which treats films as a medium of mass communication rather than as an art should be completely oblivious of the commercial realities of filmmaking. Later we hope to dissect the most pernicious article in the current *Sight and Sound*. And that should be all. Since "Stand Up! Stand Up!" we have had plenty of proof that repeated attack on the same subject from the same viewpoint become monotonous and finally ineffectual.[2]

For the rest of the term we aim to write about films rather than about criticism. The remaining three numbers will each contain an article on an important director—[Frank] Tashlin, Nicholas Ray, and [Georges] Franju—as well as pieces on other cinematic topics and reviews of films.

Ian Cameron

> "Grant me patience, just Heaven! Of all the cants which are canted in this world—though the cant of hypocrites may be the worst—the cant of criticism is the most tormenting." Opinion of *Tristram Shandy, Gentleman* (Sterne 1946: 131)

Fifty Famous Films, 1915–45 is the title of a booklet published by the BFI to provide notes for the [National Film] Archive programs at the National Film Theatre; any criticism should presumably observe the title's terms of reference.[3] Not that the booklet itself does so: it lists fifty-four films, at least five of which are certainly not famous, and one of which was made in 1914.[4] The title itself is interesting in the modesty of its claims; the Archive could have included *The Jazz Singer* (1927) or *King Kong* (1933) in its program and no one would have been able to deny that the films were famous. It has in fact included both *Storm over Asia* (1928) and *Brief Encounter* (1945). The use of the word "famous" is just a blanket; it would have been much less evasive to call the season "Fifty Great Films." In that context there would have been some sense in the note which apologizes for the nonavailability of [Charles] Chaplin's feature films: "The Archive season . . . should include *Shoulder Arms, The Kid, A Woman of Paris, The Gold Rush, City Lights* and *Modern Times*" (99). The publication of this list—and, even more, the exclusion from it of *The Great Dictator*

(1940)—can only imply a value judgment and it's a pity the Institute was not more honest about it.

I thus intend to treat the booklet as a catalog of films that are included in the Archive series either for their value as works of art or because of their historical importance. From this point of view the publication is worth examining for the light it throws on the standards and prejudices of this country's cinematic establishment.

The season covers three decades, and the numerical distribution of the films is itself interesting: the first (1915–25) is represented by seventeen films, the second (1926–35) twenty, but the most recent (1936–45) by a mere six—or five not counting *Night Mail* (1936).[5] As for directors, six are represented by more than one film: [D. W.] Griffith, [Sergei] Eisenstein, and [René] Clair have three apiece; [Erich von] Stroheim, [John] Ford (!) and [G. W.] Pabst (!!) have two. Meanwhile Hitchcock, [Fritz] Lang, and [Orson] Welles have to be content with a single film, and in each case it is not one of their best. The omission of *The Magnificent Ambersons* (1942) is perhaps the most startling gap in the entire season. But there is worse to come: [George] Cukor, [Mark] Donskoy, [Josef von] Sternberg, [Billy] Wilder, [Jean] Cocteau, and, above all, Howard Hawks and Jean Renoir are nowhere to be found; the contributions of filmmakers in Italy, Sweden, and Japan are totally ignored; and among the important genres that are either completely or virtually unrepresented are the animated film, the *film noir*, and the western. The color film was never invented.

However, in fairness it must be admitted that the difficulties involved in compiling a season of this sort are enormous—no selection of fifty films could hope to be without omissions and unbalance. There are excuses for the content of the season; there are none for the content of the booklet. In the first place it suffers from a terrible confusion over its aims. The foreword by the director of the BFI states that "it is hoped that the booklet will have some value as a permanent reference work" (n.p.).[6] It has none. There is perhaps one contribution which could be dignified by the name of journalism. But nowhere is there the slightest sign of the detailed, academic criticism which one might reasonably expect to find in a publication of this sort and from this source. If films are not to be subjected to close and intelligent study in the

National Film Archive, then there is little hope that they will be so anywhere else. A single example: *The Last Laugh* (*Der letzte Mann*, 1924), we are told, "was recognized as breaking new ground in the art of screen narration. It was particularly praised for its use of camera movement" (42–43; 42).[7] And there the subject rests.

Instead of careful analysis we are offered, in most cases, a plot synopsis, a short account of the careers of people connected with the making of the film, details of production costs and hazards which would fit quite well into a *Ben-Hur* (1959) handout, and pious liberal sentiments. Thus of the anti-Negro propaganda in *The Birth of a Nation* (1915): "A charitable view may imply indiscretion rather than malice" (1–4; 3). Could anything be daintier? Or less relevant to the quality of the film?

Another question one automatically asks—though the BFI seem to have given it no thought—is for whom this publication was intended. The answer seems obvious: the patrons of the National Film Theatre. But surely they can be supposed to have passed the stage where they need to be told that "the close shot gives us a single detail of a scene, the rest being excluded; but the rest can be supplied by other close shots of other details" (2). No; they will look in vain for an examination of technique which goes beyond this elementary Manvellian stage.[8]

In fact such scant attention is paid to technique and aesthetics that the notes in this booklet might as easily have been written about novels or plays as about films. A plot synopsis of *The Navigator* (1924) would have revealed that whereas "Robinson Crusoe cannot boil an egg because he has neither fire nor kettle—Keaton cannot boil an egg because the available apparatus is only fit for boiling three hundred." (30–32; 32). There is nowhere an indication that the writers of this booklet have realized that the film is a medium different in kind from any other.

One conviction, however, they do seem to share: things are not at all what they used to be. *The Birth of a Nation* has a "maturity and power . . . which have seldom been equalled since, despite the great technical progress made by the cinema in other ways" (2). "The handling of the actors in intimate scenes (of *Intolerance* [1916]) has seldom been equalled" (5–9; 8).[9] *Metropolis* (1927) "has a bizarre quality which the current science fiction films have never equalled" (44–46; 44). And *42nd Street* (1933) was "realized with flair and the sort of gusto that even the best musicals of to-day . . . cannot match" (73–74; 73). No wonder "the three greatest artist-innovators in world cinema remain Griffith, Chaplin and Eisenstein" (33–35; 33) with never a mention of Welles, Renoir, or [Roberto] Rossellini, let alone [Alain] Resnais.[10] Read on. "Griffith created the cinema's alphabet, Chaplin its humanity, individual and particular, and Eisenstein its intellect" (33). No, I'm not making it up.

With criticism stuck at this level one is not surprised by the absence of any attempt to define or describe a director's artistic personality; indeed two of the films in the season are reviewed without even a mention of their director's names. But one is surprised, naïvely perhaps, by the carelessness with which the whole thing has been bundled together. *The Beggar's Opera* is "the seventeenth-century operetta" (68).[11] The ending of *Blackmail* (1929) was changed "for 'commercial' reasons" (58–59; 59) (cf. Chabrol and Rohmer, *Hitchcock*).[12] Worst of all, we read within a single paragraph that in *Un Chien andalou* (1929) "the emphasis is not on movements or tricks for their own sake . . . in spite of its harrowing and pointless effects" (60–62; 62).[13]

Lack of intellect and originality go hand in hand: not once is the traditional valuation of a film challenged. The verdicts pronounced by [Paul] Rotha when *The Film Till Now* (1930) was first published thirty years ago are still being pressed into service; Eisenstein's estimate of his own work is swallowed whole. It gets worse: there are five films in the season that were made in Germany between the wars. Of these only *Die Dreigroschenoper* (*The Threepenny Opera*) (1931) is reviewed without reference to [Siegfried] Kracauer's book *From Caligari to Hitler* (1947)—other notes retail and accept without question a thesis which Fritz Lang has described as total nonsense.

But of course they would, for Kracauer's book must be a model that almost every British film critic attempts to follow, since it neglects the aesthetics of the cinema in favor of politics and sociology. We all know by now that what the cinema needs is "warmth," "heart," "compassion," "human sympathy," and a pile of other artistically expendable commodities. That is why *The Grapes of Wrath* (1940) "must mark the highest peak of achievement in (Hollywood's) long traffic with the art of the film. . . . For whatever other qualities this film may possess it is primarily a film about people, people who transcend the incidental evil and ugliness of life by their innate qualities of goodness and human courage. And when the meanness and malice of cruel men have done their worst it is the great spirit of Ma Joad . . . (et al.) . . . which remains. It is because of this positive affirmation of life that the film soars to greatness" (86–88; 87). So there you are. Run out and get yourself a positive affirmation and, cinematically, you're made. You'll have "the greatest masterpiece the screen has ever produced" (87) on your hands.[14] Fine: but don't ask me to sit through it.

I cannot pretend to believe that the attitude which exalts right-mindedness above form, style, and technique ("It is almost impertinent to refer to the production qualities of the film") (87) has grown up in order to fulfill a real need.[15] I *do* believe that British film critics have been forced to adopt this method because it is by far the easiest to practice; any fool can blather about positive affirmations. But in an art as new as the cinema it demands intellect, perception, and sheer hard work to get to grips with aesthetic questions. And these are gifts which our critics too obviously lack. They are thus driven back to their easy assumption that a great film is made by the director's having his heart in the right place. The assumption, like the booklet, and like the criticism that it so accurately mirrors, stinks.

Works Cited

Anderson, Lindsay. "Stand Up, Stand Up!" *Sight and Sound* 26, no. 2 (1956): 63–69.

Cameron, Ian, Mark Shivas, and V. F. Perkins. "Correspondence: *Oxford Opinion*." *Sight and Sound* 30, no. 2 (1961): 100–101.

Chabrol, Claude, and Eric Rohmer. *Hitchcock*. Paris: Editions Universitaires, 1957.

Gibbs, John. *The Life of Mise-en-Scène: Visual Style and British Film Criticism, 1946–78*. Manchester: Manchester University Press, 2013.

Houston, Penelope. "The Critical Question." *Sight and Sound* 19, no. 4 (1960): 160–65.

Kracauer, Siegfried. *From Caligari to Hitler: A Psychological History of the German Film*. Princeton, NJ: Princeton University Press, [1947] 2004.

National Film Theatre, *Fifty Famous Films, 1915–1945*. N.p.: British Film Institute/National Film Archive, n.d.

Rotha, Paul. *The Film Till Now: A Survey of the Cinema*. Rev. ed. London: Vision, [1930] 1949.

Sterne, Lawrence. *The Life and Opinions of Tristram Shandy, Gentleman*. Everyman's Library ed. London: J. M. Dent & Sons, [1758–67] 1946.

Filmography

Ben-Hur. Directed by William Wyler. MGM, 1959.
The Birth of a Nation. Directed by D. W. Griffith. Epoch Producing Corporation, 1915.
Blackmail. Directed by Alfred Hitchcock. Wardour Films (UK), Sono Art-World Wide Pictures (US), 1929.
Brief Encounter. Directed by David Lean. Eagle-Lion Distributors, 1945.
Un Chien andalou. Directed by Luis Buñuel. Les Grands Films Classiques, 1929.
Die Dreigroschenoper (*The Threepenny Opera*). Directed by G. W. Pabst. National-Film (Germany), Warner Bros. (US), 1931.
Entr'acte. Directed by René Clair. Société Nouvelle des Acacias, 1924.
42nd Street. Directed by Lloyd Bacon. Warner Bros., 1933.
The Grapes of Wrath. Directed by John Ford. Twentieth Century Fox, 1940.
The Great Dictator. Directed by Charles Chaplin. United Artists, 1940.
Intolerance. Directed by D. W. Griffith. Triangle Distributing Corporation, 1916.
The Jazz Singer. Directed by Alan Crosland. Warner Bros., 1927.
King Kong. Directed by Merian C. Cooper and Ernest B. Schoedsack. Radio Pictures, 1933.
The Last Laugh (*Der letzte Mann*). Directed by F. W. Murnau. UFA, 1924.
The Magnificent Ambersons. Directed by Orson Welles. RKO Radio Pictures, 1942.
Ménilmontant. Directed by Dimitri Kirsanoff. Jean Tedesco, 1926.
Metropolis. Directed by Fritz Lang. Universum Film (UFA) (Germany), Paramount Pictures (US), 1927.
The Navigator. Directed by Buster Keaton and Donald Crisp. MGM, 1924.
Night Mail. Directed by Harry Watt and Basil Wright. Associated British Film Distributors, 1936.
The Pawnshop. Directed by Charles Chaplin. Mutual Film, 1916.
Storm over Asia. Directed by Vsevolod Pudovkin. Mezhrabpomfilm, 1928.
Strike (*Stachka*). Directed by Sergei Eisenstein. Goskino, Proletkult, 1925.
Tango Tangle. Directed by Mack Sennett. Mutual Film, 1914.

Notes

1   *Sequence* was a significant British film journal, published between 1946 and 1952. Lindsay Anderson and Gavin Lambert were among its editors and contributors. In 1950, Lambert became director of publications at the BFI

and editor of *Sight and Sound*. See John Gibbs, *The Life of Mise-en-Scène: Visual Style and British Film Criticism, 1946–78* for an extended discussion of *Sequence*. Ed.

2   "Stand Up! Stand Up!" was an article by Lindsay Anderson, published in *Sight and Sound* (Fall 1956) (Anderson 1956). It was cited by Penelope Houston, the editor of *Sight and Sound*, in an article in which she attacked the *Oxford Opinion* writers (1960). They replied in a letter published in a subsequent issue (Cameron et al. 1961). Ed.

3   The individual entries are not attributed to specific writers, but the introduction notes that the booklet includes "critical assessments" by Lotte Eisner, Penelope Houston, Gavin Lambert, Ernest Lindgren, Rachael Low, Liam O'Laoghaire, Karel Reisz. John Huntley ("Introduction," n.p.). Ed.

4   This is Charles Chaplin's *Tango Tangle* (1914). Ed.

5   Perkins's figures are not quite correct here. The fifty-four films in the booklet break down by date as follows: 1914, 1; 1915–25, 22; 1926–35, 24; 1936–45, 6; and 1 undated film (Chaplin's *The Pawnshop*, from 1916). The *Night Mail* film included in the booklet is the 1936 film produced by John Grierson for the GPO Film Unit and directed by Basil Wright and Harry Watt. It is unclear why Perkins might not "count" *Night Mail*. It is a short film—but so are many of the Chaplin and Laurel and Hardy films included in the booklet. Perhaps it is its status as a documentary made for the GPO Film Unit that places it in a different category for Perkins. Ed.

6   The director of the BFI was James Quinn. Ed.

7   The booklet erroneously gives the film's year as 1925. The bracketed numbers (42–43; 42) give the page numbers for the booklet's entry on the film and the specific page of the quotation. Ed.

8   The reference is to Roger Manvell (1909–1987), the first director of the British Film Academy and author of many books on film and filmmaking. Manvell was one of the writers Perkins associated with what he called "orthodox film theory" in *Film as Film* (1972). Ed.

9   The article is quoting the film notes on *Intolerance* issued by the Museum of Modern Art Library, New York City. Ed.

10   Entry on "*Strike (Stachka)*." Ed.

11   "*Die Dreigroschenoper*" in *Fifty Famous Films, 1915–1945*, 67–68. John Gay's *The Beggar's Opera*, with music by Johann Christoph Pepusch, was actually written in 1728. Ed.

12   The reference is to Claude Chabrol and Eric Rohmer's pioneering study, *Hitchcock*, published in France in 1957. Ed.

13 Entry on "French Avant-Garde Movement: *Entr'acte, Ménilmontant, Un Chien andalou.*" Ed.

14 Quoted by Perkins from Basil Wright, in entry on *The Grapes of Wrath*, 86–88; 87. Ed.

15 Wright, 87. Ed.

THE BRITISH CINEMA (ON BEHALF OF THE EDITORIAL BOARD)

First published in Movie, *no. 1 (June 1962): 2–7.*

Five years ago the ineptitude of British films was generally acknowledged.[1] The stiff-upper-lip movie was a standard target for critical scorn. But now the British cinema has come to grips with Reality. We have had a breakthrough, a renaissance, a New Wave. More than that, we are now on the crest of a Second Wave: "In the new spirit of freedom the British cinema moves on to explore worlds outside the conventional middle-class drama . . ." All we can see is a change of attitude, which disguises the fact that the British cinema is as dead as before. Perhaps it was never alive. Our films have improved, if at all, only in their intentions. We are still unable to find evidence of artistic sensibilities in working order. There is as much genuine personality in *Room at the Top* (1959), method in *A Kind of Loving* (1962), and style in *A Taste of Honey* (1961) as there is wit in *An Alligator Named Daisy* (1955), intelligence in *Above Us the Waves* (1955), and ambition in *Ramsbottom Rides Again* (1956).

Perhaps that sounds merely peevish; we can't be *that* bad? Indeed, by comparison with most other major film-producing countries, we are not. *Mutatis mutandis* the remarks on the previous page could quite aptly be applied to the Russian, Polish, German, or Argentinian product. Here again any difference is one of ambition, not of achievement. If one can accept *Ashes* and *Diamonds* (*Popiól i diament*, 1958), *The Wolf Trap* (*Vlčí jáma*, 1958), *Stars* (*Sterne*, 1959), or *The House of the Angel* (*La Casa del Ángel*, 1957), then there is little reason to feel affronted by *Victim* (1961), *The Entertainer* (1960), *The Angry Silence* (1960), or *Look Back in Anger* (1959).

None of these films can survive comparison with the best movies from France, Italy, Japan, Sweden, and the United States. We would not suggest that every French or American film is good or even tolerable. But where are the British films that we can compare with, say, *Lola* (1961), *The Keepers* (*La Tête contre les murs*, 1959), *Vertigo* (1958), *Rebel Without a Cause* (1955), or *Man of the West* (1958)?

"Uncommercial" "avant-garde" cinema is not a requirement. Nor do we ask for a particular *type* of film. The cinema of Fritz Lang, Raoul Walsh, or Jacques Tourneur is different from, not superior to, the cinema of [Jean-Luc] Godard, Nicholas Ray, [Georges] Franju, [Joseph] Losey, [Ingmar] Bergman, or George Cukor. The request is not for a "correct" approach to the necessary subjects. It is for a cinema which has style, imagination, personality, and, because of these, meaning.

The Obstacles to Making Good Films in Britain

The reasons usually given for the badness of British movies center on the impossibility of setting up interesting projects. The big producers are not interested in adventurous pictures: they are tied to the formulae set by previous commercial successes. So any movie which aims to be even slightly different must be made on a very small budget. But even small-budget projects are difficult to set up because backers demand a distribution guarantee. This cannot be obtained for a film which has no "names," while "names" are incompatible with small budgets. Full circle. Additionally: union requirements place unnecessary burdens on the budget; guaranteed distribution depends on a censor-vetted script; and the market in Britain is so small that "unless you make a picture that will recover two-thirds of its cost outside this country, there is no hope that it can come out on the right side."

This is for the most part true and horrifying, especially when we come down to cases. Joseph Losey has been two years setting up production of

Alun Owen's *No Trams to Lime Street*. As star he has the not exactly unknown Stanley Baker. But "it's been extremely difficult to get set up. The usual complaints—'Where is the action?' 'There isn't enough sex.' 'It's downbeat.' 'It's too local.' 'It's a strictly domestic picture.' It is a character drama of the most sensitive and beautiful sort. It could be marvellous. . . . But, anyway, it's been a very great struggle." Losey also wanted to do a picture called *Israeli Love Story* with Hardy Kruger: "That, I think, we're setting up as a German-French-Israeli production; the English have all been too frightened to touch it, every single distribution set-up without exception."

Are Conditions Better Elsewhere?

We do not imagine that Losey's case is unique, and under the circumstances no one is going to blame British directors because they have not produced pictures like *Breathless* (*À Bout de souffle*, 1960), *Wild Strawberries* (*Smultronstället*, 1957), and *L'avventura* (1960). But the British cinema, as an industry dominated by near-monopolies, differs only in the size of its domestic market from the cinemas of Japan or the United States. [Kenji] Mizoguchi said: "I've been making films for thirty years. If I look back on all that I've done in that time I see nothing but a long series of compromises with the capitalists, whom we nowadays call producers, in order to make a film in which I could take pleasure. My only real desire has been to be able to make a film according to my own taste. But I have often been forced to accept a job knowing in advance that it couldn't offer the least chance of success and would mean nothing for me but an absolute failure."[2] The fact remains that Mizoguchi's long series of compromises resulted in at least three great films: *Ugetsu Monogatari* (1953), *Sanshô Dayû* (1954), and *Princess Yang Kwei-Fei* (1955).

The System Is Not a Sufficient Excuse

A comparison with the United States is even more revealing. American directors have no less trouble than British in making the films they want in the way they want. Indeed, in Hollywood's present state of evident chaos the difficulties are likely to be greater in the States than in Britain. Why, then, has

America been able to give us pictures as good as *Home from the Hill* (1960), *Rio Bravo* (1959), *Party Girl* (1958), *Heller in Pink Tights* (1960), *North by Northwest* (1959), and *Anatomy of a Murder* (1959)?

Now consider what happens to a good American director when he comes to work in Britain. We are liable to hear rumors of frustration and annoyance at working conditions here. His movie is quite likely to show signs of panicky reediting. (The general atmosphere of desperation is making this abominable practice common in both Britain and America.) Nevertheless he generally manages to make a film which reflects his ambitions, his conception, and his method rather than his conditions of work. In Britain were made Robert Aldrich's *The Angry Hills* (1959), Leo McCarey's *The Devil Never Sleeps* (1962), Howard Hawks's *Land of the Pharaohs* (1955), Nicholas Ray's *The Savage Innocents* (1960), and Hugo Fregonese's *Harry Black* (1958).

Most convincingly of all, in Britain, in 1957, on a limited budget, with a script little better than that of the average horror picture, and in spite of some awful effects work, a director of no prestige but enormous talent made one of the finest "occult" movies we have ever seen. In other words, Jacques Tourneur made *Night of the Demon* and offered us final proof that, however frustrating it may be, the British industrial system is not, in itself, a sufficient explanation of the badness of British films.

So how *can* we explain it? Primarily we would point to the general climate of opinion in Britain, and in particular to the British concept of The Good Film. The traditional British "quality" picture follows a recipe for which the ingredients are: an important and if possible controversial subject (race prejudice, the idiocy/inhumanity of war, the dignity of the individual, etc.); a popular story; a fair representation of all points of view; a resolution which makes the audience "think"; a "cinematic" treatment; and lastly, but importantly, a few "personal" idiosyncrasies (in the hope that mouthpieces will thus resemble people).

Now if this looks like the formula for *The Bridge on the River Kwai* (1957) so much the better: *Kwai* is the picture which almost all the old-guard directors would most like to make. It is also the direct product of a critical environment, of the belief that at its best the cinema offers "a good story well told."

The Woodfall Answer

The British "New Wave" is the product of a rather different, though related, belief. The awfulness of the "quality" picture was so readily apparent that the *Sequence* generation offered its own solution to the problems of the British cinema. What it needed, essentially, was a new sense of responsibility, and the courage to deal with life as it is lived on these islands; it must "come to grips with serious human relationships and with social problems." So now the new British cinema, or, more correctly, the Woodfall company, offers us a different and somewhat less rigid formula involving: a literary success on a "significant" and/or "working class" subject (*Look Back in Anger, The Entertainer, Saturday Night and Sunday Morning* [1960], *A Taste of Honey*); extensive location shooting; unfamiliar actors; and a conscientious attempt at style.

Somewhere between Woodfall and the traditional British cinema come the other New Wave films made by directors who have served the standard apprenticeship in the industry and who, in general, apply "traditional" methods to "Woodfall" subjects: Jack Clayton's *Room at the Top*; Guy Green's *The Angry Silence*; and John Schlesinger's *A Kind of Loving*.

How to Make a "Quality" Picture

What have been the practical results of these different approaches? The traditional "quality" cinema has given us a series of problem pictures dealing with, for example, race prejudice (*Sapphire* [1959]), homosexuality (*Victim*), and education (*Spare the Rod* [1961]). Their method is to devise a number of stereotypes to represent every possible attitude to the matter in hand; they have no success in their attempts to pass these stereotypes off as human beings. These pictures are particularly offensive in assuming that their holy platitudes are too loftily intellectual to be accepted by audiences unless the pill of wisdom is sweetened with spurious excitement. Thus, in *Sapphire* and *Victim*, Basil Dearden and his scriptwriter Janet Green have produced thriller-problem films which work neither as thrillers nor as examinations of a problem, and particularly not as films.

Dearden typifies the traditional Good Director: in the schematic nature of his subjects; in the appalling performances he draws from good actors; and in his total lack of feeling for cinema. He sacrifices everything to impact and, consequently, has none. Instead he gives us a compendium of all the stupid effects which are generally supposed to produce modernity. One of his specialties is the "shock" cut between sequences. In theory this gives a film pace, and pace is one of the Great Virtues. What Dearden produces, though, usually takes longer than the equivalent dissolve and looks much sillier. End of sequence; track into close-up of irrelevant detail; cut to close-up irrelevant detail of new setting; track out and begin sequence.

Perhaps we can show how little this sort of "style" is thought out, or felt, by taking a look at the way it works in Dearden's most recent picture. *All Night Long* (1962) is a contemp'ry *Othello* with an implicit racial tolerance message. At the beginning of the film a wealthy jazz lover is throwing a party to celebrate the first anniversary of Aurelius Rex, a bandleader (Paul Harris), and Delia Lane, a singer (Marti Stevens). Their arrival at the party is given a laborious build-up. We find out why in a medium shot held so long that we can only suppose we were meant to be shocked by its revelation: that Rex is a negro, and his wife is white!

In the hands of a sensitive director this could have had stunning effect. Hitchcock, for example, often does something very similar. He will trade on our prejudices to produce a shock, and then turn the shock back on us so that we are ashamed of our initial reaction. In *All Night Long*, however, the effect occurs simply because the director has not thought sufficiently about his style to realize that his method implicates him in what he is attacking.

New Places but No Sense of Place

It is in ambitious clumsiness of style that the new directors (Reisz excluded) most closely resemble the old guard; and it should be noted at this point that both Guy Green, in *The Mark* (1961), and Jack Clayton, in *The Innocents* (1961) (a pseudoambitious project), have reverted to traditional treatments of traditional subjects. Woodfall pioneered the new serious approach. To have done this must have involved considerable courage and persistence, especially since they were departing from the old schematized treatments as well as from the old ideas of what constitutes a "suitable" subject. But gratitude for the company's courage fades quickly when we are confronted with the conspicuous lack of talent in Woodfall's stock director, Tony Richardson. We would give quite a lot not to have seen *Look Back in Anger*, *The Entertainer*, and *A Taste of Honey*. Richardson's style conforms perfectly to the Lawrence definition of sentimentality: "Working out on yourself feelings you haven't really got."

Richardson, Reisz, Schlesinger, and Clayton are weakest exactly where their ambitions most demand strength: in the integration of character with background. Because of this weakness they are constantly obliged to "establish" place with inserted shots which serve only to strengthen our conviction that the setting, though "real," has no organic connection with the characters. So Richardson tarts up *A Taste of Honey* with his street games. And Schlesinger landscape-mongers in the most blatant and inept fashion. An example: the first "love" scene in *A Kind of Loving* is filmed mainly in a medium shot which shows us the boy and girl necking in a park shelter. On the walls behind and to the side of them we see the usual graffiti of names and hearts. The setting makes, in this way, a fairly obvious but relevant comment on the action. But Schlesinger has no appreciation of the power of his decor; he destroys the whole effect by moving his camera to take the actors out of the shot and isolate the inscriptions in meaningless close-up. As if he hadn't done enough damage he continues the movement until we come to rest on a totally gratuitous detail: a poster forbidding mutilation of the shelter. For all the location work, none of our directors has demonstrated a feeling for place nearly as acute as that displayed by Fred McLeod Wilcox on *Forbidden Planet* (1956).

"Before shooting a wedding scene, John Schlesinger took photographs at several churches. From these he built up an idea of an ordinary family which he used when he shot the opening scenes of *A Kind of Loving*." It is not done to quote publicity handouts in criticism. We allow ourselves to break the rule here because, accurate or not, the quote gives a very true impression of the film—and of *A Taste of Honey* and *Room at the Top*. They are films which emphasize, because they try to ignore, the distance between director and subject. They confuse research with statement; they finally look rather as *Nanook of the North* (1922) might have done if [Robert J.] Flaherty, while filming, had convinced himself that he was an Eskimo.

Reisz's *Saturday Night and Sunday Morning* is preferable to the other new movies partly because its director does not attempt to palm himself off as one of the lads, and partly because he is less addicted than his colleagues to attempts at extraneous "style." Also he knows a little about how to use actors. Other positive qualities are less easy to find, and when Reisz does try for a bit of "technique" he is no more bearable than Richardson.

The Right Sort of Films to Make

The fairground sequence of *Saturday Night* is one of the set pieces of which the new directors are so fond, and is unutterably silly. It is followed by a sequence to which Reisz obviously gave a good deal of thought: the beating up of Arthur Seaton (Albert Finney). Violence, because it is pure action, provides a very good test of a director's powers of staging. ("Fascist," no doubt, but true.) Reisz failed the test miserably. He devoted all his resources to obscuring the action, and he is not excused by the fact that the little he did let us see is very improbable. We are not saying, though it is a tenable position, that a director is obliged to show us everything all the time; we do say that action can only be obscured for a very good reason. The beating up in *The Criminal* (1960), for example, was shot in such tight close-ups that we do not see any of the blows connect. But here the technique works because tight close-ups are appropriate to a confined setting, and Losey was using them to convey the claustrophobic atmosphere of the prison cells. Also Losey has sufficient skill to let us know precisely what is happening without having to document the action. Reisz, on the other hand, gives us only the vaguest idea of events, coupled with the conviction that he did not want us to *see* what he was allegedly showing.

One guesses that Reisz was rather annoyed at having to portray violence at all. That would be perfectly in line with British opinion on the cinema which is concerned mainly with what a director ought to want to do. It is at this point that the beliefs behind the old and the new British films meet. Each is based on a preconception of the sort of film that ought to be made, whether it's a "good story well told" or "a long, hard look at the well-springs of the human condition as it displays itself in the grind of living."

For nearly fifteen years British film criticism has been concerned with "the important films to make." Thus Rotha on *Ugetsu*: "Mizoguchi, we are told, was one of the originators of the contemporary social problem film in Japan. If *The Street of Shame* (*Akasen chitai*, 1956) was an example, then he indeed deserves our praise but I cannot extend it to the period costume drama to which we are now submitted." In the same vein we find Derek Hill attributing the "failure" of the new French cinema to the fact that French criticism concentrates on *how* a film should be made, rather than on *why*.

To us this seems an eminently sane way of proceeding. In this sense, *why* he makes a film is a question for a director to ask himself in the light of his experience, his self-knowledge, and his moral convictions. *How* he expresses his personal vision, assuming that he has one, is much more a matter between the filmmaker and his audience. If thought and feeling are not to be devoted to style then we are indefinitely committed to ambitious nonsenses like *The Entertainer* and *Flame in the Streets* (1961).

At the same time we are committed to the unambitious excrescences like *The Secret Partner* (1961), *The Night We Dropped a Clanger* (1959), and *Blue Hell at St. Trinians*.[3] For the concomitant of a belief in "good subjects" is the belief that there are "bad subjects," assignments which one accepts in order to pay school fees, etc., and which are not worth any effort.

To appreciate the effect of this belief we must again compare British and American films. In this country "a little thing I'm doing for the money" is apt to turn into *Desert Mice* (1959). But a good American director will start from the same base and produce a picture like Paul Wendkos's *The Case Against Brooklyn* (1958), Don Siegel's *The Lineup* (1958), or Gerd Oswald's *Fury at Showdown* (1957). Given enough money to fill only a smallish piggy bank, a derelict airstrip, and a few clips from a silent film, Edgar Ulmer can produce a little miracle, *Beyond the Time Barrier* (1960). It doesn't happen in Britain because no one believes that a film with a title like *Beyond the Time Barrier* or *Fury at Showdown* can possibly be worth making.

The Case of Joseph Losey

Obviously a change in the climate of opinion cannot occur very quickly, and equally obvious is the fact that none of our directors is going to change overnight into an artist of extraordinary sensibility. Is there, then, any basis for hope? We believe that such hope as there is depends on two people, Joseph Losey and Seth Holt. Working in Britain under a handicap suffered by no other British director—the Hollywood blacklist—Losey has managed to produce three films that can stand comparison with practically anything that other countries can offer: *Time Without Pity* (1957), *Blind Date* (1959), and *The Criminal* (1960). All these pictures had unconvincing melodramatic plots. They were all made within the "system." They were all violated by our censor. In making them Losey had no peculiar advantage over any British director—except his talent. It was talent, and determination, which turned the stupid story provided for *The Criminal* into a deeply personal comment on, among other things, the horrors of the British prison system, the inevitable corruption of any system which relies on violence to enforce law, and the frustration of individuality in a rigidly organized capitalist society.

But Losey is an American. He has, at least temporarily, left Britain. How much indigenous talent have we which could legitimately inspire hope? Five years ago we would have named Robert Hamer (*Kind Hearts and Coronets* [1949], *Father Brown* [1954]) and Alexander Mackendrick (*The "Maggie"* [1954], *The Ladykillers* [1955], *Sweet Smell of Success* [1957]). Since then, however, we have seen nothing from either except, in Hamer's *The Scapegoat* (1959), the remains of a very good movie savaged by its distributor. We have a few young directors who have shown competence within the limits of the traditional British cinema: John Guillermin (*Waltz of the Toreadors* [1962]), Don Chaffey (*The Man Inside*), and John Moxey (*The City of the Dead* [1960]).[4] Peter Sellers has made one movie (*Mr. Topaze* [1961]), which was quite pleasant, and even thoughtfully directed. And we have Seth Holt.

Seth Holt: Taste of Talent

During all the excited commotion over the British New Wave, from *Room at the Top* to *A Kind of Loving*, when hardly six months have gone past without bringing some new "revelation," Seth Holt's *Taste of Fear* (1961) trickled by, apparently, without being very widely noticed. It was a horror-cum-mystery picture with unaesthetic contents, like a decomposing corpse. And it was indeed, by serious standards, not very good. However, we are convinced that, if any hope for the future of the British cinema exists in visible form, it comes from Holt's film rather than from—its only competitor—Reisz's. To put it simply, *Saturday Night and Sunday Morning* is a good film, and we can't imagine, on its evidence, that Karel Reisz will make a much better one. *Taste of Fear* is rather a bad film, and we can imagine Seth Holt making a masterpiece.

Excellent films have been made from mediocre scenarios—*Party Girl* is perhaps the locus classicus but there are plenty of other examples. *Taste of Fear* is a useful reminder that there is a level below which a scenario becomes untranscendable. It *couldn't*—without script changes more drastic than one guesses Hammer were prepared to sanction—have been a good film. Nothing but Holt's own word for it would convince us that he *wanted* to make it. Jimmy Sangster's story, as in *The Criminal*, is a preposterous amalgam of previous thrillers. In this case it leans especially heavily on the script of *Les Diaboliques* (1955), to which it is markedly inferior because it is full of obvious holes. Yet one certainly prefers Holt's film to [Henri-Georges] Clouzot's. What sets it apart from other British pictures? Simply that it reveals time and again a director who can create cinematically, where other directors are content with illustrating their scripts.

The distinction is as easy to see as it is difficult to explain: it has, of course, nothing to do with those collections of cute tricks that currently pass for style. We must be able to respond to the rhythm of the film. And we can point to various specific successes: the very subtle beginning with its tactful development of the relationship between Susan Strasberg and Ronald Lewis (the scenario, with its incorrigible penchant for trick endings, makes nonsense of this later on. Never mind, there is no question here of an organically successful film); the brief love scene between Lewis and Ann Todd where everything is conveyed through the handling of the actors; the tracking shot where the camera accompanies Lewis down the cliff-path to the salvaged car and communicates, in its movement, the character's growing uneasiness; Strasberg's long dinner-table speech about herself: no director has got from her before such inwardness and subtlety.

If we are less inclined to dwell on the "atmospheric" suspense effects, that is because they are easier to achieve; suffice it to say that no other British director has brought them off like this. Compare, for instance, the works of Terence Fisher (*Dracula* [1958], *The Curse of the Werewolf* [1961]), a distinction it would not be worth making explicitly were it not that our critics were generally content to lump *Taste of Fear* with all the other Hammer horrors.

The British Cinema Does Not Only Need New Subjects

Jean Domarchi said it in *Cahiers* and it seems almost too obvious to repeat: what the British cinema needs is not new subjects but new ideas about direction. The difference between *Taste of Fear* and *Dracula*, or Dearden's *The Secret Partner*, is a simple one of talent, not of subject or opportunity. It is easy to see why Domarchi described *The Angry Silence* as "un film très *Sight and Sound*"—not because *Sight and Sound* liked it (it didn't) but because it is the sort of picture that the particular critical climate represented by that publication, and endemic in this country, is likely to produce.

The Critics Must Bear Part of the Blame

We feel that *Sight and Sound* bears a graver responsibility than the editorial of its spring issue is prepared to acknowledge. "'Perhaps'—it says—'we know now, as we didn't then [three years ago], what a breakthrough might mean: we've had films as varied as *La notte* and *Il posto*, *Lola* and *À Bout de souffle* to teach us" ("Front Page" 1962). But *why* didn't we know then? *Look Back in Anger* was celebrated (Robinson 1959, 122–23; 179) in the issue of *Sight and Sound* (Summer/Fall 1959) that reviewed *Anatomy of a Murder*, *Le amiche* (1955), and *North by Northwest*, lamented *À Double Tour* (1959), and dismissed *Blind Date*, with a one-star recommendation, as a "brisk and well-made if illogical whodunit, laced with sex, class feeling and hints of corruption at Scotland Yard" ("Blind Date" 1959). If Britain needs an *À Bout de souffle*, why did Miss Houston's late assistant tell us that "by eliminating meaning and feeling, Godard has merely trapped himself in that familiar artistic *cul-de-sac*—the film all dressed up for rebellion, but with no real tangible territory on which to stand and fight" (Dyer 1961, 90)? We suspect that the "breakthrough" Miss Houston is hoping for is merely an increase in intellectual respectability, or perhaps simple snob value.

Style Is Worth Fighting For

We know that we can't have a *L'avventura* or an *À Bout de souffle* under the present system. We are much more disturbed by the fact that we are not getting equivalents for *Psycho* (1960), *Elmer Gantry* (1960), and *Written on the Wind* (1956). We relate this failure to the climate of opinion in Britain, not in the belief that a change therein will suddenly endow Dearden, Lee Thompson, or Richardson with talent; but because we hope that such a change would make it easier for our Holts, Hamers, and Mackendricks to find, initially, recognition and, subsequently, profitable employment. And we might in the end find ourselves enjoying the works of a homegrown, and home-based, Hitchcock.

We shall be on the way when British film enthusiasts are prepared to distinguish rigorously between the "haves" and the "have-nots" of talent, to champion the artists they respect, and to shout loud the names of the hacks they despise. But until it is accepted that style is worthy of passionate feeling and detailed analysis there will be no change.

Works Cited

"*Blind Date.*" *Sight and Sound* 28, nos. 3–4 (Summer/Fall) 1959: 192.
Dyer, Peter John. "*À Bout de souffle* (*Breathless*), France, 1959" (1961). *Monthly Film Bulletin: Index 1961* 38, nos. 324–35: 90.
"The Front Page." *Sight and Sound* 31, no. 2 (1962): 55.

Hazumi, Tsuneo. "Self-Assessment: An Unsatisfied Filmmaker." In *Mizoguchi the Master*, edited by Gerald O'Grady, 12. Toronto: Cinematheque Ontario, n.d. [likely 1996 or 1997].

———. "Trois Interviews de Mizoguchi." *Cahiers du Cinéma* 20, no. 116 (1961): 15–21.

Robinson, David. "*Look Back in Anger.*" *Sight and Sound* 28, nos. 3–4 (1959): 122–23; 179.

Filmography

À Bout de souffle (*Breathless*). Directed by Jean-Luc Godard. UGC, 1960.
Above Us the Waves. Directed by Ralph Thomas. General Film Distributors, 1955.
À Double Tour. Directed by Claude Chabrol. CCFC, 1959.
An Alligator Named Daisy. Directed by J. Lee Thompson. Rank, 1955.
All Night Long. Directed by Basil Dearden. Rank, 1962.
Le amiche. Directed by Michelangelo Antonioni. Titanus, 1955.
Anatomy of a Murder. Directed by Otto Preminger. Columbia Pictures, 1959.
The Angry Hills. Directed by Robert Aldrich. MGM, 1959.
The Angry Silence. Directed by Guy Green. British Lion (UK), Valiant Films (US), 1960.
Ashes and Diamonds (*Popiól i diament*). Directed by Andrzej Wajda. Kadr, 1958.
L'avventura. Directed by Michelangelo Antonioni. Cino del Duca, 1960.
Beyond the Time Barrier. Directed by Edgar G. Ulmer. American International Pictures, 1960.
Blind Date. Directed by Joseph Losey. Rank, 1959.
Blue Murder at St. Trinian's. Directed by Frank Launder. British Lion, 1957.
The Bridge on the River Kwai. Directed by David Lean. Columbia Pictures, 1957.
The Case Against Brooklyn. Directed by Paul Wendkos. Columbia Pictures, 1958.
The City of the Dead. Directed by John Moxey. British Lion, 1960.
The Criminal. Directed by Joseph Losey. Anglo-Amalgamated, 1960.
The Curse of the Werewolf. Directed by Terence Fisher. Rank (UK), Universal-International (US), 1961.
Desert Mice. Directed by Michael Relph. Rank, 1959.
The Devil Never Sleeps. Directed by Leo McCarey. Twentieth Century Fox, 1962.
Les Diaboliques. Directed by Henri-Georges Clouzot. Cinédis, 1955.
Dracula. Directed by Terence Fisher. Rank (UK), Universal-International (US), 1958.
Elmer Gantry. Directed by Richard Brooks. United Artists, 1960.
The Entertainer. Directed by Tony Richardson. British Lion, 1960.
Father Brown. Directed by Robert Hamer. Columbia Pictures, 1954.
Flame in the Streets. Directed by Roy Baker. Rank, 1961.
Forbidden Planet. Directed by Fred M. Wilcox. MGM, 1956.

Fury at Showdown. Directed by Gerd Oswald. United Artists, 1957.
Harry Black. Directed by Hugo Fregonese. Twentieth Century Fox, 1958.
Heller in Pink Tights. Directed by George Cukor. Paramount Pictures, 1960.
Home from the Hill. Directed by Vincente Minnelli. MGM, 1960.
The House of the Angel (*La Casa del Ángel*). Directed by Leopoldo Torre Nilsson. Argentina Sono Film SACI, 1957.
The Innocents. Directed by Jack Clayton. Twentieth Century Fox, 1961.
The Keepers (*La Tête contre les murs*). Directed by Georges Franju. La Société des Films Sirius, 1959.
Kind Hearts and Coronets. Directed by Robert Hamer. General Film Distributors, 1949.
A Kind of Loving. Directed by John Schlesinger. Anglo-Amalgamated (UK), Governor Films (US), 1962.
The Ladykillers. Directed by Alexander Mackendrick. Rank, 1955.
Land of the Pharaohs. Directed by Howard Hawks. Warner Bros., 1955.
The Lineup. Directed by Don Siegel. Columbia Pictures, 1958.
Lola. Directed by Jacques Demy. Unidex, 1961.
Look Back in Anger. Directed by Tony Richardson. Warner Bros., 1959.
The "Maggie" (US title: *High and Dry*). Directed by Alexander Mackendrick. General Film Distributors (UK), Universal-International (US), 1954.
Man of the West. Directed by Anthony Mann. United Artists, 1958.
The Man Upstairs. Directed by Don Chaffey. British Lion (UK), Kingsley-Union Films (US), 1958.
The Mark. Directed by Guy Green. Continental Distributing (UK), Twentieth Century Fox (US), 1961.
Mr. Topaze. Directed by Peter Sellers. Twentieth Century Fox, 1961.
Nanook of the North. Directed by Robert J. Flaherty. Pathé Exchange, 1922.
Night of the Demon. Directed by Jacques Tourneur. Columbia Pictures, 1957.
The Night We Dropped a Clanger. Directed by Darcy Conyers. Rank, 1959.
North by Northwest. Directed by Alfred Hitchcock. MGM, 1959.
No Trams to Lime Street. Directed by Ted Kotcheff. ITV (TV), 1959.
La notte. Directed by Michelangelo Antonioni. Dino de Laurentiis Cinematografica, 1961.
Party Girl. Directed by Nicholas Ray. MGM, 1958.
Il posto. Directed by Ermanno Olmi. Titanus, 1961.
Princess Yang Kwei-Fei. Directed by Kenji Mizoguchi. Daiei, 1955.
Psycho. Directed by Alfred Hitchcock. Paramount Pictures, 1960.
The Pure Hell of St. Trinian's. Directed by Frank Launder. British Lion, 1960.
Ramsbottom Rides Again. Directed by John Baxter. British Lion, 1956.
Rebel Without a Cause. Directed by Nicholas Ray. Warner Bros., 1955.
Rio Bravo. Directed by Howard Hawks. Warner Bros., 1959.
Room at the Top. Directed by Jack Clayton. British Lion (UK), Continental Distributing (US), 1959.
Sanshô Dayû. Directed by Kenji Mizoguchi. Daiei, 1954.
Sapphire. Directed by Basil Dearden. Rank (UK), Universal Pictures (US), 1959.

Saturday Night and Sunday Morning. Directed by Karel Reisz. British Lion/Bryanston, 1960.
The Savage Innocents. Directed by Nicholas Ray. Rank, 1960.
The Scapegoat. Directed by Robert Hamer. MGM, 1959.
The Secret Partner. Directed by Basil Dearden. MGM, 1961.
Spare the Rod. Directed by Leslie Norman. British Lion/Bryanston, 1961.
Stars (*Sterne*). Directed by Konrad Wolf. Boyana Film/Deutsche Film (DEFA), 1959.
The Street of Shame (*Akasen chitai*). Directed by Kenji Mizoguchi. Daiei, 1956.
Sweet Smell of Success. Directed by Alexander Mackendrick. United Artists, 1957.
Taste of Fear (US title: *Scream of Fear*). Directed by Seth Holt. Columbia Pictures Corporation, 1961.
A Taste of Honey. Directed by Tony Richardson. British Lion, 1961.
Time Without Pity. Directed by Joseph Losey. Astor Pictures, 1957.
Ugetsu Monogatari. Directed by Kenji Mizoguchi. Daiei, 1953.
Vertigo. Directed by Alfred Hitchcock. Paramount Pictures, 1958.
Victim. Directed by Basil Dearden. Rank, 1961.
Waltz of the Toreadors. Directed by John Guillermin. Rank (UK), Continental Distributing (US), 1962.
Wild Strawberries (*Smultronstället*). Directed by Ingmar Bergman. Svensk Filmindustri, 1957.
The Wolf Trap (*Vlčí jáma*). Directed by Jirí Weiss. Ceskoslovenský Státní Film/Filmové Studio Barrandov, 1958.
Written on the Wind. Directed by Douglas Sirk. Universal Pictures, 1956.

Notes

1   In his tribute to Ian Cameron, Perkins wrote of the collaborative discussions that fed into the first issue of *Movie*: "On an agenda agreed in discussion Ian wrote an editorial proclamation but it appeared unsigned. Robin Wood's authorship is evident in some passages of the lead article on British Cinema that appeared over my name." *Movie: A Journal of Film Criticism*, no 1 (2010): 1–2. https://warwick.ac.uk/fac/arts/film/movie/contents/ian_cameron_-_a_tribute.pdf (accessed June 1, 2020). Ed.

2   This is probably Perkins's own translation from the collection of three interviews with Mizoguchi published as "Trois Interviews de Mizoguchi" in *Cahiers du Cinéma* 20, no. 116 (1961): 15–21. This interview was originally recorded for radio broadcast by NHK (Nippon Hoso Kyokai/Japan Broadcasting Corporation) in 1950. The interviewer was film critic Tsuneo Hazumi (1908–1958), who also worked as a producer at Toho and Shintoho during the early postwar years (1946–50). The French text of Perkins's translation is found in *Cahiers* 20: 15 and reads as follows:

> Voici trente ans que j'exerce ce métier. Si je réfléchis à tout ce que j'ai fait de tout ce temps, je ne sois qu'une longue série de compromis et de querelles avec les capitalistes, qu'on appellee aujourd'hui producteurs, pour réaliser un film qui me plaise. Je travaillais vraiment avec le seul désir de pouvoir choisir de faire un film suivant mon goût. Mais il arrive que je sois obligé parfois d'accepter un travail, tout en sachant à l'avance qu'il ne peut offrir la moindre chance de réussite et ne m'apporter même qu'un échec absolu.

A different English-language translation of the interview appears as "Self-Assessment: An Unsatisfied Filmmaker" in Gerald O'Grady, ed., *Mizoguchi the Master* (Toronto: Cinematheque Ontario, n.d. [likely 1996 or 1997]), the newspaper-format anthology produced to accompany the traveling Mizoguchi retrospective that reached London in February 1998. With thanks to Alex Jacoby for this information. Ed.

3 Perkins has conflated here *Blue Murder at St. Trinian's* (1957) and *The Pure Hell of St. Trinian's* (1960). Ed.

4 There is no Don Chaffey film by this title. The reference might be to *The Man Upstairs* (1958). Ed.

CLIVE DONNER AND *SOME PEOPLE*

First published in Movie, *no. 3 (October 1962): 22–25.*

What can you do about a film sponsored by the Duke of Edinburgh's Award Scheme *and* starring Kenneth More?[1] Conscientious objection would seem to be the only valid reaction and, for once, one was willing to be amused by the snide journalese which passes for criticism in the *Observer*'s film columns: [after their first contact with the Duke of Edinburgh's scheme] "The Young People start doing life-saving and using Wolf Cub phrases: 'I've made a musical instrument for my pursuit,' says a 17-year-old proudly. The girls knit, which is a way of taking their minds off Going Too Far, for if you are D. of E. you mustn't go too far. People say 'D. of E.' rather as though it were the next stage on from 'C. of E'" (Gilliatt 1962, 21).

This is a very nice evocation of the film that one expects to see, a monstrous mating of *Reach for the Sky* (1956) and *The Young Ones* (1961), with a little bit of *Violent Playground* (1958) thrown in for foul measure. It bears, however, no relation at all—in terms of the minimum requirements of accuracy—to *Some People*, the film under discussion. This is not a matter of differing opinions on a particular film. Mrs. Gilliatt has not simply disliked a film that I happen to like enormously; she has attacked a purely personal hallucination, so that in the three sentences quoted above there are three quite obvious misrepresentations of what actually occurs on the screen.[2]

Obvious, that is, once one has seen the film. Unfortunately there was no magazine showing of *Some People*, and *Movie*'s writers were sufficiently daunted by the prospect outlined above to postpone seeing the picture until the last week of its London release. Hence this belated acknowledgment of the film's excellence. Anglo-Amalgamated assure us, however, that it will be quite widely shown in the independent cinemas over the next couple of months.

Some People is the most intelligent, honest, and enjoyable picture from a British director since Seth Holt's *Nowhere to Go* (1958). But it is not simply a triumph in the context of British filmmaking, which would not be difficult to achieve; it is, by any standards, a very good movie. It has a less self-conscious, and therefore more genuine, freedom than any of the films of the so-called British New Wave.

Talking to Clive Donner, its director, we were surprised by the casual way in which he dismissed the conventions of British quality cinema.

James Archibald, the producer, was approached by the Duke of Edinburgh Award Scheme to make a picture for them. They wanted a picture which brought the idea of the scheme to the attention of what the sociologists call the "unattached teenager." He and I went on a tour with the scheme's deputy director which was aimed to show us a cross-section of young people throughout the country. As a result we decided that in order to give them the film they wanted, we would have to make an entertainment picture (not a didactic documentary, because it wouldn't reach the audience it was intended for) and one in which there was no aspect of people being got at. There was obviously a propaganda requirement. The sponsors said they wanted their point made good and strong. We said they wouldn't achieve anything by being blatant about it. It would be foolish and dishonest to pretend that it wasn't there, but it would have to be there very much in proportion to the other activities—as it would be in life if this subject were to come up: the kids would talk about it, in the coffee bar scene for instance, for two or three sentences and then get on to talking about Helen Shapiro.

Donner, clearly in the film and explicitly in conversation, is more interested in characterization and narrative than in thematic statements. But he has gone far beyond the point of simply refusing to proselytize. We are encouraged to join with the characters in taking the rise out of the scheme: at one point it is described as "a scheme for giving you tea at Buckingham Palace when you've got your gold, whatever that is." Donner's aim was *to send it up rotten as often as possible. But I think that's the only way to do it. Of course it's open to criticism and we tried to treat it naturally, in a way that isn't holy. Why should you take a starry-eyed view of something which you happen to think is good?*

Some People in fact joins the long line of films, including *Psycho* (1960), *Rio Bravo* (1959), and *The Devil Never Sleeps* (1962), whose gags are a proof of seriousness. The genre has been practically extinct in Britain for a very long time.

Some People is also the first of the British life-as-it-is-lived movies to be filmed in color.

It was partly done for the entertainment value, but also because to me the convention that reality is better in black and white is just a convention, and there's no reason why you shouldn't adopt another one.

The film was made entirely on location in Bristol. We are thus for the first time informed that real people exist in all parts of England and are not just a phenomenon observable in cities to the north of Birmingham.

This was very much a reason for going there. We wanted to break away: realist drama doesn't only have to take place in the north country but you can hardly move up there without falling over a film unit. There were other reasons also. It had to be made in a provincial city, not in London. I didn't want to make it in a city where there was a traditional background of working class problems, because I don't think that the subject we're considering in the film relates so much to traditional "bad areas" but much more to the housing estates and so forth: we didn't want a town like Jarrow. Bristol was one of the places that impressed me most on our tour, and it has a considerable problem among young people. The scheme's deputy director had a lot of personal contacts there. Lastly, of course, it was very exciting visually. I could go back to Bristol and make four more pictures without feeling that I was repeating myself.

Within the British context perhaps the most exciting thing about *Some People* is that it uses its message as a pretext for presenting its characters, as against the standard practice of using "characters" as a pretext for presenting a message. This is not to suggest that Donner has betrayed his sponsors. No one who sees the film is likely to leave the cinema ignorant of the existence of the Duke of Edinburgh's Award Scheme. On the other hand, the scheme is only important to the movie insofar as it affects and illuminates the relationships of the characters. *Some People*, like most good pictures, has a basically simple plot more important in its details than its outline. But since few of *Movie*'s readers are likely to have seen the film it seems advisable, even at the risk of making the story sound silly, to provide a synopsis.

Johnny, Bert, and Bill (Ray Brooks, David Hemmings, David Andrews) are three teenagers who derive most of their pleasure, after work, from their motorbikes. As a result of an accident they are summoned on charges of dangerous driving, and their licenses are suspended. Wandering around Bristol one evening they come upon a youth club which Bill despises for offering "hymns and ping-pong" as the ingredients of an exciting evening. Inside, Bert forces open the locked piano so that Johnny can play for them. They are thrown out by the club leader and accused of being troublemakers. Johnny is furious and when the boys come upon a church he leads them inside and plays a twist number on the organ. They are interrupted by an outraged vicar (Michael Gwynne) who then hands them over to Smith (Kenneth More), the organist and choirmaster. Smith attempts to take a reasonable view of the matter. When he discovers that the boys have their own guitar group but nowhere to play he offers them the use of the church hall on choir-practice nights. They accept his offer, but Bill, who guards his nonconformist reputation jealously, is suspicious of a catch.

At the church hall Johnny meets Ann, Smith's daughter (Anneke Wills), and after a while she becomes his girl. The group is joined by two members of the choir, Tim (Timothy Nightingale) on guitar, and Jimmy (Frankie Dymon) on drums. Bill's girl, Terry (Angela Douglas), who is more interested in Johnny, completes the line-up by singing with them. Bill's suspicions, which have led him to withdraw from the group, are apparently confirmed when Smith turns out to be the local organizer of the Duke of Edinburgh's Award Scheme, to which both Tim and Jimmy belong. Smith outlines the scheme and in the argument which follows Terry and the boys, including Bill, find that they have joined the scheme simply to prove to Smith that there's nothing to it. Bill is increasingly fed up with Terry's attentions to Johnny. He suggests to Bert that they should join together in building a canoe in which, as a way of avoiding too much walking, they can carry out the expedition which is one of the scheme's requirements.

Johnny and Ann have fallen in love, but Ann breaks the relationship when she tells Johnny that she intends to go to college and that he "won't be the last." Johnny suggests that she is acting on advice from her parents and they quarrel. Bill drops out of the scheme. He tells Johnny that he is better off without Ann and that the scheme is just a plot to induce him to "conform and be happy." But when Johnny accepts Bert's invitation to join him on the canoe expedition, Bill quarrels with them. In the evening he brings a number of his friends to the church hall, where the group is practicing, and provokes a fight with Johnny. The hall is wrecked and Johnny feels that Smith holds him responsible.

Johnny searches for Bill, intending to fight, but his intention dissolves in the enjoyment of the chase around the roller-skating rink where he finds him. Bill maintains that he has done him a good turn by freeing him from his tie with the group, but Johnny insists on his right to choose his own friends and admits that he has learned a lot from Ann. He goes to see Smith outside the church hall and offers to help pay for the damage. Smith says it won't be necessary, but urges Johnny to go inside and rejoin the guitar group. "After all, they *are* your friends." Johnny eventually agrees. Although he is greeted by a shout of welcome from the group as he goes through the door, there is no suggestion of a renewal of his relationship with Ann.

The main question is, of course, what has Johnny learned. Certainly not that the gates of heaven lie just beyond the gates of Buckingham Palace. In a sense the arguments which Smith puts forward on behalf of the scheme are extraordinarily weak. It's "just a way of keeping people busy, I suppose."

I don't think that's unfair. The trouble is that there are no complete answers. There are only partial answers and a partial answer will be partial at all stages in its conception. One of the troubles about this, or any other, scheme is that there's no solid point which you can offer to justify it. I think you have to allow for a certain natural embarrassment on Smith's part because he's intelligent enough to realize this.

But the criticism of the scheme is also a criticism of our society; it can offer no really purposeful outlet for the energy which is the most obvious of the moral qualities shared by Johnny, Bert, and Bill. It can only attempt to absorb that energy so that it is not employed destructively. Bill seizes on this point in his most intelligent and forceful argument. He sees the scheme as just one aspect of the plot hatched by adult conformist society to tame people like himself and Johnny and to swamp their individuality. Johnny objects that the scheme is explicitly for the individual, not for the team. "Of course it's for the individual," says Bill, "so long as he joins the team."

On the other hand Bill's actions are inconsistent with his argument. He reduces the problem of individuality to a simple choice between two teams. He resents Johnny's association with Smith and the group not, one suspects, because it is a team but because it is the wrong team. Consequently Bill sacrifices his individuality to the stereotyped trappings of nonconformity; he exchanges, in other words, the reality for the appearance. This distinction is perhaps the most important thing that Johnny learns. At the end of the movie Bill has no answer for Johnny's decision to choose his friends wherever he pleases, even from among the "conformists."

The film embodies in its approach the thing which it shows in its narrative. It depicts the resolution of a number of class and status conflicts, and it does so naturally and honestly, with a complete lack of embarrassment or awe. There is one particularly striking piece of social observation early in the film when the boys first set up their guitars in the church hall. One of the amplifiers goes wrong and Tim comes forward and offers to fix it, but he does so apologetically in a way which reveals clearly the barrier of embarrassment and feared resentment that separates working-class grammar school from working-class secondary modern (fig. 1). In the course of the film, however, this barrier is crossed without strain. On the level of personal relationships (and he does not attempt to treat the problem on any other level), Donner suggests that there is nothing insuperable about the barriers put up by differences in social and educational background. "Some people," the song says, "ought to simmer down," and one can only hope the message will get through

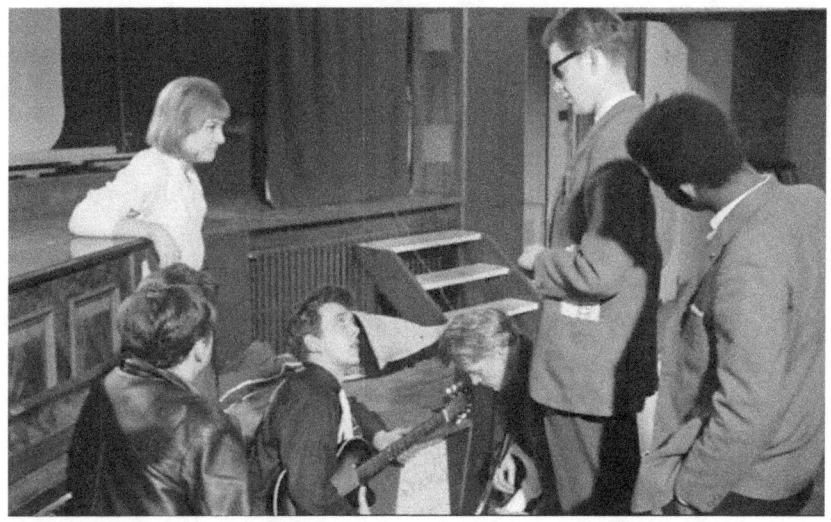

Figure 1. Tim offers to fix the amplifier

to some filmmakers. The ability to observe class differences without hysteria and renounce them without pomposity is a valuable asset.

Some People profits enormously from Donner's refusal to force the pace, to make the connections too obvious. Toward the beginning of the film the boys pass a rather chi-chi restaurant (unidentified but, in fact, Marco's), and they spend some time making fun of its patrons. Later, we learn that Johnny has taken Ann to dinner at Marco's (mentioned by name, but not shown).

The intention was to show that Ann slightly opened his eyes. He could go into Marco's, there was no difficulty. He could afford it, that was no problem, and there was no reason at all why he shouldn't take a girl there if he wanted. We did have a scene with them there originally, but we took it out because although it was a very pretty shot it didn't do much for the film dramatically.

But Donner's attitude is not one of middle-class paternalism; in fact, Ann learns at least as much from Johnny as he does from her, a point which is graphically illustrated by a sequence in which she sits in the bath fully clothed in order to shrink her jeans skin-tight according to Johnny's instructions. The whole relationship between Ann and Johnny is beautifully handled. There is no attempt to make their emotional reactions oversophisticated, and at the moment when the idea of love between them is first tentatively suggested, we realize that they are experimenting with their own feelings. Similarly, they neither meet nor part in an unduly dramatic way. Johnny and Ann are not Romeo and Juliet. "You won't be the last," and they both know it.

The camera style, like the narrative and the acting, is natural and unemphatic. Bert appears at the magistrates' court in his "best" dark suit and grey winkle-pickers. But the shoes are not thrown at the audience; in fact, they only appear in the long shots as the boys walk out of the courtroom. Donner asks quite a lot of his audience's powers of observation. It is quite often required to make up its own mind as to the characters' motivations since the director frequently does not explain them until after the event and sometimes not at all. For example, Ann tells her father that Johnny and his friends are the first boys she's known, "at least since it began to make any difference, who've ever treated me with any sort of respect." Because the boys are not particularly courteous, we have to work out for ourselves what Ann means by "respect."

On the other hand, Donner is not Preminger; he does not want to leave our reactions completely free. He intends that we should identify with the boys rather than with the representatives of adult conformism. For this reason we are introduced to Johnny at work, with Bill, and at home before we see him in his motorbike uniform.

Audience identification with the boys is so complete that there is no sympathy at all for the magistrate, who lectures them in a way which is completely sensible but entirely out of touch. One has little patience with his tired and defeated manner, but one responds wholeheartedly to Bill's vigorous "Silly old git!" as the boys march out into the street.

Some People is brilliantly acted. There is not a bad performance in the picture, and the young people are all staggeringly good, without a trace of uncertainty or theatricality. For once improvisation is evident from the naturalness, complexity, and confidence of the performances, not from the actors' embarrassment. Donner had three weeks of rehearsals before starting to shoot the film. We talked to him about two sequences where the acting is particularly detailed and spontaneous. In the first the boys are fooling around outside a bookshop.

I didn't really know what was going on. It was very roughly rehearsed but the boys worked together so closely that they could play a scene like this alongside each other and instinctively get timing and overlapping right without my having to go over it point by point in those sorts of situation. For the discussion in the coffee bar there was a scene written in the script which we rehearsed. We then revised the scene and broke it down so that everyone had his lines. Then when I came to shoot it, I squashed it all up again and made them all talk one across the other.

Although it is in no real sense a musical, *Some People* is the first British picture whose beat numbers have had any impact. The title song, in particular, is staged and edited with a splendid sense of rhythm, so that, while remaining quite credible on a naturalistic level, it comes across as infectiously as the most stylized Bob Fosse creation. In this connection one might note a remarkable piece of honesty: we hear one of the numbers, "Too Late," on a coffee-bar jukebox some time before we see it played by the group. There is no pretense that Bristol is harboring a number of teenagers who happen to be able to write as tunefully as Ron Grainer.

The sequence inside the church provides a number of examples of Donner's control of his material. He has led up to it very strongly (perhaps too strongly) so that we half expect that the boys are going to wreck the place. Once inside, however, they forget their anger in the enjoyment of their own daring. Their mood is conveyed to us partly through our identification with the actors, but also because, when Johnny gets up into the organ loft, he discovers a little game with the remote control of the stops. We share his delight in this and forget the violent atmosphere created in the scene outside the church. From this point the excitement builds up rapidly. Johnny tries out the organ. Bert makes a half-serious attempt to drag himself away. Johnny starts to play—a rocked version of Sullivan. Bert finds a surplice and puts it on. He and Bill go into a twist-cum-jive in the aisles. The camera follows Bert closely as the two boys jump around, so that the sequence culminates in the wildly anarchic image of his whirling white surplice. The vicar arrives and shouts at Johnny to come down from the loft. The sudden silence is interrupted only by the dying sigh of the organ pump as Johnny switches it off. *Some People* is full of such abrupt and adroit changes of mood.

In the past four years, Donner's abilities have been squandered on Edgar Wallace quickies. One can only hope that the success of *Some People* will have cleared the way for more profitable employment.

Work Cited

Gilliatt, Penelope. "Young England Up to Date." *Observer*, July 22, 1962, 21.

Filmography

The Devil Never Sleeps. Directed by Leo McCarey. Twentieth Century Fox, 1962.
Nowhere to Go. Directed by Seth Holt. MGM, 1958.
Psycho. Directed by Alfred Hitchcock. Paramount Pictures, 1960.
Reach for the Sky. Directed by Lewis Gilbert. Rank, 1956.
Rio Bravo. Directed by Howard Hawks. Warner Bros., 1959.
Some People. Directed by Clive Donner. Anglo-Amalgamated, 1962.
Violent Playground. Directed by Basil Dearden. Rank, 1958.
The Young Ones. Directed by Sidney J. Furie. Warner-Pathé, 1961.

Notes

1 The Duke of Edinburgh's Award is a scheme for young people, established in 1956. Participants undertake a range of activities, successful completion of which can lead to bronze, silver, and gold awards. Ed.

2 Penelope Gilliatt (1932–1993), English novelist, short story writer, screenwriter, and film critic. She wrote on film for the *Observer* from 1961 to 1967, and for the *New Yorker* from 1967 to 1979. Ed.

CENSORSHIP

First published in Movie, *no. 6 (January 1963): 16.*

The British Board of Film Censors (BBFC) is often regarded as existing for the protection of the British public.[1] In fact, it exists solely for the protection of the film industry. John Trevelyan is the industry's chief PR man in this country; insofar as there is a real opposition between art and commerce in the cinema, our censor is committed to the interests of commerce. His function is to protect the industry from hostile public opinion. He has two main enemies: the cheapjack sensationalist and the artist. Either can, for his own reasons, incur the wrath of the nation's moral guardians.

But the artist is treated more severely than the cheapjack—compare the fate of any arse-flaunting nudie with that of *Vivre sa vie* (1962) or *Blind Date* (1959). Quite right too: art is infinitely more subversive than sensationalism. These categories are not, however, mutually exclusive. The censor is at his most vicious when dealing with a film that refuses to settle comfortably into one of the pigeonholes: *Underworld U.S.A.* (1961), *The Chapman Report* (1962), *Blood and Roses* (*Et Mourir de plaisir*, 1960). Sensationalism is a necessary ingredient of all these films, and many others. By cutting their most effectively sensational sequences the censor wins the battle, not for "morality," but for philistinism.

In order to shield the industry from unfavorable publicity, the BBFC cuts "any matter likely to cause offence to the majority of reasonable people."[2] In other words, the board acts in defense of established values. One can, if one wishes, believe in the censor's sincerity when he claims not to discriminate against opinion, but his naïveté is incontestable. Any act reflects a moral attitude; any depiction of an act states a moral attitude. When he deletes a shot from a movie, the censor vetoes one viewpoint and states another. The boasted invisibility of BBFC cuts only makes the changes more insidious. In doing so, he condemns the cinema to a tedious mediocrity of opinion: for example, sex is allowed to be sordid or pleasant, but it may not be filthy or ecstatic. On the stage, our society tolerates striptease but not nudity; on the screen, nudity is permitted so long as it is ill-photographed and unattractive enough to convert any healthy male to the pursuit of handsome young sailors. Sniggers are allowed, belly laughs are banned. The movies are "free" in Britain to do only those things for which freedom is not needed. A director who is allowed to do anything (provided that it does not cause offence) has merely the illusion of liberty.

Freedom is only valuable, only in fact noticeable, when it extends to the unpopular or unacceptable point of view. Why should the movies not be free to say to adult audiences that sex is a messy drag or that cruelty is life's greatest pleasure? And if our society is so death-ridden that it needs protection from these beliefs, then is it worth protecting?

From what, in any case, does the BBFC shield us? Not from obscenity: the oil pump in *The Chapman Report* is a remarkably contemptuous symbol for copulation. Not from sadism: in *Dr. No* (1962) the audience is expected to share the hero's delight in spy-shooting. In *The Chapman Report* sex is repulsive and in *Dr. No* killing is fun, but not *explicitly*. The moment the viewpoint becomes clear, as it did presumably in the missing portions of *The Chapman Report*, Uncle John feels obliged to borrow Aunt Edna's scissors.

The enemy, then, is lucidity. We may imagine, we may suspect, we may infer, but we may not see. The BBFC indulges the most noxious obscenity of the mid-twentieth century, the will to blindness. Trevelyan's recipe for a *Quo Vadis* (1951) arena sequence is a model of pornographic filmmaking in the striptease convention. It is easier to enjoy the thought than to relish the sight of a human body being torn by a lion. The demand for a "tasteful" presentation of violence is an endorsement of violence. The desire to "purify" sex is clearly neurotic. And the pretense of moral superiority to the poor corruptibles who go to the movies is, at least, somewhat grandiose.

The fate of *The Chapman Report* is particularly disturbing because of the modernity of the film's preoccupation—with the quality, not just the fact, of sex. *Private Property* (1960), another American film with a similar subject, was banned altogether. Is the screen ever to be allowed to examine sexual relationships in detail? To put the question another way, what hope is there for an end to the present regime at the BBFC, for a classifying, but not mutilating, system of film censorship? The only ultimate solution is the legal recognition of the privileges and responsibilities of the director, as author of a film; but this is a very remote prospect. One can expect nothing from the industry itself, unless commercial pressures compel it to demand a more "liberal" censorship. In the meantime, the best we can do is to exploit the censor's sensitivity to public opinion by squawking whenever outrage is committed. Freedom of expression must be defended as vigorously as public virtue.

Filmography

Blind Date. Directed by Joseph Losey. Rank, 1959.
Blood and Roses (*Et Mourir de plaisir*). Directed by Roger Vadim. Paramount Pictures, 1960.
The Chapman Report. Directed by George Cukor. Warner Bros., 1962.
Dr. No. Directed by Terence Young. United Artists, 1962.
Private Property. Directed by Leslie Stevens. Citation Films, 1960.
Quo Vadis. Directed by Mervyn LeRoy. MGM, 1951.
Underworld U.S.A. Directed by Samuel Fuller. Columbia Pictures, 1961.
Vivre sa vie. Directed by Jean-Luc Godard. Panthéon Distribution, 1962.

Notes

1   In 1984, the organization changed its name to British Board of Film Classification. Ed.

2   Perkins may be drawing from the editorial "The Front Page" in *Sight and Sound* 29, no. 4 (1960): 59, which focused on British film censorship and included the following point: "One issue which has found surprisingly little place in the discussion concerns the theory on which our censorship operates. Its basis: nothing ought to be shown on a public screen which is considered likely to give offence to reasonable people." Ed.

FORCED TO BE FREE OR DOING BUSINESS IN A GREAT ART

First published in Movie, *no. 15 (Spring 1968): 17–19.*

Legislation on the British film industry is now being reviewed. The Board of Trade does not lack advice in drafting the measures that will come into effect in three years' time. The Monopolies Commission presented its report in late 1966. The Cinematograph Films Act was due for renewal last year. In preparation, every group with an interest to further or protect made use of the public relations networks to broadcast its case loud and, where clarity was thought desirable, clear. With new legislation postponed to 1970 the PR effort continues; at times it has seemed that the highest aim of anyone connected with movies in this country might be to have his press conference become a news item, his *Outlook* a briefing.

Movie, almost uniquely, has no special interest to promote but is eager for the survival and prosperity of the cinema: the more films that are made and shown the greater the chance that a few of them will reward critical attention. It seems worthwhile to offer some proposals and observations, especially since the public prints—failing to maintain the skepticism which is owed to all forms of advertising—have sometimes been induced to view the situation in hero-villain terms. It is important that our legislators resist this temptation. Despite the peculiar interdependence of the various interests within the film trade, each is quick to exploit any immediate advantage for its own aggrandizement or another's discomfiture. Given a shift in the balance of power, April's poor-but-honest will be happy to emerge as December's ruthless rich. And, always, for the best of reasons.

The real problems arise from fundamental conflicts within the nature of the film industry. The basic facts are familiar to us all. Movies are at once the most costly and, potentially, the most profitable form of entertainment yet devised. As a manufacturer, the filmmaker invests in a hugely expensive product, which, when completed, may prove to be worth millions of pounds or tens of pence. He will recover his investment rapidly or not at all. He is therefore concerned to see his product distributed with the greatest possible speed and system to the most profitable outlets. The pressure here is toward tightly organized chains of cinemas giving maximum exposure at minimum expense.

Equally valid arguments, however, point in the opposite direction. Each film is a unique product offering to each of its potential patrons a unique blend of lures and deterrents, to each member of its audience a unique balance of pleasures and frustrations. You can't please all of the people all of the time. So what's needed is a very flexible system which recognizes the individuality of both movies and moviegoers, and gives each picture the chance of reaching its particular audience. From this viewpoint "tight organization" looks indistinguishable from rigidity. In his role as showman, rather than manufacturer, the filmmaker would surely wish to acknowledge the variousness of audiences by advocating freedom for each cinema to select its own programs to suit its own patrons.

It's clear that the system in this country follows the more rigid pattern, making very few concessions to the claim for variety and showmanship. A complicated mesh of restrictive practices has been inherited from the years in which every operator fought to protect his right to get rich quick by limiting competition. In addition the closures and "rationalizations" of the past decade have greatly increased the dominance of the two major circuits, controlled by ABC and Rank. A film can be considered to have been distributed in this country—to have enjoyed a reasonable opportunity of earning a reasonable part of its production costs here—only when it has secured a release on one or other of these circuits. Informal ties between distributors and the circuits further limit the prospects. A film handled by, say, Twentieth Century Fox will be offered to the Odeon (Rank) circuit but not to ABC. In effect, if the film does not tour the Odeons it will scarcely be played at all. However, this fact can be interpreted variously: as evidence either of the way competition is stifled by the rigid patterns of distribution and exhibition, or of the way that the present system recognizes facts of show-business life. Given the necessity of retaining the distributor's goodwill, Rank is likely to accept any Fox film which can hope to pay its way around the circuit. On the other side, ABC—while perhaps willing to exert itself on behalf of a doubtful Warner or MGM picture—can hardly be expected to take an interest in a Fox film that was too risky even for Rank. So it would be an empty gesture if Fox were to demonstrate "competition" by offering its Odeon rejects to the ABC circuit. Every producer risks creating a totally unsaleable picture. It is not unknown for the Odeons to feel obliged to turn down movies financed, wholly or partly, by the Rank Organisation itself.

Which brings us to another aspect of the monopoly situation. Rank and ABC are not simply the dominant powers in film exhibition. Each of them is engaged also in production and distribution—they even own the studios where their pictures are made. They are thus uniquely placed in relation both to other film producers and to other cinema owners, since they command the screen space needed by the former and the films required by the latter. It would be, at least, odd if they did not attempt to turn the situation to profit by securing the best opportunities for their own films and by acquiring the most promising pictures, on the most favorable terms, for their own cinemas.

Within a structure displaying so pronounced an unbalance of power, it is necessarily difficult to distinguish a sensible enjoyment of the benefits of size and authority from unscrupulous exploitation designed to squeeze out independent competition, or from a blinkered insistence on immediate gains which may have the same effect. It is against this background that the crises of the past few years have erupted, that the Monopolies Commission has made its report, and that the government will have to legislate.

The objectives are quite easily defined, and largely noncontroversial. We wish to secure the continuance, hence profitability, of film production in this country; and to ensure that movies are available to the public, as an amenity, wherever there is a demand sufficient to make their presentation (in whatever form) self-supporting. Both these aims require us to cope with special problems arising from the dominance of the two great combines. It is open to the government either to enforce changes in the structure and control of the film industry, or to adopt measures to regulate the operation of the existing system.

Among the radical solutions that have been canvassed the most attractive is the compulsory separation of exhibition from distribution and production. The model here is the American antitrust legislation, which pushed the big production-distribution combines out of cinema ownership. Theoretically, this carries the advantage that exhibitors, liberated from financial and bureaucratic ties with producing companies, become free to choose films on their commercial merits. Such a course would not oblige the circuits themselves to operate more flexibly, nor would it reduce their domination over other exhibitors. Moreover, in this country divorcement would not have the consequences that it had in the States. There the major combines (Paramount, MGM, and so on) were pushed back into the production and distribution sector. It's certain that here, forced to a choice, Rank and ABC would opt out of production and allied activities, restricting their film interests to exhibition.

Granted that the Rank Organisation has a lamentable record in the production field and that we would not feel too acutely the loss of our Norman Wisdoms, Morecambes and Wises, Betty Boxes and *Long Duels* (1967), there remains a valid argument that forces so dominant in the relatively low-risk business of exhibition ought to accept large responsibilities in the highly speculative production arena. In other words, Rank and ABC could reasonably be asked to extend, rather than eliminate, their involvement in film financing.

Again, the existence of the vertical combines is at least defensible and probably essential in view of the standing threat to British production from America. We may be more or less conscious of this threat from year to year—at the moment it seems negligible—but it must weigh heavily in decisions on the structure of the British industry. The power of the circuits does much to offset the advantage that the size of its home market gives to

American production throughout the English-speaking world. It is surely not pure coincidence that, the States apart, Britain is the one English-speaking country to have both a tight, near-monopoly pattern of exhibition and a native tradition of feature film production. The one may be a necessary guarantee for the other.

A similar objection applies to the idea of forming a third circuit from existing cinemas. If this is to be powerful enough to compete for films with Rank and ABC, some of their cinemas will have to be purchased compulsorily. As a result many people will be cut off from ready access to the most popular films, and box-office returns to the producers of these successful movies will suffer substantial reduction. But if the third circuit offers a less attractive deal than the two majors can provide, it will have access only to pictures of dubious appeal: its one chance of survival will be to exploit its monopoly of the duds by squeezing the distributors' share of the box-office take. In neither case can a third circuit be expected to offer much encouragement to production. Nor is it desirable for the government to recognize and entrench the circuit system of exhibition.

A greater degree of flexibility could be introduced into the operation of the existing circuits by making local managers responsible for the selection of films to be shown in their cinemas. This course has everything to recommend it and is opposed only by specious arguments from the circuits themselves. Sadly, it provides no basis for legislation since a law requiring cinema-by-cinema booking is unenforceable so long as the managers are employed by circuit owners.

Short of taking cinemas into public ownership, we have now exhausted the possibilities for radical change in the industry's structure. With the mighty proviso that a nationalized cinema must in some way be protected from establishment tastes and values, we ought to be prepared to consider public ownership as a serious possibility and to advocate it if other measures prove inadequate. But, for the moment, we accept the Monopolies Commission's view that change must be sought within the existing system.

We do not, however, share the commission's optimism that the necessary changes can be effected by the industry itself. Some degree of government control is essential. Since Rank and ABC are being left to enjoy their monopoly position, limits placed on the exploitation of their power will give them little cause for complaint provided that they suffer a minimum of interference in the day-to-day running of their businesses. The Rank Organisation, particularly, should have no quarrel with measures designed to increase competition and promote private enterprise.

If reasonable machinery can be designed to correct abuses in the film business it may provide a useful model for other industries which government-urged rationalization is propelling toward monopoly. Legislation itself is not enough; the power of the combines is such as to allow them to turn to their own advantage almost any provision the law may make. Flexibility is a vital need for any system which is effectively to safeguard the claims of the independent exhibitor and the independent producer.

To meet this need we suggest the establishment of a watchdog body with defined powers of compulsion in relation to distributors and exhibitors. It must be able to make rapid investigations either on its own initiative or in response to complaints received. It must be equipped to enforce its decisions. It must not be composed of representatives of the movie trade.

The first and most important problem it will have to confront is that of restrictive practices in the supply of films to cinemas. At present any company which owns a chain of cinemas—not just Rank and ABC but much smaller and more localized concerns—is able to let it be understood that it will book a film into its best theaters only if its less profitable ones are also given preference. This means that a cinema which is badly sited, poorly maintained, and has high running costs, but which happens to be one of a chain, is given access to films before a potentially more rewarding independent outlet in the same district. As a result the better cinema may be driven out of business by its inability to book popular films before the circuit house has creamed off the audience.

It will be necessary, then, for our watchdog commission to discriminate between competing cinemas wherever it finds reason to suspect that the power of numbers is preventing them from competing on their own commercial merits. The commission will have to assess which one is, in its own right, the more attractive location and to award prior booking rights accordingly. To avoid entrenching the present circuit system, these rights will have to be applicable only to pictures which are, in any case, receiving full circuit distribution. Probably the best way of achieving the desired end will be to give the favored theater parity with a comparable cinema in another district. There will be problems of definition with this as with most of our suggestions, but we can leave definition to the professional law-drafters.

The support for the present inequitable allocation of films is the iniquitous system of bars whereby cinemas, singly or in groups, dictate the terms under which any film shown by them may be booked for exhibition by others. This practice plumbs the depths of absurd and impertinent restrictiveness when the Exhibitors' Association successfully puts pressure on the Renters' Society to refuse 16 mm film material (regardless of title) for noncommercial showing within two miles of a commercial movie house. Such infringements of the rights not only of film libraries but also of private citizens will need to be brought within the commission's terms of reference.

Machinery exists to settle disputes over bars insofar as they relate to commercial cinemas; but it is machinery run by the trade and consequently dominated by the big interests. The principal result of the barring system is to confirm the rigidity of the distribution pattern by establishing on a permanent basis the order in which the cinemas of any given area will receive the opportunity to book any given film. For example, the industry's disputes committee has recognized bars by Exeter's two (circuit) cinemas on two (independent) theaters in Exmouth. Anyone who knows Devonshire will find it hard to imagine how a film's appearance in Exmouth, either before or at the same time as its showing in Exeter, could affect business at the Rank and ABC houses. On the other hand, it may well be that during the summer holiday season the seaside cinemas are superior in commercial potential to the inland ones. And, while it is difficult to conceive of this bar's contributing to any cinema's prosperity, it obviously stands in the way of experiment with local release patterns—making it impossible for a distributor to consider, for example, a simultaneous release to all South Devon centers, which would allow maximum economy and effect in the use of common publicity media.

The most that any exhibitor may legitimately demand is that the contract under which he hires a film should clearly define the rights bestowed. He is not entitled to dictate, in perpetuity, the relationship between his and another's cinema. Yet it is this point, amazingly, that the Monopolies Commission conceded to feeble arguments presented by the trade. It recommends only a few improvements in the arbitration system, while leaving the system itself in the industry's hands. We suggest, on the contrary, that the restrictive practice of barring should be forbidden in the new legislation; and that, where it sees pressure being exerted on distributors to withhold or delay the supply of films, the watchdog commission should be charged to exert a greater pressure in the opposite direction—by requiring the supply, or the swifter supply, of films to the victimized cinema. In other words, the commission should be seen to protect, rather than limit, the distributor's right to offer his films when and where he chooses. As an extension of this function the watchdog body should be responsible for supervising competitive bids for individual films along the lines suggested in the Monopolies Commission's report.

We should not delude ourselves that these measures will transform the pattern of distribution and exhibition. They can be expected only—it's enough—to create a greater likelihood of flexibility within the present pattern.

That in itself should help out with problems at the other end of the scale—those of independent filmmaking. The producer who is not financed by either of the combines, or by one of the "tied" distributors, is in a particularly unfavorable position when he wishes to arrange the release of his film. Like anyone else, he's safe if it has obvious box-office potential; the circuit bookers do not deliberately discriminate against him. But if its commercial appeal is in doubt—which may mean if it is somewhat out of the ordinary—he enjoys none of the customary protection since the combines stand to lose neither money of their own nor valuable goodwill by refusing his picture a booking.

Compare, for example, the situation between ABC and MGM by imagining that, as a booker for the ABC circuit, you have just emerged from a screening of, say, *The Comedians* (Peter Glenville, 1967). Your personal judgment might be that the film is a fiasco and likely to send your customers into hibernation. You still have to weigh that personal judgment against the knowledge that it's a very expensive production, that MGM will therefore be eager for a wide exposure, and that the same company has lately demonstrated its confidence in your circuit's ability to sell movies by entrusting it with *The Dirty Dozen* (Robert Aldrich, 1967) and *Doctor Zhivago* (David Lean, 1965). You might, then, pause to reflect on the fallibility of a guess at what others may enjoy . . .

With an independent production it's much easier not to allow personal judgment to be confused by other considerations, much easier to say no. Our concern is not to secure a safe passage around the circuits for every independently produced stinker; no particular effort should be made to cushion the risk in what is by nature a highly speculative field. But some guarantee is needed that the decisions of the circuit bookers accurately reflect the tastes of the public. Since theoretical decisions are useless, a distributor should be entitled to demand a practical trial for a film whose appeal is in doubt. It should be the task of the watchdog to select a range of cinemas which both the distributor and the circuit accept as representative. If the picture proves attractive in these locations, provision can be made for its more general release. Both to prevent irresponsible demands on behalf of aborted projects and because there is no reason why the circuits should pay for producers' mistakes the initial trial should be granted on condition that the distributor guarantees to make good losses shown by the cinemas involved.

Again, we should not expect this measure to produce immediate or startling results; distributors' vaults will not yield up a horde of martyred masterpieces: they may not reveal even a single film which can justify commercially its claim to circuit distribution. But the likely long-term effect will be to make it a little easier for producers to be adventurous in their choices of subject and treatment, because financiers will become a little less frightened of projects which do not reflect their notions of the circuits' notions of public taste.

It does not seem to us that these proposals give the industry's establishment cause for protest (though that won't stop them protesting). In the first place, provided that the commission is given adequate powers and is prepared to act decisively in its early stages, the industry will adapt to the new conditions by anticipating justifiable complaints in order to forestall official action; so there will in all likelihood be a minimum of interference in day-to-day business. Secondly, the combines will be left to enjoy many of the privileges of their present position: they will still, for example, be free to book their own productions into their own cinemas at the most favorable times of the year.

Our present recommendations do not cover the whole scope of films legislation. The structure of government support for British production also demands revision, and there are special problems relating to the short film. On these issues also there are suggestions to be offered . . .

Filmography

The Comedians. Directed by Peter Glenville. MGM, 1967.
The Dirty Dozen. Directed by Robert Aldrich. MGM, 1967.
Doctor Zhivago. Directed by David Lean. MGM, 1965.
The Long Duel. Directed by Ken Annakin. Rank (UK), Paramount Pictures (US), 1967.

SUPPORTING THE BRITISH CINEMA

First published in Movie, *no. 16 (Winter 1968–69): 13–15.*

It's open to the government to *invent* the means of controlling the effects of the monopoly structure of film exhibition in this country. *Movie* 15 offered some suggestions here. But machinery has long existed to provide statutory support for film production. In the new legislation, due in 1970, this machinery will be reassessed. The important thing is that the reassessment should be guided by the greatest possible clarity of purpose. Because loud and large inducements are offered to embody in the legislation confusions which can be turned to profit by various sectional interests, the urgent need is for lucidity. New legislation must be shaped by a clear view of what the state intends, hopes, and—most important—is *able* to achieve through its support.

The present situation offers positive encouragement to examine the function of state support for the film production industry; we are not currently facing a crisis that demands emergency measures. On the contrary, production is enjoying great prosperity. Our studios are fully occupied and the levels of both investment and employment are high. So one aim of policy must be to ensure the continuance of this prosperity, to create a system flexible enough to forestall the possibility of future collapse. That such a crisis will sooner or later occur is almost certain, because present prosperity is built on the most precarious base.

Last year an estimated 90 percent of finance for British feature film production came from the United States. Virtually the whole of this money could be withdrawn from the British industry with alarming speed. There are few reasons to expect that American investment will remain permanently at this level. We have to be prepared for its contraction or disappearance. At the moment, we are completely unprepared. The withdrawal of American finance would mean the collapse of British production.

Two major consequences would follow from this collapse: a huge waste of resources in terms of both facilities and skilled labor; and dependence on Hollywood to fill our cinema screens. The effect of the latter on our balance of payments with the United States constitutes the chief motive for government support of domestic production. In other words, the state is concerned with the film industry *as* an industry; the purpose of its involvement is strictly economic and financial. Its interest is in the *prosperity* of the industry and in nothing else. Welcome evidence that this fact is officially recognized came recently when the Hammer Company won a Queen's Award for Industry. The award commended the success of the Hammer horrors in the export market. It was obviously not intended to acknowledge services to art, culture or international understanding.

This is not an argument against state patronage of the arts. It's an argument against mistaking support of an industry for encouragement of the artists it may or may not employ. These are separate issues. Anomaly and contradiction result from attempting to treat them as one.

Such attempts have been vigorously pursued over the past few years. Confused in purpose, they've necessarily been grotesque in prescription. For example, it is suggested that the government should support film production because of its by-products: the benefits to, among other things, national trade and prestige which immediately follow.

On trade, the argument is that British films display British goods on screens throughout the world and thus create a demand which serves the export drive.

No better supported by fact or reason are the claims made on behalf of movies as a prestige product. But they *are* more dangerous, because they can tempt the feebler mind to believe that, in supporting the industry, the state is concerned with the "quality" of its products. Note that quality in this context does not and cannot mean excellence. It means, rather, the ability to win acclaim from reviewers, festival jurors, and other pundits. And there is little reason to suppose that such acclaim promotes British political values or influence, which is what we take "prestige" to connote. If we admire *Bonnie and Clyde* (1967) the less because of Vietnam and Chicago, or view Czechoslovakia more happily when we've listened to the Soviet State Orchestra, then our powers of discrimination are in need of repair at the political level as much as the cultural.

This will have been insultingly obvious to all but PR exponents, their commercial and bureaucratic employers, and their dupes. The PR mind not only manufactures myths but is also immersed in a myth of its own: the efficacy of public relations and advertising in any and every medium, and by extension the infinite gullibility of mankind. So it would have us accept what, for its own protection, it wishes to believe: that movies can function as substitutes, in trade, for the excellence and cheapness of products or services and, in politics, for political strength and political wisdom.

Our legislators, however, will have to be readier to distinguish illusion from reality. To recognize, for instance, that there is no necessary correlation between journalists' reactions, artistic achievement, and commercial results; that none of these can be reliably predicted at the financing stage; and that the state's concern with the prosperity of the industry does not imply an interest in anything other than the profitability of its products.

So long as the film industry is significant enough in economic terms to command the government's attention, policy will have to be directed to ensure continuity of production, and so of finance. As in any large industry which requires sophisticated technical resources, continuity is vital. It is easy to close down production—and studios—in time of crisis. But to revive them in times of prosperity is both difficult and expensive.

One aim of legislation, then, must be to ensure the existence of a reserve of public finance ready to replace American or other private money at short notice. The machinery for this already exists in the National Film Finance Corporation, but is considerably run down. The NFFC is a government bank lending money to finance film production. Its funds are very depleted and its lending tends to be sporadic; between October 1966 and August of last year, for example, it had to suspend its activities to await the return of monies out on loan. It is clearly not in a position to give the necessary short- or long-term support to carry the industry over a period of crisis.

If the NFFC is to be made effective, past losses will have to be wiped out and new funds provided by the government. Its role should also be redefined so that future policy can operate without the confusions of the past and present. As a bank, its major concern is with the profitability of its investments. Only by directing its activities to this end can it serve the purpose of maintaining employment and productivity in the British Industry. Its brief should not be complicated or confused by other considerations. Investment must not be mistaken for subsidy or patronage.

In the past the corporation has spoken and acted as if it were required to make its decisions on grounds other than those of business. It has seemed to believe itself called upon to protect the picture that is culturally as well as financially "indigenous" to protect us from the supposed horrors of mid-Atlanticism. Reasonably, its interest in the kind of movie it backs should end when it has decided whether the kind is more or less likely to prove successful.

Nothing in its nature or function requires it to favor one type of movie over another. Nor should it be asked to promote "quality." The applause of journalists is relevant, in a minor way, as a bonus to commercial success; it is no compensation for commercial failure. Yet the annual reports of the NFFC demonstrate a pathetic preoccupation with reviews, festivals, and prizes: for example, the (unmerited) "international awards and almost universal praise from the critics' received by *I Was Happy Here* [1966] are offered as if to show that the investment was a good one despite the fact that 'losses are feared.'"

Something of the confusion involved can be gauged from the following statement by the corporation's managing director: "In the past we have had only a commercial criterion in considering projects; but I think we should have a second criterion, that the films we support should be films of quality which one is proud to export. I think, oddly enough, if we had had this dual criterion throughout the years we might have done better commercially than we have."

The latter part of this statement seems to recognize that the "safe" project is in fact no safer than the "risky" one. But if that's the case, as we believe, then the corporation has no need of a second criterion. It can invest in "films of quality" on commercial grounds without appealing to irrelevant issues of national pride. Implied in the opposition between "commercial" and "quality" criteria is the belief that the Quality Film is by nature more difficult for the popular audience to understand and enjoy and is therefore a more speculative investment.

The same implication underlies the proposal from other sources that the corporation should allocate a proportion of its funds to the development of "a native 'cinema of quality'" (Reed 1968: 6). As always from the British Film Institute, the assumption is that the "cinema of quality" is composed of something other than good films. The Quality Film, in this context, is seen as a distinct genre analogous with, but far removed from, the horror movie or the sex comedy. One decides to make a Quality Film in the same way, but never at the same time, as one decides to make a vampire film. It's worth diverging for a moment to emphasize (yet again) that the problem of the British cinema from a critical point of view is not that our films have tended to be of certain types, but that, within those types, the films have generally been poor. The question is not whether horror movies or farces—or Quality Films—should be made, but whether they could be *better* made. The problem cannot be resolved at government level, and we certainly shall not reach a solution by deforming a structure designed for the maintenance of an industry in order to make it a channel for the encouragement of "quality" production.

Indeed, if the government accepts the task of promoting a native "cinema of quality" within the industry, it will soon be faced with the urgent necessity of trying to promote good Quality Films as against bad ones. But if the state wishes to become the patron of filmmakers and to commission prestige productions, it should do so directly and without thought of profit. A bank is not the most appropriate channel for such an initiative.

A reconstructed NFFC will require new funds and an unambiguous directive to invest, profitably, in British production. It will also require a management which can in practice master the complex demands of that simple brief. The civil service is not the obvious breeding ground for the necessary talent but, wherever it is found, the management will need complete and guaranteed freedom from official interference over a period of years in order to establish its competence. Equally, there should be no question of the management's surviving, say, five years of unprofitable operation.

The NFFC has suggested that it be reestablished with a capital of £6 million. We cannot offer an alternative figure, but we would guess that a great deal more is needed if the corporation is to function adequately.

Though it is no part of its purpose to drive out American finance, it will have to compete to some extent with the American companies. Otherwise its opportunities will be limited to the less-promising projects which will come to it largely as American rejects. The most likely consequence would be a continuous dissipation of the funds which it will need in the event of American withdrawal.

The corporation therefore has to offer deals as attractive as that available from the American companies. So it will need to be able to put up 100 percent backing for the selected projects. Its funds must also be large enough to permit investment in numbers of films so that successes can compensate for failures, and so that it does not have to wait for receipts from one or two pictures before resuming its operation. Finally, it should be equipped to invest in every type of film; it should not be placed under the necessity of discriminating against large-budget projects.

The other major instrument of government support for filmmaking is the British Film Production Fund. In practice, this is a tax on foreign, and particularly Hollywood-made, pictures in favor of films produced in this country, so that, for example, *The Sound of Music* (1965) and *Bonnie and Clyde* contribute to the receipts of *Blow-Up* (1966) and *Witchfinder General* (1968). It's a levy on cinema admissions which is redistributed (as "Eady money") to the producing companies of British films in proportion to their box-office takings. The fund has provided a very useful stimulus to feature film production. It explains, to a large extent, the scale of American investment in British filmmaking. Some changes are, however, indicated in its distribution.

At the moment the bulk of the fund in any one year is shared by a very small number of hugely successful films like *Tom Jones* (1963), *Goldfinger* (1964), or *The Family Way* (1966). For these pictures Eady money must represent pure profit, whereas for others it could make the difference between losing and recovering the investment. It has been suggested that a ceiling should be placed on the amount that any one film can draw from the fund or that a reducing scale should be operated. But either of these adjustments would constitute discrimination against the big-budget movie. *2001: A Space Odyssey* (1968), for example, might prove more popular than *Poor Cow* (1967), but it would not recover from the fund anything like the same share of its cost. This problem can be resolved if the steps in a reducing scale are marked not by fixed sums of money but by percentages of audited production cost. The consequent reallocation of the fund would be significant, but it would not carry the suspicion of working to contradict box-office verdicts.

The purpose of the fund is to encourage investment in British-made movies. Any reconstruction must respect this fact. As much as possible of the money raised should return directly as finance for film production. The fund must not be regarded as an all-purpose money-box to be raided in favor of this or that good cause (film schools, etc.); and it should not be seen as a suitable channel for the expression of official prejudices or for the encouragement of particular kinds of production. No elements of discrimination should be built into, or derived from, its working. Those which exist at present should be abolished. Part of the fund is at present diverted to support the Children's Film Foundation.[1] Again, if the government wishes to aid the foundation's work in producing films for children, it should do so directly; otherwise the Eady fund becomes an entertainment tax whose revenues are available for general purposes tenuously connected with support for the industry.

A more serious anomaly exists in relation to the short film that highlights the futility of attempts to use commercial and industrial devices to enforce cultural discriminations. When the Eady fund was established it was decided that short films were in particular need of support. Since then the fund's payments to shorts have been inflated by treating the earnings of short films as if they had been two and a half times greater than the actual figure. The direct, though unforeseen and lamented, product of this error was the creation and entrenchment of Rank's *Look at Life*.[2]

Because the Rank Organisation dominates exhibition in this country, it can guarantee wide and regular distribution for its own products. With guaranteed distribution it can engage in regular—not to say mechanical—production of *Look at Life*. It is at least likely that the existence of the series does much to exclude other shorts from circuit distribution. And it's certain that, whatever the intention of its dedicated producers, *Look at Life* absorbs the greatest share of the money paid out of Eady to short-filmmakers.

Nothing better illustrates the absence of heroes and villains in controversies over the picture business than a comparison between the reactions to this situation of the Rank Organisation and the excluded shorts producers; the bland complacency of the former is matched by the latter's aggressive incoherence.

In none of the offered prescriptions has the most rational solution been proposed or even mentioned. This is the abolition of the "multipliers" for Eady calculations, now applied to shorts, newsreels, and second features. Statutory and financial incentives to the production of *Look at Life* and ABC's *Pathé Pictorial* would thus be removed, and economic realities could be more realistically confronted.[3] If, under these circumstances, Rank finds it worthwhile to continue the series (as it may do, since guaranteed distribution and regular production enable costs to be held low), then that's a regrettable decision which it is entitled to make. But other outcomes are possible.

Rank itself may find it convenient to enforce an increase in the supporting program's share of box-office receipts. All shorts producers would benefit. Or, because audiences pay to see feature films and because the success of the supporting program depends not on its own appeal but on that of the feature, the future of the short film may be shown to lie outside the ABC and Rank circuits. If this is really so, then the fact should be accepted.

The worst kind of mean-minded commercialism is revealed by the assumption that an (unlikely) disappearance of shorts from circuit screens is equivalent to the extinction of the short film. It's quite possible that the short-filmmaker's most rational reaction to the commercial situation (unless he is obsessed with making either money or a career) is to develop the unofficial channels of distribution represented, now, by the Film-Makers'

Co-Operative. An artist, as distinct from a businessman, will find nothing demeaning in this suggestion.

That, of course, leaves us with the plight of the exploited filmgoer so often and so cruelly victimized by the excruciating products of Harold Baim and his kind.[4] But we think it probable that the incidence of this victimization will decline, and the management and content of the supporting program be reappraised, quite soon after the removal of Eady's inducements to push out the cheapest available junk as "support" for the most successful features.

The worst (or best) that can now happen to the circuit short as the result of our proposals is the elimination of *Look at Life* and its ugly sisters. But arguments, so to speak, have been advanced that the state has a particular responsibility to nurture the commercial short film because of the benefits that will follow to the feature industry. The short picture, it is claimed, provides a fine training for the feature-makers of the future. Very little evidence supports this assumption, and there are indications to the contrary.

In the first place, a medium whose survival demands an artificially boosted economy would seem to offer a most unsuitable introduction to the requirements of the feature industry. Secondly, the economics of even subsidized shorts production generally rules out sustained work with actors—the most useful part of a director's training. The experience of West Germany is worth bearing in mind. It both operates the most elaborate system of support for the "quality" short and holds the world record (India, by some accounts, apart) for the decrepitude of its feature industry. Finally, it is true that Godard, Resnais, and Franju, for example, made shorts and then made features. But this is no proof that their experience with shorts was necessary to their ability as feature directors. On the other hand the first films of Orson Welles (*Citizen Kane* [1941]), Nicholas Ray (*They Live by Night* [1948]), and Arthur Penn (*The Left Handed Gun* [1958]) stand as evidence that a cinematic training ground is not indispensable to cinematic genius.

In the cinema a short film, like any other, is either self-justifying or expendable. The only good reasons for its presentation are that an artist wanted to make it and that an audience (of economically significant size) enjoyed seeing it.

Work Cited

Reed, Stanley. *Outlook 1968: A Report and Review by the Director Stanley Reed.* London: British Film Institute, 1968.

Filmography

Blow-Up. Directed by Michelangelo Antonioni. Premier Productions, 1966.
Bonnie and Clyde. Directed by Arthur Penn. Warner Bros.-Seven Arts, 1967.
Citizen Kane. Directed by Orson Welles. RKO Radio Pictures, 1941.
The Family Way. Directed by Roy Boulting. British Lion, 1966.
Goldfinger. Directed by Guy Hamilton. United Artists, 1964.
I Was Happy Here. Directed by Desmond Davis. Rank, 1966.
The Left Handed Gun. Directed by Arthur Penn. Warner Bros., 1958.
Look at Life. Various directors. Rank, various dates.
Pathé Pictorial. Various directors. Pathé, various dates.
Poor Cow. Directed by Kenneth Loach. Anglo-Amalgamated, 1967.
The Sound of Music. Directed by Robert Wise. Twentieth Century Fox, 1965.
They Live by Night. Directed by Nicholas Ray. RKO Radio Pictures, 1948.
Tom Jones. Directed by Tony Richardson. United Artists (UK), Lopert Pictures (US), 1963.
2001: A Space Odyssey. Directed by Stanley Kubrick. MGM, 1968.
Witchfinder General. Directed by Michael Reeves. Tigon British Film Productions (UK), American International Pictures (US), 1968.

Notes

1 The Children's Film Foundation (CFF) was a nonprofit organization founded in 1951 which made films for children in the United Kingdom. It was subsidized for thirty years by the Eady Levy and in 2012 became the Children's Media Foundation. Ed.

2 *Look at Life* was a series of short documentary films on contemporary British life, produced between 1959 and 1969 by the Rank Organisation, to be shown before the main feature in its cinema chains. Ed.

3 *Pathé Pictorial* was a series of film shorts in a magazine format that ran in British cinemas for over fifty years from 1918. Ed.

4 Harold Baim (1914–1996) was a prolific producer and director of short films in Britain between the 1940s and the 1980s. Ed.

DEVELOPING A DETAILED CRITICISM

NICHOLAS RAY

First published in Oxford Opinion, *June 14, 1960, 31–34.*

CinemaScope. Warnercolor. Low-angle shot. A deserted and littered street about half past midnight. In the right foreground of the screen stands a toy monkey whose clockwork is beginning to run down. A young man in a black suit, black tie, and white shirt lurches, drunk, toward the camera. He falls down beside the monkey and looks at it for a few moments (fig. 2). His face is that of a teenager but it is heavily lined and shows a terrible anxiety. He picks up the monkey, turns the key which protrudes from its belly, and smiles as it taps its paws together. He reaches for a piece of newspaper to use as a sheet; in a gesture of enormous tenderness he places it over the monkey's body. He moves around to lie beside it. As he closes his eyes the noise of a police siren grows louder, and the final credit appears on the screen, superfluously: "Directed by Nicholas Ray."

Superfluously because Ray is one of the few directors with a personal style which is recognized immediately and with pleasure. He is also, in English-speaking countries, the most underrated of all contemporary directors. The reasons for this are obvious enough: the majority of his films have been assignments—of the seventeen Ray pictures so far seen in England only three have been overtly serious in intention. Moreover, they are melodramas, whose importance derives not from what their characters do and say but from the way in which they do and say it, the way in which they move, talk, and look at one another. Thus the quality of his films is not literary, since it

Figure 2. The opening of *Rebel Without a Cause*

owes little to the original script, but cinematic; it results from the subjection of a frequently banal narrative to an idiosyncratic mise-en-scène.

Writing about this director presents one great difficulty, in the need to separate the various aspects of his genius: for example, the moment I begin to deal with his methods of composition, or his use of camera movement, I become involved with his meaning, since for Ray, as for any other great cinéaste, the meaning of a film is contained in its style.

Another difficulty arises from the debasement of the film critic's vocabulary: the adjective "beautiful" has lost significance through its misuse by writers on the film as a synonym for "pretty," "attractive," or even "neat," with reference to the images produced by, say, Ford and [Vincente] Minnelli. In the cinema's history there have been perhaps a dozen directors who possess the ability to create images which, combining visual delight with meaning, deserve to be called beautiful: Hitchcock and Welles are two, and Ray is another. An image by any of these directors has a virtually indefinable quality, like that which constitutes "presence" in an actor: perhaps it is best described as weight.

The beauty of a Ray picture is partly choreographic, since it depends on the movement of objects and people, of the camera or of both. Only Welles can use the moving camera as effectively as this director to provide psychological insight—in *Rebel* the camera takes us inside James Dean's eyes and mind by turning vertically 180 degrees as his mother walks downstairs toward him—and sensual joy: Cyd Charisse's dances in *Party Girl* (1958), for example.

Even more important to a Ray composition is the element of pure structure: from this point of view the experience of studying under Frank Lloyd Wright must have been invaluable. Another obvious influence is the "architectural" approach of Fritz Lang, whose work Ray admires. But there is none of that director's symmetry in his images: in fact many of them are deliberately, sometimes startlingly, unbalanced to give an effect of displacement. Ray is fond of using static masses with bold lines—staircases, doors, trees, rocks—which intrude into the frame and at the same time disrupt and unify his compositions.

The concern with matters of abstract form has been very fruitful. In the first place it has combined with an avowed love of the horizontal line in composition to give Ray a unique control over the spatial potentialities of the CinemaScope screen: there is, for example, no one who has used its extreme edges to greater effect than Ray. Also, it has enabled him to find beauty in the most appalling situations: in *Party Girl* there is a shot of a girl lying with her hands dangling in a bath full of water, which is red from the blood of her slashed wrists. Even by Ray standards it is outstandingly beautiful. Perhaps it is significant that the only other director who can manage this dual effect is Franju, another disciple of Lang.

For both the gift is essential, since it is often necessary for them to present actions which are in themselves repulsive. Ray's uncompromising depiction of acts of cruelty, violence, and bloodshed is one result of his painstaking search for lucidity. For this reason we are not spared—except by the intervention of the BBFC—any of the details of the knife fight in *Rebel*, the slaughter of Florida's bird-life in *Wind Across the Everglades* (1958), or the Gypsy marriage ritual in *Hot Blood* (1956).

The quest for lucidity has also led this director to reject the traditional methods of plot construction. Most filmmakers proceed by a series of disclosures, building their characters and situations gradually, and often holding back essential details until the last moment. For Ray this is impossible: his method is to reveal characters and relationships with maximum speed and clarity. Thus the first shot of a Ray picture will normally introduce the principal character, and by the end of the first reel all the important relationships will have been presented. *Rebel* achieved, I suspect, a record. The first shot—described at the head of this article—shows us James Dean; the second is a brief linking shot of Dean being taken into the police station; and the third introduces us to Sal Mineo and Natalie Wood. Less than ten minutes later we have learned about the family backgrounds of Mineo and Wood, and have even met Dean's parents and grandmother—again in a single shot which conveyed most of the details of a complex relationship.

Ray interests us not in the "development" of character, but in its consequences. This method of construction must have created difficulties when he made *In a Lonely Place* (1950), a film which contains many of the elements of a thriller; his solution was characteristic. The story concerns a Hollywood writer suspected of a young girl's murder (Bogart), and a woman who loves him, but is not convinced of his innocence (Gloria Grahame). Any other director, surely, would have left the issue of Bogart's possible guilt in doubt for the greater part of the film. Ray's technique is both more honest and more subtle: the audience knows that Bogart did not kill the girl; but suspense is maintained by the knowledge that he is a violent man, capable of murder if sufficiently provoked, and living under ever-increasing strain.

Clearly this technique requires brilliant acting. Requires and, as a rule, receives: the finest performances I have seen by Bogart, Dean, Grahame, Sterling Hayden, Charisse, and Wood were given under Ray's direction. He has been particularly successful in his handling of the "intractable" actor who, under weak or unsympathetic management, can either withdraw from a film (Dean, Mineo, John Ireland) or swamp it with a display of mannerism (Lee J. Cobb, Burl Ives). On his method of directing actors Ray has said, "Je ne crois pas à l'écrasement ni à la domination de l'acteur.... Seul compte une entente préalable entre le comedien et le metteur en scène. Cette entente ne peut venir que d'une lente et patiente période de persuasion.... La véritable direction d'acteurs, c'est-à-dire la possession progressive et mesurée du comédien (consentant) par le metteur en scène, doit s'effectuer hors du champ des projecteurs.... Un réalisateur lucide ne saurait obtenir ce qu'il veut d'un comedien s'il n'a pas une connaissance complète des possibilités de cet acteur. C'est la raison pour laquelle une fois l'acteur choisi, je me fais projeter plusieurs de ses films pour tenter de pénétrer ses qualités et ses tics et de jouer avec, d'en tirer avantage" (Douchet 1960: 7).[1]

One of Ray's peculiar achievements with actors is to help them appreciate the way in which behavior is influenced by environment and is altered by apparently insignificant changes in it: the time of day, for example. A man will not react in the same way at ten o'clock in the morning and at ten o'clock at night. Because Ray realizes this, he is one of the very few directors who can produce night scenes in which the night is felt as something more than the absence of sunlight. In *Rebel* he goes even further by setting one sequence under the artificial night of a planetarium while preserving the feeling of early afternoon.

This sequence also demonstrates Ray's talent for conveying the general implications of a particular episode. He draws a close parallel between the isolated and insecure condition of his characters, and that of the whole of mankind in the universe. While the audience at the display greets the end of the world with nervous contempt the commentator rambles on sententiously—". . . destroyed as we began in a burst of gas and fire . . . the earth will not be missed . . . and man existing alone himself seems an episode of little consequence." Throughout the film the planetarium is used to give a wider reference to the action. When Corey Allen is trapped in his car as it rushes toward the edge of a cliff, the music depicting the end of the world returns. Mineo, thinking himself abandoned by his only friend, takes refuge in the planetarium and is killed as he runs from it. In the film's final shot the camera tracks back to a general view of the building.

Ray achieves a similar, though less spectacular, effect through use of actions and dialogue which express several, often contradictory, meanings. He is specially shrewd in his employment of the inappropriate or even absurd gesture. Jim Backus lecturing his son on the insignificance of his problems ("In ten years you'll look back on all this and laugh at yourself for thinking it was so important") starts to worry over a file which he has removed from his briefcase.

The exploitation of the inappropriate is not confined to the direction of the actors, but is a vital part of Ray's camera and editing technique. Sometimes he shoots an entire sequence "incorrectly," in a way that no ordinary craftsman could tolerate. An interview between Natalie Wood and

Edward Platt, a police officer in the juvenile division, is filmed in cross-cut close-ups, which, as anyone who has seen *The Big Country* (1958) knows, *must* not be used on the 'Scope screen. Worse still, Ray ignores one of the basic rules of correct editing by cutting from one shot to the other with the dialogue, so that there is no sound to cover the abruptness of the shot changes. The only possible defense of this crazy technique is that it is completely effective in conveying the isolation of Wood, and the officer's failure to establish contact with her; a spatial relationship is withheld until a personal one has been formed. A remark of Franju's is very relevant to this "wrongness" in Ray's technique; talking to Truffaut about *Les Quatre cents coups* (1959) he said: "Vous faites un film qui montre des maisons de correction, faites des incorrections cinématographiques, c'est dans la ligne, dans le ton du film. On ne peut pas faire un film contre la correction correctement, non?" (Truffaut 1960).[2] Of course not, and the same goes for Nicholas Ray. It would be wrong to make a film about dislocation and unconventionality in a conventionally flowing style.

And this is the principal subject of his films. Their heroes are "displaced" persons who share the "vulnerability so profound as to be moving, almost frightening" which Ray noticed in James Dean. They are men whose isolation is emphasized by their membership of a group which stands apart from society and often outside the law: the teenagers of *Rebel*, the gipsies of *Hot Blood*, and presumably the Eskimos of the as-yet-unseen *Savage Innocents* (1960). Indeed their nonconformism is such that they reject the conventions even of these unconventional groups: Dean shocks a gang whose chosen weapons are switchblades and stolen cars by threatening its leader with the shaft of his car jack. They habitually express themselves in terms of violence. In *Wind Across the Everglades* Christopher Plummer declares his abhorrence of the slaughter of the jungle birds by tearing the feathers from the hat worn by an overdressed woman. But for Ray violence can often be an act of tenderness, as it is in Dean's attack on his father or Bogart's on his agent. This is just one of the contradictions inherent in Ray's work. Another is that between the self-destructiveness of his heroes, and their struggle to survive both nature and the physical and psychological violence of men. This struggle is often concentrated in a sort of trial by ordeal, like *Rebel*'s "chicken run." It forms the climax of *Wind Across the Everglades*, where Burl Ives agrees to stand trial in Miami if Plummer can take him in without turning his back or falling asleep, and without losing his way through swamps he has never before entered. The circumstances are usually such that an unambiguous victory is impossible, since the hero can only survive on terms which make his own life even less worth preserving.

In all this Ray is presenting an extension of what he seems to regard as a general human predicament. If his characters are violent it is because "there is violence in each of us"; if they are isolated it is because isolation is part of human nature; and if they are self-destructive it is because they feel very deeply the disadvantages of being human. From the double threat of isolation and subjection Ray sees only one means of escape—by way of a relationship between people who understand one another well enough to conquer loneliness without sacrificing individuality. But this is achieved rarely, and at a cost.

Ray, then, is intensely pessimistic. That his pessimism never slips over into self-pity is due to his insistence upon individual responsibility. If Ray's characters are victims then they are victims not of society but of their own defects or, at best, their own humanity: often their fault lies in seeking assistance where there is no chance of finding it. This is one respect in which *Rebel Without a Cause* has been misinterpreted, by emphasizing a single aspect of the film to the exclusion of all others. To say that it blames parents for the sins of their children is quite incorrect. It is clear that the parents of Dean, Wood, and Mineo are unequal to the needs and demands of their children, but the children are not for that reason excused responsibility for their actions, any more than in *Party Girl* Robert Taylor is excused by the injury which crippled him in *his* childhood. The sequence in which Dean declares his own share of the guilt for the death of Corey Allen is one of the most moving in the film. Dean's mistake during the first half of the picture (and the mistake for which Mineo pays with his life) has been to make strong demands on people who are by nature incapable of meeting them. Finally he himself realizes this, and his last words to his parents—"This is Judy. She's my friend"—are at least as much a renunciation as an acceptance. The "one day," beginning for Jim Stark in trouble and confusion, but ending for the first time in something different, is also the day on which he ceases to regard his parents as Mom and Dad and begins to look upon them as ordinary people, no better and no worse than most, but for him quite useless.

The world of Nicholas Ray is lonely, harsh, and violent, dominated by an almost Hobbesian pessimism: but it has consolations in moments of courage, tenderness, and humor ("Hey, you forgot to wind your sundial!"). It is a happy thought that we have not yet seen the finest work Ray is capable of producing. *The Savage Innocents*—which he considers his best film to date—reaches England in July. *King of Kings* is now in production and expected to be better still. A wonderful prospect.

Works Cited

Douchet, Jean. "Le Gros plan de la semaine: Nicholas Ray: *Les Dents du diable* sont mon meilleur film. Maintenant je vais tourner à Madrid la vie du Christ." *Arts/Spectacles*, no. 773 (4 May 1960): 7.

Truffaut, François. "Petit journal du cinema." *Cahiers du Cinéma* 18, no. 104 (1960): 43–46.

Filmography

The Big Country. Directed by William Wyler. United Artists, 1958.
Hot Blood. Directed by Nicholas Ray. Columbia Pictures, 1956.
In a Lonely Place. Directed by Nicholas Ray. Columbia Pictures, 1950.
King of Kings. Directed by Nicholas Ray. MGM, 1961.
Party Girl. Directed by Nicholas Ray. MGM, 1958.
Les Quatre cents coups (*The 400 Blows*). Directed by François Truffaut. Cocinor (France), Zenith International Films (US), 1959.
Rebel Without a Cause. Directed by Nicholas Ray. Warner Bros., 1955.
The Savage Innocents. Directed by Nicholas Ray. Rank, 1960.
Wind Across the Everglades. Directed by Nicholas Ray. Warner Bros., 1958.

Notes

1 "I don't believe in crushing or dominating the actor.... What counts is a prior understanding between performer and director. This can only come from a period of slow and patient persuasion.... The real direction of actors, that is

to say the gradual and measured (consenting) possession of the performer by the director, must be made away from the field of the spotlights. . . . A clear-sighted director can't get what he wants from a performer without a detailed knowledge of their potential. This is why once the actor is chosen, I screen several of their films to try to understand the qualities and mannerisms that can be worked with and used to one's advantage" (trans. Edward Lamberti). Ed.

2 "You make a film that shows reformatories, using 'incorrect' film technique, that's in the line, in the tone of the film. You can't make a film 'correctly' that's against correction, right?" (trans. Edward Lamberti). Ed.

CHARM AND BLOOD

First published in Oxford Opinion, *October 25, 1960, 34–35.*

Hitchcock customarily offers value for money, of course, but one doubts whether he has ever before treated the customers with such extreme generosity as he does in his latest film. The *Psycho* bargain offer comprises two crimes, two heroines, two murders, two Anthony Perkinses—even, in fact, two complete films. The second is the one to which the title refers and the one which Paramount is selling. It deals with Norman Bates's attempt to shield his mother from the consequences of her homicidal mania. The first film is Hitchcock's free offer in the sense that it is not a film which many people would pay to see divorced from its present companion (cf. the commercial failure of *The Wrong Man* [1956]).[1] The story is as shapeless as an autobiography. An ordinary girl steals forty thousand dollars and drives away to join her lover. She is obliged to break her journey at a motel, and in the course of a conversation with its proprietor decides to return the money. That's all: no great soul-searching, no "drama," and not even a good strong climax. But the second film has already started. Norman is upstairs fetching his wig and meat axe.

In prefacing the story of Norman Bates (Anthony Perkins) with that of Marion Crane (Janet Leigh) Hitchcock has not only taken commercial advantage of *Psycho*; he has also strengthened its impact. The weakness of most thrillers is that one expects the hero or heroine, the biggest star name on the credits, to remain alive until at least the final sequence of the picture. In the first twenty minutes of *Psycho* Leigh is made the center of interest and sympathy; her sudden and violent removal from the scene leaves the spectator completely unprepared for whatever may follow.

At this point, and at several others in the film, one can feel Hitchcock's amusement at what he is doing. The film starts with a joke: a series of titles announcing the precise place, date, and time (2:43 p.m.) introduce a love scene to which time, date, and place are, at least, incidental. As the film progresses the mirth becomes increasingly sinister. "Dirty night," remarks Bates, welcoming Marion to the motel; and in the sequence immediately following Marion's descent to the bottom of the quagmire, one of the good citizens of Fairvale is heard to insist that "insect or man, death should always be painless." Was ever laughter in a cinema hollower than that which greets Vera Miles's assertion—before she goes off to talk to Mrs. Bates—that she can "handle a sick old woman"?

Hitchcock's delight in the macabre aspects of his subject is apparent; but so is his impatience with its whodunit side. There is no one, I suspect, who enjoys a good mystery less than Alfred Hitchcock. Admittedly he does not here go to the same lengths as in *Vertigo* (1958) to dispel any doubts as to who did what how (then he quite simply showed us, half an hour before revelation time) but he stops not far short. On at least five occasions Norman Bates acts as he must do if he has just ceased, or is about to commence, being Mother. The first conversation we hear between Norman and his dear old mum has the unnatural sound of underrehearsed dialogue. And even when Perkins was playing female impersonation for laughs—in *The Matchmaker* (1958)—he dared not swing his hips so outrageously as he does in the shot of Norman mincing upstairs prior to taking mother down into the fruit cellar. Hitchcock makes his contempt for "mysteries" quite explicit in the sequence which purports to explain Norman's behavior. The explanation is delivered by the most unsympathetic of all the film's unsympathetic characters; the sequence is interesting only in that it is deliberately tedious, and the description of Norman's psychological state is not simply ludicrous—it is downright untrue to the facts as we have observed them. The psychologist claims that though Bates was often "all Mother" he was never "entirely Norman": this is nonsense. So much so that even on second or third experience of the film one sees Perkins—for example, at the time when he disposes of Marion's car—as a devoted son hiding the traces of his mother's crime, and not for one moment as Norman Bates doing the same thing on his own account.

This is a tribute to a portrayal which is beyond praise. Perkins has often been magnificent but he has never given a performance to equal this one. His stutterings, his embarrassment at his mother's outburst, his fury at Marion's suggestion that Mrs. Bates be "put someplace," his panic when the private investigator shows dissatisfaction with the story he has been told—all these things are more than convincing; they are deeply moving. Much of Perkins's success must be attributed to the control of one who is commonly thought not to be an "actor's director." In *Psycho*, Hitchcock has gained a set of performances as telling and concerted as we have seen in any film since *The Trouble with Harry* (1955). The acting is at its most spectacularly brilliant in Perkins's duologues with Janet Leigh and Martin Balsam. With only a few minutes of screen time at his disposal Balsam (the private investigator) conveys a complete image of a man whose humanity has been drained away by a lifetime of standing with his foot in someone's door. And in the milk-and-sandwiches conversation between Leigh and Perkins, Hitchcock reveals with frightening clarity the layers of tension, built up between two charmingly candid young people who both have a great deal to hide: even Tennessee Williams is here outclassed in the business of demonstrating the presence of something unspoken.

Acting of this sort and standard could only have been obtained under conditions of honesty such as I have stipulated earlier. That is one of the reasons why *Psycho* is so much better on second than on first viewing: the first time it is only a splendid entertainment, a "very minor film" in fact. But when one can no longer be distracted from the characters by an irrelevant "mystery" *Psycho* becomes immeasurably rewarding as well as much more thrilling.

Hitchcock's technique in *Psycho* is as sharp and brutal as his instrument of murder. The style of the greater part of the film is a strange blend of lewdness and puritanism which betrays an attitude of scandalized amusement—the misanthropic attitude, indeed, of a gossip. Only a gossip could relate with such evident relish the tale of "that awful business down at the Bates Motel." Only a gossip would discover so many juicy details with which to embellish such a story. Only a gossip, come to that, could consider such a story to be "full of charm and blood. Lots and lots of blood" (Domarchi and Douchet 1959, 28; translation mine).[2]

A gossip's style is entirely appropriate to *Psycho* since its themes are those that preoccupy such people—appearances and respectability. In the Marion Crane story we are concerned with theft not as an immoral but as an illegal act. Marion robs a hideous-natured old man who has stated, "I never carry more than I can afford to lose." That she has no qualms of conscience Hitchcock shows by his brilliant use of a device which I had always thought insupportable: the superimposed voice is justified in this case because it is employed not so much to express the character's thoughts as to show her reaction to them. By everything that concerns the possibility of being caught and exposed Marion is disturbed almost to the point of nausea; but the thought of her repulsive victim's discomfiture brings a smile irresistibly to her lips (fig. 3). In the first few minutes of the film we hear Marion insist upon the necessity of preserving one's respectability, and a few hours' experience of life as a fugitive—haunted by the fear that she may be acting as if there is something wrong—is sufficient to reestablish her belief that respectability, though "mostly hard work," is worth the effort.

Figure 3. Marion's smile

The Norman Bates story shows the other side of the picture: it may be advisable to present a false front to society but it is fatal to do so to oneself. At the end of the film Norman has become completely engulfed by his own lie. How much of the responsibility he must bear for this we cannot know since we are told little about his past that we can safely believe: our information comes almost entirely from a psychologist to whom Mother has told as many lies about Norman as Norman used to tell about her. He or she, Bates is a liar to the end.

Shortly before the end of the picture (on a second viewing, I insist) we are faced with a final question: How does a film which I believe is accurately described as a work of gossip attain the stature of a work not just of art—Hitchcock's genius guarantees that much—but of great art? The answer depends upon one further subtlety in Hitchcock's technique; the director has interposed between himself and the audience a second personality—that of the gossip. Once or twice in the course of the film we are confronted with an image which questions our whole response to the picture and forces us to ask whether this is really so amusing. I am thinking in particular of Norman's tired and isolated silhouette stretching above the quicksand. In the last three images—Mrs. Bates, the skull, and, again, the quicksand—the director steps forward in his own person to give the question a double negative. It is not a fit subject for a gossip; it is fit only for a tragedian. And that is what Hitchcock finally shows himself to be.

Works Cited

Domarchi, Jean, and Jean Douchet. "Entretien avec Alfred Hitchcock." *Cahiers du Cinéma* 17, no. 102 (1959): 17–29.
Wood, Robin. "Psychanalyse de *Psycho*." Translated by Louis Marcorelles. *Cahiers du Cinéma* 19, no. 113 (1960): 1–6.

Filmography

The Matchmaker. Directed by Joseph Anthony. Paramount Pictures, 1958.
Psycho. Directed by Alfred Hitchcock. Paramount Pictures, 1960.
The Trouble with Harry. Directed by Alfred Hitchcock. Paramount Pictures, 1955.

Vertigo. Directed by Alfred Hitchcock. Paramount Pictures, 1958.
The Wrong Man. Directed by Alfred Hitchcock. Warner Bros., 1956.

Notes

1 This was the first serious appraisal of *Psycho* published in English. Just a month later, Robin Wood's enthusiastic article on the film appeared in French (*Cahiers du Cinéma* 19, no. 113 [1960]), after being turned down by *Sight and Sound*. Ed.

2 The original, from which Perkins presents his translation, reads: "Plein de charme et de sang. Il y aura beaucoup, beaucoup de sang." Ed.

WORDS AND MUSIC
Two Recent Cukor Films

First published in Oxford Opinion, *November 1960, 26–27.*

Walter Lang (*The King and I* [1956], *Can-Can* [1960], and similar disasters) was originally announced as the director of *Let's Make Love* (1960); he left the film—before shooting started, according to Fox—and George Cukor took over. Charles Vidor (*A Song to Remember* [1945], *Love Me or Leave Me* [1955], *The Joker Is Wild* [1957]) receives the direction credit on the titles of *Song Without End* (1960); he died in the early stages of shooting, and again Cukor took over. These facts, as well as the material offered, indicate that Cukor regarded both films as "assignments." Though they are both directed with more than routine efficiency, *Song Without End* is much less interesting than *Let's Make Love*. It is, in any case, a "producer's film," combining an international cast with visibly expensive locations and technicians—Wong Howe, for example, as cameraman. Its only apparent noncommercial purpose is that which the script attributes to Liszt: "To bring great music to more people." Not a very promising basis for a film, and, for the most part, Cukor seems to have contented himself with securing the decency of its technique and performance, and the inoffensiveness of its vulgarity. In fact, Vidor might well have made a more entertaining movie of "The Story of Franz Liszt" than Cukor has done. Vidor evidently conspired to a baroque style, but lacked the technical virtuosity essential for success in that line; the result was an ornate vulgarity which would have suited *Song Without End* perfectly. Cukor is too sophisticated for this sort of picture; his attempt to give the film tone has deprived it of the doubtful amusements (e.g., "Long time no see, Johann") customarily associated with the genre.

Let's Make Love is much more amenable to Cukor treatment and a very enjoyable film; but it is not in the same class as many other comedies by this director—*Born Yesterday* (1950), say, or *Adam's Rib* (1949)—mainly because of the dull patches in the script, by Norman Krasna of *Who Was That Lady?* (1960). But even if the standard of the best sequences had been maintained, it is still unlikely that it could have provided ideal material for Cukor. Although it has several points of contact with the comedy of character in which this director has established his mastery, and it observes its backstage setting with a sardonic romanticism reminiscent of many of his most likeable films (*The Actress* [1953], *Les Girls* [1957]), the entire plot depends upon the sort of device which one imagines that Cukor finds unsympathetic—mistaken identity of the most outrageously improbable sort.

Given these scripts Cukor seems to have decided to make the most of the episodes which interested him personally without worrying too much over the effect on the complete films. Hence in both pictures the best sequences—which are superb—are achieved at the expense of overall structure. This is particularly so of *Song Without End*. Aided by Geneviève Page's excellent performance, Cukor has made the Countess's panic at her desertion by Liszt so genuine and painful that the conventionally tearjerking romance between Bogarde and Capucine, which occupies the latter two-thirds of the film, seems all the more tediously confected.

In one of *Let's Make Love*'s most delightful sequences Bing Crosby attempts to instruct Yves Montand in the art of putting across a popular song ("You and I will know you're out of breath, but she'll think it's very sexy"). But once Crosby has turned an undistinguished ballad, "Incurably Romantic," into vocal gold there is little pleasure in hearing Frankie Vaughan's leaden interpretation of the same number. Again, in two of Montand's dialogues with Marilyn Monroe and Tony Randall, Cukor has made the predicament of his central characters much more convincing and important than the story which contains them; partly for this reason the plot maneuvers of the last fifteen minutes are rather irritating.

The acting in both films is practically perfect. But this does not mean a great deal for *Song Without End* because the script gives the actors few opportunities to transform its stereotypes into believable people. Bogarde should, however, be credited with a portrayal of Liszt that goes far beyond the prescribed line of duty: he does communicate an intense passion for music, and his furious "Seductive!" shouted in disgust at the Mannheim Orchestra is memorable. Those who have seen *Pat and Mike* (1952) or *Born Yesterday* will need to be told little about the acting in *Let's Make Love* beyond the fact that it has enough gaiety and charm to vitalize much feebler scripts than Krasna's, and that Monroe has finally abandoned the rather synthetic pathos which marked some of her most recent performances: she is, in consequence, both funny and touching.

On the other hand, each of the films has, amazingly, to contend with bad acting in a minor part. Lyndon Brook's Wagner in *Song Without End* is ludicrously conceived and ineptly acted; more seriously, each appearance of Frankie Vaughan in *Let's Make Love* provokes annoyance or embarrassment. The best numbers survive their involvement with this supremely talentless performer only because Cukor is established as the one director who is nowadays willing and able to film song and dance with real excitement. No musical since *The Pajama Game* (1957) has offered anything as enjoyable as Monroe's "My Heart Belongs to Daddy" or even the "Let's Make Love" duet. The numbers are shot in Cukor's post–*A Star Is Born* (1954) manner: splendid color and lighting effects; a camera which glides with the slick elegance of a Cyd Charisse; and a brilliant use of small areas of the wide screen—it never suggests that the director would have found the old three by four ratio more congenial. Cukor is almost unique in his avoidance of the backstage musical's most obvious temptation: the expansion of the numbers into production routines, which would look cramped on the stage of the Colosseum. The dances in *Let's Make Love* are the more effective because they could quite conceivably be produced in a small off-Broadway theater-in-the-round with a minimum of stage props and an efficient lighting system.

The setting of *Let's Make Love* has allowed Cukor to return to what appears to be a favorite theme (cf. *A Star Is Born*, *It Should Happen to You*

[1954]): the humiliations of public, and especially theatrical, life. Among the many indignities in which the billionaire Jean-Marc Clement (Montand) is involved through pretending to be an actor, the following are notable: being obliged to caricature himself as a rooster, complete with "cock-a-doodle-do"; being reprimanded for his failure to suggest ardor in a love song addressed to an actress with whom he is genuinely in love; and being trained to be funny under the impatient tutorship of Milton Berle. In the most painful episode of all, he gets the bird for his attempt to entertain the crowd of professional entertainers with an old and unfunny joke: it is reminiscent of the cruelest sequence of *A Star Is Born*—the fan-club funeral of James Mason—in its demonstration of the callousness which possesses people when they become members of an audience.

These are not the most characteristic moments of *Let's Make Love* but, together with some trenchant observations on the advantages and disadvantages of affluence, they do seem to belong to the few aspects of the script which held a personal significance for the director. It seems likely that *Song Without End* and *Let's Make Love* were principally important for him in providing two box-office winners with which to reestablish his commercial reputation. From that point of view they have obviously succeeded; and if neither of them can be classed with the best of Cukor's work, the latter is enjoyable enough to provide an acceptable substitute until the real thing comes along.

Filmography

The Actress. Directed by George Cukor. MGM, 1953.
Adam's Rib. Directed by George Cukor. MGM, 1949.
Born Yesterday. Directed by George Cukor. Columbia Pictures, 1950.
Can-Can. Directed by Walter Lang. Twentieth Century Fox, 1960.
Les Girls. Directed by George Cukor. MGM, 1957.
It Should Happen to You. Directed by George Cukor. Columbia Pictures, 1954.
The Joker Is Wild. Directed by Charles Vidor. Paramount Pictures, 1957.
The King and I. Directed by Walter Lang. Twentieth Century Fox, 1956.
Let's Make Love. Directed by George Cukor. Twentieth Century Fox, 1960.
Love Me or Leave Me. Directed by Charles Vidor. MGM, 1955.

The Pajama Game. Directed by George Abbott and Stanley Donen. Warner Bros., 1957.
Pat and Mike. Directed by George Cukor. MGM, 1952.
A Song to Remember. Directed by Charles Vidor. Columbia Pictures, 1945.
Song Without End. Directed by Charles Vidor. Columbia Pictures, 1960.
A Star Is Born. Directed by George Cukor. Warner Bros., 1954.
Who Was That Lady? Directed by George Sidney. Columbia Pictures, 1960.

KING OF KINGS

First published in Movie, *no. 1 (June 1962): 29–30.*

Most of the adverse criticisms of *King of Kings* (1961) have been made elsewhere, and many of them are valid: the process work and postsynchronized sound are bad, the decor is often unhelpful, and the music always terrible. There's no need to repeat it here. In addition, censorship has interrupted the action, motivation, and design at several points. Nicholas Ray has simply been unlucky with "production values."

But the film does have faults which are entirely the director's responsibility. In particular, Ray has editorialized too much. Exaggerated camera angles emphasize points which have already been made clear. The death of Herod (Gregoire Asian), for example, is filmed in extreme high angles intended to convey Ray's moral judgment: but we have *seen* Herod order the slaughter of all the newborn children in Bethlehem—additional comment is superfluous. The angles here, and elsewhere in the film, are dictatorial; they leave no room for us to make up our own minds.

This is against the tone of a film which draws heavily upon our ability to make connections. For example, when Salome (Brigid Bazlen) demands the Baptist's (Robert Ryan) head we are reminded of Antipas's (Frank Thring) treachery to his father. He stumbles drunkenly on the steps where the dying Herod had groveled: we are expected to remember Antipas's words, "A king who cannot walk to his own throne is no longer a King, father." Similarly Ray indicates a contrast between John the Baptist's treatment of Salome and Jesus's (Jeffrey Hunter) treatment of Mary Magdalene (Carmen Sevilla):

Salome and Magdalene wear clothing and jewelry of the same color for the comparable sequences. The suggestions made by Ray's staging (and particularly by his use of contemporary references) are embodied in the narrative, not imposed upon it.

Ray's decision to direct *King of Kings* was a considerable surprise. He could not expect to transform this story, as he did with *Party Girl* (1958) or *Bigger than Life* (1956), into a vehicle for personal expression. The film makes it plain that he was attracted not by the possibility of "interpreting" the story of Jesus but by what was already in the story: the first statement and trial of Christian principles. Within this context, however, *King of Kings* does relate in theme to other Ray pictures.

It is inevitably concerned with the problem of communication which Ray sees (we are not obliged to agree) as the principal theme of his movies. The tragedy of Judas (Rip Torn) in *King of Kings* is partly that he looks for a magical solution to his country's problem (cf. James Mason in *Bigger than Life*) but mainly that he fails to understand the practical meaning of the ideas which he accepts. Throughout the film Jesus is dogged by incomprehension: one man is ready to accept his challenge to cast the first stone at Magdalene; many who hear the Sermon on the Mount are baffled by his refusal to call on God to destroy the Romans; even toward the end the disciples themselves cannot see why he should have to die.

Jeffrey Hunter's Jesus is diametrically opposed to the other Ray heroes in his certainty of his purpose in life. The film emphasizes Christ's—and Mary's (Siobhan McKenna)—knowledge and acceptance of his destiny. Hunter's performance admirably conveys Jesus's awareness of his mission; for example, at the moment when Judas is received among the disciples Hunter's voice and movement combine acceptance with regret in a way which shows clearly that he recognizes Judas as his future betrayer.

The central characters of Ray's previous movies, on the other hand, have been victims of confusion: either, like James Dean in *Rebel Without a Cause* (1955), they have not been sure what they are looking for, or, like Robert Taylor in *Party Girl*, they have looked for it in a self-defeating way. Hence the sad irony of "I know where I'm going" on the soundtrack of *They Live by Night* (1948). Ray's preoccupation with moral and psychological confusion is expressed in *King of Kings* by the contrast between Jesus's certainty and the tormented vacillation of Lucius and Judas.

It is typical of Ray that, in filming *the* bestseller, he should wish to avoid everything familiar. Hence his rejection of the great religious paintings as a basis for the film's design; hence also the bewilderment of those critics, notably Mrs. Gilliatt, who seem to think that a biblical movie must be a running, jumping, and standing still El Greco.

Instead of devoting his energies to providing tableaux Ray has concentrated (with his writer, Philip Yordan) on making the events and issues significant for a twentieth-century audience. For this reason the characters of Barabbas (Harry Guardino) and Lucius (Ron Randell) have each been built up on the basis of a single clue in the New Testament; and for this reason the motivation of Judas's betrayal has been altered. To put it simply, and with all respect to the original authors, the moral conflicts expressed in the New Testament are not very interesting and not at all complex: Judas has only to decide between being faithful to Jesus and making a bit of pin money. By involving Judas in the movement to free Judea from Roman domination, and motivating the betrayal in that way, Ray and Yordan have faced us with more complex and significant issues; they have also, like few filmmakers, recognized that Christianity is not an easy or comfortable way of life.

The whole film, in fact, has been designed as a meeting of two incompatible ways of life: one based on violence and oppression, represented equally by the court and the rebels; the other based on love and resignation, represented by Jesus and, in various degrees, his followers. Their conflict is expressed in a consistent symbolism which is made explicit by Barabbas. He rejects the idea of enlisting Jesus to further the zealots' cause: "He speaks only of peace. I am fire, he is water. How can we ever meet?" In the same sequence the ultimate superiority of water over fire is shown in the cooling of a red-hot sword. There is little point in detailing all the appearances of this symbolism; a few examples will show how completely it is integrated with the narrative. The first appearances of John the Baptist, the adult Jesus, and Simon Peter (Royal Dano) come in shots which have a background of water. John and Jesus are seen in this way because Jesus has come to the river to be baptized, Simon Peter because he is fishing when Jesus calls him. Herodias's complaint against

Herod's attentions to Salome is made while a juggler is walking behind her throwing firebrands—during a court entertainment. Barabbas, summoning the attack on the Antonia fortress, climbs the waterwheel in the center of the square—because that is the highest accessible place from which to address the crowd.

King of Kings is acted in two distinct styles which embody its opposed ways of life. The violent, neurotic life of the court is expressed in a detailed, almost naturalistic, style with elaborate interplay of gesture, intonation, and expression. The gentle, affirmative life of Mary, Jesus, and the disciples is shown in a simpler style of broad, confident gestures. There is no detail here: when Joseph says he has been told to take Jesus away into Egypt, Mary simply gets up and says, "Then we will go." There has been no attempt to give Jesus a "personality"; Jeffrey Hunter *represents* Jesus, but has resisted any temptation to "act" the part.

The simplicity of the sequences centering on Mary and Jesus brings the film very close in feeling to the great religious folk ballads. There has always been a "folk" element in Ray's pictures: in their directness of language and symbolism; in their acceptance of death and suffering as the necessary conditions of life: and in their straightforward statements of the ambiguous. The heroes of many Ray pictures are near relations to the "brave and desperate boys" of folk song, and *Johnny Guitar* (1954) is exactly one of those "sad songs about kissing and killing" that Burl Ives enjoyed in *Wind Across the Everglades* (1958).

Similarly, Ray's use of an elemental (fire/water, dark/light) symbolism, and the directness of his style in the Christian sequences of *King of Kings*, evokes "The Cherry Tree" or the Corpus Christi Carol. In this connection it is interesting that the ballad-makers were not afraid to elaborate upon the gospel story: in "The Cherry Tree" the unborn Jesus cries out from his mother's womb to protest Joseph's cruelty to Mary.

There is not space in a short review to examine in detail Ray's approach to the problem of the "big" picture. But perhaps a brief look at one of the biggest sequences will give some indication of his method. The problems in filming the Sermon on the Mount are sufficiently obvious: it is purely verbal; its audience is huge and potentially impersonal. Ray has rejected the obvious, static method of staging the sermon. Instead his camera accompanies Jesus, in a series of short tracking shots, as he walks down the side of the mountain talking to groups of people in turn. The statements and exhortations of Matthew's account have been converted into a series of questions and answers that involve the crowd organically in the scene and allow us to judge the effect of Jesus's words. Ray gives added meaning to the words by inserting shots to remind us of their special significance for various members of the sermon's audience: thus on "the good shepherd lays down his life for his sheep" Mary's reaction brings us close to the reality behind the words. Visually the course of the sermon is marked by the progressive integration of the figure of Jesus into the crowd: the more he becomes accepted as a man among men, the more closely he becomes a part of the crowd compositions. But, at the end of the sermon, one very striking shot of people hurrying away down the mountain conveys a visual impression of disintegration: we are prepared for Barabbas's dismissal of Jesus's message as "words!"

Filmography

Bigger than Life. Directed by Nicholas Ray. Twentieth Century Fox, 1956.
Johnny Guitar. Directed by Nicholas Ray. Republic Pictures, 1954.
King of Kings. Directed by Nicholas Ray. MGM, 1961.
Party Girl. Directed by Nicholas Ray. MGM, 1958.
Rebel Without a Cause. Directed by Nicholas Ray. Warner Bros., 1955.
They Live by Night. Directed by Nicholas Ray. RKO Radio Pictures, 1948.
Wind Across the Everglades. Directed by Nicholas Ray. Warner Bros., 1958.

WHY PREMINGER?

First published in Movie, *no. 2 (September 1962): 11. ("Why Preminger?" introduced eleven articles in* Movie, *no. 2, on Preminger's films.)*

The films of Otto Preminger are so different from those of any other director that an investigation of Preminger's work tends to dwell as much on what it is not, as on what it is. Most obviously, and for many critics most damningly, Preminger does not solicit affection for his characters. His films are cold. "Warm" and "cold" are not, however, evaluative terms. A film is no more condemned by its lack of warmth than by its lack of suspense, or violence, or stereophonic sound.

Certainly Preminger refuses to *love* his characters. His refusal also to condemn, admire, despise, inflate, or to patronize them is less often remarked. His aim is to present characters, actions, and issues clearly and without prejudice. He is concerned to show events, not to demonstrate his feelings about them. This objectivity is a mark of his respect for his characters and, particularly, for his audience. He presupposes an intelligence active enough to allow the spectator to make connections, comparisons, and judgments. Preminger presents the evidence but he leaves the spectator free to draw his own conclusions.

He has, then, "nothing to say"? Not at all. But his method and his attitude are identical. His films are about ways of reaching decisions—on facts and on courses of action. They both advocate and embody a method of looking at people and events. Preminger is the enemy of preconceptions, snap judgments, closed minds. In order to enjoy Preminger's films the spectator must apply an unprejudiced intelligence; he is constantly required to examine the quality not only of the characters' decisions but also of his own reactions.

Preminger rejects every stylistic, emotional, or narrative distortion. He gives us no information about his characters except what we can deduce from their actions. We can only grasp the reality behind surface appearance by looking clearly and intelligently at the appearance itself, by appreciating that the appearance *is* a reality.

Thus Preminger is committed to exact and lucid presentation. Action and character cannot be falsified or exaggerated in order to emphasize the theme. In his three most recent pictures Preminger has brought epic subjects (justice, nationhood, democracy) down to the human scale; ideas are only judged by their results in human behavior.[1] Any ideas which the director wishes to examine must therefore be embodied in, not imposed upon, the story. Hence the vital importance which Preminger attaches to his scripts. All that he wishes to say or show is in the development of his narrative and the moral evolution of his characters.

Narrative and treatment are Preminger's equivalent of content and form. The visual beauty of his films does not come from his compositions, which, though usually attractive, are always dictated by the need for complete lucidity. It is rather a result of the involvement of the camera in the physical and moral movement of the characters. Fluidity (of development, not indecision) distinguishes Preminger's visual style as it distinguishes his narrative method and his moral attitude.

Filmography

Advise and Consent. Directed by Otto Preminger. Columbia Pictures, 1962.
Anatomy of a Murder. Directed by Otto Preminger. Columbia Pictures, 1959.
Exodus. Directed by Otto Preminger. United Artists, 1960.

Note

1   The three films were *Anatomy of a Murder* (1959), *Exodus* (1960), and *Advise and Consent* (1962). Ed.

THE MAN WITH THE GOLDEN ARM

First published in Movie, *no. 2 (September 1962): 20.*

Everything from acting to editing is done well in *The Man with the Golden Arm* (1955). It could serve as the model of the well-made film on a forbidden subject. But, except in the sequences which center on the Kim Novak character, it is both apart from and inferior to the rest of Preminger's work. Its setting is artificial. Its approach is subjective. It is a mood film; and Preminger has normally concentrated on action and character, leaving atmosphere to take care of itself. Also its characters' decisions are constantly predicted in the camerawork and music so that the film has the spurious inevitability that we least expect to find in a Preminger movie.

Superficially Frankie Machine (Frank Sinatra), the drug addict, has much in common with the obsessed heroes of, for example, *Laura* (1944), *One Man Mutiny* (a.k.a. *The Court-Martial of Billy Mitchell*, 1955), and *Exodus* (1960). Unlike Billy Mitchell or Ari Ben Canaan, however, Frankie's powers of moral decision are not heightened but destroyed by his (entirely physiological) obsession. The story of *One Man Mutiny* could not exist without Billy Mitchell's belief in air power. Frankie Machine's drug addiction could be excised from *The Man with the Golden Arm* without affecting the film's real subject: his relationships with his wife and with the girl in the flat downstairs. His obsession is only important because it robs him of the ability to choose. And for Preminger there is no drama without choice.

Filmography

Exodus. Directed by Otto Preminger. United Artists, 1960.

Laura. Directed by Otto Preminger. Twentieth Century Fox, 1944.

The Man with the Golden Arm. Directed by Otto Preminger. United Artists, 1955.

One Man Mutiny (a.k.a. *The Court-Martial of Billy Mitchell*). Directed by Otto Preminger. Warner Bros., 1955.

RIVER OF NO RETURN

First published in Movie, *no. 2 (September 1962): 18–19.*

Matt Calder (Robert Mitchum) leaves his farm, beside the River of No Return, and rides away upstream.[1] He arrives at a camp, which has mushroomed following a gold strike. The camera follows Matt as he rides through the camp; this shot provides a number of keys to Preminger's method. The position of the camera, behind Matt, leaves the character free; it does not anticipate (and therefore predict) his actions. The camera movement is complex, because it follows Matt through a number of changes of direction; it conveys both the turbulence of the life in the camp and Matt's preoccupation. Also, the shot is *complete*. It is not broken up by atmospheric inserts. It ends when it ceases to provide the clearest view of the situation. Montage is ignored and a magnificent fluidity results.

Matt stops at a trading post to enquire for his son Mark (Tommy Rettig), who was to have been delivered to him there. He learns that Mark's guardian has abandoned him and joined the gold rush. We cut to a shot of a small boy wandering through a tent gambling saloon. Mark Calder, obviously, but the conclusion imposed by the cutting is a matter of narrative fact. Before leaving Mark hands a guitar to Kay (Marilyn Monroe), the saloon showgirl. The gesture conveys Mark's acceptance of Kay and her profession. During Kay's song Matt enters the tent; he shows no interest in Kay or in the amenities of the saloon, and leaves to continue his search. Mark is given two pails of beer to carry to the barber's shop. A drunk shoots holes in them. Matt walks up and floors the drunk.

Mark says he is waiting for his father, whom he does not know. Matt's question—"Would it be all right if he looked like me?"—indicates his anxiety for approval of himself and his way of life. From this point the film's protagonists are engaged in constant comparison of the moral worth of opposed attitudes and actions. Mark is pleased but wary. He demands proof of Matt's identity. Matt shows him a picture of his mother.

Mark insists, despite his father's reluctance, on saying goodbye to Kay, "the lady who sings in the saloon." When they arrive in her dressing room Kay is cleaning the red satin shoes she wears on stage. She condemns Matt as a bad father for "leaving a kid running round a crummy place like this." She refuses the money Matt offers for having looked after Mark. She goes onstage. Matt is disturbed by the admiration with which Mark watches her. Eventually he takes his son out of the saloon.

When Kay returns to her room she finds Harry Weston (Rory Calhoun), the gambler she is in love with. There are no subjective shots here to "place" Kay's love for Harry, just as there were none to establish Mark's admiration for Matt and Kay. These emotions are simply observed in the action and dialogue. Harry has won a claim in the middle of the richest strike, but he must get to Council City quickly in case his opponents try to prevent his registering it. No horses are available so Kay gives him the money to buy a raft. They will make the journey by river. Harry's plans for a life of luxury are contrasted with the image of life on the farm, which Matt offers his son as they ride out of the camp. End of first statement.

Development section. Mark is helping his father with the plowing. Matt warns him against trying to go too fast: "Sometimes you have to back up and go around." Matt's attitude is developed when he explains what led him to take up farming: "If a man doesn't know what he's doing or where he's going the best thing for him is to back up round and start all over. I thought I'd start with the ground." Mark says he would like a rifle when they sell their first wheat. He asks whether they will be rich like the men finding gold. "No, but we'll beat those that don't find it." When he asks why Matt left home so suddenly and didn't send for him sooner after the death of his mother Matt evades the issue by starting a shooting lesson.

"What's important?" "To hit the target." "When?" "The first shot." "Why?" "Because I might not get another." This episode summarizes our experience of Matt: he is leisurely and methodical, he makes his decisions entirely according to the rules, and he is eager for his son to approve and adopt his way of life. The lesson is interrupted, by the sight, first, of, Indian fires on the mountains above the farm, and then of a raft in trouble on the rapids. Matt saves Harry and Kay. As Harry lifts Kay from the raft, she drops the bundle which contains most of her "things" into the water. Kay's gradual loss of the physical tokens of her way of life has great symbolic significance. But Preminger is not overimpressed. The bundle simply floats away off-screen while Harry brings Kay ashore. It would be wrong to describe this as understatement. The symbolism is in the event, not in the visual pattern, so the director presents the action clearly and leaves interpretation to the spectator.

Matt forms a rapid (hasty?) judgment on Harry and Kay—an extension, in part, of his contempt for all the prospectors, and in part of his antipathy to their respectively opportunistic and instinctual approaches to life. He tells Harry that the raft journey is suicidal but he will neither lend nor sell his horse and rifle because of the danger from the Indians. Harry steals the rifle and forces Mark to get the horse. He rejects Matt's request to take the boy because he cannot afford the delay. When Matt tries to fight Harry knocks him out with the rifle butt. The attitudes to Harry's action are presented from all three points of view. In particular Kay's emotional arguments ("The gold doesn't matter that much"; "He's hurt"; "He saved our lives") culminate in her completely sentimental decision to wait at the farm until Harry returns.

Harry leaves. The Indians attack. Matt, Mark, and Kay escape on the raft to attempt the river journey. The Indians set fire to Matt's cabin. The fire is seen from the raft as it is swept downstream. This is the first subjective shot in the film. Like all those which follow it is used to unite, not to differentiate, the characters' points of view.

Description and comment for all that happens on the journey would more than fill this magazine. Briefly, Matt admits to Kay that he intends to "go after" Harry, whose offence is capital. In attempting to explain, though not to excuse, Harry's "one mistake," Kay reveals her knowledge that Matt was imprisoned for shooting a man in the back. Mark overhears and will not accept Matt's explanation that he did it in order to save the life of a friend: Mark condemns his father by the rules which Matt has been teaching him to regard as absolute. Matt is now in the same offensive/defensive position as Harry and Kay.

In the course of the journey, there are significant changes in the behavior of Matt and Kay. Kay begins to assume some of Matt's mannerisms, and Matt begins to be capable of Kay's sort of emotional decision: when Kay faints from cold and exhaustion Matt is persuaded by his son's concern to light a fire, although it is likely to draw the Indians. But in other respects Matt's actions become increasingly similar to Harry's. His life is saved by two men, Colby and Benson, who are looking for "a card sharp called Weston." (We are never told whether Harry in fact cheated them.) Colby invites Kay to go to Council City with them; since they have horses and rifles she will have a chance of surviving the journey. Kay declines: "I'd rather have no chance, with him." Matt and Colby fight. Matt gets Colby's knife and, holding it at his throat, tells Benson to hand over one of their rifles (cf. Harry threatening Matt with his rifle and telling Mark to hand over Matt's *only* means of defense).

Matt is baffled by Kay's decision. He asks why she refused Colby's offer. "You have to ask? A man like that?" "What's a man like Weston?" "How would you know anything about him? You only know the one crazy thing he did. You can't even see the difference!" This conversation occupies part of a long take in a medium shot which favors neither point of view. The judgments are completely subjective; they are important mainly as part of the characterization. The spectator decides whether, for example, there is a moral difference between Weston and Colby.

Similarly we are gradually shown that neither Matt's reliance on law and reason nor Kay's on emotion has proved completely satisfactory. Kay expresses a distaste for the life of the saloons that Preminger nowhere endorses. The film leads us to the conclusion not that Kay's life is wrong in absolute terms, but that it is wrong (because unproductive) *for Kay*.

At the end of the journey, as the raft drifts toward Council City, Kay asks Matt to talk to Weston: "Give yourself the chance to find out." Matt refuses, but he agrees to let Kay talk to Harry alone.

Developing a Detailed Criticism • 119

Finale. Matt, Mark, and Kay are walking toward the center of town. Kay wears Matt's leather jacket; she has lost every vestige of her own way of life except the red shoes and the guitar. The latter is a neutral object: it can accompany both the brashly erotic "File My Claim" and the lyrical "Down in the Meadow." Kay reverses her first judgment on Matt; she says that all his actions have been dictated by his love for his son.

They arrive at the general store. Matt enquires for Harry. The storekeeper says he is in the saloon, and then offers Matt credit for all he needs to rebuild the farm. Kay crosses the street to find Harry. Great care is taken to involve the store and the saloon organically in the movement of the sequence. They are both parts of the same world: it is possible to choose, or compromise, between the ways of life they symbolize.

Kay finds Harry in the saloon playing cards. She tells him that Matt is waiting for him: "He could kill you and no one would blame him. I told him you were desperate. I think he believed me at last. Now you've got to tell him." Harry reluctantly agrees to talk to Matt. He produces a gun "in case he's hard of hearing." Kay makes him put it on the bar and he goes to leave the saloon apparently unarmed.

In the store Mark refuses his promised rifle present. Matt goes out, unarmed, to meet Harry. Halfway across the street Harry draws a revolver from inside his coat and fires at Matt. Matt takes cover but Harry corners him. There is a shot and Harry falls dead. Mark has shot him in the back with a rifle from the store. Kay comforts Mark and tells him that he had no choice in what he did. As Matt approaches she takes the rifle from Mark and puts it in the rack. She leaves the store and crosses the street in front of Matt and Mark to enter the Black Nugget.

Coda. Kay has returned to her former life. The camera moves out from a close-up of her shoes as she sits, gaudily dressed, on top of a piano. At the end of her song Matt comes in, lifts her down from her perch, and carries her, with her guitar, out of the saloon. He puts her down beside Mark in the front of a cart. "Where are you taking me?" "Home." Matt climbs up and drives off. As they move away Kay takes off her shoes and throws them down in the road. The film ends, like *Anatomy of a Murder* (1959), as the camera tracks in to a close-up of abandoned footwear.

Filmography

Anatomy of a Murder. Directed by Otto Preminger. Columbia Pictures, 1959.
River of No Return. Directed by Otto Preminger. Twentieth Century Fox, 1954.

Note

1   The year of release of *River of No Return* was 1954. Ed.

MERRILL'S MARAUDERS

First published in Movie, no. 2 (September 1962): 32.

When this is all over I'm going to line my children up against a wall and tell them what it was like here in Burma . . .

In life and on film Samuel Fuller has been many things: among them war correspondent (*The Steel Helmet* [1951], *Fixed Bayonets!* [1951]), pulp novelist (*Pickup on South Street* [1953]), and crime reporter (*House of Bamboo* [1955], *The Crimson Kimono* [1959]). With *Verboten!* (1959) and *Merrill's Marauders* (1962), the two Fuller pictures most recently released in Britain, the persona has changed again. These movies suggest illustrated lectures. Newsreel extracts, documents, maps, and animated diagrams are used to clarify the narrative and to emphasize its actuality. This development of his method, now that it has occurred, seems a logical step in Fuller's progress toward a form which combines personal statement with historical reconstruction.

In one respect, though, Fuller does not change. The director of *Merrill's Marauders* is as much a sensationalist as the director of *The Steel Helmet* or, presumably, as the author of *Burn, Baby, Burn!* (1935).[1] He sets out to surprise or shock his audience both visually and emotionally. Thus the success of his movies can almost be calculated from the number of trouvailles which they contain: *Merrill's Marauders* is very successful indeed.

There are, however, any number of talentless directors who devote their creative energies, such as they are, to the pursuit of impact. Fuller is distinguished from these by the fact that he sacrifices neither clarity nor credibility in order to create his effects. Compare, for example, *The Wolf Trap* (*Vlčí jáma*, 1958), *The Death of a Cyclist* (1955), and *Room at the Top* (1959), where action and gesture are so subordinated to the struggle for visual impact that they become ludicrously artificial. When Fuller wants a sunset in the background to a close-up of a Burmese girl he achieves the shot by changing the camera's position, not the actress's.

If they don't cry I'll beat the hell out of them.

Fuller's method is sensational also in another, more literal, sense. He wants his audience to experience, rather than observe, the events and emotions with which his film deals—to know, not simply what happened in Burma during the Second World War, but "what it was like here." The director intends that we should identify with his characters in their physical and psychological exhaustion; that we should feel the truth of the doctor's diagnosis of "A.O.E.—accumulation of everything"; that we should know subjectively what moves the sergeant to tears at the moment (beautifully realized by Claude Akins) when he experiences his first ordinary human contact after weeks of fighting and struggling through the jungle.

Audience identification is achieved through the unity of rhythm between the action and the presentation. The attack on the railhead at Shaduzup is filmed with a rapidly moving camera and edited for maximum ("machine-gun") impact on our eyes and nerves. But after the battle long takes and slow ("exhausted") camera movements involve us in the soldiers' fatigue.

Fuller's art is built on contradiction. The themes of *Merrill's Marauders* are expressed in the opposition between, for example, the total exhaustion of the soldiers after the capture of Shaduzup and the determination of Brigadier Merrill (Jeff Chandler) to take them on to help the British at Myitkyina. At every point in the chain of command the decision to go on to Shaduzup, and from Shaduzup to Myitkyina, is first resisted and then implemented. The film's strength comes from our identification with both actions.

> "When you're at the end of your rope, all you have to do is make one foot move out in front of the other." "If you can breathe you can fight."

Fuller is concerned in this film, as in his Western, *Run of the Arrow* (1957), to establish a relationship between moral and physical stamina. Merrill radios headquarters to drop supplies, but he realizes when the planes are on their way that the Japanese will be drawn by the falling parachutes. He orders his men back into the swamps. "Chow-hound" (Will Hutchins) remains behind against orders and is shot by the Japanese as he seizes one of the packages. The futility of his assertion of an individual will is underlined by Fuller's use of his camera to contradict Chow-hound's movements.

In contrast: a dying soldier asks Merrill, "Did Lemchek get through?" But the soldier *is* Lemchek. Men renounce individuality when they become soldiers. They are fighting machines, but they are fueled by emotion. In the final stage of the trek to Myitkyina, Eleanor, the point platoon's mule, collapses. Her attendant, "Muley," rather than see her destroyed, himself carries her load. His emotions, concentrated in his devotion to the animal, sustain him until he has exhausted all his energy and he dies.

In *Merrill's Marauders* Fuller shows leadership as the ability to inspire an emotion which, like Muley's, can summon up a man's last reserves of strength and will. There is very little reference in the conversations among Merrill's troops to the military purpose of their struggle. Merrill's decisions are dictated by the strategic importance of the Burmese campaign, but his men fight out of loyalty to their leader, rather than to an idea.

Fuller's war films are unlike any other director's in placing their emphasis upon order. A Japanese machine-gun post is *systematically* destroyed by a series of advances under smokescreen cover. Even the chaos of the battle at Shaduzup, in and around the maze of concrete blocks which protects the railhead, is only apparent: a hand grenade can still be thrown along a chain of men until it reaches the soldier who is technically placed to make the most efficient use of it.

The sequence of relaxation after this attack includes one of Fuller's most stunning images and perhaps his most successful attempt at providing an "objective correlative" for his attitude to war. Lt. Stockton (Ty Hardin), commander of the point platoon, staggers toward a stream which runs past the native village. He stops at its edge and places his helmet, ammunition belt, and rifle in a neat pile on the ground. Then he slumps forward, face first, into the water.

Filmography

The Crimson Kimono. Directed by Samuel Fuller. Columbia Pictures, 1959.
The Death of a Cyclist. Directed by Juan Antonio Bardem. Janus Films, 1955.
Fixed Bayonets! Directed by Samuel Fuller. Twentieth Century Fox, 1951.
House of Bamboo. Directed by Samuel Fuller. Twentieth Century Fox, 1955.
Merrill's Marauders. Directed by Samuel Fuller. Warner Bros., 1962.
Pickup on South Street. Directed by Samuel Fuller. Twentieth Century Fox, 1953.
Room at the Top. Directed by Jack Clayton. British Lion (UK), Continental Distributing (US), 1959.
Run of the Arrow. Directed by Samuel Fuller. Universal Pictures, 1957.
The Steel Helmet. Directed by Samuel Fuller. Lippert Pictures, 1951.
Verboten! Directed by Samuel Fuller. Columbia Pictures, 1959.
The Wolf Trap (*Vlčí jáma*). Directed by Jirí Weiss. Ceskoslovenský Státní Film/Filmové Studio Barrandov, 1958.

Note

1   Fuller is credited as Sam Fuller for this novel, the title of which, on the first-edition hardback cover, is strikingly presented as "burn, *Baby*, burn!" (New York: Phoenix, 1935). Ed.

AN IMPORTANT RE-RELEASE
George Stevens' *Giant*

First published in Movie, *no. 4 (November 1962): 33.*[1]

Many people have expressed surprise at *Movie*'s antipathy to the work of the senior Oscar winners. We in turn find this surprising; the more so when Preminger asks, in evident bewilderment, why we should regard William Wyler and David Lean as fifth-rate artists.[2] We expected the creator of *Anatomy of a Murder* (1959) and *Advise and Consent* (1962) to be among the first to condemn the overcalculation of their films. Certainly it is difficult to reconcile his definition of successful direction ("You wouldn't be aware that the director did anything intentionally") with an admiration for filmmakers who strain to make everything "effective."[3] Their compositions, movements, lighting, cutting, and, especially, soundtracks are cheaply exploited in an all-out assault on our responses. (Wyler's *The Loudest Whisper* [US title: *The Children's Hour*, 1961] uses even silence bombastically.) The films of Wyler, Lean, [Fred] Zinnemann and Co. work, if at all, only so long as one ignores *how* they work. Their effects vanish, like some minor psychological disturbance, as soon as they are understood.

I am not attempting to make a plea for the functionless, disorganized movie whose only claim on our attention lies in its "spontaneity." After all, I acknowledge the supremacy of the arch-calculator, Hitchcock. But

Hitchcock's effects survive inspection. No matter how one *explains*, say, the Albert Hall sequence of *The Man Who Knew Too Much* (1956), the excitement and the mystery remain, and, ultimately, refuse analysis. Perhaps the important difference is between calculating in order to communicate experience (Hitchcock) and calculating in order to impose it (Wyler, etc.).

The Wyler school of quality direction also betrays itself by its concentration on inessentials. Atmosphere and "point" customarily take precedence over what is important, the action—in, for example, the final gunfight in Wyler's *The Big Country* (1958). This, I suspect, is one of the reasons for the critical reputation which Wyler enjoys. He is just the man for critics who think that action is rather vulgar (see the reviews of any Walsh film) and who do not realize that they are *praising* Nicholas Ray's *Party Girl* (1958) when they remark on its "lack of period atmosphere."

George Stevens is another of Hollywood's "most respected craftsmen." But it is not only this fact which makes one consider him as a member of the Wyler-Zinnemann clan. At his worst, and that is often, he victimizes his audience as unscrupulously as anyone. On the other hand, one does go to a Stevens movie hopefully, because even his most crudely calculated pictures have contained sequences which suggest a sympathetic personality striving to emerge from the welter of effects. *Shane* (1953) exploits a patronizing "boy's-eye view" of its characters, but it does achieve real feeling in the sequence where Van Heflin and Alan Ladd uproot the huge tree stump. *The Diary of Anne Frank* (1959) occasionally takes time out from contemplating its own pathos to give us in, for example, Shelley Winters's outburst over the damage to her fur coat, a genuinely observed incident.

Giant (1956) reverses the pattern of Stevens movies. Here one objects to many details of treatment, but the film as a whole remains extremely likeable. It has a remarkable simplicity of method. In the opening shots two contrasted ways of life are summarized in the transition from the yellow-brown Texas landscape to the greenery surrounding Leslie's (Elizabeth Taylor) home. Most of the film (and practically everything that is good in it) has a family-album feeling, quite close to that of *Meet Me in St. Louis* (1944) but far removed from the sententiousness associated with "blockbusters." Many of the best scenes deal with family occasions—weddings, birthdays, funerals, Christmases, and so forth. Again it is the simplicity, the ordinariness, even, that strikes one. The middle-aged Jett Rink (James Dean) is characterized by his arriving on a business visit to the home of Jordan Benedict (Rock Hudson) unaware that it is Christmas Day. Two ways of life are contrasted through two ways of serving breakfast.

The episodic structure of the film and the long time-span (twenty-five years) that it covers make its sequences virtually autonomous. Because of this, it is easy to forget the miscalculations: the unnatural "explosive" silence which descends on the hamburger joint when the Mexicans enter, or the cat thrown across the set purely for effect (i.e., superfluously) when Rink and Benedict are about to fight.

Stevens's tendency toward facile point-making is restrained in *Giant* by his respect for his leading characters. The personal relationship, for once, is more important than the ideas which it symbolizes. Jordan and Leslie are in love five minutes after the film begins and they remain so until the end. They are able to compromise even when their strongest convictions are involved. Stevens is not always capable of this degree of humility in relation to his audience. But it is very pleasant to hear him resolve an argument on an important matter of principle with "Take off your hat, honey!"

Works Cited

"Interview with Otto Preminger." *Movie*, no. 4 (November 1962): 18–20.
Mayersberg, Paul. "An Important Re-Release: George Stevens' *Giant*." *Movie*, no. 4 (November 1962): 31–32.

Filmography

Advise and Consent. Directed by Otto Preminger. Columbia Pictures, 1962.
Anatomy of a Murder. Directed by Otto Preminger. Columbia Pictures, 1959.
The Big Country. Directed by William Wyler. United Artists, 1958.
The Diary of Anne Frank. Directed by George Stevens. Twentieth Century Fox, 1959.
Giant. Directed by George Stevens. Warner Bros., 1956.
The Loudest Whisper (US title: *The Children's Hour*). Directed by William Wyler. United Artists, 1961.

The Man Who Knew Too Much. Directed by Alfred Hitchcock. Paramount Pictures, 1956.
Meet Me in St. Louis. Directed by Vincente Minnelli. MGM, 1944.
Party Girl. Directed by Nicholas Ray. MGM, 1958.
Shane. Directed by George Stevens. Paramount Pictures, 1953.

Notes

1 This is second of two articles on *Giant* in *Movie*, no. 4 (the other is by Paul Mayersberg), marking the film's re-release. The two articles appeared together under the shared title "An Important Re-Release: George Stevens' *Giant*." Ed.

2 This may have been part of the discussion with Preminger that led to the interview in *Movie* 4, but the exchange does not form part of the published interview. Ed.

3 In the *Movie* 4 interview, Preminger says: "I believe that the ideal picture is the picture where you don't notice the director, where you are never aware that the director did anything deliberately" (1962, 20). Ed.

UN-AMERICAN ACTIVITIES

First published in Movie, *no. 5 (December 1962): 3–6.*

Samuel Fuller's Underworld U.S.A. *(1961), like* Verboten! *(1959), has not been given a circuit release. Instead it has appeared unpublicized at a number of suburban cinemas in a double bill with* I Love, You Love *(Io amo, tu ami, 1961). Even if there were not a shortage of new films this would still be a waste of one of the best of the year. It is worth traveling to the most sordid and inaccessible cinemas to see it.*

Underworld U.S.A. is Samuel Fuller's most brutal picture. It adopts the methods of the crime reporter more completely than either *Pickup on South Street* (1953) or *The Crimson Kimono* (1959). The film has the urgency of an on-the-spot report: Fuller's images reproduce with extraordinary accuracy the texture of newspaper photographs. A little girl is knocked off her bicycle and killed in a motor "accident." We see the same shot twice: first when the murder is committed, and later as a photograph on the front page of a newspaper.

Fuller has carried his search for impact further in this than in any other of his films. Every shot is a smack in the eye. Every cut is a shock cut. Is a "shock dissolve" a contradiction in terms? Perhaps, but Fuller has always exploited contradictions and *Underworld U.S.A.* contains a number of shock dissolves. The picture's jolting style fulfills no *dramatic* requirement; it is willed by the director, not imposed by the narrative.

The end justifies the style. Fuller's films have a moral (propagandist, if you like) purpose. They celebrate energy, often collective, as in *Merrill's Marauders* (1962), but here individual. Style and content are united in an attack upon the film's audience, the American public. Fuller has, one suspects, little sympathy for anyone who lives vicariously in the cinema. A verbal equivalent for his camera's attitude would be "Don't just sit there. Do something!"

Underworld U.S.A. provides a portrait of the American public more scathing even than that painted in Kazan's *A Face in the Crowd* (1957). Gullible, apathetic, and gutless, the American people have allowed "the punks" to take office. The totalitarian threat to the democratic way of life comes not from communism (as in *Pickup on South Street*), and not from fascism (*Verboten!*) but from organized crime. A vast syndicate, masquerading under the title of "National Projects," controls vice and labor rackets. Like other big business corporations, it is rigidly hierarchic. Earl Connors (Robert Emhardt) coordinates the work of the departments headed by Gela (Paul Dubov, i/c drug-traffic), Gunther (Gerald Milton, labor) and Smith (Allan Gruener, prostitution). Connors himself takes his orders "from the Coast." The syndicate keeps power by murder and intimidation; by bribery (Gunther objects to Smith's paying a police chief $5,000 because "it's more than I give my union bosses"); and by maintaining "a legitimate business facade from basement to penthouse."

The syndicate's methods are so successful that Driscoll (Larry Gates), the head of a federal crime committee, finds it impossible to get people to testify. Although bribery and murder account for the unwillingness or inability of key witnesses to give evidence, the syndicate's strongest weapon is public indifference. Driscoll describes the chief of National Projects as "shrewd, warm, charitable—an animal!" and Connors himself tells a board meeting of the syndicate: "There'll always be people like Driscoll. There'll always be people like us. As long as we keep books and subscribe to charities, we'll win the war. We always have."

We hear of only one example of successful opposition to the organization, and that is the result of democratic action. Smith is loosing his grip over one of the unions because "the Locals are kicking our men out of office." In Fullerian politics the strength of a democracy is proportional to the energy and vigilance of its individual members. *Underworld U.S.A.* shows the outcome of a decline in those qualities.

There are both external and internal indications that Fuller regards such a decline as a matter of historical fact. In *Pickup on South Street*, which was made in 1952, the "lowest" members of society—pickpockets, informers, prostitutes—were willing to die rather than help America's enemies. But now, in *Underworld U.S.A.*, even the most "decent" characters (the term is relative) are indifferent to the struggle. This contrast is the more striking in that *Underworld*'s businessmen are strictly comparable, in their methods and behavior, with the "commies" of *Pickup*.

Within the film also, time plays a very important role. When he is twelve years old Tolly Devlin (Cliff Robertson), the film's hero, sees his father beaten to death by four punks. By the time that he is grown up and ready for revenge three of the punks have become leaders of a vice monopoly. There is no reason why the story should be constructed in this way unless Fuller intended the time lapse to be interpreted historically.

Fuller is not alone in his view of recent American history. Allen Drury's novel *Advise and Consent* (1959) also portrays the United States citizen as "too complacent and uncaring." He says (and I quote for the relevance of his point, not the beauty of his prose),

> A universal guilt enshrouded the middle years of the twentieth century, in America; and it attached to all those who participated in those times. . . . It rested . . . not least upon the ordinary citizen and his wife, who somehow didn't give quite enough of a damn about their country in spite of all their self-congratulatory airs about how patriotic they were. Nobody could stand forth now in America and say, "I am guiltless. I had no part in this. I did not help bring America down from her bright pinnacle." For that would be to deny that one had lived through those years. (Drury 1961, 33).

Tolly Devlin also does not give a damn about his country; he helps Driscoll simply in order to achieve his personal revenge on Gunther, Gela, and Smith, his father's murderers. He saves a prostitute, Cuddles (Dolores Dorn), from Gus (Richard Rust), who has been detailed to dispose of her because she knows too much: "I saw Mr. Smith kill a dame, a hustler." He persuades Cuddles to testify against Smith, and he insinuates himself into the syndicate. Driscoll concocts a document stating that Gunther has declared his readiness to squeal on his associates. Tolly gives Gela the document, which he claims to have stolen from a safe in the crime committee's building. Gunther is rubbed out. Driscoll now decides to call a temporary halt in Tolly's activities in order not to arouse the syndicate's suspicions. But Tolly is eager to settle with Gela, so he himself invents a list of meetings between Gela and Driscoll and delivers it to the syndicate's boss, Connors. In order to provide "verification" of this evidence Tolly tells Driscoll that Gela is ready to make a deal. Driscoll visits Gela at his home. The meeting is observed by one of Connor's spies and Gus is sent to eliminate Gela.

Tolly's revenge is now complete, and for him the fight against National Projects, a purely personal affair, is over. He never grasps the social meaning of his actions. His usefulness is a by-product of his emotions. In this he resembles other Fuller heroes. Widmark the pickpocket in *Pickup on South Street* falls in love with Jean Peters and then helps the police to defeat a Communist spy ring because his girl is threatened. Angie Dickinson, the Eurasian prostitute in *China Gate* (1957), refuses to help the French in Indochina: "As far as I'm concerned you and the hammer-and-sickle boys can go fight it out among yourselves." But she gives her life helping to destroy a Communist supply dump when the French promise to send her son to America. She tells the boy's father, an American soldier, "You came here to fight for a Chinese baby. You don't give a damn about the French."

Similarly, Tolly tells Driscoll that with the death of Gela their "partnership" has ended. He is deaf to Driscoll's request that he stay with the organization long enough to finish Connors: "What do *I* care about Connors? That's your headache." But he has fallen in love with Cuddles, and when Gus visits him with orders to assist in her murder his emotions are again involved. Now he turns Gus over to the police and suggests they check the bullets in Gela's body against Gus's revolver; previously he had refused to name Gela's killer. He goes to National Projects and kills Connors, but is himself mortally wounded by Connors's bodyguard. He dies, ambiguously heroic, beneath a poster which reads "GIVE BLOOD NOW" (fig. 4). As Cuddles is led away from his body she is told: "You've got a job to do. You've got to sing on Smith. You've got to finish the job for Tolly or he died for nothing."

It is one of the many contradictions in Fuller's work that the most necessary social actions are performed by the most antisocial characters for the most unsocial reasons. The complicity of the law in Tolly Devlin's scheme of revenge is totally opposed to Francis Bacon's classic statement of political ideals: "Revenge is a kind of wild justice; which the more Man's Nature runs to, the more ought Law to weed it out. For as to the first Wrong, it doth but offend the Law; but the Revenge of that wrong, putteth the Law out of Office" (1909, 14).

In *Underworld U.S.A.* the law is "put out of office" by a general indifference and timidity, and restored by individual violence. There is nothing in this which defeats the film's purpose as a fable of democracy. Fuller's statement is quite clear: a democracy whose citizens, for whatever reason, neglect their moral (i.e., political) duties can survive only fortuitously, as a result of individual (i.e., undemocratic) action. Fuller is supported in his indictment of "the ordinary citizen and his wife" not only by Allen Drury on the right but also on the left, by Norman Mailer: "A stench of fear has come out of every

Figure 4. Ambiguously heroic

pore of American life, and we suffer from a collective failure of nerve. The only courage, with rare exceptions, that we have been witness to has been the isolated courage of isolated people" ([1959] 1972, 271).

It is necessary to emphasize the film's effectiveness on its most obvious level partly because Fuller is often, and too glibly, characterized as a simple fascist; but mainly because not to do so would be to rob *Underworld U.S.A.* of its peculiar force. Fuller is not an "underground" director whose films actually *do* the opposite of what they overtly *say*. His ambiguity is such that he makes opposites coexist. Thus he celebrates democracy at the same time—and with as complete sincerity—as he celebrates the most violent individualism.

In this context it is notable that the society depicted in *Underworld U.S.A.* relates more directly to [Thomas] Hobbes's "tyrannical" theory of state than to any of the more democratic political philosophies. The syndicate has gained what Hobbes would call "Common-wealth by Acquisition" (2006, 171). The Federal Committee is ignored because "the Obligation of Subjects to the Sovereign, is understood to last as long, and no longer, than the power lasteth, by which he is able to protect them" (218). "Where a man is . . . in the power of the enemy . . . the Obligation of the Law ceaseth; because he must obey the enemy or dye" (296).[1] The syndicate places the choice between obedience and death very clearly before any man who is tempted to help the crime committee. Apart from the hero and Cuddles, only one character in the film is willing to betray the syndicate and he does so when he is already on his deathbed in a prison hospital. After the death of Gela, Tolly tells Driscoll that he intends to give Connors his resignation but "none of his subjects by any pretense of forfeiture can be freed from his subjection" and Driscoll tries to make Tolly realize the fact: "You'll never be able to start from scratch unless you help us put Connors away."

In *Underworld U.S.A.* Fuller creates a Hobbesian society in which the syndicate rules because "desire of ease disposeth men to obey a common power," but proposes a hero who refuses to obey the Hobbesian laws. One of Hobbes's basic premises is that man is ruled by reason. Fuller rejects this idea: his characters are most admirable when least reasonable. They ignore Hobbes's law of nature, a "generall Rule, found out by Reason, by which a man is forbidden to do, that, which is destructive of his life" (2006, 128). Fuller's hero puts a very low premium on his own life and comfort; his actions are dictated by emotion, not by reason, and his extreme individualism prevents him from making those compromises with his environment which reason would dictate.

At the start of the film the twelve-year-old Tolly refuses to "fink" on the men who murdered his father. "I don't want no help from you cops," he tells Driscoll. "I'll get those punks my own way." Tolly is absolutely committed to the principle of Do It Yourself. There is no necessity for him to deal with Connors personally at the end of the film. He knows more than enough to put Connors away by testifying to the committee.

Tolly's independence is the more striking because organizations and values are very similar on both sides of the struggle. The first thing Driscoll remembers, when the grown-up Tolly phones him, is that he was "the boy who wouldn't fink." Loyalty is the quality most respected by both Driscoll and Connors. When he learns that Gela is ready to sell him out Connors becomes almost pathetic. "Find Gus," he says, and his voice is heavy with regret. National Projects, with its executive swimming pool and gray-suited accountants, is just like any other big corporation. Tolly asks Gela for a job and says, "I'd like a future with your organization."

Cuddles tells Tolly that she wants him for her husband: "We've got a right to climb out of the sewer like other people. We could quit our way of turning a buck." But Tolly is not "like other people." It is impossible to imagine him fitting into any "normal" place in society. Even when Gela is dead and Tolly is able to accept Cuddles's proposal, he believes that marriage is "the only good partnership." Fuller's hero only exists in a state of war. In *China Gate* a soldier says, "This is the only life for me, even if I have to die to live it." This hero is destroyed as soon as he ceases to fight; either he dies or the film ends.

Communist, gangster, or fascist, the identity of the enemy is irrelevant. Fuller's hero goes where the fighting is. Almost any "organization" will do, because organizations destroy individuality. Tolly's progress from orphanage to reform school to prison is horrifyingly conveyed in three close-ups of file cards being typed with his name and age. Fuller evidently detests cold reason. And it is the rational nature of totalitarian systems that makes them abhorrent. Gus, the syndicate gun, is all the more chilling because he is not a psychopath; he kills without enjoyment. He likes children, but when it becomes necessary to murder a little girl, he does so with no emotion at all.

Tolly Devlin, on the other hand, fights and kills with emotion; and he *is* a psychopath. Fuller makes the neurotic motivation of his actions quite explicit in the dissolve from Tolly's hand gripping a sheet during a nightmare vision of his father's death to Tolly's hand gripping the lock on a safe he is burgling. Sandy (Beatrice Kay), who represents the off-beat mother figure familiar from *Pickup on South Street* and *The Crimson Kimono*, is horrified when Tolly tells her of his revenge plans: "You're a grown-up man now. Act like it!" And later she tells him, "You're sick!" In his relationship with Cuddles, Tolly is almost a whore. Here, as in *Pickup on South Street,* Fuller has produced some amazingly brutal "love" scenes. In the first of them Tolly tenderly prods at a bruise on Cuddles's cheek while drawing from her Gus's telephone number, which he repeats as eagerly as if the numbers were cherished words of love.

Underworld U.S.A. goes further than any other Fuller movie in depicting the hero as a psychopath: his heroism is a product of his sickness. Here again Fuller finds an unlikely collaborator in Norman Mailer. In this century, Mailer says, man's only sane course is "to accept the terms of death, to live with death as immediate danger, to divorce oneself from society, to exist without roots, to set out on that uncharted journey into the rebellious imperatives of the self. In short, whether the life is criminal or not, the decision is to encourage the psychopath in oneself, to explore that domain of experience where security is boredom and therefore sickness" (1970, 271).

For Tolly Devlin, though, it is not a decision but a compulsion. Tolly wants Gela to know why and how he is going to die: "There's one punk left, Mr. Gela, and that's you." In witnessing the death of Gela, Tolly exorcises his neurotic demon. He is now able to accept Cuddles's love, which he had previously abused and ridiculed. But he is destroyed at the moment when he is restored to psychological health. He has been invulnerable because of his "freedom" from normal emotional attachments: in settling with Connors, Tolly is for the first time recognizing a responsibility to another human being; and in doing so, he is killed.

But even in death, Fuller's hero has not ceased to fight. The film ends on a zoom into a close-up of Tolly's clenched fist. (This has been a visual motif throughout the film). The propaganda purpose of Fuller's pictures is to instill into a democracy the vigor of his hero. The ideal would be a compromise between Tolly's individualism and the needs of society. But Fuller is not concerned with ideals. Instead, the tension of equal and opposite forces, each dangerous and each salutary, maintains his world in its spectacularly perilous equilibrium.

Works Cited

Bacon, Francis. "Of Revenge." In Francis Bacon, *Essays, Civil and Moral*. Vol. 3. New York: P. F. Collier & Son (Harvard Classics), [1625] 1909–14.

Drury, Allen. *Advise and Consent*. New York: Giant Cardinal, [1959] 1961.

Hobbes, Thomas. *Leviathan: Or The Matter, Forme and Power of a Common-Wealth Ecclesiasticall and Civil*. Mineola, NY: Dover, [1651] 2006.

Mailer, Norman. "The White Negro: Superficial Reflections on the Hipster." In *Advertisements for Myself*, 269–89. London: Panther, [1959] 1972.

Filmography

China Gate. Directed by Samuel Fuller. Twentieth Century Fox, 1957.
The Crimson Kimono. Directed by Samuel Fuller. Columbia Pictures, 1959.
A Face in the Crowd. Directed by Elia Kazan. Warner Bros., 1957.
I Love, You Love (Io amo, tu ami). Directed by Alessandro Blasetti. Dino de Laurentiis Cinematografica, 1961.
Merrill's Marauders. Directed by Samuel Fuller. Warner Bros., 1962.
Pickup on South Street. Directed by Samuel Fuller. Twentieth Century Fox, 1953.
Underworld U.S.A. Directed by Samuel Fuller. Columbia Pictures, 1961.
Verboten! Directed by Samuel Fuller. Columbia Pictures, 1959.

Note

1   Perkins originally conflated quotations from two books of Hobbes's *Leviathan*. Ed.

HAWKS COMEDIES

First published in Movie, *no. 5 (December 1962): 21–22.*

In his interview with Peter Bogdanovich (1962), Howard Hawks criticizes *Bringing Up Baby* (1938) for just the quality which makes it one of the screen's greatest comedies: "If only the gardener had been normal . . ." That would have been a cardinal error. Standards that would be relevant to, say, Cukor's naturalistic comedies are quite inapplicable here. Cukor's comedies are funniest when they are most "real," but Hawks's depend on the reversal of all our preconceptions about character and behavior. Thus in Cukor's *Born Yesterday* (1950) the "dumb blonde" reactions come from a dumb Brooklyn blonde (Judy Holliday). In *Bringing Up Baby* they come from an intelligent Connecticut society girl (Katharine Hepburn). Hawks's achievement is to create a world in which the abnormal is the norm and where, in consequence, the rational seems outrageous. In this world a postman's reaction to your announcement that you are about to be married is not "Congratulations!" but a somber "Don't let it throw you, buster."

The Ransom of Red Chief, Hawks's contribution to the Fox omnibus picture *O. Henry's Full House* (1952), is a concentrated exercise in the reversal of normal patterns of behavior. Its heroes, two "confidence men without confidence" (Fred Allen and Oscar Levant) kidnap a little boy, "J. B." Dorset. They are observed in this by the child's mother. She offers a languid commentary: "Now they're puttin' a sack over his head. . . . Now they're takin' him away." Her husband sways placidly in his rocking chair. "Must be strangers," he says. Mom wanders away with an apathetic "More'n likely." J. B. terrorizes and humiliates his captors. Mr. Dorset demands a cash payment before he will take his son back. The kidnappers pay the ransom—their entire savings. As Slick Sam hands over the money he tells the Dorsets, "You gotta gold mine in that boy."

Red Chief turns inside out all the devices of a "mechanics of crime" picture. *Monkey Business* (1952) and *I Was a Male War Bride* (a.k.a. *You Can't Sleep Here*, 1949) similarly proceed with a remorseless logic from very simple premises. What if the elixir of youth endowed its discoverers with the mental as well as the physical attributes of youngsters? What if the protocol devised for the transport of war brides to the States were applied to the *husband* of an American service woman?

Bringing Up Baby has no such premise. Its plot is either nonexistent or frantically complicated, as you wish. Turn it inside out and it would still be crazy. In every other respect, though, the Hawks law of reversal applies. David Huxley (Cary Grant) learns that Katharine Hepburn has gone off to catch not her aunt's tame leopard "Baby," but a ferocious circus beast who has recently mauled its trainer. "Poor darling Susan," he says. "She's in danger and she's helpless without me." Cut to an exasperated Susan determinedly dragging said beast up the steps of the local constabulary. The most consistently "reversed" of the characters in *Bringing Up Baby* is Major Horace Applegate, a big-game hunter (Charles Ruggles). He is presented as an effeminate pedant who cannot distinguish between the cries of leopard and loon. He is also a coward and a rotten shot.

Normal relationships as well as consistent characterization are overturned. *Monkey Business*, like *Red Chief*, reverses the adult-child relationship. George Winslow, the eight-year-old baritone, overcomes by a neat piece of blackmail Hugh Marlowe's reluctance to act as maypole for a gang of infant savages: "Don't you like children?" "Of course." "Why are you mean to them, then?"

Most of all Hawks likes to upset the relationship between the sexes. Cary Grant, the Male War Bride, resents the fact that a soldier's wolf whistle is meant for his wife, not for him. In *Monkey Business*, under the influence of the youth drug "B-4," he goes off on a spree with Marilyn Monroe. When he returns, his wife (Ginger Rogers) observes that his face is "breaking out in red blotches." "That's not red blotches," he insists. "That's lipstick." Ginger Rogers, in her turn, consumes B-4 and becomes a shy virgin. She drives her husband from the bedroom of the hotel to which they have returned for a second honeymoon. The cord of his pajama trousers is caught in the slammed door. When he draws attention to his predicament, she takes the cord and puts a knot in it. The symbolism is unstressed, but clear and beautiful.

The hero of *Bringing Up Baby* is completely dominated by women. Firstly by Alice, who regards a chaste peck on the cheek as a violation of public decency: "What will Professor LaTouche think!" The professor is a tolerant man. "After all," he concedes with an understanding smile, "you *are* getting married tomorrow." Alice rules out David's tentative suggestion that they might perhaps have a honeymoon. Nothing, *nothing*, must be allowed to distract him from his work for the Stuyvesant Museum of Natural History. He is no less ruthlessly exploited by Susan. A psychiatrist has told her that "the love impulse in man frequently reveals itself in terms of conflict." David shows some mild irritation at, among other things, having his car stolen and wrecked, and at being tripped up in the bar of the Ritz Plaza Hotel. Therefore, according to Susan's free-association method of reasoning, he is in love with her. Therefore he must be tricked into escorting her to Connecticut a couple of hours before his wedding is due to begin. And once there, of course, he must not be allowed to escape. So deprive him of his clothes.

Susan's mind here works along true Hawksian lines. A course of action, once decided upon, must be carried through (as [Jacques] Rivette says) *jusqu'au bout*. Hawks's motto for comedy seems to be: "Everything in excess." Thus, once Cary Grant has been labeled as a war bride, male, it can only be a matter of time before we see him in skirts. But, happily, Hawks is not willing to leave the matter there: the uniform which his wife borrows must be a nurse's. And why put him in nurse's uniform if he is not to do any nursing? So let him be called on to assist at a childbirth. Similarly, in *Monkey Business*, what could be more natural than that the "ten-year-old" Cary, having had his face covered in whitewash, should use it as the basis for an Indian war paint? Then he can join in a children's game and suggest scalping his wife's one-time sweetheart, Hugh Marlowe. Now George Winslow must step forward to ensure that the rules are obeyed: "You can't scalp anybody unless you do a war-dance first.... That's no good. You gotta sing when you do it!"

Bringing Up Baby is one of the most "excessive" of Hawks's films. (The other is *Gentlemen Prefer Blondes* [1953]). "I'll be with you in a minute, Mr. Peabody," David shouts to his influential golf partner as he leaves the course. The words are repeated many times, with uncertainty giving way to desperation, as he becomes ever-more frantically involved with Susan. They are last heard as he walks closely and speedily behind her through the doors of the Ritz Plaza Hotel. Susan's loss of the rear panel of her evening dress is thus concealed but David's top hat (trampled) and frock coat (torn) are clearly displayed.

In this chaotic world language aids confusion, not comprehension. Susan attempts to account for her "theft" of another woman's purse, "but it never will be clear," says David, "as long as she's explaining it." She either ignores or overexploits verbal logic. When David protests that she has just taken his golf ball and is about to drive his car away, she asks, "You mean this is your car? *Your* golf ball? *Your* car? Is there anything in the world that doesn't belong to you?" She uses words mainly for camouflage: when David emerges from the shower and asks what has happened to his clothes, she says that the gardener is taking them into town to be cleaned. "Well, stop him. I've got to leave here immediately." "But, David! You can't leave here without your clothes!" She tells her aunt what she really means by this apparent nonsense: "If he gets some clothes, he'll go away. And he's the only man I've ever loved." Susan's is a logic of the emotions, not of the syllogism. All that she does, however crazy it seems, is justified rationally by her love for David. As Hugh Marlowe says in *Monkey Business*, "The language may be confusing, but the actions are unmistakable."

Humiliation plays a very important part in all of Hawks's comedies, a humiliation the greater because its victims are established as persons of a certain dignity. I see no need, however, for the assumption that this director's view of the world is pessimistic. All comedy is more or less "black." Hawks has simply learnt the lesson of Stan Laurel: if you wear a bowler hat, it's all the funnier when you slip on a banana skin. His comedies do not lament human degradation so much as celebrate human resilience. *I Was a Male War Bride* is the blackest of the comedies. Its hero is relegated to the final position on the transit order, after dogs, cats, canaries, and other domestic animals. But even he retains enough of his human dignity to protest when his wife starts to make a wig for him from a horse's tail: "Can't you at least take it off the mane?" he asks.

In *Monkey Business*, humiliation is the direct result of a refusal to accept life's terms. Charles Coburn drags his secretary, Marilyn Monroe ("Anyone can type!"), to the laboratory with him to see the success of an experiment in rejuvenating an aged chimpanzee. "Look at that old chimp, Miss Laurel," he splutters. "Eighty-four years old. Fourteen years older than I am! And just look at him!" A husband and wife suffer "maladjustment, near-idiocy, and a series of low-comedy disasters" when they return to youth. But they learn from their experience and come to regard B-4 as "the most dubious discovery since itching powder, and just about as useful." For a genuinely pessimistic treatment of the subject of *Monkey Business*, see Nicholas Ray's *Bigger than Life* (1956), which, with the substitution of cortisone for B-4, is virtually a remake of Hawks's picture.

David Huxley certainly sheds a good deal of surplus dignity in the course of *Bringing Up Baby*. He wanders around the middle of the night, wearing an ill-fitting suit with the trousers rolled up, no socks, and carrying in one hand a butterfly net, in the other a croquet mallet. He becomes so accustomed to associating Susan with disaster that when she appears in the museum with the lost brontosaurus bone his immediate reaction is panic flight. But even David finally realizes "one catastrophe after another" actually constituted "the best day I ever had."

Work Cited

Bogdanovich, Peter. "Interview with Howard Hawks." *Movie*, no. 5 (December 1962): 8–18.

Filmography

Bigger than Life. Directed by Nicholas Ray. Twentieth Century Fox, 1956.
Born Yesterday. Directed by George Cukor. Columbia Pictures, 1950.
Bringing Up Baby. Directed by Howard Hawks. RKO Radio Pictures, 1938.

Gentlemen Prefer Blondes. Directed by Howard Hawks. Twentieth Century Fox, 1953.
I Was a Male War Bride (a.k.a. *You Can't Sleep Here*). Directed by Howard Hawks. Twentieth Century Fox, 1949.
Monkey Business. Directed by Howard Hawks. Twentieth Century Fox, 1952.
O. Henry's Full House. Directed by Henry Hathaway, Howard Hawks, Henry King, Henry Koster, and Jean Negulesco. Twentieth Century Fox, 1952.

HATARI!

First published in Movie, *no. 5 (December 1962): 28–30.*

Hatari! (1962) provides a digest of the Best of Howard Hawks. It has the tame feline from *Bringing Up Baby* (1938), the warpaint gag from *Monkey Business* (1952), the target-practice game from *Red River* (1948), and the song "Whiskey Leave Me Alone" from *The Big Sky* (1952). Its characters, situations, and much of its dialogue come directly from *Rio Bravo* (1959). Obviously John Wayne, John T. Chance in *Rio Bravo*, remains John Wayne, as Sean in *Hatari!* But one can also equate Elsa Martinelli with Angie Dickinson, Hardy Kruger and Gerard Blain with Dean Martin and Ricky Nelson, and even Red Buttons with Walter Brennan.

Hatari!, like *Rio Bravo*, has plenty of action and very little plot. The narrative is a simple pretext for the presentation of a number of relationships which fascinate Hawks. The western had a strong central situation which disguised its lack of narrative unity. But *Hatari!* gives us only a series of incidents that occur during one hunting season on an East African game farm. It starts with the failure to catch a rhinoceros. Toward the end (climax?) a rhino is caught. Then Sean marries Dallas (Martinelli).

Within this loose framework the film's only real coherence comes from the personality of its director. Hawks has always used his films to celebrate the things he likes. For example, the ritual slapstick of the whitewash sequence in *Monkey Business* is an obvious homage to Laurel and Hardy. One of the hunts in *Hatari!* is quite "irrelevantly" interrupted so that Sean can show Dallas a water hole belonging to the Maasai tribe. As "cinema" this may be impure, but it is pure Hawks. Sean talks about the Maasai: "They'll work all day getting that water up, but when it comes to repairing it, they won't touch it. They're cattlemen, too proud to dig."

Hawks abandons a tight dawn-to-midnight construction of narrative in favor of a much more meaningful unity. His personality dominates even the smallest incidents. When Dallas corrects Kurt (Hardy Kruger) in his recital of the "The Old Folks at Home," he offers her the freedom of the piano, but with the warning "You'd better be good." And she is, of course. The style of the director is the style of the man. This point emerges very clearly from the Bogdanovich interview (1962). Most directors surprise one by the incompatibility of what they say in their interviews and what they do in their films. But Hawks speaks like the author of *Rio Bravo* and *Hatari!*

Hatari! offers perhaps the most perfect illustration of the "adventurer" approach to filmmaking. The director goes off to Africa with some friends. They enjoy themselves, and bring back a movie. The film is not only *about* an adventure, from the audience's point of view; it is an adventure for its makers. Some stunning close shots of pounding rhino and buffalo make it clear that it is no less dangerous for the film's crew to hunt wild animals with a camera than it is for the film's heroes (and actors) to hunt them with ropes and rifles.

But if *Hatari!* is the ultimate adventurer picture, it fits somewhat less easily into the action genre, subspecies safari movie. "If," says Rivette,

> Hawks represents all that is best in the classical American cinema, if he has ennobled each genre by making in turn the best gangster film (*Scarface* [1932]), the best air film (*Only Angels Have Wings* [1939]), the best war film (*Air Force* [1943]), the best Western (*Red River* [1948]), and finally the best comedies (*Bringing Up Baby, Ball of Fire* [1941], *Monkey Business*), it is because he has always known, in each case, how to take what is essential and great from the genre and to mix his personal themes with those which American tradition had already deepened and enriched.

But equally noticeable is the way in which Hawks has, on occasion, destroyed genre. In *Hatari!*, sequences which (according to the rules of the African genre) ought to be menacing are played as comedy. Ostriches rather than, say, leopards are the animals which provoke chaos by escaping from their cages. And a sequence that ought to be funny—Dallas's exit pursued by an elephant—is rather sad. When "Indian" (Bruce Cabot) is, almost fatally, gored by a rhinoceros, Pockets (Red Buttons) says "a big Band-Aid" will fix it. Hawks never asks for *one* reaction to an event. Instead he uses a mixture of conflicting reactions to produce one total response: enjoyment.

For Hawks enjoyment is the vital criterion, in style as in life. His camera is at the service of the audience rather than of, for example, an idea (Losey) or an investigation (Preminger). It stands in moderate proximity to the action and at a natural angle. There is virtually no "montage"; the shots are changed when a new angle provides a more convenient view of the subject. Hawks is not "cinematic," happily, since that term has come to imply nothing more than an overindulgence of the cinema's powers of distortion and concealment.

Sean returns home drunk after hearing that Indian will live. He enters his bedroom and begins to undress. "Before you go any further," a female voice says, "I think I should tell you that you are not alone." Sean switches on the light and sees Dallas in his bed. Given this sequence to film, most directors would have wanted the audience to share Sean's amazement. The shooting would therefore have been arranged to exclude Dallas from the frame or keep her in darkness until some point after she has begun to speak, But, as *The Thing* (1951) amply demonstrates, Hawks does not indulge in false "shocks." We see Dallas in the foreground of the shot as Sean enters his room. Nothing is lost through this honesty in the presentation. The sequence is all the funnier because Sean's bewilderment conflicts with the matter-of-fact attitude of Dallas and the sobriety with which the director handles the episode. It is a part of Hawks's genius that he can achieve through complete honesty what many others fail to achieve *because* of their use of "cinema."

Hawks lets the action dictate to the camera rather than vice versa. But in style as in everything else, it pays to advertise. There are still those who will regard no man as a stylist if he presents subject, verb, and object in that order. Consider the opening shots of *Hatari!* First we see Sean, Pockets, and Luis (Valentin de Vargas) in a truck on the African plains. Sean is looking off-screen through his binoculars. Then we see close shots of Sean and Pockets. Next we are introduced to Kurt and Indian. They are in a jeep on another part of the plains. Close shot Kurt. Close shot Indian. Back to a medium shot of Sean's group. As Sean swings his binoculars to the right the camera takes up the movement and turns away to reveal a herd of wildebeest. Subject, verb, object. Seven shots, no dialogue, but Hawks has presented the situation with perfect clarity and considerable excitement.

If style is the marriage of vision and lucidity then Hawks is one of the cinema's greatest stylists. His presentation and his heroes have the same qualities. His refusal to distort is merely the negative manifestation of his acceptance of the natural world: there is no compulsion to make it significant, more decorative, more heroic, more *anything* than he finds it. At the hospital Luis asks how long it takes for the doctor to give his verdict on Indian. "As long as it takes," says Sean. Hawks must be the least neurotic of all great artists. Significantly, he has shown no interest in psychological problems. Wayne's desire for revenge on his "son" in *Red River* and Martin's victory over the bottle in *Rio Bravo* are presented in terms of morality rather than psychology.

Hawks's respect for professionalism is reflected in the pace of his films. Like his heroes he takes the shortest route to the desired end. Sean and his friends go to a bar to wait for news of the Indian's blood transfusion. There is no prolonged build-up of tension. Instead Hawks dissolves into a shot of the group sitting in the bar only a few seconds before the phone call comes through.

It is not so much the skill as the attitude of the professional that Hawks admires: "Just a calm acceptance of a fact." In *Rio Bravo* Ward Bond listens to Wayne's account of his resources and asks, "Is that all you've got?" "It's *what* I've got," replies Wayne. The Hawks hero does what he can with the materials at his disposal. Angie Dickinson cannot fire a rifle but she can save the sheriff's life with a well-thrown flower pot. And in *Hatari!* Pockets, who is afraid of animals, captures five hundred monkeys by applying his knowledge of "vectors, trajectories, centrifugal forces, and stuff like that."

But facts must be known before they can be accepted or applied. For this reason the heroes of Hawks's films are constantly testing their abilities and, particularly, their limitations. They have to see how far they can impose their own terms on nature and on life. In comedy this necessity shows itself in, say, Cary Grant's determination that a brontosaurus bone reside in a museum rather than in the ground where nature put it. In *Hatari!* the struggle is symbolized in the job of transferring wild animals from their natural surroundings to the world's zoos.

A man can only learn his limitations from his own experience. Hence the characters in *Hatari!* display a sort of constructive brutality in their personal relationships. Dallas insists that she can look after herself standing in the back of the truck from which Sean catches giraffe. Sean does not argue with her; she has to find out for herself. Later Dallas apologizes for making a fool of herself. "Well, at least you know it," says Sean, "but I don't think you can talk your way out of it again." Dallas, like the other Hawks heroes, is given *one* chance to learn for herself.

In their relationships with one another, also, the characters of *Hatari!* have to find out how far they can go. Conversely they insist on the recognition of their abilities and dignity. When Pockets wants to hear the details of his triumph in monkey catching repeated for the umpteenth time, Sean obliges without hesitation because "he earned it." But Chips Maurey (Gerard Blain) will not give the blood needed to save Indian's life until Kurt has apologized for insulting and assaulting him. He will not even accept an apology from Kurt's boss. "I'm sorry. But *he's* going to have to ask me."

One final similarity between Hawks and his heroes: the ability to grasp the essentials of a situation. Sean asks Dallas why she is crying. Dallas says she got a "scrotch" going through the bush. Wayne corrects her pronunciation. "Scratch or scrotch," says Dallas, "it hurts!"

Filmography

Air Force. Directed by Howard Hawks. Warner Bros., 1943.
Ball of Fire. Directed by Howard Hawks. RKO Radio Pictures, 1941.
The Big Sky. Directed by Howard Hawks. RKO Radio Pictures, 1952.
Bringing Up Baby. Directed by Howard Hawks. RKO Radio Pictures, 1938.

Hatari! Directed by Howard Hawks. Paramount Pictures, 1962.
Monkey Business. Directed by Howard Hawks. Twentieth Century Fox, 1952.
Only Angels Have Wings. Directed by Howard Hawks. Columbia Pictures, 1939.
Red River. Directed by Howard Hawks. United Artists, 1948.
Rio Bravo. Directed by Howard Hawks. Warner Bros., 1959.
Scarface. Directed by Howard Hawks. United Artists, 1932.
The Thing (a.k.a. *The Thing from Another World*). Directed by Christian Nyby. RKO Radio Pictures, 1951.

ROPE

First published in Movie, *no. 7 (February 1963): 11–13.*

"It's a very bad thing for a film-maker to repeat himself. If you repeat a success, it's no longer any good. The most important thing, after a lot of experience, is to change as much as possible" (Domarchi and Rohmer 1961, 8). "I try not to fall into the trap of any formula. I feel that this could be deadly for me. I would get bored, perhaps without really knowing it, because it would become too easy. . . . It's this that makes my profession so exciting: the challenge that comes up every hour if you work on new things" ("Interview with Otto Preminger" 1962, 18). Cukor and Preminger are only two of the many directors who have spoken of the need to vary their subjects in order to keep their freshness of approach. Of the twenty-five films Hitchcock has made since he went to the States in 1939, all except two are thrillers. But Hitchcock, conscious of the dangers of his situation, has provided himself with a variety of techniques and forms, rather than of genres. In each of his major films he has challenged himself to solve a self-imposed problem.

The problem in *Rope* (1948) is, of course, the ten-minute take, and the challenge is to produce, without the use of editing, a movie that is undeniably "film."[1] Although there are ten cuts in the movie, only the first of them occurs at the will of the director. The others are unavoidable because the film has to be changed: in the camera after ten minutes, and in the projector after twenty. The reel changes on the projector are not disguised: Hitchcock simply cuts to a new camera setup. Between each projector change, however, there is a changeover on the camera. The break in continuity here is camouflaged by joining the two reels during a momentary blackout: for example, the camera follows behind one character until the frame is blacked out on his back—change—he leaves the frame and the camera continues its movement toward another character. Unfortunately only the last of the five changeovers managed in this way is completely satisfactory. The first is spoiled by a sudden acceleration in the acting pace after the join, the other three by incomplete blacking out. The failure here is not in technique (the blackouts, although arbitrary, are never ludicrous) but on a technicality: after ten minutes of movement, the actor or the camera just misses the position necessary for perfect masking of the frame.

The changeovers take up perhaps forty seconds of an eighty-minute film. They are worth mentioning for two reasons: they stand as evidence against the conviction, fostered by the perfection of his three most recent films, that Hitch can do no wrong; and they qualify, however minutely, the master's success in solving his chosen problem.

In every other respect his triumph is complete. The film opens with a high-angle shot of a street in a prosperous-looking residential area. The camera draws back over a balcony and pans across until we are staring at a long window with its curtains drawn. There is a scream, a moment's pause. Cut inside the darkened room to a close-up of a young man's face as he chokes to death. Track back to reveal his murderers, Phillip (Farley Granger) and Brandon (John Dall). From the moment we enter the apartment everything proceeds in perfect continuity until the last "shot" as Phillip and Brandon, guarded by their friend and betrayer Rupert Cadell (James Stewart), await the entry of the police.

Continuity in lighting. Having placed David's body in an antique chest, Brandon opens the curtains to let in the early evening sunlight. In the next hour and a quarter the light gradually fades and we are drawn into the blackness of night. The changes in lighting are so subtly executed that we sense, rather than observe, the nightfall.

Continuity in sound. As the "signature of the artist" on his work of art (the murder) Brandon gives a party. The guests are David's father, Mr. Kently (Cedric Hardwicke); his aunt, Mrs. Atwater (Constance Collier); his fiancée, Janet (Joan Chandler); his best friend, Kenneth (Douglas Dick); and his ex-tutor, Rupert. Even when there are only two characters on the screen, we hear constant reminders of the others' presence through the wisps of conversation and laughter which drift in from other rooms.

Continuity, above all, in action and movement. Here, Hitchcock achieves his most brilliant, amusing, and, at the same time, agonizing effects. The camera follows Brandon from the sitting room to the dining room as he carries the rope with which David was strangled. Brandon goes into the kitchen as his housekeeper, Mrs. Wilson (Edith Evanson), comes out. And in the half-second of the swinging door's rebound we see Brandon put the rope away in a drawer (fig. 5). Most alarming of all is the sequence which depends upon the immobility of Hitchcock's elsewhere very mobile camera. Brandon decides to "make our work of art a masterpiece" by serving dinner in the sitting room, from the chest which contains David's corpse. The books which were to have been displayed on the chest are transferred to the dining-room table. After dinner, while the guests speculate on the reasons for David's nonappearance, Mrs. Wilson begins to clear the chest.

Figure 5. The swing door's rebound

A deep-focus shot from behind the chest allows, or compels, us to watch Mrs. Wilson's three journeys to the kitchen with the empties, and back to the sitting room with the books which she will want to place in the (unlocked) chest. The framing of the shot, with only Rupert's back on the extreme right of the screen, prevents us from knowing whether Mrs. Wilson's work is being observed by anyone else in the room.

Suspense is anxious waiting. Delay is therefore a vital weapon in Hitchcock's armory. *Rope* exploits continuity as a means to delay (cf. the use of the Storm Cloud Cantata in *The Man Who Knew Too Much* [1956]). In the course of the party Rupert becomes increasingly suspicious that Phillip and Brandon are somehow involved in David's nonappearance. As he leaves, Mrs. Wilson passes him a hat. He is so preoccupied that he does not notice that it is too small for him. Mrs. Wilson's laughter makes him realize his mistake. He looks inside the hat and the camera tracks in to show us what he sees: David's initials. A tilt up to Rupert's face shows his reaction.

This is the classic montage layout, and one can legitimately consider the presentation as three shots: medium shot—a man looking; close-up—what he sees; close-up—his reaction. Alternatively, the normal long-take method of presentation, in the gospel according to [André] Bazin, would be to hold the camera at medium shot to Rupert, keeping him clearly visible while the hat is brought into the foreground of the frame (e.g., Rupert could turn toward the camera in order to bring the hat into the light). Here the montage would be performed by the eye of the spectator, tracing the same course as Hitchcock's camera, but much more rapidly.

The true originality of *Rope* lies not in the initial decision to use the ten-minute take, but in the method of using it—sacrificing the "best" points of both [Vsevolod] Pudovkin's montage and the Welles/Wyler long take. Montage allows the director to control the apparent speed of an event while ignoring strict continuity, but also makes the spectator aware of his subjection to the will of the director. If Hitchcock had cut between his three shots he would have been compelled to move much faster: the time which is "wasted" on the journey to and from the close-up of the hat could not have been absorbed in a long static shot. The spectator would have felt annoyed rather than frustrated. The camera movement allows Hitchcock to extend the delay between the latter two shots, and at the same time to make the spectator feel, incorrectly, that he is at the mercy of an event rather than of a director: it is not Hitchcock's fault if it takes this long for the camera to travel from the hat to Rupert's face.

The effect is perhaps best appreciated by contrast with a similar moment where a reel change forces the director to use a direct cut. During dinner, before Rupert's suspicions have been fully aroused, Brandon tells a story about Phillip's expertise in chicken-strangling. The camera moves in to isolate Phillip in close-up as he becomes increasingly panic-stricken. When Brandon's story reaches its climax Phillip bursts out with "That's a lie!" The cut here, to a reaction close-up of Rupert, momentarily drops the tension. In the first place, the essential question is answered almost before one has had time to ask it: Has anyone noticed the significance of Phillip's outburst? Secondly, a good deal of the suspense in the film comes from the fact that one is seldom sure just where one is being taken by any particular camera movement. The cut sacrifices both the anxiety and the delay which aggravates it.

In *The Magnificent Ambersons* (1942) or *The Best Years of Our Lives* (1946), the long take has the advantage that it opens up the frame and, in giving greater freedom to his eyes, increases the spectator's detachment. But freedom and detachment are the feelings which Hitchcock least wants to induce. Instead, he again exploits the "weakness" of the process—the strict and laborious continuity which makes the *Ambersons* ballroom sequence, for all its brilliance, look pretty phony. Deep focus delighted Bazin for its simultaneous juxtaposition of objects and events to provide a one-shot montage. Hitchcock uses it to show us a single action in detail, as Mrs. Wilson clears the chest, and deliberately excludes from the frame the other elements in the dramatic situation.

He destroys the detachment of the long take by a technique which, without resorting to subjective camerawork, makes us share in the characters' feelings. When he is alone with Mrs. Wilson in the sitting room Rupert questions her about the strange behavior of Phillip and Brandon. The camera moves back from a close-up of Rupert, the sound of his conversation fades, and, when the camera reaches medium shot to Rupert and Mrs. Wilson, Phillip enters the foreground of the frame. The unintelligible whisperings which we now hear make us share in Phillip's panic at what Mrs. Wilson may be revealing. Similarly, the camera movements often adopt the style of the characters, so that we identify with Brandon's arrogant exhibitionism through the obvious cleverness of the rope-into-drawer business, or with Phillip's frightened submissiveness as we follow him following Brandon from sitting room to kitchen. And, as Rupert's investigation progresses, the camera style becomes ever-more closely identified with him in its tentative and fearful probings. Significantly, while Hitchcock rejects the deep-focus, long-take method of *Kane* and *Ambersons*, Welles adopts the Hitchcockian technique, to integrate montage with camera movement and exploit the suspense-generating properties of spatial and temporal continuity in the opening sequence of *Touch of Evil* (1958).

To say that Hitchcock's use of the long take is essential to the suspense in *Rope* is to justify the technique only for those sequences in which suspense is an immediate object. The wider justification requires a wider context. *Rope*, like *Rear Window* (1954), is restricted to a single set. In *Rear Window* Hitch devotes his ingenuity to devising ways of breaking the camera's confinement. But in *Rope* he has the opposite aim. The long take is his main method of making us feel the confinement of his characters. Hitchcock's insistence on a slow continuity builds such claustrophobia that even the "light comedy" episodes of the film become oppressive. As the film proceeds, the restriction of movement in the flat increases. Before the guests arrive the camera moves back and forth several times through the sitting room, hallway, and dining room. Then the movement is restricted to the sitting room and hallway. Finally, after Rupert returns to confirm his suspicions, we are confined to the sitting room only.

The claustrophobia mounts continuously to give tremendous emphasis to the climax of the film when Rupert opens a window to summon the police by firing a revolver into the night air. At this moment, as [Claude] Chabrol says (Chabrol and Rohmer 1979, 94), one can almost feel a gust of fresh air blowing in from the dark street. The claustrophobia is relieved at this point because the delayed but inevitable retribution has finally been set in train. Much of the suspense in the film comes from the tension between our identification with the murderers and our desire to end our incarceration. Hitchcock makes it clear that we cannot have it both ways. We enter the apartment to witness the commission of a crime, we are to be held there until the crime is exposed. By steadily increasing our confinement, he makes us want the exposure. In Hitchcock's world every crime and, more important, every sin brings retribution. For the first, the revenge of society symbolized by the sound of the approaching police siren. For the second—"Did you think you were God, Brandon?" screams Rupert—damnation: the light of the neon sign across the street, flashing green, red, and white, invades the apartment and turns it into a ghastly image of hell. But Rupert is in there with Phillip and Brandon. Why?

In *Rope*, as in *North by Northwest* (1959), the functions of the villain are divided between three characters representing the planner, the administrator, and the executor of evil. Phillip is the executor—it is he who actually strangles David. He is continually receiving orders from Brandon, the administrator: the murder, the party, the dinner from the chest were all devised by Brandon. But Rupert provided the inspiration. As tutor to Brandon and Phillip he introduced them to the Nietzschean concept of the superman, to the idea that "murder is a crime for the masses but a privilege for the few." But Rupert, as Brandon observes, "could have invented, and he could have admired, but he never could have acted."

Rupert's responsibility is made clear in a number of ways. Hitchcock likes to give his film a central compositional motif: in *Vertigo* (1958), the spiral; in *Psycho* (1960), the circle. Here he uses the triangle. When Phillip and Brandon are on the screen together the compositions are usually either triangular—one character leans over toward the other in submission (Phillip) or domination (Brandon)—or such as to presuppose the existence of a missing "third point" (e.g., Brandon in the right foreground watches Phillip answering the phone in the center background, and the left side of the screen stands empty). The compositions in *Rope* are unbalanced not—as usual in Hitchcock—because they are "too big for the screen," but because they are incomplete. Several times in the course of the movie Rupert approaches Brandon and Phillip, usually from behind, and completes the compositional triangle. At one point the triangle becomes a straight line, which illustrates graphically the chain of responsibility: we start with Phillip in the background between Brandon and Rupert; Brandon moves across, obscuring Phillip; Rupert advances to stand over the chest, obscuring both Brandon and Phillip. At the end of the film, the triangle is completed and stabilized. Rupert, having summoned the police, walks back to the chest, draws a chair up to it and sits in the center foreground. He leans over the chest protectively as if to say, "Keep away. It's mine!" Phillip and Brandon are held to the left and right of the background (fig. 6).

The whole film could be seen as Rupert's attempt to find his place in the scheme of things. He himself remarks that he is the odd man out at the party. All the other characters in the film, except Mrs. Wilson, can be paired off neatly. Significantly, Rupert is the only guest who pays any attention to Mrs. Wilson. As the other guests leave, Rupert makes a tentative movement toward Phillip, as if not sure to which group he belongs. Consistent with his position, Rupert is the great interrupter: he is the only one of the guests who arrives unannounced. He interrupts Rupert's attempts to play the piano, twice; he interrupts numerous

Figure 6. The triangle is stabilized

conversations; and he interrupts the final preparations for the disposal of David's body.

Rupert's complicity in the murder is further underlined by a large number of correspondences between his actions and attitudes and those of Phillip and Brandon. Throughout the film he is held between the two emotional states represented by Phillip (panic) and Brandon (exhilaration). At the climax, his response is the product of these two states—fury. Rupert is related to Phillip: they both cut their hands and bind their wounds with a handkerchief. He is related to Brandon: by his habit of examining and enjoying other people's reactions, by his sense of superiority.

Most of all, though, by his sense of humor which is malicious and morbid. Brandon: "David *was* a Harvard undergraduate. That might make it justifiable homicide." Rupert: "Hotel employees are in the death by slow torture category." The difference is that Rupert, despite his insistence that he's a "very serious man," is never anything but flippant about his beliefs. At the height of an argument with Mr. Kentley about the rights of men of superior intellect, Brandon appeals to Rupert for support. But Rupert backs out hastily and suggests that Mr. Kentley be taken to look at Phillip's book collection. It is Brandon who translates theory into action. After Rupert has uncovered David's body, Brandon again appeals to him: "Phillip and I have done what you and I have talked." But by putting it into practice Brandon has converted Rupert's theory from a philosophical daydream into a moral nightmare. Rupert is unable to accept the implications of his beliefs. He is horrified when he sees David's corpse. Horror only turns to anger when Brandon insists on the logic of his action. But Rupert still does not abandon his claim to superiority; he merely shifts its basis to make it moral rather than intellectual: "There must have been something deep inside you from the very first that would let you do that thing."

But Rupert is not the only character whose ideas and wishes are disastrously realized. In the last minutes of the film Phillip tells Brandon, correctly, "It's what you wanted: somebody else to know." Brandon and Phillip murder for the sake of excitement, and the sensation of heightened experience. But it is heightened experience which gives them away. Rupert's suspicions are aroused because both Phillip's timidity and Brandon's arrogance are exaggerated. And when Rupert appears to be dismissing his suspicions, Brandon alerts him again because of his desire for excitement. He asks Rupert what he would do if he had to dispose of David's body, and in thinking the problem out Rupert hits upon Brandon's solution—the chest.

I do not think that Hitchcock aims at "making the unacknowledged wishes of the protagonists come true in order to show how wrong they are," as Ian Cameron suggests in *Movie* (1963, 12). Hitchcock is not, in this sense, a moralist. He is not telling us that we ought not to be amused by the idea of murder; after all, he encourages us to share in the film's black humor. Hitchcock's films, with rare exceptions like *The Wrong Man* (1956) and *The Man Who Knew Too Much*, are demonstrations of the power of evil. All of us inevitably express evil desires. "Everybody," says Brandon, "*talks* about committing the perfect murder." But, also inevitably, every human desire, however wicked, will somewhere and somehow be realized: "Nobody commits a murder just for the experiment of committing it. Nobody except us."

Rope makes us feel the power of evil. Night descends and "nobody feels quite safe in the dark." The film is an inverted mystery; because we already know the rational answer to the constant cry of "What's going on here?" the simple facts cease to provide a sufficient explanation. Our faith in cold logic, like Rupert's, is shaken. Hitchcock offers his film as evidence against Brandon's assertion that "good and evil, right and wrong, were *invented* . . ."

Evil *is*.

Works Cited

Cameron, Ian. "Hitchcock 2: Suspense and Meaning." *Movie*, no. 6 (January 1963): 8–12.
Chabrol, Claude, and Eric Rohmer. *Hitchcock: The First Forty-Four Films*. Translated by Stanley Hochman. New York: Frederick Ungar, [1957] 1979.
Domarchi, Jean, and Eric Rohmer. "Entretien avec George Cukor." *Cahiers du Cinéma* 20, no. 115 (1961): 1–11.
"Interview with Otto Preminger." *Movie*, no. 4 (November 1962): 18–20.

Filmography

The Best Years of Our Lives. Directed by William Wyler. RKO Radio Pictures, 1946.
Citizen Kane. Directed by Orson Welles. RKO Radio Pictures, 1941.
The Magnificent Ambersons. Directed by Orson Welles. RKO Radio Pictures, 1942.
The Man Who Knew Too Much. Directed by Alfred Hitchcock. Paramount Pictures, 1956.
North by Northwest. Directed by Alfred Hitchcock. MGM, 1959.
Psycho. Directed by Alfred Hitchcock. Paramount Pictures, 1960.
Rear Window. Directed by Alfred Hitchcock. Paramount Pictures, 1954.
Rope. Directed by Alfred Hitchcock. Warner Bros., 1948.
Touch of Evil. Directed by Orson Welles. Universal-International, 1958.
Vertigo. Directed by Alfred Hitchcock. Paramount Pictures, 1958.
The Wrong Man. Directed by Alfred Hitchcock. Warner Bros., 1956.

Note

1   This was the term most commonly used for many years when writing about *Rope*. Ten minutes was the maximum exposure time that could be achieved by the film magazine held in the 35 mm camera. The actual length of the shots in *Rope* varies from about 4.5 minutes to 10. Ed.

THE CINEMA OF NICHOLAS RAY

First published in Movie, *no. 9 (May 1963): 4–10.*

All our critics distinguish, more or less explicitly, between commercial and personal cinema. The distinction is occasionally valid, often silly, and always dangerous. It is quite legitimate, for example, to point out that Nicholas Ray has frequently been obliged to work from a scenario with which he was not satisfied: *Run for Cover* (1955), *Hot Blood* (1956), *Party Girl* (1958); that many of his films have been mutilated after completion: *The True Story of Jesse James* (UK title: *The James Brothers* [1957]), *Bitter Victory* (1957), *Wind Across the Everglades* (1958), *The Savage Innocents* (1960), *King of Kings* (1961); and that the stories of *The Lusty Men* (1952), *Johnny Guitar* (1954), and *Bigger than Life* (1956) might look uninviting on paper. But film is not paper, and never can be except in the wishful imagination of a critic who regards his eyes only as the things that he reads with. The distinction between personal and commercial cinema has become a weapon for use against films which do not impress by the obvious seriousness of their stories and dialogue. The director's contribution is as irrelevant to the critical success of *They Live by Night* (1948) and *Rebel Without a Cause* (1955) as it is to the critical neglect of *Johnny Guitar*, *Bigger than Life*, or *Wind Across the Everglades*. It is nonsense to say that in *Party Girl* Ray's talent is "squandered on a perfect idiocy" (Louis Marcorelles in, of all places, *Cahiers du Cinéma* [1959, 40]).[1] The treatment may or may not have been successful: there is no such thing as an unsuccessful subject. Ray has himself criticized the literary preoccupations of some screenwriters. "'It was all in the script' a disillusioned writer will tell you. But it was never all in the script. If it were, why make the movie?" (1993, 191). The disillusioned writer and the insensitive critic are alike in discounting the very things for which one goes to the cinema: the extraordinary resonances which a director can provoke by his use of actors, decor, movement, color, shape—of all that can be seen and heard.

Primarily, one sees and hears actors. Ray's films contain a number of performances which can be called great because they give complete characterizations: Bogart (*In a Lonely Place* [1950]); Mitchum (*The Lusty Men*); Dean, Wood, and Backus (*Rebel Without a Cause*); Burton (*Bitter Victory*); and Plummer (*Wind Across the Everglades*) spring immediately to mind. But the director's control is proved not so much by the perfection of individual performances as by the consistency with which Ray's actors embody his vision. This consistency is the result—it's an ancient paradox—of the director's search for the *particular* truth of each *particular* situation. Johnny Guitar's isolation is depicted in such specific terms that we appreciate, without directorial emphasis, the wider significance of his remark, "I've a great respect for a gun and, besides, I'm a stranger here myself." In *They Live by Night* Cathy O'Donnell is unable to put her watch right because "there's no clock here to set it by." The remark has a specific, complex, dramatic context. We are aware, as the character is not, of its more general relevance for a girl who was "never properly introduced to the world we live in."

Ray works with his actors in such a personal way that he is able to utilize what we are accustomed to regard as their defects. The aggressiveness of Susan Hayward (*The Lusty Men*), the arrogance of Robert Wagner (*The True Story of Jesse James*), the coldness of Cyd Charisse, and the self-conscious charm of Robert Taylor (*Party Girl*): these are all used to intensify situations and convey meanings. Ray is not unique in using actors for their weaknesses as well as their abilities, but he is in the very good company of Hitchcock and Cukor.

Throughout any Ray movie one finds a complete mastery of the—often contradictory—action which *expresses* more than it does, the ability to convey an idea through a gesture, a hesitation, a movement of the eyes. Much of the meaning of *King of Kings* is contained in its intricate pattern of looking, glancing, and staring. Salome's motivations are revealed almost entirely in these terms. The first image of *Rebel Without a Cause* conveys a whole history of confusion and undirected tenderness in the protective gesture with which James Dean draws a newspaper over the body of a toy monkey. *Wind Across the Everglades* expresses the concept of understanding and compromise between two civilizations through the hero's action in sharing a "peace cigar" with his Seminole friend.

Again, while insisting on Ray's genius in conveying the general through the particular, the abstract through the concrete, I have no wish to claim that it is uniquely his gift. It is simply the ability that distinguishes the true filmmaker from the pseudodirector who provides "photographs of people talking." And it is an ability which one feels not just in Ray's direction of his actors but in his use of the entire vocabulary of film.

Time and Place

There are very few directors, for example, who have as great an appreciation of the suggestive powers of decor and locale. Critically, of course, one observes the appropriateness of place to action and theme. But beyond this, when the right location has been found, one becomes aware also of the influence of place on action. Decor, in Ray's films, is the entire visual environment, including (and here he is unique) the time of day.

It is Ray's intense sensitivity to time that makes one feel the night as more than the absence of sunlight. *Rebel Without a Cause* contains the most striking example of this sensitivity in its first planetarium sequence; here Ray makes us feel the intrusion of an artificial night into mid-afternoon. The sense of time is especially heightened in this sequence, but in fact it informs the entire structure of the film. Night is the time of confusion and insecurity, the time when parents are asleep. The film begins at night, with a young man falling down drunk in the middle of a dark street. We follow him through two other "nights": the artificial one in the planetarium and the real one during which James Dean engages in the "chicken run"—itself an extraordinary evocation of confusion, the blind and dangerous rush along the path to extinction. By contrast, morning offers the prospect of a new beginning, a journey in search of a new lucidity. On the first morning, Dean hopes for a fresh start because he is beginning life at a new school. His hopes are frustrated in the following "nights." But the next morning contains a more definite promise. It is dawn, the true beginning of day, rather than nine a.m. The film ends on an image of the renewal of life and effort, as the camera draws back to reveal a man walking toward the planetarium to begin his day's work.

Ray's use of decor to illuminate specific situations can best be seen in the various ways that he has employed the particular concept of "upstairs." In *Johnny Guitar* upstairs represents isolation. The saloon owner, Vienna (Joan Crawford), has completely divorced her public from her private life; the former is lived on the ground floor amid the drinks and the gambling tables, the latter in her upstairs retreat with its more delicate, feminine decor. She is quite explicit about the distinction. Standing halfway down the stairs, gun in hand, she wards off the posse which has come to search her place: "Down there I sell whisky and cards. All you can get up these stairs is a bullet in the head." In the last shots of the film, Johnny Guitar is shown helping Vienna to break through her isolation: he supports her as she walks down a (different) flight of stairs to rejoin the other characters.

In *Bigger than Life*, as in *The True Story of Jesse James*, upstairs suggests both the possibility of a normal family life and the temporary retreat from responsibilities. Travel posters decorating the walls become more exotic as they progress from the Grand Canyon, by the front door, to Bologna, on the top landing. Upstairs represents the desire of the middle-aged schoolmaster (James Mason) to "get away sometime." *Rebel Without a Cause* uses upstairs to point Jim Backus's failure as a husband and father. His son is shocked and hurt to find him, aproned, outside his bedroom and on his knees. He is timidly mopping up the mess he has made by dropping the supper tray he was bringing to his wife. The choice of place, as much as the conviction of the performances, makes us appreciate James Dean's anger and anguish.

Structure

But places and objects have a structural as well as an evocative or a symbolic value. Ray takes full advantage of this in the architecture of his images. In *The Lusty Men*, Arthur Kennedy, against the wishes of his wife (Susan Hayward), abandons the impoverished security of his job as a ranch hand and becomes a rodeo rider. It is a life without stability, lived in station wagons and trailer parks. In one sequence, Susan Hayward goes to a party at a hotel. Ray shows her sitting in front of a curtain, with a good deal of nervously exuberant action going on behind her. The shot describes her dissatisfaction with the new way of life and her longing for a secure home: the curtain has a symbolic value of its own—the fabric is very "domestic" in its design—but it also divides the image vertically, to separate her from the environment which she wishes to renounce.

Ray frequently uses static masses with bold lines—walls, staircases, doors, rocks—which intrude into the frame and at the same time disrupt and unify his images. In particular he uses objects in order to enclose his characters, to produce a frame within the frame. In *Bigger than Life* James Mason takes overdoses of the cortisone which has been prescribed for his heart complaint. Under their influence he becomes the victim of a delusion of intellectual and moral superiority which threatens to destroy his family. The frame is in perpetual movement: closing down, for example, on Mason during the argument with his wife which provokes one of his seizures; closing down on his son as he struggles to placate Mason by solving some far-too-difficult problems in arithmetic; opening up again for a moment of respite after the solution has been found. Through his use of line and structure Ray produces "compositions which somehow make concepts as abstract as those of liberty and destiny both clear and tangible" (Godard on *The True Story of Jesse James* [1986, 60–61]).[2]

The turbulence of the frame is the product of the three sorts of cinematic movement: of the actors, of the camera, and of the shots—the montage. If there is a single idea which dominates Ray's technique (and therefore his philosophy, but that comes later), it is the opposition of conflict and harmony. For example, a Ray movie is instantly recognizable as such by the director's extremely individual use of editing. Many of Ray's camera movements appear to be incomplete. Any simple guide to moviemaking will tell you that a traveling shot must have a beginning, middle, and end. Often Ray uses only the middle: the camera is already moving at the beginning of the shot, and the movement is unfinished when the next shot appears; or if the movement *does* end, it falls somewhere short of its apparent goal. Whole sequences are often built up from these "incomplete" shots so that the montage becomes a pattern of interruptions in which each image seems to force its way onto the screen at the expense of its predecessor (e.g., the introduction of Scott Brady's gang in *Johnny Guitar*). Ray is one of the most "subjective" of all directors. The world he creates on the screen is the world seen by his characters. His dislocated editing style reflects the dislocated lives which many of his characters lead.

Even a sequence composed mainly of static shots will frequently be interrupted by cutting in a close shot of a character who is, to all appearances, only peripherally involved in the immediate action: Johnny Guitar into the first confrontation of Vienna and Emma (Mercedes McCambridge); Viveca Lindfors into a discussion between John Derek and James Cagney in *Run for Cover*; Salome into the trial of Jesus before Herod Antipas in *King of Kings*. The effect has a remarkable duality. The abrupt cut contributes to a feeling of dislocation, of disharmony. But, through its integration of an apparently extraneous element, it suggests also a hidden unity.

The use of color in Ray's films, too, depends largely on the concept of harmony. He does employ colors in the classical, and excellent, manner of Cukor and Kazan, for their emotional effect: in the first reel of *Bigger than Life* the dissolve from the predominantly gray shot as Mason leaves school to a screen virtually covered with the glaring yellow of parked taxis makes us feel the strain that is imposed on him by performing two jobs each day. But more characteristic is Ray's manner of selecting colors for the extent to which they blend or clash with background. Although the reds which Charisse wears in *Party Girl* have an autonomous emotional value, their effect comes principally from their relation to the other colors in the shot: spotlighting her among, and isolating her from, the somber browns of a courtroom; blending with, and absorbing her into, the darker red of a sofa on which she sleeps. Cornel Wilde's revolt against the traditions of his Gypsy family in *Hot Blood* is expressed through the clash between the conventional color of his jacket and the gaudy "Gypsy" upholstery of the chair on which he places it.

Direct Speech

This sort of direct statement is common in Ray's films because he believes (unfashionably perhaps, but so much the worse for us) that the cinema is a medium of communication, and that clarity is of prime importance. The directness of Ray's approach is reflected in the construction of his screenplays. The principal characters in his films are presented as quickly and economically as possible. The first shot will usually introduce the hero, and by the end of the first reel all the important relationships will have been presented. There are exceptions to this rule—*The Savage Innocents* and *King of Kings*, for example—but they only occur when the nature of the story itself makes it inapplicable. The exposition at the beginning of *Rebel Without a Cause* is amazing in its speed and lucidity. The first shot behind the credits is a close-up of James Dean as he lies in the road; the second is a brief linking shot as he is taken into the police station; and the third introduces us to Sal Mineo and Natalie Wood. Less than ten minutes later we have learned about the family backgrounds of Mineo and Wood and have even met Dean's parents and grandmother—again, in a single shot which conveyed most of the details of a complex relationship.

The desire for direct communication also distinguishes Ray's use of symbolism. His images are never obscure; many of them are derived from nature, like the references to fire and water in *King of Kings* or to rock and wind in *Johnny Guitar*—the first time we see her, Emma looks as if she is being carried along by the wind and for the rest of the film she acts entirely according to impulse. These symbols are felt rather than noticed. But when Ray wishes to convey an idea he is not squeamish about using an extreme image. Emma exploits the murder of her brother as a pretext for hounding Vienna; as she rides at the head of a lynch mob her funeral veil is lost in the dust of the horses' hooves. James Mason abuses cortisone to induce an inflated sense of his own significance: we see him pump life into a wilted football.

This use of extremes is not confined to symbolism. It involves the camera, most notably in the shots in *Rebel Without a Cause*, *Hot Blood*, and *Wind Across the Everglades* which carry subjectivity to its logical conclusion; they show the inverted images which their heroes see and, in *Rebel*, the camera turns vertically through 180 degrees as James Dean swings his body around to sit upright. In *Johnny Guitar*, and at times in all his films, Ray uses extreme situations and extreme actions to provide an almost diagrammatic representation of ideas, characters, and conflicts. Christopher Plummer expresses his disgust at the slaughter of the Everglades' wildlife by snatching the feathers from the hat of an overdressed woman and asking how she'd like it "if this bird wore you for a decoration." Lee J. Cobb, the gangster boss of *Party Girl*, shoots holes in a portrait of Jean Harlow, when he learns of her marriage. One of Vienna's bartenders walks into a medium shot and looks straight into the camera to tell us he's "never seen a woman who was more like a man." Howard Da Silva smashes Farley Granger's dream of domestic bliss (*They Live by Night*) as he smashes one of the trinkets on his Christmas tree.

The Blind Run

Such directness, such extremes of expression, would result in the merest onthebeachified brain fodder if they were not controlled by a profoundly personal vision.[3] But in their context they form a moving testimony to the courage and lucidity of a filmmaker who communicates his preoccupations on the screen with poetic intensity. Every one of Ray's "devices" has its correlative in some aspect of his sensibility.

But, conversely, the majority of his films will make little sense to anyone who goes to the cinema simply to hear a good script well read. One must respond to the textures of Ray's films before one can understand their meanings. One must appreciate their dynamics before one can see, embodied in their turbulent movement, an ethical and poetic vision of the universe and of man's place in it. In *Rebel Without a Cause* Ray uses the planetarium to draw a close parallel between the isolated and insecure condition of his characters and that of the whole of mankind in the universe. Members of the lecture audience view the depiction of the end of the world with indifference, contempt, or terror. But the commentator rambles on: "Destroyed as we began in a burst of gas and fire . . . the earth will not be missed . . . and man existing alone himself seems an episode of little consequence." It is against this concept of a man's life as an episode of little consequence, rather than against society, or his family, that Dean rebels.

Ray's original title for the film, *The Blind Run*, reflects a view of life as a too-rapid journey under no guidance, with no apparent direction or purpose. The actions of Ray's characters are conditioned by this view. Some of them, like the director, engage in a search for an alternative, for a real unity dominating our seemingly chaotic, unstable, and indifferent world. Others, failing in the search, accept chaos but with no equanimity: there can be few more anguished statements on film than Burton's in *Bitter Victory*: "I kill the living, and I save the dead." *Run for Cover* shows Matt Dow (Cagney) as a man who is able to come to terms with the world because he has found an interior stability which few of Ray's characters are privileged to share (fig. 7).

There is one reaction to the harsh realities that Ray presents which invariably leads to disaster: the refusal to recognize life's terms. In *The Lusty*

Figure 7. A man able to come to terms with the world

Men Robert Mitchum, a retired rodeo rider, goes back to the shack in which he spent his childhood, "looking for something I thought I'd lost." The door is locked. At the film's climax he returns to the arena because he needs to prove himself: "I used to buy my own booze. . . . A fella just likes to see if he can still do it." In the sequence before he signs on for the contest, a commentator describes the opening parade through the Texan town as "an exciting display of old glory." Mitchum dies from injuries received in the arena. The final failure and death of Jesse James results from his increasingly fantasistic way of life: he attempts to divorce his two characters, as Jesse and as the respectable small-town family man, Mr. Howard. His band disintegrates during a bank raid which fails because it takes him too far from home. Mason's abuse of cortisone very nearly causes him to murder his son. At the end of the film Mason can only regain sanity if he can base his life on its realities rather than on a comforting illusion: "If he can remember everything that happened, and face it, he'll be alright."

The acceptance of life's terms involves the acceptance of turmoil and change. Ray's characters share his sensitivity to time. Vienna tells the posse, "I intend to be buried here—in the twentieth century!" But Emma's quarrel with Vienna is partly caused by her desire to resist change: "You'll never see a train run through!" Christopher Plummer rejects an invitation to contribute to the development of Miami: "Progress and I never got along very well." And Richard Burton describes a tenth century Berber village disdainfully as "too modern for me."

Progress contributes to the instability of our lives. Emma opposes the extension of the railroad because it will destroy the isolation which protects her. In one very violent and moving speech she says that the trains will bring "farmers. Dirt farmers! Squatters! They'll push us out! . . . You're gonna find you and your women and your kids squeezed between barbed wire and fence posts. Is that what you're waiting for?" Even Emma, who early in the film announces her intention of killing Vienna, has her justification.

There are no pure villains in Ray's pictures. There are simply, and more dramatically, failures of communication and understanding. In *Run for Cover* Viveca Lindfors says that the wife who divorced James Cagney "must have been bad." "No," says Cagney. "She just hated the sight of me." Each man acts, with whatever degree of lucidity, according to his own code or his own deepest needs. Almost every man acts from a position of profound uncertainty and insecurity. Because he is insecure in his own estimation Ray's hero often seeks to win or retain his self-respect through the admiration or submission of his fellows; but this struggle only increases the instability of personal relationships. An unambiguous victory in the battle for prestige is impossible, since it inevitably makes the victor's life less worth living: Herod Antipas is haunted by guilt because he has granted Salome's request for the head of John the Baptist rather than "let it be known that the word of a king is worthless."

Men will make almost any sacrifice in order to protect their prestige. In *Bitter Victory* Curd Jürgens is unable to act at a vital moment in the attack, which he commands, on a German headquarters. Richard Burton tells him that "what happened tonight has nothing to do with me, that's (a matter) between you and you." But Jürgens is sure that his men regard him as a coward. He risks his life, by drinking from a well that he suspects has been poisoned, in order to demonstrate his courage.

Ray's films contain a large number of variations on man's appreciation of his insecurity. In *Party Girl* Robert Taylor, as defense counsel for a gangster (John Ireland), is able to secure an acquittal against the evidence by giving the jury a sense of superiority: he wins their pity for himself—by exaggerating his lameness—and for his client, by suggesting that the press has already condemned him without trial (and therefore deprived the jurors of their right of decision). In a precisely parallel situation in *Run for Cover* we are shown John Derek's self-destructive willingness to exploit the sympathy of others. He also is lame. In an attempt to win the pity of James Cagney he leans toward him across a desk exactly as he did, on the floor, when making his first attempt to walk without crutches. Christopher Plummer in *Wind Across the Everglades* says that he has been given no choice but to arrest the leader of the feather-pirates (Burl Ives). In fact, he was offered in public a warrant for Ives's arrest, provided that he would serve it personally. Inuk (Anthony Quinn), the Eskimo hero of *The Savage Innocents*, uses a man's fear of contempt positively, in order to save his life. He shames a trooper into putting his frozen hands inside the hot stomach of a husky by asking if white men can stand pain.

The need for acceptance by society, with its conformist pressures, inevitably conflicts with the desire to live one's life according to one's own code. The heroes of *Johnny Guitar, Wind Across the Everglades,* and *The Savage Innocents* are nearly destroyed in the attempt for recognition on their own terms. Ray's adventurers are adventurers not by choice, like the Hawks or Walsh heroes, but through interior compulsion. They are "displaced" persons whose isolation is emphasized by their involvement with a group which stands apart from society and, often, outside the law. Indeed, their nonconformism is such that they isolate themselves even from these unconventional groups: Dean shocks a teenage gang whose chosen weapons are switchblades and stolen cars by threatening its leader with the shaft of his car jack.

But even though a man may choose isolation, as an escape from the pressures of society, it can never be a permanent or satisfactory solution. In *Johnny Guitar* and *Party Girl* we are shown a man and a woman, both deeply dislocated, withdrawn characters, both intensely vulnerable, each trying to escape isolation and restore self-esteem by earning the respect of the other. *Johnny Guitar* contains a sequence of extraordinary power in which Johnny and Vienna are alone together for the first time, after a long and painful separation. Each of them hides emotion in a cynically contrived "dialogue," designed to test the other's feelings without involvement. Johnny tells Vienna, "Lie to me. Tell me you've waited," and Vienna "reads" his words back to him, saying exactly what she's asked to say but trying to suppress every trace of feeling. Similarly, the relationship between Robert Taylor and Cyd Charisse in *Party Girl* starts with injured pride and mutual resentment. But it is built gradually through a series of tests until each is able to provide the conditions of trust and respect which the other needs. It is only through such a relationship, based on instinctive sympathy and explicit dependence, that Ray's characters escape the double threat of isolation and subjection.

The delicate balance needed to create and sustain any harmonious relationship can only be achieved at cost, and it is in constant jeopardy. The useful extension of a character's emotional or moral range can only follow the painful destruction of those barriers which are intended to protect him, but which in fact oppress him: false relationships, unjustified hopes, and outmoded rules of conduct. In *Rebel Without a Cause* James Dean looks for guidance and support from a father who is by nature incapable of providing them. Eventually, through anguish and tragedy, he is forced to accept the realities of his situation. Only then can he begin to build a more useful relationship.

A Stranger Here

"Often," says Burl Ives in *Wind Across the Everglades*, "the longest way round is the shortest way through." But often Ray's characters attempt to find an easy way out of their difficulties. Like Mason in *Bigger than Life* they mistake the panacea for the cure. Or, like Arthur Kennedy in *The Lusty Men*, they allow a method to become an end in itself. Kennedy and his wife long for the security represented by "a place of our own." As a shortcut toward this goal, Kennedy competes for the prizes of the rodeo arena. But the prestige which he earns there sidetracks him from his house; he buys a trailer, a symbol of permanent instability. Similarly, the laws and conventions which a society devises are valuable insofar as they meet its particular needs. But they are too easily regarded as moral absolutes; and they can only provoke chaos and injustice when applied beyond their necessarily limited context. In the first half of *The Savage Innocents* we are shown a life lived in strict accord with the terms dictated by the Arctic environment. But a missionary comes to the Eskimos, Inuk and Asiak (Yoko Tani) to persuade them that the Lord—a character who has played no previous part in their lives and whose existence corresponds to no felt need—is angry with them for living in sin: a concept which has never suggested itself to them. Inuk is himself disgusted by the missionary's refusal of the traditional hospitalities of his race and in particular of Asiak's loving services. In his anger he accidentally fractures the missionary's skull. Much later, when Inuk has forgotten the entire episode, troopers come to arrest him and take him away to be tried according to laws of whose existence he was unaware, and whose authority he does not recognize: "My father's laws have not been broken." The conflict in the latter part of the film is entirely the result of an attempt to impose on an alien way of life rules which have become stronger than the men who made them.

Asiak speaks for Ray when she tells the trooper that "when you come to a strange land, you should bring your wives and not your laws."

The rigidity with which men enforce their particular codes is a further response to insecurity. Ray's films show man as an intruder in a turbulent and indifferent, or hostile, universe. His hero often journeys into a primitive landscape like that of the Everglades in search of a lost certainty, a lost harmony between man and his environment. But he brings with him his own inner conflicts, which make that harmony unattainable. Burl Ives and Christopher Plummer represent opposite responses to nature, the former wanting to be its master, the latter its servant. Ray looks for an integration of these attitudes, toward an ideal relationship of man to nature like that of man to man, in which the struggle for domination is resolved by the recognition of interdependence.

But such a harmony can only be attained when a man finds the purpose of his life in the conquest neither of nature nor of his fellows, but of himself. For this is the one conquest which does not imply a defeat or need a victim. In *King of Kings* Ray uses a dissolve during the temptations in the wilderness which absorbs the figure of Jesus into the earth. By coming to terms with himself, and only in that way, man is able to come to terms with his environment.

This is not simply a moral point. Ray has often shown us characters who are, psychologically, incapable of attaining stability and who, like the heroes of *Bitter Victory* and of *Wind Across the Everglades*, become victims of the basic rule of nature—the survival of the fittest. Ray makes his moral judgments from a position of sympathy and understanding: while we recognize the defects and conflicts which destroy his heroes, we are forced to recognize them also in ourselves and in our society. Until recently one might justifiably have supposed that Ray found these contradictions so deeply embedded in men's personalities as to forbid any real stability. His most successful films were also those whose attitudes seemed the most pessimistic: their resolutions were unconvincing when they were not either tragic or extremely ambiguous. One could not believe that the hostility of the world, so concretely depicted, was entirely the reflection or the product of the hero's neurosis.

Ray refuses to guarantee the futures of his characters: at the end of *Johnny Guitar, Rebel Without a Cause,* and *Bigger than Life* the hero has reached a point from which he may progress toward a more meaningful and ordered existence. But we are not permitted to believe in any magical transformation of his personality. Even after the death of Sal Mineo at the climax of *Rebel Without a Cause,* James Dean's agonized cry of *"I've* got the bullets!" symbolizes for us the continuation of his inner conflict. There is always the danger that the hero will again fall back into chaos and self-destruction.

The danger is no less real at the end of *Party Girl,* but it is less oppressive. One feels, for the first time, that the hero has recognized it and is therefore better equipped to deal with it. Also, Robert Taylor has reached, by the middle of the film, the position which other Ray heroes attain only at the end. Because we have seen him survive and grow through several trials we are more confident of his ability to survive the hazards of the future.

This is not a purely formal achievement. It suggests, rather, a considerable extension of the director's range. In the two films since *Party Girl—The Savage Innocents* and *King of Kings*—one still finds the anguish and confusion of *Rebel Without a Cause* or *Bitter Victory.* But at times in both films anguish has been replaced by passionate placidity. All Ray's films balance an immediate conflict against an ultimate unity, but his more recent work suggests a place for man within that unity.

Works Cited

Godard, Jean-Luc. *Godard on Godard*. Edited and translated by Tom Milne. New York: Da Capo, [1972] 1986.

Hoveyda, Fereydoun. "Nicholas Ray's Reply: *Party Girl*." In *Cahiers du Cinéma— Volume 2: 1960-1968: New Wave, New Cinema, Re-evaluating Hollywood*, edited by Jim Hillier, 122-31. London: Routledge & Kegan Paul, 1986. First published as "La Réponse de Nicholas Ray," *Cahiers du Cinéma* 18, no. 107 (1960): 13-23.

Marcorelles, Louis. "Lettre de Londres." *Cahiers du Cinéma* 16, no. 94 (1959): 40.

Ray, Nicholas. "I Hate a Script." In *I Was Interrupted: Nicholas Ray on Making Movies*, edited by Susan Ray, 189-93. Berkeley: University of California Press, 1993.

Filmography

Bigger than Life. Directed by Nicholas Ray. Twentieth Century Fox, 1956.
Bitter Victory. Directed by Nicholas Ray. Columbia Pictures, 1957.
Hot Blood. Directed by Nicholas Ray. Columbia Pictures, 1956.
In a Lonely Place. Directed by Nicholas Ray. Columbia Pictures, 1950.
Johnny Guitar. Directed by Nicholas Ray. Republic Pictures, 1954.
King of Kings. Directed by Nicholas Ray. MGM, 1961.
The Lusty Men. Directed by Nicholas Ray. RKO Radio Pictures, 1952.
Party Girl. Directed by Nicholas Ray. MGM, 1958.
Rebel Without a Cause. Directed by Nicholas Ray. Warner Bros., 1955.
Run for Cover. Directed by Nicholas Ray. Paramount Pictures, 1955.
The Savage Innocents. Directed by Nicholas Ray. Rank, 1960.
They Live by Night. Directed by Nicholas Ray. RKO Radio Pictures, 1948.
The True Story of Jesse James (UK title: *The James Brothers*). Directed by Nicholas Ray. Twentieth Century Fox, 1957.
Wind Across the Everglades. Directed by Nicholas Ray. Warner Bros., 1958.

Notes

1 Fereydoun Hoveyda quotes Marcorelles as claiming that in *Party Girl* Ray's is "a prodigal talent wasted on rubbish" (1968, 127). Ed.

2 This is the wording as translated in *Godard on Godard* (1986), probably the most accessible English translation. Ed.

3 The reference is to *On the Beach* (1959), directed by Stanley Kramer. Ed.

55 DAYS AT PEKING

First published in Movie, *no. 11 (July/August 1963): 4–6.*

Provided that the producer's resources and the technicians' abilities are equal to the demands of the project, the quality of an immodest spectacular is determined in exactly the same way as that of a thrifty quickie: by the quality of the direction. It is not surprising, therefore, that *55 Days at Peking* (1963) is the best of the Big Ones currently on offer. It is superior to its only rival—*How the West Was Won* (1962)—to the extent that Nicholas Ray's direction here surpasses that of a substandard Henry Hathaway.[1]

This is not to claim that everything seen at Peking is preferable to anything seen in the West, nor that any film by Ray surpasses every film by Hathaway. Film is too complex and temperamental a medium to allow any general statement more than approximate value, and spectaculars are particularly liable to raise questions of directorial responsibility: the credits of *Peking* give unusual prominence to the second unit, which boasts not only a director but a "Director of Operations" as well.

The existence of a second unit need not, however, imply the periodic impotence of the director: *The Vikings* (1958), *The Savage Innocents* (1960), and *Barabbas* (1961), among others, have shown that the large-scale picture can be in all essentials the work of one man, provided that the second unit understands and respects the director's intention for the layout of a sequence and the design of movement within it. But *55 Days at Peking* contains a number of sequences which quite clearly have not been subject to this sort of control. They are in no sense the work of Nicholas Ray. In fact, both the action and the filming are so ill-organized in these sequences as to deny the presence of any direction at all.

The entertainment value of zealous devastation ensures our enjoyment of the picture's most spectacular scenes. But only two of the "action sequences" have any real value as film. One, the attack on the Chinese arsenal, shows Ray's hand in its smallest detail—for example, in the spiderish way the attackers scurry across open ground (cf. Ray's *Bitter Victory* [1957]). The other sequence shows how the foreign troops drive the Boxer forces from their position of advantage in a combined assault by fire wagon and cannon fire. One guesses that here Ray was able to supervise the filming simply because the action is placed and the rhythm controlled with a precision notably lacking in the other sequences of destruction and military strife.

On every level of beauty, significance, and enjoyment the best scenes in the film are those that belong most completely to Nicholas Ray. A rolling plate in Ray's ballroom sequence is a more effective *spectacle* than a burning fortress filmed by the second unit simply because it serves a dramatic and emotional purpose within the total composition of the scene. The impact of the big fire, on the other hand, depends entirely upon the scale of the event and is in no way heightened by its presentation in a conventionally edited series of photographs.

At this point it becomes necessary, in justice to the film, to point out that for about 60 percent of its length it is directed by Ray at top form. Time and again one is staggered and exhilarated by the masterly way in which a sequence is worked out, and nowhere more than in the film's magnificent opening.

The first sequence takes its form from a musical idea (splendidly realized by [Dimitri] Tiomkin) which in turn owes something to Charles Ives—a battle of brass bands. In the legation compound at Peking the troops of eight foreign powers hoist their flags to the raucous accompaniment of their respective national anthems. Ray's camera climbs, glides, and dives from one group to another, organizing the sequence into a meaningful visual, as well as aural, cacophony; and in a series of crane shots as the camera climbs to follow the rising flags, the director plays on the conflict between the vertical subject and the horizontal image to produce an effect of instability and displacement.

The sequence has another, more disturbing, effect which perhaps embodies the director's intention for the whole movie: by presenting some petty gestures of national vanity on the consciously grand scale associated with blockbusters, Ray prepares us for a struggle of epic futility.

In its qualities of irony, invention, and control, also, this opening prepares us for the film. The freedom and daring with which Ray is accustomed to treat the wide screen are as much in evidence as ever. He wastes little energy in overcoming the "limitations" with which the "scopes," "visions," and "ramas" terrorize so many filmmakers even in 1963. Instead his camera remains at liberty, "to hunt for the truth of the scene."

Some part of Ray's originality obviously comes from his recognition that there is nothing in the size, ratio, or clarity of the 70 mm image which need prevent intimacy or hinder a director in examining the small-scale action. Beyond this, Ray evidently feels that personal conflicts and hidden motivations can be revealed as clearly in a scene of mass action as in a sotto voce duologue. The events in Ray's films are not given autonomous value. They exist primarily as the reflection and product of individual character. The dramatic conflicts are always an extension of the conflicts between, or within, the characters. This fact sets Ray apart from [Vittorio] Cottafavi, Vidor, Fleischer, and others for whom a spectacular is justified principally by its spectacle. The arena sequences in Fleischer's *Barabbas* have *and need* no important external meaning: one is excited by the choreography and technique of the contest, not by its significance. But in, for example, the ballroom sequence of *Peking*, Ray is not concerned to present an *abstract* pattern of color and movement. He arrives, very beautifully, at such a pattern, but it is a by-product, not the objective, of his method.

The essential pattern here is one of intrusions. The legation ball itself, at which the military two-step is played with disinterested vigor by a Chinese band, represents an attempt to establish the customs and values of the English aristocracy in an alien landscape. But the European decor is in turn disrupted by the arrival of the resolutely Chinese Prince Tuan (Robert Helpmann) and his troupe of Boxer acrobats: they offer an entertainment which, in its energy and violence, is distinctly at odds with the formality of the occasion. Finally, the American Major Lewis (Charlton Heston) shatters both the English and the Chinese disciplines by ignoring the rules of their respective games and—pointlessly—converting diplomatic hostilities into open warfare. The pattern of visual conflicts established here is reversed in the following sequence when Lewis and the Russian baroness, Natalie Ivanoff (Ava Gardner), enter a deserted Chinese temple to dance together under the eye of the alien gods.

The ballroom scene, in its contrasts of public gesture and private motive, provides the film's most complex sequence. But *Peking*, like any other Ray movie, is full of moments in which characters, attitudes, or emotions are concentrated into their most direct visual form. Thus the years of rejection and uncertainty which have marked the childhood of Teresa (Lynne Sue Moon), the orphaned daughter of a Chinese woman and an American soldier, are summarized in one characteristic gesture—the arm tentatively outstretched toward any possible source of acceptance and security. Or again, Matt Lewis's quick glance at Natalie's extravagant dress is enough to contradict, for us, her claim that she is "not in uniform" and to change the significance of Matt's reply: "I like things fine the way they are" is now carried beyond the immediate context of polite flirtation to become a statement of Matt's refusal to risk emotional involvement. Through the extreme symmetry of his compositions within the imperial palace, Ray emphasizes the unreal position occupied by the Empress (Flora Robson). The unnatural balance of the images betrays the artificial and inhuman balance which the Empress attempts to impose, but which cannot accommodate the realities of personal and political conflict: the desired pattern is broken, visually, by the protagonists' refusal to adopt the symmetrical positions appropriate to the Empress's decor.

In her self-imposed isolation from human contact the Empress resembles Matt, and the direction links the two characters by presenting each, at times, within the circular design of a window, a door, or a tunnel. The character of the hero is, in fact, the most obviously personal aspect of the film. Matt understands swords, guns, fortifications, and strategy; but he is bewildered and frightened by the more complex tactics involved in human relationships. His public bravery is the result, and the shield, of his private cowardice. His extreme sensitivity toward his own feelings makes him extremely insensitive to anything else, and this blindness colors even his public actions. As a result, even at their most intrepid and "glorious" his actions tend to be futile (the attempted rescue of a missionary) or foolish (the attack on the unarmed leader of the Boxer acrobats).

The sympathetic disrespect with which Ray treats his hero, the insistence on Matt's emotional incompetence, plays a large part in evading the sentimentality threatened by the scenario. One notices Ray's originality most in precisely those sequences which promise the worst in embarrassment and cliché. The "romance" between Matt and Natalie is undermined by the hero's inability to find the necessary words or actions (their one kiss is a notably brutal and inexpert affair) and destroyed by the consistent absence of passion. Matt wants a "soldier's woman": a whore, not a lover.

Similarly, Ray's most complete triumph over obvious emotionalism occurs in the film's most treacherously booby-trapped episode—when Matt is required to inform Teresa of her father's death. Ray sidesteps the invitation to pump the tears and presents the scene from Matt's point of view instead of the child's. Matt has been advised to tell Teresa as he would like a child of his own to be told. But he does not even tell her what has happened. Instead he forces the girl to extract the truth from him in a grim game of question and answer, and then comforts her by saying that she knew it would happen sooner or later. Embarrassed by the possibility that she may betray some emotion, he picks up a child's doll and stares at it while he speaks. By taking the emotional tone from Matt's inadequacy rather than Teresa's vulnerability, Ray has certainly not destroyed the pathos of the scene; but he has underscored it with an irony which stops just short of really cruel humor.

The qualities which make *55 Days at Peking* such a satisfying film are mainly the qualities of Ray's direction. Its defects, which make it Ray's least satisfying film since *Run for Cover* (1955), are mainly attributable to the crippling disease known as Producer's Twitch. It is unfortunate that, in a key role, Elizabeth Sellars gives the standard English interpretation of gallant frigidity. It is inevitable that Peking, reconstructed on the outskirts of Madrid, lacks something in authenticity. But it is not necessary for a producer to lose his nerve when he either is making or has made such an entertaining movie. Nevertheless, *Peking* carries all the stigmata of a large-scale picture ruthlessly and ruinously mutilated at some stage in its production. Attitudes, especially

Chinese attitudes, are stated, not dramatized. Characters and relationships developed in the first half are brushed aside in the second. Motivations become obscure. Sequences of entirely different emotional weight are inappropriately juxtaposed. One scene is composed of shots belonging to two sequences, of which one takes place in broad daylight and the other at night. Ava Gardner's untimely death is produced in the laboratories by freezing the frame when she closes her eyes (or was she just blinking?). All this foolishness leaves a number of unanswered questions of directorial intention. Why is color progressively withdrawn from the images? How much weight should one give to Matt's final acceptance of responsibility for Teresa? Why *does* he accept it? And so on.

For his butchery, and because producers are only vulnerable at the bank, one would like to believe that Samuel Bronston was about to lose a few shirts on the film. Unfortunately, from this point of view, what he has left is so excitingly filmed that his crimes are likely to be handsomely rewarded.

Filmography

Barabbas. Directed by Richard Fleischer. Columbia Pictures, 1961.
Bitter Victory. Directed by Nicholas Ray. Columbia Pictures, 1957.
55 Days at Peking. Directed by Nicholas Ray. Allied Artists, 1963.
How the West Was Won. Directed by John Ford, Henry Hathaway and George Marshall. MGM/Cinerama, 1962.
Run for Cover. Directed by Nicholas Ray. Paramount Pictures, 1955.
The Savage Innocents. Directed by Nicholas Ray. Paramount, 1960.
The Vikings. Directed by Richard Fleischner, United Artists, 1958.

Note

1 Hathaway was one of three credited directors on *How the West Was Won*; the others were John Ford and George Marshall. Hathaway directed three of the film's five segments. Ed.

CHEYENNE AUTUMN

First published in Movie, *no. 12 (Spring 1965): 36–37.*

John Ford's name traditionally heads the list of artists who have managed to integrate themselves into the Hollywood machine and function successfully as creative filmmakers within its commercial structure. Ford himself has never seen it that way. As early as 1936, he made a public statement of his discomfort: "It's a constant battle to do something fresh. First they want you to repeat your last picture.... Then they want you to continue whatever vein you succeeded in with the last picture. You're a comedy director or a spectacle director or a melodrama director. You show 'em you've been each of these in turn, and effectively, too. So they grant you range. Another time they want you to knock out something *another* studio's gone and cleaned up with" (Eisenberg 2001, 257–58).

His film reveals with depressing clarity the nature and extent of the restrictions which the industrial system places on personal communication. Its relative, and glorious, failure demonstrates the contradictions inherent in the commercial machine and exaggerated by its current modus operandi.

The story of the Cheyenne nation's fifteen-hundred-mile trek from the government reservation in Oklahoma back to their Yellowstone homeland had long fascinated Ford as a potential movie subject. He made several unsuccessful attempts to set it up as a medium-budget production. Eventually the only way to convert the project into reality was to turn it into a blockbuster.

Beyond a certain figure, every extra dollar on the budget represents an additional strain on the executive's nerves. Every scene has to be double-checked for consumer appeal. The temptation to "improve" the work of the men actually making the film seems to become irresistible. In return for their huge investment Warners doubtless anticipated another "great Western in the classic Ford tradition." Ford delivered a film designed to question that tradition and to destroy the legend which, of all people, he himself has been most instrumental in creating. Whereas the budget was supposed to have guaranteed an action-packed epic, Ford centered the film on the moral development of a hero too human to be heroic: few of the most important scenes involve more than two or three characters.

Thus betrayed, Warners set about bringing the film into line with every philistine's image of what a blockbuster ought to be. Where Ford wanted something much more intimate and evocative, Alex North was called in to provide a self-consciously epic score. The picture was cut for action, many of the more personal sequences being jettisoned in order to build up the movie's spectacular aspects. Scenes which Ford had intended for drastic pruning (particularly those with Karl Malden, which now appear overemphasized) were retained. Others, more vital to Ford's conception, landed on the cutting-room floor: Sal Mineo's important role has been reduced to skeletal dimensions. One sequence, mentioned in the synopsis and essential to the plot, is quite absent from the film as released.

Cheyenne Autumn (1964) thus joins the list of the cinema's great ruins; we are more profitably employed examining its greatness than lamenting its mutilation. There's no need, at this stage, to detail its demonstrations of Ford's genius: those of us who had imagined that we could see legitimate objections to his method were silenced, and finally, by *Donovan's Reef* (1963). Each scene, discounting the excesses allowed to Malden, is realized with precision and intimacy, the direct emotional appeal embedded in the details of the action. The pattern and meaning so firmly established in the organization of the scenes has not been allowed to emerge fully from the organization of the narrative. But, as in Minnelli's *Two Weeks in Another Town* (1962) or Ray's *King of Kings* (1961), the power and beauty of the separate sequences contradict, where they do not excuse, the incoherence of the total structure. On the train out of Shinbone the aging senator Ranse Stoddard, the legendary *Man Who Shot Liberty Valance* (1962), contemplated the transformation of the Western landscape: "Look at it, Hallie. It was once a wilderness. Now it's a garden." The central question remained open: Were we to admire or to regret the transformation? In *Liberty Valance* Ford developed an exciting tension between a story which celebrated the submission of the Old West to the rule of law and order, and a style which evoked nostalgia for the primitive nobility of its untamed frontiers. This ambiguity, essential to the entire western legend, is resolved in Ford's own terms by *Cheyenne Autumn*.

The central subject here is the attempt to impose an inhuman discipline on a deep, anarchic emotion. For the Cheyenne, the determination to repossess their native land is unreasoned because unquestionable: a necessity which operates beyond the reach of logic and to which the desire for comfort, for life itself, is subordinated. Disaster is provoked by the inability, or the refusal, of others to acknowledge the force of their determination. The action of the film constitutes a series of destructive efforts to cultivate the wilderness of human feeling and make it submit to the orderly patterns of a garden.

Where the needs of the Cheyenne, which are felt rather than thought, can only be understood through sympathy, decisions based on calculation become invalid and destructive. True judgment of the situation is prevented in various ways: by administrative convenience; by economic interest (the dollar patriots and the land-grabbers); by abstract conceptions of duty (Widmark, initially) and order (Malden); and by the exploitable nature of the conflict. The "*New York Globe*" decides to give editorial support to the Indian cause, but as a means to increase circulation by adopting a different line, not through an understanding of the Cheyenne position. Among the Indians themselves, the first battle is precipitated by a young brave (Sal Mineo) eager to use the conflict to promote his courtship of another man's wife.

In the film's opening sequence the Cheyenne gather at the army outpost to await the arrival of a posse of politicians who are expected to do something to implement the promises made to the Indians. A soldier is dispatched in order to signal the approach of "those gentlemen from the East." Ford holds the shot until man and horse become a small speck in a huge landscape. Throughout the movie emphasis is placed on the distance between the men who make the decisions and the people whom these decisions most directly concern.

Cheyenne Autumn develops a theme which has frequently found expression in Ford's work: time and again, at least from *Stagecoach* (1939) to *Donovan's Reef*, judgments not based on sympathy and personal involvement prove to be incomplete and destructive. Where most of us are accustomed to regard detachment as a prerequisite of true judgment, Ford finds the two qualities incompatible: judgment is a function of sympathy. This makes him the least Brechtian of directors. It may also explain why he has so often, not just risked, but courted the accusation of sentimentality: he does not want to allow us a detached, unemotional, and so to his mind false view of his characters' experiences.

The conflict between detachment and sympathy is traced in the evolution of Captain Archer (Richard Widmark), and in the tension between an obligation to carry out orders based on abstract calculation and a personal experience which convinces him that the orders are unjust. At the start of the film he is aware that the Indians have been betrayed; he wants "every big-wig in Washington" to see how miserable the reservation is. But his involvement does not go beyond a reasoned belief that something needs to be done to correct an administrative error. By traveling over the same territory and enduring the same hardships in his pursuit of the Cheyenne, he comes to understand, sympathize with, and finally share their determination. It is only when the secretary of the interior (Edward G. Robinson) has heard Archer's personal account and abandoned the attempt to deal with the problem by remote control from Washington that a solution becomes possible.

"This is the West, sir. When the legend becomes fact, print the legend." Thus the newspaper editor in *Liberty Valance*. *Cheyenne Autumn* again complements the earlier picture by showing the less-happy results of printing the legend. Throughout the film the legendary reputation of the Cheyenne as bloodthirsty savages distorts the facts and prevents the sympathetic consideration which their case deserves. It takes Archer a long time to realize that *these* Indians are no longer the proud warriors of former times, but a collection of hungry wanderers who just want to go home. The Western myth continually asserts itself as a destructive force: a cattle man shoots down an unarmed brave who has come to beg for food because he "always wanted to kill me an Indian" and because an Indian scalp would enable him to silence the bragging of the old-timers.

As a portrayal of the degeneracy of the Old West, the end of its heroic era, the Dodge City episode (which has been mistaken for a simple piece of irrelevant fun) summarizes the movie's themes, though in a lighter vein. Based, like the main story, on a true episode in US history, the battle of Dodge City illustrates the Western legend operating, this time, to grotesque rather than tragic effect. The citizens believe the wild tales about the scale of the Cheyenne "revolt" and prepare to evacuate their inadequately garrisoned town. The evacuation is led by men who, having known the West in the old days, realize the folly of the general panic. Wyatt Earp (James Stewart) and Doc Holliday (Arthur Kennedy) conduct the evacuation in picnic spirit, but it turns into a rout when the citizens observe a single forlorn Indian riding along disconsolately in the distance.

Earp himself may be less gullible, but he is scarcely more heroic than the other Dodge citizens. With no more great battles to fight, no antagonists worth more than passing attention, the aging marshal, short-sighted and effete, sits around in the saloon and plays a tetchy game of poker, content to accept his 10-percent cut of the town's gambling take. Miss Guinevere Plantagenet (Elizabeth Allen) attempts to revive memories of a meeting during the old days back in Wichita, but without success. It was all, we gather, too long ago. The heroes are tired; which is why the organization men have taken over.

Work Cited

Eisenberg, Emanuel. "John Ford: Fighting Irish." In *John Ford Made Westerns: Filming the Legend in the Sound Era*, edited by Gaylyn Studlar and Matthew Bernstein, 255–60. Bloomington: Indiana University Press, 2001. First published in *New Theatre* 3 (April 1936): 7, 42.

Filmography

Cheyenne Autumn. Directed by John Ford. Warner Bros., 1964.
Donovan's Reef. Directed by John Ford. Paramount Pictures, 1963.
King of Kings. Directed by Nicholas Ray. MGM, 1961.
The Man Who Shot Liberty Valance. Directed by John Ford. Paramount Pictures, 1962.
Stagecoach. Directed by John Ford. United Artists, 1939.
Two Weeks in Another Town. Directed by Vincente Minnelli. MGM, 1962.

VIVRE SA VIE

First published in The Films of Jean-Luc Godard, *rev. ed., edited by Ian Cameron, 32–39. London: Studio Vista, [1967] 1969.*

"Suppose that for some reason or other I wanted to bring into a film a Sorbonne professor of the history of philosophy. There would certainly be nothing to prevent my having him talk about Kant's teaching. But that would be a ridiculous abuse of film, from an aesthetic viewpoint. Why? Because the spectator does not go to the cinema in order to listen to discussions" (Marcel 1954).

Toward the end of *Vivre sa vie* (1962) the philosopher Brice Parain speaks at some length to the movie's heroine (Anna Karina) and to its audience about the problems presented by the inadequacies of language as the medium of thought and communication, and by human failures in the use of language. He talks about the teaching of Kant and the nineteenth-century Germans, and their significance in the history of philosophy. He discusses the relationship between errors, lies, and truth.

It is quite possible that this episode in Godard's film was directly inspired, or provoked, by the dogma quoted above. Certainly much of the film's force and value come from its determined attack on preconceptions about the nature of cinema and how a film ought to behave.

In particular *Vivre sa vie* upsets the notion of a correct balance between the word and the image. The rule that it most consistently flouts is the rule that, in the cinema, "essentially a visual art," the important statements are to be made by the picture. There are a number of sequences where the image is made to serve the interest of the spoken word, most notably the section in which passages from a treatise on prostitution are recited in question-and-answer form. Here the dialogue offers all the essential information while the images themselves take over the normal functions of a commentary.

The film is constructed very largely as a series of dialogues on which Godard's camera plays a suite of variations, offering both an actual mise-en-scène and a string of suggestions as to how one *might* film a conversation. This impression is heightened by a substantial continuity of decor—five of the heroine's encounters take place in café-bars and the similarities of setting and action serve to point up the differences in presentation. As a filmmaker, Godard remains a critic speculating on the nature of film and the possibilities of direction. One of his concerns, here and elsewhere, is to test the relative strengths of language and the movie image as media for various forms of communication.

An aspect of Godard's "ridiculous misuse" of the cinema in *Vivre sa vie* is the film's refusal to settle into any single category. On one level it is a documentary about prostitution. Moving on from there, it is a "dramatized documentary," using its central character to present a typical case history. But the case history is extended into pure fiction to become the story of a young woman seeking her place in an elusive and alien world. At its most fictional the film again becomes documentary—as sketches of life in Paris in 1962 and as a portrait of Anna Karina.

The various approaches alternate and, occasionally, fuse. Thus the generalized treatise on the lives of prostitutes acts also as an account of Nana's life and carries us over a gap in the narrative: the development and decay of her relationship with a ponce, Raoul (Sady Rebbot). Similarly, the opening sequences, which offer a very personal account of the disintegration of Nana's world, contribute as well to the case history through their schematic portrayal of stages in her drift toward prostitution.

But while it is important to recognize the existence of these and other relationships between the film's various strands, the overall pattern remains one of disconnection and contradiction:

It is in the narrative with its leaps in time, its arbitrary succession of incidents, and its rapid oscillations of mood—Nana's desperate submission to "The First Man" is followed by joyful contentment in a meeting with an old friend Yvette (Guylaine Schlumberger), which gives way to the indulged nostalgia of a jukebox song, which breaks off into the violence and panic of a terrorist machine-gun fight.

It is in images which mirror Nana's precarious relationship with her environment by showing her in close-up against flat and unstable backgrounds (walls, mirrors, windows) so that she exists in a goldfish world, at the same time engulfed by and detached from the life around her. Writing her letter in a café, Nana seems to be sitting in front of a window which overlooks a wide, tree-lined street; but the "view" turns out to be a lifeless photographic wallpaper.

It is in the mismatching of image and soundtrack—particularly of the image and the spoken or written word: a passage quoted from a romantic novelette is set against a candid-camera shot of the city streets.

It is in the gratuitous nature of camerawork which frequently defies any notion of natural harmony between action and presentation. Swaying and shifting in random patterns, the camera follows the process of Nana's mind but ignores the demands of "logic" and the expectations of the audience. Scenes whose action is static are filmed with a mobile camera, but the precise nature of the camera's movements is so far irrelevant to the recorded settings, faces, movements, and gestures that the various treatments could be interchanged from scene to scene without affecting our knowledge or understanding of the action in any substantial way.

It is in the conflict between a narrative which offers the killing of Nana as something completely arbitrary (the point is that it's pointless) and a series of references (Joan of Arc, Porthos, "The Oval Portrait") which by prediction make her death a formal necessity.

It is, above all, in the contradiction between the movie's structure and its tone. The framework is one that suggests Brechtian detachment: a series of twelve tableaux, each introduced by a caption summarizing, explaining (or questioning), its content. The images themselves have an austerity of lighting and composition that recalls the [Robert] Bresson of *Pickpocket* (1959). Yet this apparently austere and endistancing form is at the service of a rich and gloomy romanticism. The clashes of mood and incident, the separation and titling of the twelve episodes, serve not to clarify or emphasize a central thesis but rather to stress discontinuity and to force on our attention the *absence* of a binding idea or program.

In effect, Godard's approach turns the absence of a Subject into the main theme of the film. For it is the essence of his romanticism, and part of his debt to Nicholas Ray, that in denying or destroying the expected connections and coherences he hints at a hidden (or lost) harmony. His manner of insisting on the absence of a visible pattern comes close to suggesting the presence of one that is invisible.

Such deliberation is in the chaos of the surface, so emphatic is the conjunction of incompatible elements, that the film seems to aspire to a level of vision at which everything would become intelligible and coherent. Given that this level of vision may be imagined but is not attained, *Vivre sa vie* operates at the point where the romantic begins to yearn for the greener grass of mysticism. At times "Her Life to Live" seems not to be the ideal title; the picture reaches out for something more along the lines of "His Wonders to Perform"—reaches out, but has not the nerve (equals courage or effrontery) to grasp. The approach to mysticism is the result of nostalgia, not of conviction: Joan of Arc is a contrast as well as a comparison. In Nana's world, gods are lost property that can be remembered but never reclaimed. For the most part the film, like its heroine, is driven back onto the simple slogan "That's how it is." *C'est comme ça*—elevation of No Comment into a moral and intellectual necessity—recurs with a range of emotional colorings as assertion, assent, acceptance, submission, and anguish.

But these different attitudes are not represented with equal force. When Nana is at her most contented, in the conversation with Yvette ("Everything is beautiful. . . . Things are what they are") the scene is embittered by its reference to Resnais's documentary on the Nazi extermination camps: Nana's repeated "I am responsible" echoes the repeated "I am not responsible" in *Nuit et brouillard* (*Night and Fog*, 1956). And there is certainly nothing on the film's affirmative side to balance the pointless brutality of the final scene. In light of the details which Godard invents to heighten the cruelty of Nana's end, *c'est comme ça* becomes a statement of impotent despair.

To Nana herself the words offer a formula permitting escape from the responsibilities of thought and communication. She talks about accepting responsibility for all her actions, but in a tone of total complacency. Her most pleasant moments arrive when she can just be, feel, or do, without being required to examine or explain her actions and motives. Her relationship with the Young Man (Peter Kassovitz) is happy, but (because?) it denies complexity—it is still at the stage where a difference of opinion can be dissolved by a declaration of love. By contrast, the failure of her relationship with Paul (André S. Labarthe) is accompanied by attempts at explanation, understanding, and self-justification. Nana believes that life ought to be simple. Where it is not, she is often prepared to force it to seem so by refusing to think or communicate. Her attitude is opposed in the film by Brice Parain.

Godard's own position remains ambiguous. The passage quoted from the novelette which offers the destruction of logic as a solution is not presented as Nana's point of view. It is offered as directorial comment. But here, as in *Alphaville* (1965), it is difficult to determine how seriously the attack on ordered thought is intended. One possibility is that Godard sees "logic" as thought divorced from its necessary context of feeling. That would be consistent with the effect of the "treatise on prostitution" where the images restore the emotional overtones excluded from the dialogue's bare statements of fact. Still, the opposition between cold reason and blind agitation seems both simple and arbitrary. There are other alternatives which the movie ignores.

Vivre sa vie is not alone among Godard's movies in presenting words, thought, and logic as the enemies of feeling. But perhaps, given the character and temperament of its heroine, the film could not do otherwise. For Nana is a sleepwalker, another of Godard's Preminger women. She relates to the heroines of *Whirlpool* (1950) and *River of No Return* (1954) in much the same way as the heroine of *Pierrot le Fou* (1965) relates to Carmen Jones (*Carmen Jones* [1954]), or as the Jean Seberg of *À Bout de souffle* (*Breathless*, 1960) relates to the Jean Seberg of *Bonjour Tristesse* (1958) and the Jean Simmons of *Angel Face* (1953). It is this which makes nonsense of the publicity statement (which Godard seems to have endorsed) claiming that *Vivre sa vie* is about a woman who "sells her body but retains her soul." If "soul" is to be taken to mean individuality, that's precisely what Nana lacks. She has little sense of who she is. When she writes her letter she has to check up on the facts even of her appearance. She is a stranger to herself: "'I' . . . is someone else," she tells the police interrogator. A touching anxiety to be recognized as "someone special" serves to point up her uncertain notion of her own identity.

Unable to achieve a definition of herself or her aims, Nana drifts—in complicity with the world that would make her an object. Her story is the story of what happens to her, not of what she does. Only in the final episode does she actually decide on a course of action, when she makes up her mind to leave Raoul's organization and go to live with the Young Man. Presumably, though the point is not clear, that decision leads to her death.

This reading of the narrative allows us to draw together certain strands in the film's pattern of devices and references. The scene in which Nana reaches her decision is the one where dialogue is suppressed in favor of subtitles. The silent movie treatment here refers us back to the quotation from [Carl] Dreyer's *Passion of Joan of Arc* (*La Passion de Jeanne d'Arc*, 1928) and Nana's identification with Joan. The direct parallel is that Nana, like Joan, feels herself driven by forces which she can neither oppose nor comprehend. But Dreyer's sequence also shows Joan learning of the imminence of her execution. By echoing Joan's ordeal in the scene of Nana's decision, Godard's subtitles connect the concepts of choice and of death. This in turn creates a relevance for Brice Parain's story of Porthos the musketeer; Dumas's hero brought death upon himself when, for the first time, he contemplated his action; Godard's heroine brings death upon herself when, for the first time, she exercises her will.

However, in suggesting these interpretations I am conscious of choosing the least unlikely connections rather than of elucidating meanings developed convincingly in the film's structure. Godard's fragmented method of narrative robs us of the stable framework that we need in order to make sense of the formal pattern. (In *Les Carabiniers* [1963] and *Alphaville* the structure of fable operates similarly to convey ideas with clarity but without offering a sense of their relevance to any actual situation.) By presenting as a film a series of sketches for a film, Godard protects himself from having to make a complete statement about any of his subjects. No filmmaker can be blamed for refusing to commit himself to a single line of thought. The trouble here is that Godard also evades the need to investigate any of the possibilities in depth.

Thus, while the film's greatest strength lies in its examination of a temperament, Godard's devices continually destroy context so that Nana's oscillations of mood and attitude fail to cohere into a portrait. We need, for example, a quite firm understanding of Nana's relationship with the Young Man if we are to comprehend its value for her and its relevance to the film. Yet the key scene is scarcely realized at all. Much of it is given over to the recital of a[n Edgar Allan] Poe story of which the meaning for the picture is, on one reading, very thin and, on another, very silly. The remainder is the subtitled conversation; here the device stylizes to such an extent that the relationship is removed from life and reality. We are left to speculate at just the point where we need to know.

So often, in *Vivre sa vie*, Godard's fresh approach betrays him into following impulses that a more "cautious" director would have abandoned as the subject began to impose its own shape and discipline. Perhaps the basic fault is Godard's unwillingness to allow the movie the degree of anonymity that a fully coherent work assumes. Instead he plays with film as he plays with ideas, very personally. Both games are conducted with passion, curiosity and elegant skill. But the context is severely limiting.

Work Cited

Marcel, Gabriel. "Possibilités et limites de l'art cinématographique." *Revue Internationale de Filmologie* 5, nos. 18–19 (1954): n.p.

Filmography

À Bout de souffle (*Breathless*). Directed by Jean-Luc Godard. UGC, 1960.
Alphaville. Directed by Jean-Luc Godard. Athos Films, 1965.
Angel Face. Directed by Otto Preminger. RKO Radio Pictures, 1953.
Bonjour Tristesse. Directed by Otto Preminger. Columbia Pictures, 1958.
Les Carabiniers. Directed by Jean-Luc Godard. Cocinor, 1963.
Carmen Jones. Directed by Otto Preminger. Twentieth Century Fox, 1954.
Nuit et brouillard (*Night and Fog*). Directed by Alain Resnais. Cocinor/Cosmo Films/Argos Films, 1956.
The Passion of Joan of Arc (*La Passion de Jeanne d'Arc*). Directed by Carl Theodor Dreyer. Gaumont, 1928.
Pickpocket. Directed by Robert Bresson. Lux Compagnie Cinématographique de France, 1959.

Pierrot le Fou. Directed by Jean-Luc Godard. Société Nouvelle de Cinématographie, 1965.
River of No Return. Directed by Otto Preminger. Twentieth Century Fox, 1954.
Vivre sa vie. Directed by Jean-Luc Godard. Panthéon Distribution, 1962.
Whirlpool. Directed by Otto Preminger. Twentieth Century Fox, 1950.

AMERICA AMERICA

First published in Movie, no. 19 (Winter 1971–72): 35–38.

The action of leaving home provides the central metaphor in Kazan's work. His best films (by which I mean *East of Eden* [1955], *Wild River* [1960], and *Splendor in the Grass* [1961]) encourage the development and elaboration of the metaphor because that action is at the center of their plots. The drive is away from the false security of the family, away from a stability which may sometimes be real but is always stifling, away from acquiescence in the static toward an engagement—reluctant, resigned, eager, or confused—with the dynamic of mobility and change.

In this context *America America* (*The Anatolian Smile*) (1963) is an indispensable testament, a giant expansion of the metaphor so that "home" is not just family but country and culture, and leaving it involves not a crossing of thresholds or rivers but a migration across landscapes and oceans with survival and arrival equally unsure.[1] Appropriately it is a very American story, the easterner journeying to and across the frontier in search of the promised land. Stavros Topouzoglou (Stathis Giallelis) is the man who shot (or became) Liberty Valance.

For Stavros, America represents the dream of a fresh start. Though he learns much on his quest, he never learns the vanity of this dream. In America, he believes, he will be washed clean. There at last, and rebaptized as Joe Arness (an immigration official's *corruption* of "Hohannes," itself an assumed identity but one that denotes purity), he has apparently achieved his goal, having abandoned the tokens of his former life—the fez, the hamal's harness—and acquired a new uniform of dress and mannerism. But "in some ways it's not different here." The bribes and cages are constant. Subjection remains even if its basis has shifted a bit. The Greek in Anatolia was victim of an oppression primarily racial, political, and religious. In America, his subjection retains a racial aspect and acquires a linguistic one but is mainly economic, hence escapable: all it needs is luck, energy, determination, and obsessive individualism, a ruthless and exclusive concentration on self-interest. The tip-gatherer's smile of Stavros the Yank offers a new, aggressive, and mercenary gloss on the smile of the Anatolian Stavros with its suggestion of anxious complicity in his own exploitation, of proclaimed gratitude and inner revulsion.

Like other forms of communication, gestures, and most notably the smile, are always suspect since they present the calculated public announcement more often than they mirror the reality of the private response. Kazan's characters are only occasionally betrayed by surprise or the intensity of inner pressures into speaking truths in their words or actions. For the most part, the director has them reveal themselves most clearly to us at precisely those moments when they most assiduously conceal or disguise themselves from one another. When Stavros blurts a truthful "yes" to his fiancée's asking whether he will leave her, the dramatic focus is not the content of the statement—we have the information already—but its context, and the shock with which it is received by a hearer who had sought reassurance.

As it mingles self-knowledge and self-contempt in predicting betrayal, the announcement is equally shocking to the speaker, trapped into so sudden and naked a presentation of truth by the correspondence between the spoken dialogue and his inner monologue of self-accusation: Since the question puts Stavros's thoughts so exactly into words, what more natural that that he should speak his answer out loud? The actual presence of the questioner is an amazing intrusion, akin to diary reading and keyhole peeping. It has the special unfairness of reality—Kazan's treacherous reality—in which those who reveal themselves or lapse from deviousness and hypocrisy necessarily offer themselves for vilification. To be open is to be vulnerable. The truth can always be represented as shameful, so the only place for honor is "safe inside me," shielded from the opportunistic contempt of the other. Of course, Kazan is not counseling withdrawal and hypocrisy: if he has any "advice" to offer, it is that honor is a debilitating pursuit; but he does not suggest that it is humanly possible to escape from concern with honor and public justification.

What interests him dramatically (to judge from what he presents with the greatest force and conviction) is the situation in which physical or psychic survival demands defiance of assumptions deeply entrenched within and around the actor, most of all where the very act of defiance is as shocking to the defier as to the defied. If understanding is a key issue with Kazan, it is not on account of a Renoir-like acceptance of all actions and attitudes as justifiable from the viewpoint of the doer, but because they are all equally open to attack, equally the product of confused and largely indefensible motives. "Explain yourself" is an imperative but also an impossibility since "you have to be a person like I am to understand."

This tension is one of the sources of Kazan's strength and force. His movies convey nostalgia for purity and innocence, disdain for the more or less culpable passivity which the maintenance of purity demands. Stavros is grimly educated away from his father's Christian fetish of inoffensiveness but cannot cease to judge his own acts by his father's standards; the struggle to escape the shame of enslavement as one of the "Greek subject peoples" is also an accumulation of new guilts and spectacular degradations. When some of these are cataloged by Aratoon Kebabian (Robert H. Harris), Stavros's ostentatious refusal to listen is simultaneously an assertion of indifference, an accusation of hypocrisy, and an admission that the facts are too shameful to be faced.

What Stavros would most like is to "start this journey over," to make a fresh start on the quest for a fresh start. Unable to annihilate the present and past, he concentrates on future glories to nullify (thus redeem) his life so far. Hence his earlier confusion of identity and intention in "I will, I am, I will, I am, I will." Ironically Kazan makes Garabet (John Marley)—the dismissive audience for Stavros's fantasy of personal redemption—offer the extension of the fantasy into the wider sphere of politics with his "one idea for this world. Destroy it and start over again . . ." Kazan embeds the attraction of the dream of the clean sweep, eradication of the past, in films which insist on unending confrontations with history, personal and national. Garabet's "fire and flood" cannot disrupt the continuity of past and present. Persons and nations can never start from nothing, and nothingness is the only purity.

Purity is associated with the inactive, the negative, and therefore with the ultimate negative of death or the ultimate negation, the death in life of subservience and self-sacrifice. So Kazan's "good" characters are selfless in the full ambiguity of the term. They have to be marginal characters because they exist only in subdued relation to the other, their energies directed with sporadic vehemence toward becoming what others believe or wish them to be. Thus, and most movingly, Thomna's (Linda Marsh) eagerness to play her allotted role in her father's plan involves accommodating herself totally to Stavros's desires: "I want everything to be the way you want it to be. . . . I'm a good girl. . . . I'll do whatever you tell me." Thomna is "good" because she allows herself no opportunity to be anything else, though even she will face—between scenes—the fact that loyalty to Stavros involves a small betrayal of her father. She is "good" because there is nothing she wants for herself. She has no independent hunger and that is only in part, if importantly, a reflection of her material circumstances.

Hohannes the beggar (Gregory Rozakis), the other "good" character, is so much Thomna's opposite as to be virtually the same. Although he has an independent aim (America) he will not trouble the world in its pursuit. Where Stavros learns to demand and take, Hohannes will only ask and accept. The one thing he imposes on the world, and that involuntarily, is the awareness of his imminent death. Ultimately he embraces even that fate in the most self-effacing way: dropping out of life without disturbance and yielding his identity for Stavros's use at the very time when Stavros is most aggressively imposing his presence and energy upon the world through the defiant display of the shipboard dance. In the terms of Kazan's vision, it is no accident that Hohannes is a doomed character from his first appearance. His nobility and humility cannot be dissociated from the compliance that makes him a perfect victim.

The tensions in Kazan's attitude are apparent in a construction which makes Stavros's success depend upon the sacrifices of Thomna and Hohannes, and in a presentation which gives Stavros his greatest dignity and stature at the moment when he betrays his ambition: by warning Thomna not to trust him and by refusing her offer to let him make off with her dowry. But even this dignified refusal is ambiguous, since it arises from the pride which prefers giving and taking, selling (even himself) and stealing, to receiving. Stavros is prepared to scour garbage for food but not to beg. He has learned only too well, from his father, from his Turkish "brother" Abdul, not to be beholden—that gifts bestow uncomfortable obligations on the recipient and that obligation opens the way for imposition.

Since the issue of survival is central to the film, it is finely appropriate that the various shades of offering and receiving, giving and taking, imposing and depriving are activated through a recurrent concern with the acquisition and consumption of food. But the food image has a wider appropriateness in the context of Kazan's abiding preoccupation with the conflict between appetite and obligation. If Kazan makes a commitment here, it is through a style which identifies him with the impatience and hungry energy of his characters' most forceful moments. Ultimately the restless vigor of his shooting and editing may reflect an uneasy preference for compromised action over passive purity, but tension is permanent because his films are "stretched" between aspiration and contrary recognition.

In extreme form, the aspiration is to a complete and guiltless renunciation of the family; it is to be without a past, to achieve full liberation from the home. The source of anguish is given a vivid image at the start when Stavros's mother drives him along the alleys of the village away from danger back to the security—and enclosure—of home, yelling, "You're not a child any more. Why should I have to take you by the ear?" From the parental viewpoint, maturity and responsibility are equated with voluntary submission; adulthood implies the acceptance of values and identities which have to be imposed on children. The parental plan is to reproduce and thus validate themselves in their children; they bring the full force of obligation into play behind resistance to developments which hazard this endorsement-by-duplication. The deviant child is caught between his own need and the imposed identity of which renunciation is seen to imply attack. The explosive cycle of development and obstruction, constantly renewed as rebel sons become anxious fathers and underdogs emerge as overlords, ensures that identity is achieved, if at all, with maximum pain and struggle.

There is no guiltless outlet for energy except in a vehement conformism. That allows an untroubled immersion in the communal shame of the herd. Otherwise, vitality and "conscience" are in permanent conflict because energy is always, like the wild river, destructive. Kazan is with Ella Garth (Jo Van Fleet) against dams but he is also appalled (if fascinated) by the operations of that power which must constantly affirm itself by seeking and crushing new opposition. The counterparts of active power and challenge are passivity on the one hand, but on the other a stubborn persistence impressively unshaken by circumstance, humanity, or reason.

Just such a reserve of contained energy allows Stavros to evade a succession of imposed identities other than the one—American—which he recognizes. The issues of identity and destructive energy unite in the finely conceived scene between Stavros and his grandmother (Estelle Hemsley). She sees him initially as a good (harmless) Greek like his father, warms toward him after he has demonstrated violent determination and authority, but, despising his inability to attack and rob her, concludes that he has insufficient force to impose himself and his desires upon the world; he is not "bad" enough. She sends him back home with a disappointed "Be what you are."

In this injunction she ignores reserves, potential, and development, seeing identity as a fixed quality—a mistake which costs Abdul his life. (Kazan believes in changes of character—unlike Fuller, Ray, Walsh, Welles, and others with whom he shares the concern with energy—but does not suggest that the changes can be controlled from within.) Identities, simple categories which "cover" the whole of a complex humanness, are continually imposed in Kazan's movies as characters claim knowledge of circumstances and insight into motives which are essentially private. Most often the imposition is an attempt by one character to absorb another into his scheme of life without disruption, by assigning an identity which fits the other comfortably into his own plan. All Kazan's active characters have schemes and determinations (or "arrangements") which can be realized and maintained only with the collaboration, connivance, or submission of others. The collision of incompatible schemes is a focal point of Kazanian drama.

Aleko (Paul Mann), father of Thomna, has a scheme—a typically paternal scheme in that it depends on the perpetuation of the status quo. It is built on contentment, on waiting and watching as the years pass without alteration in the mode of life; and it presupposes a happy acceptance of the existing hierarchy by all who enter it. So it is radically opposed to Stavros's impatient vision. The scene in which Aleko presents his scheme, hoping to win Stavros's unreserved acceptance, is probably the finest in the film. The balance of sympathies is beautifully adjusted, the tension finely held as Aleko, almost in reverie, but calculating too, outlines a gentle plan of life which encompasses even Stavros's death: "And when we die, we will die properly—surrounded by women looking after us." In film terms, it is a very long speech but it never suggests soliloquy. The ensemble is so precisely dramatized and graded that, while no weight is subtracted from Aleko's words, the scene is at no time reduced to a talking head. Particularly fine is the nervous grace of Thomna's movement between the two men, the eager but tentative submission of her father's plan to Stavros implicit in her gestures as she sits on the arm of Stavros's chair, between the two men, puts her hand on his shoulder, and looks across to Aleko. As Stavros is drawn into Aleko's vision, he reaches up to hold Thomna's hand, now *around* his shoulders; a full acceptance of Thomna is necessarily a commitment to her father's scheme. The temptation is seductively rendered so as to give full weight to the guilt and resolve in Stavros's troubled affirmation that Aleko's vision offers "all a man should *want*."

Gratitude would outweigh accuracy, however, if one suggested that the entire film was on this level, although much of it is little short. In this picture, as in *The Arrangement* (1969), Kazan faces but does not entirely solve the problem of the director-writer, the temptation to produce the "perfect" script which leaves too little to be done with the film. For example, the scene with the grandmother remains as I've described it, a fine conception; but its realization is rather weak. The weakness is not so much a matter of inadequacies of acting and postsynchronization, disturbing as these are, but in a treatment which gives the ideas controlling each movement precedence over the movement itself—the actions have a rather bare independent life.

America America [the novel by Kazan] is a poor novel crying out to become a great movie. *America America* is too respectful of its source material. The writer's leisurely complexity of connection between episodes may create too little room for the director's density of relationship within them. The episodic construction, which carries Stavros through a series of encounters with one character at a time, is at times monotonously linear, and it is a great weakness in the script (as Kazan material) that Stavros escapes the physical presence of his father at such an early stage. As a result, the direction is sometimes underloaded, no doubt to the satisfaction of those mildness lovers who choke on the richness of *Eden* or *Splendor*. Yet if *America America* is flawed, even disappointing, in its too frequent sobriety, it remains, as I said at the start—indispensable.

Filmography

America America (UK title: *The Anatolian Smile*). Directed by Elia Kazan. Warner Bros., 1963.
The Arrangement. Directed by Elia Kazan. Warner Bros.-Seven Arts., 1969.
East of Eden. Directed by Elia Kazan. Warner Bros., 1955.
Splendor in the Grass. Directed by Elia Kazan. Warner Bros., 1961.
Wild River. Directed by Elia Kazan. Twentieth Century Fox, 1960.

Note

1   *The Anatolian Smile* was an alternative title used in the United Kingdom. Ed.

PART 2
1981–2016

FILM CRITICISM

Principles and Practice

MOMENTS OF CHOICE

First published in The Movie, *no. 58 (1981): 1141–45.*

Orson Welles filmed the sleigh-ride scene for *The Magnificent Ambersons* (1942) neither in a studio nor on location. He insisted on building his set inside the largest available refrigeration plant. The landscape he required could have been simulated at RKO just as convincingly and much more cheaply. What could justify such costly self-indulgence? What gain could it possibly bring to the film? Were Welles's actors so incompetent that they needed to be frozen stiff before they could bring conviction to a winter scene?

There is an answer, and it is visible on the screen. In subzero conditions, unlike those on a hot soundstage, the breath of players (and ponies) freezes in the air to a visible vapor. That is an important effect, since it goes with the soft white landscape to make the scene felt as one of natural purity. The sharp freshness of its air, made present this way, provides an all-the-more-telling site for the appearance of the horseless carriage. Here, in a scene whose nervous jollity is only touched with foreboding, it is a joke that the vehicle sullies the countryside with racket and filth. But there is nothing frivolous about the contrast between the heavy black fumes of the machine and the silvery human breaths that vanish on the air. It states the vulnerability of the complacent small-town aristocracy to the impact of a new technology.

The very breath of an actor can be made significant when the director places it in an expressive relationship with the other aspects of the scene. It can contribute to the effectiveness of the moment—building the sense of a threatened and fleeting purity—and it can establish a visual theme: the Amberson lifestyle is progressively submerged in an industrial wilderness of smoke, metal, speed, and mechanical din. Though the choices are seldom as costly (and only sometimes as rewarding) as Welles's here, directing a film is always about making choices of this kind—hundreds of them every day and at every stage in the translation from script to screen. Many of the choices are matters of craft. The director works to make the scenes vivid and varied, so as to achieve an arresting presentation of the characters and their story. Flaws in the casting may have to be disguised. Dull spots in the writing and sagging passages in the construction of the screenplay may need to be enlivened. Cunning may be required to stretch limited resources: in *Letter from an Unknown Woman* (1948), Max Ophuls had to construct the living world of late nineteenth-century Linz on the back-lot set that Universal had been keeping going as an all-purpose Mitteleuropa exterior since *All Quiet on the Western Front* (Lewis Milestone, 1930).

The most promising script, judiciously cast, will still fall flat if the director is unable to get all the elements of the production working together—either in harmony or in lively contrast—so that the end result flows when it is played to an audience. If it does not work on the screen, we are likely to think that there was not much of a story or that the performances were lacking. But often the fault lies in the director's inability to find a style that brings the material convincingly to life. Just as often, it is the director who should take the credit for our belief that we have seen a credible and forceful story with colorful and engaging characterization. In terms of the package and its ingredients, there is not much that separates *The Reckless Moment* (1949), *Johnny Guitar* (1954), or *Written on the Wind* (1956) from dozens of mediocre products of the Hollywood machine. The crucial factor is the direction of Max Ophuls, Nicholas Ray, and Douglas Sirk.

Old Hollywood was well aware how much its product stood to gain, as entertainment, from a style that rendered its drama effectively and made it look, move, and sound as if it had a *sense of direction*. It expected directors to be capable production managers and to complete their work on time, on budget, and without major damage to studio morale. But it also valued and rewarded the ability to control performance, image, and editing so as to create moods and viewpoints through which the story could persuade and grip the audience. Very seldom would a director's career suffer from a noisy insistence on getting a particular fabric for the set, a particular lens for the camera, or a particular casting for an apparently insignificant role. Directors were paid to believe that every little thing mattered—and to prove it by their results.

One minor instance is the choice of props. At the start of Nicholas Ray's *Party Girl* (1958), chorus-girl prostitutes are paid for their services at boss Rico Angelo's party with a gift of powder compacts. The glittering compacts are discarded as soon as they have been emptied of the hundred-dollar bills inside. Later Rico (Lee J. Cobb) settles accounts, at a presentation dinner for his "ambitious" underling, Frankie Gasto (Aaron Saxton), by beating him about the head with a gold-plated miniature pool cue inscribed "From Rico to Frankie." At the film's climax, Rico's threat to disfigure the heroine is teasingly developed as he unpicks the tinsel and tissue wrapping from a bottle of acid. Throughout the picture, then, elaborate gift-wrapping serves as a cover for payments, bribes, assaults, and threats. Ray presents an image of gangland Chicago as a world of disguise whose characters are constantly hiding the true nature of their transactions from themselves as well as from others. The props are one means through which he was able to remodel a fairly routine gangster assignment into a film about pretexts.

If objects may be dressed, performers nearly always are. Dress offers the characters' conscious or unconscious self-presentation and may define social role or financial circumstance. A fur coat provides Max Ophuls with an image for the rewards and limitations of the role of bourgeois housewife in *The Reckless Moment*. Although the coat is "her own," Mrs. Harper (Joan Bennett) cannot dispose of it at a point when she is in desperate need of cash. It is too much part of her uniform, her identity, as the wife of a successful architect. A vital moment is conveyed when she manages to persuade her hitherto rebellious daughter to borrow it: she has at last cast her offspring into the "womanly" role of decorative servitude. The daughter can now be sent out into the world—or to the movies with the "boy next door"—as a replica of her dutiful mother.

The same director in *Caught* (1949) uses three different coats to depict the options open to his indecisive heroine: the extravagant mink of a Long

Island hostess; a plastic mac for the poor-but-honest nurse; and a "sensible" cloth coat, warm and becoming but not showy, for the unassumingly loyal doctor's wife. The use of dress here goes beyond working as a simple but effective visual presentation of changing circumstances. It helps also to define an attitude to those changes. What is important is that none of the garments represents the heroine's "natural" character. Each of them gives her a role which she will try, or be forced, to live in.

Dress is a vital element in deciding how the film will look. But it is only one element, and its design needs to be related to the visual context determined by the choice of locations and the construction of sets. In *Some Came Running* (1958), the textures and colors of the decor stake out three different worlds in which the hero moves. In the downtown section, the director Vincente Minnelli said, he wanted the audience to feel that it was living inside a jukebox. The design yields a raucous contest between harsh metallic colors.

A justly famous scene in *La Règle du jeu* (*The Rules of the Game*, 1939) gains much of its effect from Renoir's use of decor. At the start of a country-house party, the aristocratic hostess, Christine (Nora Gregor), is obliged to confront the gossip surrounding her relationship with a young aviator, André Jurieu (Roland Toutain). She does this by introducing him to her other guests as a group, with a speech in praise of pure friendship. The scene is set in the château's entrance hall, and the decor is a perfectly credible arrangement of doors, pillars, and open space. But Renoir's disposition of his actors and camera turns the space into a theatrical arena as Christine takes André "center stage" to present him to the others, grouped at a little distance to constitute the audience, while her husband and his friend look on anxiously and at last proudly from "the wings." The sense of Christine's performance as one governed by strict rules, where a wrong move threatens disaster, emerges from another visual parallel that the decor permits: the camera sees the floor, with Christine and André moving across its black-and-white marble tiles, as a chessboard. The power of the scene largely derives from the tension between Christine's nervously awkward sincerity and the demand implied by the theater/chess game image for the precise execution of a delicate maneuver (fig. 8).

Figure 8. The entrance hall as chessboard

Physical aspects of production like decor and dress can help the actors to feel themselves into their roles. But the detail of performance that brings the characters to life—movement, gesture, intonation, rhythm—has to be established on the set. Here the director's job is, particularly, to hold each and every moment of performance within a vision of the scene as a whole so that the impact and effectiveness of *today's* scene is not achieved at the expense of what was filmed last week or what remains to be shot. The continuity of the end product is, most often, an impression that has to be constructed and protected in spite of the radically discontinuous method of shooting. (The first day's work may be on scenes from the final pages of the script, and the leading man may be speaking his lines to an off-screen heroine who is due to join the production in a fortnight's time.) The pacing of a scene may seem just right in itself, but how will it look when the audience reaches it halfway through the film? Directors work in the knowledge that nothing is right "in itself" but only in relation to the developing design. Balance and proportion are crucial.

The task here begins with the casting. The famous Hollywood "chemistry" was usually publicized as an aspect of star teams like Hepburn and Tracy; but it applies to all casting, right down to the smallest roles. When the young fugitives get married in Nicholas Ray's *They Live by Night* (1948), the scene exploits, in systematic parody, all the elements of the conventional presentation of a white wedding. The casting of Hawkins, the local justice, whose business is marriage, is clearly crucial. Greed (extortionate greed leaning toward but never quite toppling over into criminality) is what the character must mainly evoke. Conventional casting would therefore suggest a fat man whose figure could represent an unrelentingly capacious appetite. By giving the role against type to scrawny, piping-voiced Ian Wolfe—a starved sparrow rather than a satiated vulture—Ray shades the notion of greed away from indulgent avarice and makes it an anxious habit born of insecurity.

The casting of the star parts is a matter on which the director might or might not be consulted. For instance, Max Ophuls did not first agree to direct *Letter from an Unknown Woman* and then decide that the heroine's role should be offered to Joan Fontaine. He had to decide whether he wanted to make the film, given that Fontaine was to play the lead. In case of conflict, the producer carries more weight over casting decisions than the director: Ray had to accept Germany's top star, Curd Jürgens, as a British officer in his World War II film, *Bitter Victory* (1957). More often than not, the director's notion of ideal casting for leading parts will be compromised by the constraints of schedule and budget.

Once on the set, however, directors have all the freedom that their imagination, tact, and persuasiveness can provide. Large statements can be made with small gestures. In the opening scene of *Caught*, the car-hop heroine is apparently sharing a harmless dream with her roommate when she fantasizes a chance meeting with a handsome young millionaire. But what is calculating and predatory in this innocence is conveyed by her punctuating her words by making idle passes with a flyswatter while lying open-legged on the bed. What is blind in her calculation, too, emerges from her complete inattention to her own gestures and their evident meanings.

Suppose that you were planning the first few minutes of a film whose central issue is to be the uncertainty of emotion, a story of passion dogged by mistrust in which only the strength of feeling (not its nature) remains constant. You want to establish that neither hero nor heroine is sure whether the man's embrace is protective and loving or threatening, murderous.

That was Ray's problem at the start of *In a Lonely Place* (1950). His answer was to give the same gesture to three different characters within the brief space of the scene that establishes the film's Hollywood setting: each of them approaches another character from behind and grasps his shoulders with both hands. The first time, it is a perfunctory and patronizing greeting whose pretense of warmth is a bare cover for the assertion of superiority. Then, between the hero and an old friend, it conveys intimacy and genuine regard. Finally, when a large-mouthed producer uses the shoulders of the hero himself as a rostrum from which to publicize his latest triumph, it is seen as oppressive and openly slighting. These moments are significant in their own right, but their deeper purpose is—in a perfectly ordinary context—to dramatize the ambiguity of gesture itself.

The work of film direction, as it has so far been considered, is not fundamentally different from that of directing for the stage. But in movies everything is designed to be filtered through the eye of the camera and remade in the patterns created on the cutting bench. Just how far a characterization may result from the director's control over the camera—even when the role is as well cast and expertly played as Judith Anderson's menacing housekeeper, Mrs. Danvers, in *Rebecca* (1940)—is nicely indicated by Hitchcock's description of his design.

He said that the figure of Mrs. Danvers "was rarely shown in motion. If she entered a room in which the heroine was, what happened is that the girl suddenly heard a sound and there was the ever-present Mrs. Danvers, standing perfectly still by her side. To have shown Mrs. Danvers walking about would have been to humanize her."

The camera's frame and the editor's scissors provide the means whereby the director carves a particular path through the world constructed on the set. Thus at the start of Ray's rodeo picture, *The Lusty Men* (1952), we are shown a selection of the displays in the opening-day parade through the center of a modern Texan town. The camera's viewpoint constantly encompasses the solid fronts of banks, shops, and offices as the permanent background of the passing show. Then, in ordering the succession of images, Ray moves systematically back through time, taking us from tractors and decorated lorries, through covered wagons and mule trains, to a band of fancy-dress Indians war-dancing along the city streets. When we get to the rodeo itself, the film has set it up as a show that attempts to extend the life of images from the past in a drastically transformed present.

Selection and sequence are the keys to viewpoint that the director controls. It is a strategic decision, for instance, never to identify members of the rodeo's audience as individuals but always to view the spectators distantly as an anonymous mass. The place that might be occupied by shots of audience reaction is taken by images of the professionals in the commentary box, and of the harshly impersonal metallic cones of the arena's loudspeaker system. The audience becomes one large component of a machine whose appetite is spectacle and danger and which runs without regard for the particular human material it devours.

Cutting and camera movement are both means through which direction shifts and manipulates viewpoint. Yet their effects, the kinds of statements they make, are very different. To cut from one object to another is to assert continuity across a chopped-up time and space. Hitchcock does this spectacularly in *Strangers on a Train* (1951). His montage makes a single sequence out of contrasted events in two towns and on different time scales: the hero's battle in a tennis tournament is intercut with the villain's struggle to regain possession of an incriminating cigarette lighter.

To shift the frame via camera movement, on the other hand, is to impose an order of perception on objects which exist in a continuous time and space so that they could, in principle, be seen all at once. In *The Lusty Men*, Ray introduces his rodeo-star hero in a shot which starts with the camera looking in through the gate of a bullpen. The animal charges along its track to halt at the gate with its eyes glinting in fierce close-up. At this the image tilts upward to frame Mitchum above the animal, preparing to mount (fig. 9). A direct contrast is drawn between two kinds of strength—the power of a natural force, and the force of human determination. But the camera's movement

Figure 9. Mitchum above the bull

links these two images in comparison as well as contrast. For all his apparent mastery, as we look up to him outlined against the sky, Robert Mitchum is like the bull in being contained within the structures of the rodeo: his image, too, is framed, hemmed in, by the wooden posts of the bullpen.

The movement and angle of the shot give a precisely calculated degree of overstatement to the assertion of mastery. Within fifteen seconds Mitchum will be floundering, injured, in the dirt of the arena. His previous inward smile of self-satisfaction at the commentator's tribute to his prowess, his pose of confident virility as he tightens his belt on the words "one of the all-time rodeo greats," are opened up to irony by the camera's too hearty endorsement of his supremacy.

Ironic overstatement like this is a possibility for the director because the expansiveness of a film style is so much a matter of balance, of what happens when you put together, in a particular way, a posture, a facial expression, an off-screen voice, and a camera viewpoint. At the very center of the director's job is this task of coordination. Direction works with the various talents of highly skilled artists to ensure their contributions meet in a coherent design. The photographer may devise ingenious ways of lighting a confined space so as to give it a sense of room and air. The ingenuity will yield little if the designer has been working to develop an image of claustrophobia.

In postwar Hollywood, directors often enjoyed considerable freedom *within* their assignments—much more than their freedom to choose and develop subjects or to initiate production. So long as they were thought to be making the best possible job of the given package of story, stars, and resources, they were likely to meet with little resistance to their ideas about how a film should look, sound, and move.

But even this freedom has strict limits. Those were still the days of the classic approach, which valued formal design only so long as it supported the spectator's involvement, understanding, pleasure, and belief in the narrative. Moreover, quite strict notions of what was appropriate were in play. A brasher, gaudier array of color was thought more suitable for musicals than for, say, light comedy. Melodrama, which aimed to carry its audience over the top, with heightened situations and excessive passions, offered a corresponding license to explore the possibilities of a flamboyant visual rhetoric.

Many directors seem to have lived quite happily within these prescriptions, being ready to exert their skills within a range of genres to achieve effective versions of the accepted manner. The limitation of such adaptable know-how was that it would seldom carry a film beyond the qualities of the package originally handed down by the studio. A movie directed by, say, Michael Curtiz would be neither more nor less than the sum of its carefully blended ingredients. Sometimes that was enough. It is no mean praise to say that *Casablanca* (1942) was as good as its script and cast.

But it is probably fair to claim that Curtiz's best films achieve a dramatically effective *manner*, rather than a style. The various elements of the film are harnessed only to a reliable judgment of what will make the story work. More is possible. The films of Ophuls, Ray, and Sirk, among others, are there to demonstrate how, with no sacrifice of movie-craft, the director can bind the movie together in a design that offers a more personal and detailed conception of the story's significance, embodying an experience of the world and a viewpoint both considered and felt. At this point, manner becomes style.

Filmography

All Quiet on the Western Front. Directed by Lewis Milestone. Universal Pictures, 1930.
Bitter Victory. Directed by Nicholas Ray. Columbia Pictures, 1957.
Casablanca. Directed by Michael Curtiz. Warner Bros., 1942.
Caught. Directed by Max Ophuls. MGM, 1949.
In a Lonely Place. Directed by Nicholas Ray. Columbia Pictures, 1950.
Johnny Guitar. Directed by Nicholas Ray. Republic Pictures, 1954.
Letter from an Unknown Woman. Directed by Max Ophuls. Universal-International, 1948.
The Lusty Men. Directed by Nicholas Ray. RKO Radio Pictures, 1952.
The Magnificent Ambersons. Directed by Orson Welles. RKO Radio Pictures, 1942.
Party Girl. Directed by Nicholas Ray. MGM, 1958.
Rebecca. Directed by Alfred Hitchcock. United Artists, 1940.
The Reckless Moment. Directed by Max Ophuls. Columbia Pictures, 1949.
La Règle du jeu (The Rules of the Game). Directed by Jean Renoir. Gaumont, 1939.
Some Came Running. Directed by Vincente Minnelli. MGM, 1958.
Strangers on a Train. Directed by Alfred Hitchcock. Warner Bros., 1951.
They Live by Night. Directed by Nicholas Ray. RKO Radio Pictures, 1948.
Written on the Wind. Directed by Douglas Sirk. Universal Pictures, 1956.

FILM AUTHORSHIP
The Premature Burial

First published in CineAction!, *nos. 20–21 (Summer/Fall 1990): 57–64.*

In spite of the wide range of meanings of "author" within and beyond film theories it is often assumed that we know pretty well what constitutes an authorship approach to critical practice and that its products in criticism are easy to spot. You might say that it has its promotional counterpart in "Alfred Hitchcock's *Psycho*" and that some of its discomforts are registered by "Neil Simon's *The Heartbreak Kid*: An Elaine May Film."

It would be less easy to state the propositions implicit in various authorship approaches. Possibly they would rest on a common understanding that the director's work is a determining factor for the qualities and meanings of most, or most of the good, films. That is a basis of much of my own work. Still, I do not call myself an auteurist and I can be tetchy when others do. I think it is necessary to observe a distinction between auteurism and other practices of director-centered criticism. Auteurism and auteur theories declare their descent from the great polemic initiative of Andrew Sarris and his transformation of the "*politique des auteurs*" from *Cahiers du Cinéma*. To my mind auteurisms are defined by a common feature, which is also a crucial error: their exaggerated concern with the continuities and coherence across the body of a director's work. This feature is assumed in, and thereby distorts, most attempts at theoretical discussion of the director's role and its consequences for criticism. The emphasis on repetition (the "author-code" traced from film to film) is what marks off versions of auteurism and auteur theory from other views of cinema which acknowledge and celebrate the central creative role of the director. Auteurism does not just observe or welcome continuity from film to film; it insists on continuity.

It is understandable that auteurism was born into this error. It emerged from a desire to confront and overturn an accepted view of (particularly) Hollywood movies as machine-made in style and either empty or baleful in content. In its Anglo-American versions it had to challenge assertions like the following: that the name of Vincente Minnelli could usefully serve to evoke the second-rate studio product—the film about which it would be silly to be thoughtful; that it would be frivolously eccentric to offer *Vertigo* (Hitchcock, 1958) as one of the great achievements of its year, and that a film's content could be cleanly equated with its plot-subject.[1]

That was the context into which claims for the quality and individuality of, say, *Psycho* (Hitchcock, 1960) and *Written on the Wind* (Douglas Sirk, 1956) had to be entered, and it is just possible that without the momentary plausibility of auteur theory the critical victories over "taking Hollywood seriously" would not have been won. There were some powerful blocks to be removed. One of them was formed by the combination of the notion that "art . . . can only be the expression of the experience and vision of a single man, the creative artist" (Lindgren 1963, 192) with an entrenched and preferred view of the director's role in Hollywood that bore little relation to actuality. That view generalized the conditions of work of the director of a Monogram serial; it ignored the great differences in production circumstance from film to film; it yielded the image of a director who functioned only during the period of principal photography and was thus excluded from the screenplay, casting, and major design as well as from scoring, cutting, and sound editing at the end. An assumed knowledge of the production acted as the guarantee of the "critical" perception of Hollywood's inferiority.

Perhaps more crucially, there was no established or developed practice of what we now understand as textual analysis in film. An appreciative interest in the detail of the realization of a film by Hitchcock or Sirk was incomprehensible; it could be received only as a dilettantiste preference for decorative form over substantial content, and dismissed as a conception of film art that involved "shoving bits of style up the crevasses of the plots" (Kael 1971, 148).

Evidence in support of the theory that authorship was possible under Hollywood conditions of production had to be offered to a readership unlikely to be convinced by argument from style—constructed, too, by critics underequipped with models or resources for stylistic discussion. Instead a demonstration of authorship that did not depend upon the detailed articulation of form was derived from the continuities of theme and viewpoint across the body of a director's work. This evidence was all the more useful for being nearly statistical. It indicated the director's name as the variable associated with differences in theme and motif between otherwise similarly constituted movies; it could be pursued to reveal those same themes and motifs as characteristic of that director in films that embraced a range of genres, collaborations, and production circumstances.

Identified in these ways the film director could become the *auteur*, in a coinage devised by Andrew Sarris both to acknowledge the French sources of the argument and to distinguish the film author from the authors of literary works and screenplays. The auteur was successfully entered in evidence against the belief in a Hollywood where the director was a mere functionary more or less effectively processing material imposed by the studios, producers, writers, and stars.

So far so good, but on the verge of a breakdown. When the "auteur" was produced on the basis of recurrence, an observation about authors—that their works often display striking continuities and coherent development—was transformed into a test of authorship, a qualification for author status. The material invoked as a demonstration of authorship sidled into use as a definition of authorship. Thus Sarris offered as the "second premise of the *auteur* theory . . . the distinguishable personality of the director as a criterion of value" (1971, 136).

Almost thirty years later it is not difficult to refine Sarris's formulation so as to hold on to what's important in this insight, as in "the achievement of eloquence and coherent viewpoint through direction is a major source of value."[2] But Sarris continued: "Over a group of films, a director must exhibit certain recurring characteristics of style which serve as his signature." This, which offers itself merely as an expansion of the first claim, shifts the focus from the single film—which might be valued for the "personality" of its direction—to the group; and it carries the notion of value in its slide, making "recurring characteristics of style" a quasi-aesthetic requirement.

This slippage recurred often in Sarris's auteurism, as here in his later essay, "Toward a Theory of Film History": "The auteur critic is obsessed with the wholeness of art and the artist. He looks at a film as a whole, a director as a whole. The parts, however entertaining individually, must cohere meaningfully" (1968, 30). Here the requirement for coherence between the parts of a film is extended to become the more dubious demand for coherence between the various films that make up a director's career, as if the two modes of coherence were, if not identical, closely related. The centrality given to propositions of this kind separated auteurism from other modes of understanding of the possibilities of authorship in film. In advancing his "pattern theory" (34) Sarris knew, of course, that, while the critic may use the director's repetitions to prove or identify authorship, repetition cannot be what the director uses to achieve authorship.

But then Sarris knew a great deal that he could accommodate only on the margins of his theoretical statements. He knew, for instance, that his concept of the auteur depended on aesthetic assumptions and critical values that he had not been able to integrate, and that authorship cannot be offered as a "criterion of value" if it is no more than a perception of resemblance between films. He shows this in the way that he offers his patterns and recurrences now in terms of themes and motifs, now in terms of quality: "'That was a good movie,' the critic observes. 'Who directed it?' When the same answer is given over and over again, a pattern of performance emerges" (35).

At issue here is the manner in which auteurism relates two distinct sets of propositions and observations. The first set concerns ways in which the director's work may be crucial for the achievement within the single film of values like economy, unity, eloquence, subtlety, depth, and vigor. This is the point at which auteurism has things to say about the connection between the good film and good direction. The second set of perceptions and arguments is about recurrent themes in a director's films considered as a series. This is the point at which auteurism has things to say about good direction and the director's involvement with themes, viewpoints, and methods of sufficient personal significance to carry over from film to film.

Sarris's auteurism was preferable to its successors because it acknowledged and tried to incorporate the issue of quality. In later formulations that issue was repressed. At the same time the insistence on repetition grew so that what had been given an exaggerated role within Sarris's theory was offered as the theory itself.

When Peter Wollen attempted to accommodate auteurism to structuralism in his 1969 *Signs and Meaning in the Cinema* (1972, 104) repeating patterns were all; anything else was "irrelevant . . . non pertinent . . . secondary, contingent, to be discarded," since beyond the identification of recurrent structure nothing was accessible to criticism: "We can merely record our momentary and subjective impressions" (105). Wollen offered one of the most emphatic but weird statements of the auteurist claim that you cannot understand one of a director's films until you've seen them all: "It is only the analysis of the whole corpus which permits the moment of synthesis when the critic returns to the individual film" (104).

A problem with this view is that it makes the production of its desired object impossible. If perceptions within the single film have no critical value, it is not sensible to aggregate them across films, so you cannot get started. You need some ground for the claim that a feature is pertinent in one film before it becomes interesting that it is repeated, and before it becomes observable that it is varied, in another. Wollen's method accepted as critical data only such "oppositions" as those between wilderness and garden, nomad and settler, book and gun. While they can be used with extraordinary richness, these are commonplaces of our culture, and their use, far from being specific to a director or a genre, is by no means specific even to the movies. The mere presence of these "oppositions" in a film does not declare their pertinence, and no more does the trick of binarism or the posture of dialectic which favors "oppositions" over tensions, conflicts, or contrasts.

Any aspect of image and sound, and any feature of the world that can be presented audiovisually, is available for expressive use. Thus walking and riding can be conceived as oppositions, and their difference is available for shaped presentations at various levels of prominence. It might be the barest indicator of a difference in energy, wealth or status. But in *The Magnificent Ambersons* (Orson Welles, 1942), walking and riding (as well as different kinds of riding, in carriage/sleigh and automobile) are systematically in play from the start, in car-borne Eugene's (Joseph Cotten) unsuccessful wooing of Isabel (Dolores Costello), out walking with Wilbur (Don Dillaway) and the dog. Later the two great long-take sequences that track Lucy's (Anne Baxter) journeys with George (Tim Holt) down Main Street draw on the difference for contrast and emotional color: as a pedestrian in the second Lucy has an independence from George not available to her as his passenger, in the first (figs. 10 and 11).

Then again, in *Letter from an Unknown Woman* (Max Ophuls, 1948) there is a pronounced though not absolute patterning of Lisa's (Joan Fontaine) walking alone against her riding in a carriage with a man, a patterning that is strongly relevant to the issue of her freedom. But if it were not relevant to some issue in the film it would hardly count as either an opposition or a

Figure 10.

Figure 11. Lucy with George: from passenger to pedestrian

pattern. It would simply be unstartling data on occurrences of locomotion in old Vienna.

Welles's and Ophuls's use of walking/riding as a motif can be observed in these films without reference to any question of recurrence. The relevance of recurrence will be something to be pondered in relation to views of *Liebelei* (Ophuls, 1933), say, or *The Reckless Moment* (Ophuls, 1949). How far it is significant will depend not on the number but on the character and centrality of its uses. You could say that the opening of *Touch of Evil* (Welles, 1958) was founded on the opposition of walking (Mike and Susie Vargas [Charlton Heston and Janet Leigh]) and riding (Linneker, the woman, the bomb, perhaps the camera). Formally the contrast is important for its contribution to the shifting rhythms of the shot. But is it a founding motif, or, rather, a local device for the exposition of other more significant themes—like the interweaving of the random and the determined? If we can derive any help from a comparison with *The Magnificent Ambersons* we should take it, but the question will need to be pursued as one about *Touch of Evil*. Without a (provisional, as always) resolution there, the issue is not available for setting into an overview of Welles's work.

Wollen seemed to claim that discussing a pattern found across a number of films was more secure than discussing a pattern found within one. The necessity for this claim arises from three aspects of his "structuralist" auteurism: its confusion over value, its picture of intention, and its rejection of collaboration.

Authorship and Excellence

Wollen's account offered no explanation of the coincidence by which the *auteurs* he mainly discussed appeared in his "pantheon" of directors, among the ten best in the American cinema. But it is clear that he wanted to erect a peculiar separation between questions of value and questions about authorship. Thus John Ford is "a great artist, beyond being simply an undoubted *auteur*" (102) and "there is no doubt that the greatest films will be not simply auteur films but marvelous expressively and stylistically as well" (113). I take it that they had to be "marvelous as well" because auteur status was entirely a matter of repetition, and thus not eligible as a component of greatness. In Wollen's context the "auteur film" had to mean something like "an instance of the repeating pattern identifying the auteur." Offering that as a necessary condition of greatness showed the same kind of confusion as the uncertain location of the "richness" valued in John Ford's work (102): in the individual film or in the relations between the films comprising his body of work.

I hope it is clear that the problem was not that questions of value were allowed an incoherent presence but that a doomed and distorting attempt was made to exclude them from the argument. The term "author," when used of a film director, is almost inevitably a term of acclaim; it is an honorific title—like "artist"—at least as much as it is description. To speak of the film author, then, and to deny evaluation will most often be to invite confusion. Similarly, it is likely that a coherent presentation of authorship would need to state how authorship is recognized (as achievement) in the single film before going on to show how it may be observed (as recurrence and development) in bodies of work.

The authorship discussion sets a context in which to ask what characterizes a director is to ask what is characteristic of his best work. What a director does well is at least as important as what he does often. That is a matter of skill, certainly, but one that goes beyond skill to embrace such values as eloquence, subtlety, vividness, and intensity. Adequately to describe a director's authorship involves an exposition of these and other qualities. A characterization of Hitchcock could not sensibly ignore his brilliance with scenes and moments centered on attempted concealment and threatened exposure, including a dazzling stream of variations on the theme, fear of giving oneself away. Another feature, one which well illustrates the possibility of a fusion (form and content), is his skill in opening up gaps between the surface meaning of an image and the other meanings offered the spectator through the structure of understandings that the film has built. Often this takes the form of a contradiction between what characters say, and what we understand by their saying it—but the saying need not be in words.

One of many such moments in *Notorious* (1946) comes just after counter-spy Alicia (Ingrid Bergman) has stolen the key to the forbidden wine cellar from the key ring belonging to her Nazi husband, Alex (Claude Rains). This is on the night of the party at which Alex means to introduce his bride to Rio society and Alicia means to introduce her morbidly guarded lover and Secret Service contact Devlin (Cary Grant) to the wine cellar. Alex emerges from the bathroom as his wife moves away from the dressing table with key in hand. He asks her for forgiveness for his expressions of jealousy over Devlin and takes her hand to plant in its palm a formal kiss—a courteous mask on the passion that we know he feels, and, as a mask, a measure of his uncertainty. (He can never quite believe his luck in having Alicia fall for him. Poor Alex.) This gives way to Alicia's gesture of passion as she throws her arms around him in a longing embrace—and thus forestalls his discovery of the purloined key in her other hand. Alex's formality denies passion, Alicia's impulsiveness denies calculation; but we are shown (and shown that we are shown) the formality, the passion, the convincing enactment of impulse, and the calculation.

As a structure of concealments by the characters and revelations by the film this scene is representative Hitchcock—that is, representative of pleasures and insights regularly offered by Hitchcock's best work.[3] The particular brilliance of the scene is its discovery of the means to embody its themes in a concentrated, clear, and forceful image. We see Alicia pretend passion as a cover for her deception of Alex. The assertion of commitment and the act of betrayal are fused into one vivid moment. But more than that, the moment in part "explains" the absent Devlin, because the image that Alicia presents to us here is the image of Devlin's panic. This is the "honeymoon scene," the scene from the honeymoon that we didn't see, where Alicia proved her aptitude for duplicity in love. A man who allowed himself to love such a woman might know only that her desire was plausible, never that it was real. (And Devlin is a man to whom such a doubt is, shall we say, paralyzing. It robs him, for instance, of the power of speech.)

A theme or conflict arrestingly presented in a moment of film, like this, cues us to notice its reemergence and development elsewhere. The material becomes a motif through the quality of the presentation. We would not observe as a recurrent opposition some contrast that appeared as inert data on no matter how many occasions. All directors—it might be in the nature of the medium—are dealing all the time with oppositions between stillness and movement. It is not possible for these features of the image to be dramatically irrelevant. But in Ophuls's work movement is so constantly manifest or implied that instances of stillness—often as paralysis, sometimes as hesitation—can be extraordinarily charged. Think of the meeting in the snow in *Letter from an Unknown Woman* and the suspended moments when the camera moves in, with Stefan, approaching a Lisa immobilized by joy and longing. Think of the urgency, in *Lola Montès* (1955), of "Don't move!" as various men attempt what is finally achieved, the halting of Lola's restless explorations. Or think of Ford and the end of *My Darling Clementine* (1946) where movement (Earp's [Henry Fonda]) and the fixity (Clementine's [Cathy Downs]) give the sense of a parting—rather than recording the bald fact of it—by showing the one who leaves from a viewpoint matched to that of the one who remains: this image is of Earp going and of Clementine being left behind, rather than of Clementine staying. A view of Ford's authorship focused on a tension between settlement and wandering derives from the force of this imagery, and the similar force of departures, separations, and homecomings in other Ford movies. Most films include a fair amount of coming and going. Plenty of directors supply "photographs of people leaving." The eloquence which constitutes the going and staying as a motif is a product not of repetition but of mastery. (One might guess that the mastery has its source in emotional commitment but those whom the thought upsets are at liberty to ignore it.)

To identify an opposition as a motif is to offer a judgment that the film gives it weight and significance. One part of this involves the recognition of a rhetoric; but since—Alicia's lesson—any set of gestures is available for purposes of fraud, another part involves an acknowledgment of the rhetoric as fitting and earned.[4] The issue of the expressive and the genuine cannot be sidelined while we determine authorship. Wanting a value-free auteurism is like wanting one's ice a bit warmer.

Structuralized auteurism as "a principle of method, which provides a basis for a more scientific form of criticism than has existed hitherto" was radically incoherent about value—and used a deal of bluster to cover itself. Thus, Geoffrey Nowell-Smith, having scored a point-blank bull's eye against the notion that "every film that is a *film d'auteur* is good, and every film that is not is bad," went on to urge analysis organized around the basic fact of authorship, a quest for the "defining characteristics of an author's work" (1967, 10). But was this author simply the director, any director? Obscured here was the question whether all films display the patterns characteristic of their directors. If only some do, that would indicate a special quality in the director's work and point to authorship as an achievement rather than a plain fact.

The flight from evaluation is all the more strange in view of the sources of auteurism. One of the functions of constancies of theme and style had been to establish not just the individuality of the auteur's work but also its integrity and sincerity. That was in response to the prevailing image of the Hollywood director as sometimes gifted but always tarnished: his talents and vision compromised, sold out or prostituted in the cause of giving the industry what it wanted.

Authorship and Intention

Wollen's first presentation of his auteur theory shifted fluently between outlining procedures for the identification of auteurs and—something else altogether—presenting considerations relevant to the possibility of directorial authorship in the cinema. Despite later disclaimers, much of the chapter would make no sense divorced from a project to explain why direction can confer authorship (in material on composition and performance) and how the director's authorship can be submerged (in references to structures of finance and production).

One way of understanding Wollen's auteurism here is as a means of recovering contact with the director's intentions, obscured and confused as their expression is by the impact of commerce and collaboration. In major respects Wollen conceded the anti-Hollywood case. Only through decipherment could the director's intentions be discerned in films which were indeed compromised by studio control, censorship, unsympathetic collaborators, and so forth. The image of the palimpsest and the concept of "noise" were invoked similarly.[5] Where a [Pauline] Kael might assert that noise is all you get from Hollywood movies, Wollen seemed to offer auteurism as a filter to clear our access to the auteur's film.

Wollen chose Hawks and Ford as his main examples—oddly, since studio interference was seldom a great problem for either of them. Indeed, the chapter gave no examples at all of the workings of critical noise removal. But it is clear that Wollen's arguments drew on a controlling model of authorial intention that was nowhere articulated or examined.[6] In this model the design of a movie is established first of all in the author's mind. The purpose of filmmaking is to reproduce a set of preformed mental images, and the process is the more or less compromised realization of these images on celluloid. The key question then is whether the originating mind is the director's or—the only alternative envisaged—the screenwriter's. The relevance of "composition and performance" is that Wollen saw only two sources for the film's design, "the original screenplay or novel" and "the mind . . . of the *auteur*" (1972, 113). So long as you forget what films are actually like, either of these can be conceived as the place where the film is composed. And structuralized auteurism can become a method of stimulating one's imagination of what a director's films would be if, being more completely authored, they corresponded more closely to the films composed in his mind.

Authorship and Collaboration

This view of intention omits the process of filmmaking with its opportunities for revision, development, and discovery of intentions. In Wollen's version of authorship the subject that the director treats derives solely from an original written source. Actors, landscapes, settings, gestures, intonations, movements, qualities of light, faces, dress, and props were excluded from consideration. They belonged to "execution" and "performance" and were not entertained as subjects that might engage a director's constructive interest and become subjects of the film. That reflects a bad auteurist habit of regarding anything not invented by the director as some kind of threat to his authorship. Even Sarris, close to his brilliant suggestion that we see direction as "a very strenuous form of contemplation," offered the assumption that the given personalities of the Marx Brothers must detract from McCarey's authorship of *Duck Soup* (1964, 37).

For Wollen the process of filmmaking was the site only of compromise, noise, "impoverishment and confusion" (1972, 105). The important possibility excluded here is that authorship of movies may be achieved not despite but in and through collaboration. To take an extreme instance, Sternberg's authorship largely consists in his explorations of Marlene Dietrich and is not at all diminished by the fact that she was his discovery rather than his invention. Who would suggest that we get more of Hawks or McCarey or Hitchcock if we remove Cary Grant from *Monkey Business* (1952), or *The Awful Truth* (1937), or *Notorious*? A director unable to make use of the individuality, the personal skills and attributes of his collaborators is likely to be to that extent, or on those occasions, a poor director.

Elia Kazan is interesting on this: "I think there should be collaboration, but under my thumb! I think people should collaborate with me" (Ciment 1973, 7). Then, on *East of Eden* and James Dean: "His face was wonderful and very painful . . . but I realised there was great value in his body . . . it had so much tension in it. . . . Dean had a very vivid body; and I did play a lot with it in long shots. . . . Julie Harris was wonderful. I wanted to make it so that her face, what's in her face, is the key to the picture. . . . Her face is the most compassionate face of any girl I've ever seen, and I stressed it.

I contrasted her face and [Raymond] Massey's which was a piece of wood" (125–26).

The director's authorship cannot be produced by eliminating the results of collaboration. Either film direction allows modes of collaboration that can yield authorship, or the concept of authorship is inappropriate. An authorship theory must find room for processes that may enable the director to take responsibility for discoveries, incorporating them into the film's intention. It must allow for the possibility that a movie may be enriched, rather than impaired, by changes from an original concept—wherever that is located. It must allow for the fact that many directors establish their authorship by seeking enrichment and fostering change.

The Authority of the Critic

It is in the line of auteurist development that when Wollen abandoned the first statement of his theory he inflated yet further its dependence on repetition. In the revised edition of *Signs and Meaning in the Cinema*, his new Conclusion claimed to clarify but in fact contradicted much of the first statement. In particular he moved to break the incriminating connection between the auteur and the notion of authorship. With a scattering of inverted commas the auteur became a pure critical construct whose existence lay entirely in patterns of repetition. Famously, "Fuller or Hawks or Hitchcock, the directors, are quite separate from 'Fuller' or 'Hawks' or 'Hitchcock,' the structures named after them, and should not be methodologically confused" (1972, 168).

Left to our own devices we might not have been in peril of mistaking a critical interpretation of a group of movies for either a human being or a professional function. That the divorce between John Ford and garden/wilderness, etc., had to be so solemnized was the consequence of Wollen's having erected the auteur film as the film the critic makes: "Renoir once remarked that a director spends his whole life making one film: this film . . . it is the task of the critic to construct" (1972, 104). The use of "construct" here is rhetoric, not a mere slip from "imagine and describe." In a number of places Wollen invited us to confuse what a director makes for showing on a screen with the products of a critic in the medium of words. But because the structures of oppositions had by the time of the 1972 Conclusion lost any rational connection with the nature and purpose of a director's actions, the director himself became a quite metaphysical entity, one that produced a structure in movies "through the force of his preoccupations" (167). Instead of confronting the problem of intention raised by the relation between the "auteur structure" and a director's choices and designs, Wollen fell back on an immaterial force with all the explanatory power of an ectoplasm.

The Death of the Auteur

Auteur theory ends here, reduced to a set of hints on how to construct an auteur without reference to a director's authorship. The auteur had dwindled into a construct tagged with a director's "name" on unspecified grounds. There was a general and understandable reluctance to volunteer life support when even this whittled-down auteur succumbed to attack. The corpse was already headed for the boneyard when the Death of the Author was pronounced. But the Death of the Author says nothing about the continued usefulness of analogies between filmmakers and the writers of novels and poems. When the figure of the author was borrowed from literature, authorship there was not perceived to be in question: calling the director a film author signified that under conditions that make the achievement remarkable he had achieved the authority in his film that a novelist acquires by putting down his pen.

More importantly, the death of the auteur is without the drastic consequences that some have imagined for the theory and practice of director-centered criticism. There has never been substantial connection between auteur theory and critical practice, even in places where the theory was pronounced. Wollen's readings of Ford and Hawks were not products of his theory—the theory was too ramshackle to have any products. Rather, the theoretical claims were sustained by their parasitic relation to a fresh, lively and suggestive reading of Ford's work and an occasionally amusing parody of Hawks's.

So I do not share the belief that "structural analysis of auteurs has produced important results" (Buscombe 1981, 31). And I deny that "the sustained and theoretically decisive critique of *auteurism*" (if it existed or could exist) would provide grounds for deploring the "persistent authorial discourse [which] runs through from publicity . . . even to academic discussion . . . where it is nominally barred." (Lapsley and Westlake 1988, 127). If the authorship approach is inadequately theorized (as against what?), yet is used in the production of "evaluations and interpretations which are frequently impressively . . . perceptive" (Caughie 181, 29), that conjuncture might have more implications for the agenda of theory than for the practice of criticism.

The significant development of the notion of authorship in the cinema is not to be found in successive constructions of an auteur methodology. Currently auteurism seems to be credited with achievements in criticism, while achievements in criticism are discounted because of the inadequacies of the auteur theory. There's symmetry in that but not justice or reason or profit. A side effect of auteurism has been the creation of an author of straw as a distractingly easy target. Attacks on the auteur can be conducted as an auto-da-fé, useful in the suppression of those internal or external voices that would otherwise persist in raising problems about the director.

One remarkable passage in *Signs and Meaning in the Cinema* is that in which Peter Wollen mentioned and dismissed an auteur criticism stressing style and mise-en-scène (1972, 78–80). The maneuver was performed with a strange shiftiness, corresponding, I suppose, to a desire to deny any route to a discourse on film authorship other than through the "structural approach." Certainly mise-en-scène was little considered in deciphering Hawks and Ford. So let's return to the final images of *My Darling Clementine*. A prominent feature is a rough wooden fence that stretches out inconclusively into the landscape of Monument Valley, enclosing nothing. Fences were evidently an important resource to Ford; their expressive possibilities were explored in a range of films, including *Drums Along the Mohawk* (1939), *Tobacco Road* (1941), and *Young Mr. Lincoln* (1939). Here the fence is the last vestige of the town's impact on the terrain and it is associated with Clementine. She does not walk to its end and as a result she is held precariously within the town while Earp is seen with backgrounds of the open road and sky. The fence is taller than Clementine, its uprights reinforce the sense of her erectness—a certain strain in her poise—and its strong perspective helps stress the distance to the horizon. At the same time, being made of widely spaced, unmatched timber, it is heavy but insubstantial and already suggestive of its own decay. The fence helps to enclose Clementine firmly within a moment which is also fleeting.

Would Ford have been surprised to have been told that the fence was a significant element in his image? I think that is much harder to believe than that he would have roasted the assistant who failed to have the fence built, the carpenter who made it too neatly, or the cameraman who offered to frame, light, or focus the shots so as to deemphasize its place in the image. We can assume that Ford well knew what place the fence would occupy at the distances and with the lights and lenses chosen. In deciding to print those takes and use this one, Ford was authorizing the effects and meanings of the image, including those contributed by the fence. On the other hand he might not have been quick or willing to articulate in another medium, like speech, aspects of the meanings of what he had made in the medium of film. Pressed about what he intended he would have been entitled to point at the screen. There he could see as well as I could, or better, what the fences meant. He had no responsibility, however, for the results of my or any critic's or viewer's efforts to articulate some facets of its presence and meanings.

There is a further point here that I think has some bearing on the canvassed transfer of authority from the author to the reader. The film director is, like all creators, his work's first audience. He can try it out on himself and take it through a long series of adjustments and refinements to get as close as he can to a work that satisfies him, that does what he wants it to do. One way of understanding the director's role is to see him checking and adjusting the elements of the film as each of them is taken to its point of registration so as to satisfy himself of the ways in which in their developing context they respond to an active reading. It's a scrutiny keyed to the question, "How does this moment play for a spectator who assumes that what's on the screen is precisely and in all its aspects a finished and authorized work?" I am not willing to suppose that Ford—or Hitchcock or John Sturges or Rudolph Maté—was a less alert, adept, or responsive reader of films than any critic.

When a moment of film achieves the unlikely enchantment of unity where it is sustained and enriched by the stresses and tensions that could split it apart, we have every reason to suppose that the moment achieves the intentions of the person who gave it direction. The critic who claimed to perceive meanings that were "unconscious and unintended" would surely face an obligation to show how he came by his knowledge, and according to what picture of the intended and the conscious. It would be absurd to insist that the critic can construct, in words, an opposition such as between the nomadic and the settled that was inaccessible, in images, sounds, and invented action, to the filmmaker. That would not be a death of the author but a license to critical vampirism. The logic that acknowledges powers of invention and construction in the reader cannot withhold them from the author.

One thing more: a theory of film authorship might usefully set out to explain why so many of those directors who have achieved authority within a single film (through a structure of authored moments) turn out to have done so repeatedly—and often in strikingly coherent terms.[7]

Works Cited

Buscombe, Edward. "Ideas of Authorship." In *Theories of Authorship: A Reader*, edited by John Caughie, 22–34. New York: Routledge & Kegan Paul, 1981.

Caughie, John. "Introduction." In *Theories of Authorship: A Reader*, edited by John Caughie, 9–16. New York: Routledge & Kegan Paul, 1981.

Ciment, Michel. *Kazan on Kazan*. London: Secker & Warburg, 1973.

Kael, Pauline. "Circles and Squares: Joys and Sarris." In *Perspectives on the Study of Film*, edited by John Stuart Katz. Boston: Little, Brown, 1971.

Lapsley, Robert, and Michael Westlake. *Film Theory: An Introduction*. Manchester: Manchester University Press, 1988.

Lindgren, Ernest. *The Art of Film*. 2nd ed. London: Allen & Unwin, [1948] 1963.

Nowell-Smith, Geoffrey. *Visconti*. London: Secker & Warburg, 1967.

Roud, Richard. "The French Line." *Sight and Sound* 29, no. 4 (1960): 166–71.

Sarris, Andrew. *The American Cinema*. New York: Dutton, 1968.

———. "Notes on the Auteur Theory in 1962." In *Perspectives on the Study of Film*, edited by John Stuart Katz. Boston: Little, Brown, 1971.

Wollen, Peter. *Signs and Meaning in the Cinema*. 3rd ed. London: Secker & Warburg, [1969] 1972.

Filmography

The Awful Truth. Directed by Leo McCarey. Columbia Pictures, 1937.

Drums Along the Mohawk. Directed by John Ford. Twentieth Century Fox, 1939.

Duck Soup. Directed by Leo McCarey. Paramount Pictures, 1933.

East of Eden. Directed by Elia Kazan. Warner Bros., 1955.
Frenzy. Directed by Alfred Hitchcock. Universal, 1972.
The Heartbreak Kid. Directed by Elaine May. Twentieth Century Fox, 1972.
I Confess. Directed by Alfred Hitchcock. Warner Bros., 1953.
Letter from an Unknown Woman. Directed by Max Ophuls. Universal-International, 1948.
Liebelei. Directed by Max Ophuls. Metropol-Filmverleih, 1933.
Lola Montès. Directed by Max Ophuls. Gamma Films, 1955.
The Magnificent Ambersons. Directed by Orson Welles. RKO Radio Pictures, 1942.
Monkey Business. Directed by Howard Hawks. Twentieth Century Fox, 1952.
My Darling Clementine. Directed by John Ford. Twentieth Century Fox, 1946.
Notorious. Directed by Alfred Hitchcock. RKO Radio Pictures, 1946.
Psycho. Directed by Alfred Hitchcock. Paramount Pictures, 1960.
The Reckless Moment. Directed by Max Ophuls. Columbia Pictures, 1949.
Tobacco Road. Directed by John Ford. Twentieth Century Fox, 1941.
Touch of Evil. Directed by Orson Welles. Universal-International, 1958.
Vertigo. Directed by Alfred Hitchcock. Paramount Pictures, 1958.
Written on the Wind. Directed by Douglas Sirk. Universal Pictures, 1956.
The Wrong Man. Directed by Alfred Hitchcock. Warner Bros., 1956.
Young Mr. Lincoln. Directed by John Ford. Twentieth Century Fox, 1939.

Notes

1. All these references are to Richard Roud, "The French Line" (Roud 1960), an article unusually sympathetic, for its time and place, to claims for Hollywood directors.

2. Changing Sarris's "criterion" to my "major source" is a way of indicating without debating an unease about the concept of an evaluative "criterion."

3. Is it also representative that he so often fumbled courtroom scenes? They seem to me to provide the feeblest moments in *I Confess*, *The Wrong Man*, *Vertigo*, and *Frenzy*.

4. The obverse of this is that the shame of the studio inserts in *The Magnificent Ambersons* and *My Darling Clementine* is not that Welles and Ford could never have made them but that they could have made them and retained them in their final cuts only through an extraordinary failure of judgment or control. In my experience Welles was never as crude as the Anne Baxter close-up in *Ambersons* and Ford seldom as clumsy as the kiss shot at the end of *Clementine*.

5. "Palimpsest . . . twice-used writing material, where partly erased early writing can be seen below more recent writing." G. N. Garmonsway, *The Penguin English Dictionary*, 2nd ed. Harmondsworth: Penguin, 1969.

6 This model of intention has much in common with the one extensively derided in Wollen's 1972 Conclusion, 156–64.

7 While I hope not to have committed plagiarism, I am aware of this article's indebtedness—too pervasive to be specifically noted—to stimulus received from work by William Rothman and Stanley Cavell, especially his essay "A Matter of Meaning It" in his *Must We Mean What We Say?* (New York: Scribners, 1969) *and* from George M. Wilson's *Narration in Light* (Baltimore: Johns Hopkins University Press, 1986).

MUST WE SAY WHAT THEY MEAN?
Film Criticism and Interpretation

First published in Movie, *nos. 34–35 (Winter 1990): 1–6.*

Leonora Eames, ex-waitress, has been picked up by millionaire Smith Ohlrig and is riding in his car. As he drives, too fast for her comfort, she answers his mocking quiz about her studies at the Dorothy Dale School of Charm. (This is in Max Ophuls's *Caught*, 1949, with Barbara Bel Geddes and Robert Ryan, screenplay by Arthur Laurents.) Leonora lists some of the skills she has learned, ending with:

> ". . . posture and social usage."
> "Social what?"
> "Usage. You know, conversation, etiquette, how to pour tea, how to listen to music, how to . . . please watch the road."

When she speaks of pouring tea and listening to music, she makes two swift gestures. First she raises her right hand daintily to lift an imagined teapot, then she opens her hand and shifts it earward with two fingers extended, meanwhile tilting her head and disconnecting her gaze from any supposed object of attention (figs. 12 and 13). In a different context, this second gesture could signify that the thought of music reminds Leonora of some old enchantment. By showing what music now means to her, it could help the film affirm the value of Leonora's education and of her achievement in working her way through school. Note that the gesture evokes music of a particular kind—Leonora does not snap her fingers or drum on her knees here. The kind is one she associates with a world of wealth, refinement and esteem accessible only in dreams or by magic. (American readers will know whether to confirm my sense that pouring tea—as distinct from coffee— may also have connoted an alien world of Europeanized pretension.)

The two gestures displayed for Ohlrig ("This is what I've learned") are also part of a reverie for Leonora ("This is how it could be if . . ."). But their succession, immediate and without differentiation, exposes something else—the belief that listening to music is, like pouring tea, a matter of the appropriately graceful gesture, a question of self-presentation. Leonora has learned that "how to listen to music" means how to assume the posture in which it is advantageous to be seen while (posh) music is being played.

Figure 12. The first gesture

Figure 13. The second gesture

Further aspects of context help to point the meanings. In the face of Ohlrig's sarcasm, Leonora is defending the Dorothy Dale regime, so these are what she understands as the best claims she can advance. She has not been made aware of anything that a woman might derive from music beyond an occasion for looking delightful. Leonora's exposition of the value of her education also shows her ignorance of its shallowness. Had she made her gestures while in eye contact with Ohlrig, she could have been sharing a knowledge of their falsity. The lack of depth to her fantasy is confirmed by the abruptness with which she can switch back to a concern with Ohlrig's driving. "Please watch the road" entails "Please look away from me" and thus suggests Leonora's unease in her performance.

The passage I have described lasts less than fifteen seconds. My description is far from exhaustive, but I believe that it is accurate and illuminating. In order to describe Leonora's gestures I have had to interpret them. The image would not be evoked, or properly spoken of, by a more extensively physical account. (A moment-by-moment plot of the intricately patterned and unavoidably meaningful eye movements performed by Bel Geddes and Ryan would be tedious and unrevealing.) It is necessary to reflect on what the gestures mean and where they come from. The camera cannot directly show what is in Leonora's mind, but her aims and feelings are as much a part of the narrative of *Caught* as the fact that she is sitting in a millionaire's car. Films like this are made on the premise that audiences can see the implications of the acts, words, and silences of movie characters. When, toward the end of our sequence, Leonora tells Ohlrig, "I know that you've never been married before," our understanding of the wish betrayed by "before" has to be at least the equal of Ohlrig's if we are to comprehend the hostility in his response. We must be alert to both the wish and the hostility if we are not to be baffled by the twenty seconds without interaction that the film holds before the image dissolves.

No neat distinction can be drawn between the meanings that Leonora offers to Smith Ohlrig, that Bel Geddes offers to the camera and that the film offers to its audience. An appreciation of this sequence should encompass all three. The aptness of the writer's invention in having Leonora include "how to listen to music" in her catalog of social usage; the skill of Bel Geddes in enacting, via a tiny beat after each "how to," the split second of recall that betrays Leonora's gestures as unspontaneous and insecurely learned; the precisely graded camera position that gives prominence to the listening gesture while allowing us to see enough of the tea-pouring (partially obscured by the steering wheel in the foreground) to supply the informing context: these are all achievements in the construction of meaning.

This assertion has its place at the head of an issue of *Movie* given over to essays in revaluation, where questions of artistic method, structure, and effect are regularly posed as suggestions about meaning. But it is also directed at some of the arguments and more of the attitudes in David Bordwell's *Making Meaning*, a book whose animus against interpretation seeks justification in a claimed concern for form and style. Criticism that tries to explore what films express, it insinuates, "does not exist on a sensible footing" (1989, 255) and should now give way to the work of the "film poetician."

It gives an early indication of the tact with which it will present the interpretive process when it suggests (Bordwell 1989, 8) that the "point" of *The Wizard of Oz* (1939) might be found to be explicit in its last line of dialogue: "There's no place like home." Such a reading presents film as a mere relay for meanings and requires an imperviousness to the complexity of cinematic expression. It involves a refusal to balance the affirmation in the words spoken by Dorothy Gale (Judy Garland) against the anxious entreaty in her tone and against other information that the film supplies: that the Kansas farmyard was indeed a place not remotely like home, a place lacking in courage, sensitivity, hope, and color, where the only singing that could be done was a lonely cry of yearning for something better. It also involves both blindness to the way that "There's no place like home" follows another more obviously mistaken affirmation—Dorothy's "I'm not gonna leave here ever, ever again"—and deafness to the backing musical sequence where a brief snatch of "Be it ever so humble . . ." gives way to a complete and emphatic restatement of "Somewhere over the rainbow." In order to understand the kind of ending this is you have to find at least some place for these aspects: "Kansas"—which relevantly resembles "Oklahoma" in the following year's *The Grapes of Wrath*—has equivalents for all the major inhabitants of Oz except the good witch; there are no indications that Kansas has found so much as the guts to confront, let alone the resources to defeat, Miss Gulch; Dorothy has had to put great effort into following the requirements of the spell that she repeats (the formula "There's no place like home")—as if hypnotizing herself so as not to resist, and she was explicitly reluctant to leave a world in which she had found not only mirrors to the confusions and malign authority of home but also experiences of joy and companionship unique to Oz; although it is stated that her death had seemed likely, no one in Kansas is sufficiently moved by Dorothy's recovery to do more than pat her hand—for any warmth of contact she can still turn only to her dog. My understanding of all this involves a sense—mindful of the actress at the center of it—that it is a far from merry thought that a child can be emotionally dependent on, and relieved not to be separated from, an environment answering so meanly to her needs for closeness and comfort. So I suggest that tears at this conclusion are not tears of unmitigated joy and that our emotions are gravely misrepresented in allegations of an uncomplicatedly "happy ending." I think the contrary claim is most likely to be advanced out of a false view of what a 1939 MGM family musical would have been obliged to serve up by way of resolution.

To contend that a critic might usefully take a cozy homily as the "literal" meaning of *The Wizard of Oz* would be only a grain less misleading than to say of *Psycho* (1960) that "you might take its explicit meaning to be the idea that madness can overcome sanity. You might then go on to argue that *Psycho*'s implicit meaning is that sanity and madness cannot be easily distinguished" (Bordwell 1989, 9). If you went on thus, you would surely deserve one of Mrs. Bates's best collusive/derisive grins, not just because it's rather late in the century to be trying to tag *Psycho* with a single "point," as if it were an unnecessarily elaborate candidate for Aesop, but also because the explicit/implicit distinction is so patently vacuous: we see Marion Crane lose and regain control over the relationship between her aims and her actions; equally, we share as well as see the failure of a range of characters to realize that Norman Bates is other than an overly devoted Mother's boy. The difficulty of distinguishing sanity from madness is a meaning in *Psycho* because it is several times a fact in *Psycho*. It is no less or more "explicit" in the film than the sense that it would be awkward for a bashful young man to be unable to complete the concealment of a stolen car and more severely embarrassing if the owner's corpse happened to be in the boot.

I say these things so as to suggest alternatives to some of the claims and definitions in *Making Meaning*. The book's subtitle, *Inference and Rhetoric in the Interpretation of Cinema*, indicates the reach of its ambition. It sets out to explore first the processes by which we arrive at our understanding of the nonobvious meanings of movies, then the ways in which this understanding is developed and expressed in forms adapted to the requirements of a particular audience. The book aims to contribute to the development of critical theory and to widen the rather limited circuits of Marxist/Freudian reference within which *théorie courante* preferred to operate. Bordwell wants to oblige film studies to take note of stimuli available both from relevant disciplines like cognitive psychology and from other outstanding bodies of cultural scholarship like the work of the art historian E. H. Gombrich.

He draws on searchlight-not-bucket approaches to perception in order to build an alternative to those notions of the film spectator's passivity that have served to glamorize the actively reading critic and the habit-busting art film. These designs would suffice to suggest a significant intervention from the coauthor of two books—*Film Art* (Bordwell and Thompson 1979) and *The Classical Hollywood Cinema* (Bordwell, Staiger, and Thompson 1985)—whose acceptance has been impressive on both sides of the Atlantic. But *Making Meaning* is not alone in declaring its opposition to *théorie courante* while being continuous with some of t.c.'s more dubious features.

The book is stuck in the familiar skepticism that constitutes a major and dispiriting strain in critical theorizing. Thus it deals happily in the notion that interpretive criticism "produces a model film," but it offers knowing signals of the distance from which it feels required to contemplate "that posited entity the 'film itself'" (Bordwell 1989, 143). The model film is "inevitably an approximation," but nothing suggests what the model could approximate to, in a world which might or might not contain films themselves.

The clarity of Bordwell's argument is asserted and enacted rather than achieved, largely because two of the book's main aims are incompatible. First, it wants to survey what critics do when they produce interpretations—rather than what they imagine or declare themselves to do—and to conduct the survey "holding partisan debates in abeyance" in a posture that aspires to an "ethnographer's calm curiosity." The book's preface asks us to suppose that "in order to study critical practice as such, we must pretend that all theories are correct, all methods are valid, and all critics are right" (xii). Once convinced that a study of critical practice is worth having at the price of such a pretense, we have further to accept that the processes of interpretation are the same across all films and without respect to the quality of the outcome. It is a nice point whether this would be an achievement of calm or of catatonia. We can know that we are surveying appropriately selected instances of interpretive practice only if we know what to count as an interpretation, as against a synopsis, a delusion, or a parody. That is a matter of judgment. It involves issues of value by logical necessity rather than because the surveyor is unavoidably subjective. To suppose that the meaning-making processes which yield the illumination in the best work of (to take only recent American examples)

Stanley Cavell, William Rothman, or George M. Wilson are the same as those that grind out some of the poor specimens cited by Bordwell demands a great leap, but who would envy the faith?

Internally contradictory as it is, this value-freed project is quite at odds with another goal. Bordwell wants to show that his survey has ended up providing support for his "belief that the great days of interpretation-centered criticism are over" (xiii). In this cause he props up many of his ostensibly representative samples of critical product in the Aunt Sally frame. They are required to demonstrate critical routines, but also to show "what a routine activity criticism has come to be." Bordwell's practice runs counter to his precepts, since at each major stage his procedure presupposes what he aims to prove. There is an uneven contest between some of the book's claims and the tendency of its structure and rhetoric continuously to demean and diminish the work of criticism. Its most consistent and probably intended effect is to portray interpretation as a boringly repetitive impediment to our understanding of cinema.

Bordwell's account is absolutely bound to a view of the interpreting critic as a propounder of hidden meaning. It allows interpretation to bother itself only with meanings held to be "implicit" or "symptomatic," and these it opposes to whatever a film "directly states." It does not specify what it would mean for a fiction film to "speak directly," even though it is constrained to put quotation marks around the words and can give only two instances: "There's no place like home" from *The Wizard of Oz* and "a stereotyped visual image such as the scales of justice" (8).

Taken seriously, this would involve the belief that the "literal meaning" of a film is the literal meaning of any statement spoken in it, or the conventional meaning of any stereotyped visual image shown. My remarks on the end of *The Wizard of Oz*, even if regarded as applying a few splashes of depression to the picture's uplifting finish, illustrate the problem here. Statements always come in a context which guides the assessment we can make of them. When they occur in a movie, what we make of them (how literally, so to speak, we take them) depends on the way we understand them to function in a context that has been elaborately constructed. If *The Wizard of Oz* secures conviction for Dorothy's last words, it must have found ways of characterizing them as authoritative—minimally, they need to be heard as sincere and sensible and not substantially qualified by the film's other data. Compare (as Bordwell does not, though he mentions it only a few lines later when defining the category of implicit meaning) the psychiatrist's performance at the end of *Psycho*. The irony here is in part achieved by presenting the spokesman figure not as the indifferently embodied voice of expertise but as a personality with a conceited sureness of his understanding, in a film in which the last of a series of similarly convinced statements was Lila Crane's (Vera Miles's) "I can handle a sick old woman." When we regard any statement ("Madness! Madness!," say) as an attempt to subsume everything in a film under a single rubric, we are responding to indications no more "direct" than those that give Lila's claim an ironic inflection.

To take any character's assertion as unmediatedly representing the film in which it occurs is to hallucinate figure without ground. Bordwell avoids recognition of the absurdities here by ignoring the problem of the terms in which a movie could be reckoned to offer "direct meaning," to "state," or to "say" and rushing on to construct the special category of the implied in opposition to the stated rather than, where it would make more sense, to the shown. Though he sneers a little freely at critics who personify the camera (as if the image might—ho, ho—sometimes be taken to indicate a human viewpoint), he is apparently unabashed by his construction of the film with a tongue.

I suggest that a prime task of interpretation is to articulate in the medium of prose some aspects of what artists have made perfectly and precisely clear in the medium of film. The meanings I have discussed in the *Caught* fragment are neither stated nor in any special sense implied. They are filmed. Whatever else that means (which it is a purpose of criticism and theory to explore) it means that they are not hidden in or behind the movie, and that my interpretation is not an attempt to clarify what the picture has obscured. I have written about things that I believe to be in the film for all to see, and to see the sense of.

Such a view is greatly at odds with the notion that "broadly speaking, all criticism is 'allegorical' in looking for another meaning than the one overtly presented" (Bordwell 1989, 195). I claim that a meaning presented is a meaning made overt within the chosen medium. A process like story-making in transmitted images develops as a medium because artists explore its possibilities for "making overt," which in large degree means its capacity to imply. In other words, implication is a form of expression, not of concealment.

The Bordwell version of criticism depends on a travesty of "the dominant framework within which critics understand interpretation. The artwork or text is taken to be a container into which the artist has stuffed meanings for the perceiver to pull out" (2). When we progress from stuffed meanings to hidden meanings we lose a relatively advanced concept of form 'n' content that pictures the container as a jam jar, since it offers a limited display of the goodies within. The container becomes rather more like a vault that withholds access to meaning and keeps sense out of sight. Under this conception, it is hardly surprising if interpretation involves doing violence to form, since the viewer is required to act as a safe-blaster in order to get within reach of anything significant.

It can be useful to point out how we mislead ourselves with confused notions of content. But if there is a general tendency to fall into a particular kind of error, it is not helpful simply to stage a celebration of (others') obtuseness. The error is likely to indicate a real and shared problem. Some of our difficulties over form and content run in parallel with difficulties over the relationship between the film as a whole and the particular aspect that, at any one time, is our center of attention. (Just such a difficulty would, I suppose, lead one to mistake the words of a character for the voice of a film.) Other hazards are presented by the relationship between the understanding of a film manifested in our response and enjoyment and the understanding that is expressed in an articulated appreciation. Bordwell writes as if there is only a problem of public rhetoric here, a problem of making one's articulation acceptable and persuasive to others, but there is regularly a more important problem with oneself, of finding the words that fit one's sense of the moment or the movie.

Opposed notions of critical rhetoric relate to opposed views of what interpretation may be. For Bordwell, rhetoric functions to render an already formed argument persuasive. That depends on seeing interpretations as intended proofs, designed to achieve internal coherence and to be assessed on the page or in the lecture theater. Some of Bordwell's discontent with interpretation seems to originate in his belief that if its operations had any merit they would be rigorously logical. Thus some of David Thomson's remarks on *Lola Montès* (which deserve the greatest credit for their early contribution—in *Movie Man*, 1967—to our understanding of Ophuls) are deemed eligible for reduction to a mock syllogism (Bordwell 1989, 300n36): a lordly footnote then remarks, "As I have laid it out the chain of inference is formally invalid." Laying criticism out with an assault of that kind is easy but pointless. Thomson's understanding of the film is at no moment posed as a proof. No intratextual interpretation ever is or could be a proof. Most often, it is a description of aspects of the film with suggested understandings of some of the ways they are patterned. Rhetoric is involved in developing the description so that it evokes a sense of how, seen this way, the film may affect us, or so that it invites participation in the pleasure of discovering this way in which various of the film's features hang together. But the ultimate appeal for conviction is to the reader's memory and renewed experience of the film.

That is why I reject Bordwell's market-oriented view that plausibility and originality are the criteria by which the practice of interpretation is governed. Originality matters very little except as a sales point. A claim for the novelty of one's view can very quickly become an assertion of its outlandishness. Plausibility is fine as the charlatan's measure of credulousness in the audience, but plausibility that persists through a renewed and alerted contact with the data is something else again. That will mean that the critic's account was accurate in respect of the elements of the film that it invoked. As I illustrated with *Caught*, those elements can never constitute a description of the whole. So there is a further judgment to be made, of the degree to which the whole is illuminated by the critic's account of the parts and the logic of their configurations. Once I have seen some meanings in a gesture, I have taken one step forward. My understanding of the film may continue to grow, but completion cannot be more than an aim. That is because completion would have to consist of accounting for all the data, but what will come to count as data cannot be known. I cannot now tell what may in the future come to notice as needing to enter into my understanding.

The same goes, too, for the whole of any part because, no matter how small the part, it can never in itself be exhaustively—wholly—described. Nor could one ever be done with the possibility of discovering material elsewhere in the film that stands in a qualifying relation with some disregarded feature of the chosen moment. Perhaps there is an important pattern in *Caught* connecting the occasions when its characters are shown sitting in enclosed and/or mobile spaces; there certainly is a structured series of moments in which, as here, Leonora submits herself to hostile interrogation by a man. Indeed, a key question for our broader understanding of the film is how far it presents its other main character, the liberal doctor Quinada (James Mason), as offering Leonora an alternative to or another version of Ohlrig, since the doctor's questions, gifts, and accusations strikingly parallel the millionaire's.

That suggests another important dimension of meaning. The demand that interpretation follow formal rules of inference results from understanding the critical process as extracting from the movie statements which are hidden but which otherwise resemble messages such as "There's no place like home." Most often, the interesting meanings of films are not like this at all. They consist rather in attitudes, assessments, viewpoints—balances of judgment on the facts and behavior portrayed. As I see *Caught*, Ophuls—for it is he!—offers us neither contempt nor indulgence in reflecting with caustic burnout on the limited understanding that Leonora has developed in her severely limiting world. The ability to work in this way depends on the resources that can be discovered in film to shade information and grade effects, to suggest the weight that is to be attached to any particular observation.

In this area, Bordwell's account of interpretation has been derailed by his drawing on cognitive psychology in some of the more mechanical forms that have developed—as one psychologist puts it—under the spell of physics envy. In particular, he arrives at a picture (as well as several diagrams) in which the items of information on which the critic draws to construct a reading exist in the film as "cues," some of which the critic picks up and some of which are ignored. I am not at all convinced that the quest for meaning is a narrow and concrete enough goal to be compared with, say, the perception of depth—and even there I understand the notion of a cue to be under some stress. But I am sure that the screened data cannot usefully be represented as prepackaged with a determination of which items are to serve as cues. A cue is not a cue unless it is picked up, but if we retreat to speaking only of potential cues we are then talking of everything that the film contains. Moreover, shading and grading are such crucial devices for establishing the relative importance of data, none of which is totally without meaning, that it seems destructive to represent all the cues as having the same size and weight, and standing immune from interaction.

Filmmakers continuously develop the repertoire of devices through which to adjust the prominence with which they present an item of information to its importance in the film's scale of values. (But we should observe that there is no level of prominence that could constitute concealment.) Ophuls judged that the succession of Leonora's gestures was worth including in the performance and in the image. It was worth the space it would occupy in a glancing moment in which the second gesture only would be presented to our unobstructed view, within a medium shot favoring Leonora. The image's prime concentration is on the faces and voices of the characters, with Ohlrig dominating the foreground but with Leonora the more clearly and fully visible. The hand gestures thus deemphasized nevertheless attract notice because, at the moment of happening, they provide the largest movement on screen. They were not judged to merit isolation in a close-up, or in a closer shot of Leonora which lasted only for the duration of the gestures. These are decisions against using the moment to see Leonora derisively. The framing and editing procedures offer the gestures as supplementary information, relevant but without the key significance of the dreamy, bedazzled, and throatily sexual response Leonora has to the other main thing she knows about Ohlrig: "And you're rich . . ." "How rich?" ". . . Oh, very rich." That needs a big close-up, the only image in the sequence completely excluding Ohlrig even when he speaks, edited so that the shot starts immediately before "And" and ends right after "very rich."

I want to develop this point by looking at an earlier section of *Caught*, one whose delicacy will not be apparent in a description since it depends precisely on the balance of prominence between various elements. It is in the opening sequence, where Maud Eames (who has not yet assumed the name "Leonora," nor been given that of "Lee") is speaking to her bed-sit-sharing mentor Maxine (Ruth Brady) of her hopes of escape from car-hop drudgery via the social education available from Dorothy Dale. Maud has been washing her feet and is sprawled across her bed toweling them while Maxine washes up at the sink in the background. During an extended take the camera moves in on Maud, excluding Maxine (who becomes the off-screen voice of practical cynicism) as she indulges a fantasy of working as a model in a fashion store. When she has finished drying her feet, and while the conversation is still of mundane matters, she reaches out idly to take hold of a flimsy metal flyswatter. She fiddles with this throughout her daydream, turning it in her hand, rubbing it against her thigh, and tapping it on her knee. "And then one day in walks a handsome young millionaire.... And he's standing at the perfume counter, and then suddenly he turns around and sees me...and we don't say a word for a long time."

At no time during this does Maud pay attention to her gestures. She is not swatting an imaginary fly. Indeed, her fiddling with the flyswatter seems to indicate boredom and aimlessness rather than a killer instinct. But on "sees me" she makes the most forceful of her taps with the flyswatter and then, in the pause as she bites her lower lip with pleasant thought, holds it still in a way that would indicate—if she were attending to her actions—that she had achieved or imagined a hit.

The flyswatter gestures are a particularly brilliant invention whereby the film suggests what is calculating and predatory in Maud's innocently naïve reverie. Note that a different character would be constructed for Maud in this exposition, if she saw what she was doing and made a connection between her thoughts and her gestures. The effect could, too, be a great deal cruder. Maud could be shown in pursuit of a real fly, with a killing made on the word "millionaire."

But Ophuls has shaded the moment with complex cross-meanings. That Maud's fantasy is, at an only just unrecognized level, one of exploiting her sexuality is indicated by showing her on the bed with her legs open. However, the bed also relates to material circumstances—it's the apartment's one comfortable seat—and neither Maud's posture (across the bed with her head propped against the wall) nor her working girl's dress of rolled-up jeans and plain shirt strongly conveys allure, or any attempt at it. Similarly, the camera's track in to construct an isolated image of Maud-at-dreaming is counterbalanced by the noises off: not just Maxine's harsh interjections but also the grubbily material sound of clattering plates and sloshing water from her dishwashing. Ophuls's chosen sound-balance is emblematic of his precisely tuned effects, since he uses the relative loudness of the impacts of flyswatter on trouser leg to characterize the relative force, and establish the relative prominence, of Maud's gestures.

I have to recognize that I have little idea what in all this could be identified as a cue or as a "unit of meaning." Nor can I see any way for the subtleties of the scene to be comprehended within Bordwell's mechanism of interpretation, which requires the application of preformed arrays of concepts ("semantic fields") to itemized signifying data ("cues"). As in many other efforts to put work in the humanities on a Sensible Footing, the task is assumed to involve drawing criticism closer to the natural sciences but according to an all-clocks-and-no-clouds model that scientists themselves reject. Bordwell would have to ask what it was about my concept of "naïvely romantic daydreaming" that made me see relevance in a flyswatter. His systems (endlessly recycling old information) cannot account for the metaphorical process whereby what I know about fly swatting may be used to show me something new about romance. I see no reason for theory, or poetics, to deny the reality of those aspects of our understanding that psychology cannot currently explain. Nor has any good reason been advanced for preferring the development of grand schemes of "interpretive practice" to improving our understanding of a single great movie.

How much of what I say about *Caught* is true and useful can be known only by checking against the film, particularly so as to see if you find that my description gives these moments valid meanings in their appropriate weights. You might discover aspects of the car scene to convince you that I have missed the point of the musical reference and that, say, one of its effects is to show how the Dale school has equipped Leonora to use masquerade so as to resist recruitment into the regime of bourgeois culture.

Remote as that possibility seems to me, it usefully illustrates the way that intratextual understanding depends on extratextual information not only about facts but also about values. I have assumed *Caught* to address an audience that could relate Leonora's gesture to its conviction of the benefits of musical understanding and thereby share an assessment of her absorption of music into the department of airs and graces. So my interpretation of the moment tries to define a set of internal relationships in the light of beliefs about the appropriate viewing perspective that are grounded inevitably in history (about which I have said nothing) and values. The image characterizes what Leonora has learned about music, but offers the characterization for assessment within even more complex terms of judgment. My reading depends on the sense that the moment draws on, and to varying degrees activates, notions of social pretense, true feeling, musicality, attentiveness, spontaneity, and control, but does not strongly invoke what Leonora may have gained by being taught how to avoid the more humiliating kinds of concert-hall gaffe. In respect of both the characterization and the valuation, judgments are made for which one could offer support but not proof.

We are all fortunate that it is not often necessary to go into this degree of detail in order to specify the grounds of our understanding. This musical reference might be invoked only to connect with the way another character uses a piano rendition of a Strauss waltz as a weapon against the heroine, or to support a broad understanding of the film as reflecting on the relationship between materialism and an impoverished cultural life.

An interpretation will be adequate or not in relation to the particular purposes for which it is advanced, and in relation to the particular aspects of the film that it claims to cover. Insofar as it hopes to illuminate a whole film or body of work by drawing attention to overall patterns and representatively eloquent detail, an important test of its validity and usefulness will be the degree to which we can internalize it and use it to enrich our contact with the film. That is one reason why response is of critical rather than merely sentimental importance. Films are constructed so as to address our minds in the knowledge that mind is much faster and more comprehensively perceptive than intellect. The starting point for my inspection of the *Caught* fragment was a desire to figure out what it was in the moment that made me smile. The evidence of feeling demands an acknowledged place in the process of interpretation. Without it, learning to construct readings of films becomes as empty an achievement as learning about music at the Dorothy Dale school.

Works Cited

Bordwell, David. *Making Meaning: Inference and Rhetoric in the Interpretation of Cinema*. Cambridge, MA: Harvard University Press, 1989.

———, Janet Staiger, and Kristin Thompson. *The Classical Hollywood Cinema: Film Style and Mode of Production to 1960*. New York: Columbia University Press, 1985.

———, and Kristin Thompson. *Film Art: An Introduction*. 9th ed. Reading, MA: Addison-Wesley, [1979] 2009.

Thomson, David. *Movie Man*. London: Stein & Day, 1967.

Filmography

Caught. Directed by Max Ophuls. MGM, 1949.
The Grapes of Wrath. Directed by John Ford. Twentieth Century Fox, 1940.
Lola Montès. Directed by Max Ophuls. Gamma Films, 1955.
Psycho. Directed by Alfred Hitchcock. Paramount Pictures, 1960.
The Wizard of Oz. Directed by Victor Fleming. MGM, 1939.

THE ATLANTIC DIVIDE

First published in Popular European Cinema, *edited by Richard Dyer and Ginette Vincendeau, 194–205. New York: Routledge, 1992.*

I want to examine some consequences of setting up popular European cinema as a category for scholarship. Popular cinema might be thought a contradiction in terms. "Cinema" carries more of the elite status of art with it than "films" or "movies"; it also emphasizes the institutional and industrial aspects of film production and exhibition while significantly excluding television. Cinemas have owners and managements; they belong—usually—to corporations, never to filmgoers. One attends the cinema as a customer or at most a patron. The institutions of cinema determine what is available for one's patronage: the choice between *Batman* and the latest *Indiana Jones* could appear quite marginal.[1] "Let the buyer beware" governs the purchase of a cinema ticket more powerfully than it rules in most consumer transactions; satisfaction is not guaranteed and no compensation is offered if the items purchased prove unsuitable or cause distress.

Popular cinema brings with it the sense of "popular culture," but only the "mass culture" sense. It has to exclude that part of popular culture which depends on communal involvement in making and circulating songs, jokes, games, and stories. There is no folk cinema to parallel folk music or folktale since access to the apparatus of production is so restricted by its cost and complexity. Even the creators can use the apparatus only as employees and under conditions governed by stringent contractual arrangements. The contract here is not with the people, however conceived, but again with the financiers. The absence of contract between the supplier and the consumer is in stark contrast with the abundance and complexity of contracts between the various agencies of manufacture. On the other hand the industry presents itself as giving the public what they want. Whatever one's skepticism toward this suggestion of creation by proxy, it also strains belief to suppose that the interests of cinemagoers have been without influence on the form and content of movies.

A Darwinian model would show this influence working as an adjudication at the box office to determine the viability of mutations generated by the film industries as they try to repeat and vary past successes, and to avoid replicating past failures. Ticket sales have been interpreted as guidance in terms of projects and personnel (not only, though importantly, stars and star combinations) with sufficient perceived force to give rise to the notion that "you're as good as your last picture."

But the products of a selection-survival system offer an imperfect mirror of audience desires since box-office arbitration can come only in those forms and between those films that the structure of the movie business promotes or accepts. (That is one reason why popular cinema is almost always the current cinema.) Film industries have never been entirely governed by perceptions of what the public wants; systems of censorship presuppose an appetite for the products whose supply they restrict. The internal dynamics of movie-making communities put other values into play alongside and sometimes in preference to immediate financial considerations; prestige attaches to forms of work in ways that can be out of harmony with the drive to profitability.

Moreover, the movie business supplies only what it can supply, since it suffers worse problems of quality control than any other manufacturing industry. Think of the financial disasters incurred by attempts to respond to the successes of *The Sound of Music* (1965), *Funny Girl* (1968), and *The Deer Hunter* (1978). Box-office indications of a desire for funnier comedies and more suspenseful thrillers are without effect since it was never by design that the producers offered a yawn a minute. We can never know what parts of the British audience in the Rank-Korda era might have been open to or eager for British movies created in independence from the values and propensities of the London theatre. The British industry was so constituted (in partial reflection of British society) that it did not generate the mutations to put to the test. The British Gainsborough Studios melodrama of the 1940s, for instance, was available only in a form where an energetic politeness set the limit on the enactment of passion. The sad distinction of the Gainsborough movies was to rediscover the stiff and insipid within the luridly contrived. We cannot know whether that was part of their appeal, or a tolerable drawback.

Movies may be commercially successful without being widely or greatly enjoyed. A film that fails does so in the terms set by the structures of the industry and not necessarily because it is incapable of offering pleasure. Thus "popular" may be thought to evade—where "commercial" would confront—the difficulties of characterizing the products of a mass medium as a cinema of the people.

Yet "of the people" is important for its emphasis on a constituency. A film may be popular/well-liked or popular/well-attended through its appeal to the prosperous, the powerful, and the conventionally cultured. Popular cinema, though, is importantly a category of access identifying films whose comprehension and enjoyment require only such skills, knowledges, and understandings as are developed in the ordinary processes of living in society—not those that come with economic or cultural privilege. The terms of access unite the formal with the cultural since what is learned in the ordinary processes of life varies with place and time. Thus a film fully accessible to its French audience will no longer belong to the popular cinema when it arrives in England equipped with subtitles. To correlate the meanings of words printed on the image in English with the inflections of foreign speech, so as to arrive at a vivid understanding of dramatic interaction, calls for abilities not acquired in the ordinary processes of English life. The significance of the passage from *vous* to *tu* is effortlessly registered by any French spectator, and quite recondite for an English audience. Conversely, English audiences will have a nuanced alertness to speech patterns that imply dramatically significant variations in economic and social status.

Factors of those kinds contribute to the processes whereby movies popular in their countries of production enter the structures of art cinema abroad. It is an advantage of the access approach that it can account for the presence within popular cinema of many films—*Raise the Titanic* (1980) and *Absolute Beginners* (1986) would be British instances—which have been neither popular/well-attended nor popular/well-liked. Of course there is some circularity in the notion of access that I have advanced, since what is learned in the ordinary process of life includes what can be routinely derived from the mass media.

The popular can legitimately be polarized against the esoteric but not against the good or the bad and not against art, unless restricted address and exclusivity—availability only to specially developed skills and knowledge—are definitive for one's understanding of what art is. This would limit the art of film to the generic and commercial structures of the art cinema, and would thereby exclude many of the finest pictures.

Historically such a limitation has been in force. The sense of the popular has often been of work which does not so much meet the needs of the people (positively valued) as feed the appetites of the mob, understood as debased and mindless. The figure of the "lowest common denominator" has been much used to characterize the appeal of the mass media to a coarse and uninstructed taste. The corollary to a suspicion of the accessible has been a valuation of the "difficult" and the "experimental," with these latter seen as the product of the more properly artistic motivations. The tendencies to imagine that quite distinct impulses, aims, and processes operate in the production of popular movies and of film art perhaps reflects a secularized hangover from the belief in art as the product of divine inspiration. A recently as 1981 the sociologist Janet Wolff could comment on "our commonsense view of the artist as genius, working with divine inspiration" (1981, 25). Divine inspiration is an all-or-nothing concept; we can hardly expect it to occur in small or moderate quantities or variously adulterated by mundane calculation. Thus the art/commerce divide may have some of the shadings of the opposition of the sacred and the profane as well as the class connotations of the noble and the base.

Within British culture the aesthetics of R. G. Collingwood reflected this kind of absolutism, insisting on a separation between art ("art proper") and amusement. Amusement was one of "three kinds of art falsely so called" (1938, 11) and was identified as a form of corruption. But Collingwood was only more rigorous than most in enforcing a division that ran right through the alarmist discourses on mass entertainment. There was some instability within these discourses between the view that the art of the film was degraded by the demands of its low audience and the belief that the popular taste was being corrupted by continuous exposure to vile work.

> The producing companies made their great mistake when they decided to cater for the taste of the music-hall patron. . . . The cinema lost a public who loved it for itself and what it meant to them. . . . In place of the old filmgoer there arose a new type of audience, a vacant-minded empty-headed public who flocked to sensations, who thrilled to sexual vulgarity, and who would go anywhere and pay anything to see indecent situations riskily handled on the screen. (Rotha 1949, 129–30)

That was presumably not regarded as a hysterical view, since it occurs in what served as the standard English-language history of cinema from its first publication in 1930 through the revised edition of 1949 until the mid-1950s. What I think it encapsulates—certainly in extreme form and perhaps too neatly—is an image of the bad audience, the public of the lowest common denominator, as members of an alien class. Evidently if the features of this audience were projected on to the films it favored one would expect nothing of major—or even modest—artistic interest to be visible.

For some British commentators the image of the popular audience as threateningly other was matched by the foreignness of the popular films, overwhelmingly American. If the clients were an undiscriminating class, their supply came from a whole society which was held to lack class and culture.

An article that proposed a picture of the audience in apparent contrast with Paul Rotha's of 1930 was written for the 1947–48 edition of the *British Film Yearbook* by C. A. Lejeune, then the recognized leader of highbrow British film reviewers. Called "A Word in Friendship," the article offered itself as a warning and defined its own sense of precarious context: "Now, at the beginning of 1947, the British film industry is standing at the parting of the ways. Its present position is secure. Its past record is proud. Its future is a matter of urgent speculation" (1947a, n.p.). Lejeune went on to warn of the dangers of competing with Hollywood on its own grounds and so becoming its parochial echo. Commercial wisdom was claimed to indicate a rejection of Hollywood's methods which were both curiously artificial and out of touch with reality.

> British audiences . . . are probably the most sensible and selective audiences in the world. . . . The thousands of British men and women and boys and girls, who will tell you today that they prefer British films, will tell you just why they prefer them. And the reason is nearly always the same—because they are more "real"; because they deal with the sort of people we know; behaving in a way we understand; against a background of the things we cherish and recognize. (1947b, 31–32)

This portrait of the audience, apparently so different from Paul Rotha's, in fact carried most of the same implications. Like Rotha, Lejeune imagined the audience as stable and coherent, always in the same mood, and having the same objectives—as one audience. But the most interesting aspect of Lejeune's picture is that it was knowingly false. It strategically ignored the mediocre commercial performance of some highly approved movies. Lejeune herself in acclaiming *Brief Encounter* (1945) had declared "I doubt very much if it will be generally popular. . . . Nothing the producers can contrive is going to make *Brief Encounter* an understandable film for the practical millions" (1947a, 161–62). More boldly still, her picture wished away the box-office triumph of critically despised British films like *Madonna of the Seven Moons* (1945) and *The Wicked Lady* (1945). Instead "Hollywood" was made to stand for the popular trash that a sensible and selective audience could be expected to reject. My point is not to examine the particular conjuncture that made this strategy useful, but to indicate the availability—for a wide range of polemical purposes—of the equation between Hollywood and the worthless popular, even when it was made in Britain. Hollywood cinema, on this view, was overpaid, oversexed, and over here.

"Over here," at least, is surely right. If we take an audience rather than a production perspective, popular European cinema must include—and will in many or most places be dominated by—Hollywood products. American pictures provide the striking exception to the rule pronounced earlier whereby movies popular in their countries of production enter the structures of art cinema abroad. Research, as relevant to American as to European interests, could well pursue the problem of the mysterious accessibility of the Hollywood film. I believe it would at some point confront questions as germane for *Liebelei* (Germany 1933) as for *Notorious* (US 1946), as pointed in *It Happened One Night* (US 1934) as in *La Grande Illusion* (France 1937), of the processes whereby the finest popular movies reconcile availability to a relaxed enjoyment—often but wrongly characterized as passivity—with a densely worked structure that can reward close, most sustained, and informed scrutiny.

The popular, considered in terms of its ranges of accessibility, is aesthetically and critically neutral. Accessibility can be an artistic as much as a commercial aim, but that a work is broadly or narrowly accessible says nothing of the values that may be found in it once access is achieved. The kind of attention a work requires is not identical with the kind of attention it may reward. Value is neither ruled out nor guaranteed.

Not long ago this point had to be stressed in resistance to a blanket condemnation of commercial cinema. More recently it has come to need affirming in face of the tendency within academic film studies to reject aesthetics except as sociological data on formations of taste. Various groups of movies have been proposed for rescue from critical neglect on the grounds that their success suggests and their internal structure confirms the closeness of their issues and images to the concerns of their audience. A relevant instance is that of the Gainsborough melodrama which a growing number of revisionist essays on British cinema offer for sympathetic reassessment. The defense typically presents the claim that the contemporary reviewers' derision of Gainsborough reflected an inability to take popular culture seriously. I have chosen to discuss *Love Story* (1944), whose screening at the Warwick Popular European Cinema conference held it up for scrutiny in the light of the understanding that "most European countries have produced a vigorous tradition of popular film . . . fully as capable of high aesthetic achievement as Hollywood."[2]

The contemporary press—with Lejeune prominent among them—poured scorn on this film and on its plot, which contrives a wartime romance between a dying concert pianist and an invalid airman doomed to lose his sight. But such extremities of condition and coincidence, with the indifference to mundane probability that makes them usable, provide the conventional basis for the eloquence of the best weepies. The reassessment of melodrama that has progressed with the development of film studies has involved a validation of the expressive possibilities in narrative contrivance and in boldness of formal and emotional design.

Moreover, the thematic material of *Love Story* is far from trivial. Lissa (Margaret Lockwood) faces the issue of what can count for her as the fulfillment of her life, and faces it urgently in the immediate prospect of death. Kit (Stewart Granger) presents the male action hero wedded to stereotypically masculine sources of self-esteem but threatened with incapacity and banishment from the valued sphere of prowess. Each of them confronts conflict between the private realm of romance and the social arena of the war effort as the ground on which fulfillment and consolation are to be sought.

These are significant issues, and the twists of the film's narrative and imagery draw in plenty of others. But then, snobbish prejudice aside, it is hardly believable that any film could appeal in the way that, in 1944, *Love Story* did to a very large British audience unless it made contact with hopes, anxieties, beliefs, and concerns whose pertinence was widely felt. It is not credible that a dramatic entertainment might elicit a strong or wide response while being thematically empty or insubstantial.

But to say this much is not to establish that the film treats its themes intelligently or honestly, nor that it realizes the potential of romantic melodrama by developing depth and subtlety within its broadly and boldly drawn effects. *Love Story* strains after emotional force by repeating established information with ever more insistent emphasis. The resulting imagery is flat and grossly contrived, as when the film reminds us of Lissa's consciousness of doom by answering a close-up of her distracted frown, during a romantic buggy ride along a Cornish lane, with an inserted viewpoint of a graveyard.

What particularly distinguishes *Love Story* from the more trenchant and inventive romances is the absence of a critical or even an inquiring perspective on the motives and perceptions of its lovers. Most damagingly, the film can do nothing with its pivotal contrivance, the lovers' silence. Kit will not tell Lissa that he is going blind; Lissa will not tell Kit of her terminal heart condition. Acts of concealment are a constant but unexplored center of the dramatic action. Lissa takes Kit to be a coward because of his apparent disengagement from the war effort. A mine accident allows him to prove his courage and then Lissa discovers him practicing his Braille. Kit claims to have dreaded her reaction of pity and he gives that as the motive for his deception. Pity is lavishly displayed in Lissa's movements and intonations, but the film observes no moment of concern over this realization of Kit's worst fear, nor—the lively alternative—does it follow up the possibility that Kit may have misrepresented or misrecognized his own motives. (Pity is an emotional currency, I suppose, that it is not prepared to bring under scrutiny.) If *Love Story* were alert, and were expecting its audience to be alert, it would also need to do something at this point about Lissa's continued deception of Kit. But "Why didn't you tell me?" at the scene's start and "Thank you for telling me" at its end are not allowed to provoke Lissa into an inspection of her own silence, or to prompt the film to an independent valuation. Indeed the immediately following scene has her enter into a dumb bargain that involves further deception of, and separation from, Kit. Inability to find an animating dramatic focus for actions crucial to the plot deprives *Love Story* of the subtext that can deepen and enrich the romantic tearjerker.

The subtexts that the film does have carry it from ineptitude to ugliness. It is oppressive and dishonest in pursuit of propagandist goals. So Kit's detachment from the war effort has to have the alibi of sickness if it is not to be contemptible. No other position is acknowledged and the appetite for disapproval that disfigures so much of English life and culture is meanly indulged. Lissa's resolve to become Kit's lover is shaken when he refuses to manage the dangerous but patriotically significant mining works. She is troubled as, once more, the pony trap carries them along a lane. They come upon a squad of war-wounded soldiers out for a hike on their sticks and crutches. The lantern-slide function of two insert shots of these cheerful, bandaged simpletons is confirmed by Lissa's declaring that she can't go on, and objecting to Kit's attitude "after what we've just seen," as if someone, somewhere, might have needed a visual aid to remembrance that the war has victims.

This exploitative and hectoring rhetoric is called in to validate Lissa's decision that she will not, after all, be sharing Kit's bed. The device gives an early indication of the film's unrecognized project, which is to divert sexuality onto sacrifice and military heroics. At the picture's end when surgery has lifted the threat of blindness, and other impediments to (however brief) union have finally been dissolved, the film celebrates Kit's reenlistment in the air force much more emphatically than it welcomes the satisfaction of desire. All talk of living for the moment resolves into a decision to marry, which then yields no image of fulfillment in love. Instead the film affirms its preference for transferred gratification by moving straight from the accepted proposal to the image of Lissa standing alone on the Cornish cliff tops and fondling her wedding ring before waving to the flight of bombers that passes over her head.

The final choice of distance over intimacy, and aggression over tenderness, is made on behalf of an England depicted with great complacency in rigidly hierarchical terms. Every public incident is handled with a steady concentration on the needs and concerns of the officer class. When an emotional crisis delays a theatrical performance a slow hand-clap is started by an aged squire (A. E. Matthews) and taken up by the crowd until it is converted to applause by the intervention of the mine owner (Tom Walls). When the mine falls in, the escape attempt below ground is managed by Kit in partnership with the owner and with virtually no reference to the skills or judgments of the miners themselves; above ground, all interest in the progress of the rescue is filtered through Lissa and another of Kit's friends, the actor-manager Judy (Patricia Roc), as if their status as upper-class outsiders gave them sure title to first news of events. The crowd of Cornish wives and colleagues at the pit head are present precisely as extras who dutifully yield all initiative along with the foreground of action. This blinkered concentration on the privileged treats their interests alone as serious and real. The film clearly looks forward to business as usual at the end of the war. Rapture itself turns out to be an elite preserve in Kit's proposal of marriage: "Happiness such as we can have is worth grasping. . . . If you can stand on the highest peak for one moment you've had what most people strive in vain for all their lives."

Evidently my contempt for this film could be misplaced. No critical case is ever conclusive, but the critical discussion would have to be advanced through descriptions and understandings like—even if opposed to—those I have offered. It cannot be resolved through an appeal to the adjudication of the box office or by demonstrating the neatness of the picture's fit with some particular reading of cultural history.

On the other hand, while *Love Story* is, on my account, a bad film, it was surely not bad to enjoy it. The "bad audience" view seems to assume that the work is relished for precisely those aspects that the commentator deplores: it is the badness of bad work that is taken to constitute its appeal. Thus one could proceed from the observation that at the end of *Love Story* Lissa's entranced affirmation that she will "never be afraid any more" has no connection with the preceding two hours' drama in which fear has not been the declared or implied source of any of her actions. Lissa's declaration will be understood—correctly, in my view—as a climactic instance of the film's emotional opportunism whereby effect is pursued without a disciplined regard for relevance or shape. But a spectator who invests emotion in this moment is surely not responding to its incoherence. It seems more likely that the crudity passes unnoticed by an audience immersed in the grand (and not contemptible) aspirations embodied in Lissa's vow. Willingness to take the film's devices for granted would allow an unchecked response to the fantasy of release from timidity and anxious expectation. The crudity, the exploitation of feeling that is unearned dramatically, is not—on this account—the source of the fan's enjoyment (though it may be the precondition for the abundance and variety of big emotional moments throughout the film). It would be, rather, passed over in the focus on against-the-odds romantic fulfillment. Stewart Granger:

> My next epic was a film called *Love Story*, shot on location in my beloved Cornwall. On the train I shared a compartment with the director who asked me what I thought of the script. Not knowing he'd written it, I told him it was the biggest load of crap I'd ever read. . . . I was wrong of course. It was a smash hit and there wasn't a dry eye in the house. (1981, 75–76)

If it is not to trap itself in a position as contradictory as that of *Love Story's* star, film studies will need to find ways of reconciling its critical and its sociocultural aspects. That will involve discussing the appeal of shoddy work without recourse to assumptions of depravity or feeble-mindedness in the spectator, but also without attempting to redeem the work by giving it undue credit for being what it must always be, a product of its time. An incautiously erected category of popular European cinema threatens to aggravate the difficulty rather than contribute to its solution. If it is not constructed as a category of access (which would for good reason acknowledge a polarization against avant-gardism) but is established in opposition to the art/auteur film, then it risks reconstructing within the discussion of European movies the old opposition between European art and Hollywood show business. Many films by directors such as Lang, Lubitsch, Ophuls, Renoir, and Visconti can be excluded from the category of the popular only, I would have thought, by declaring them too good! It is important to dismantle the opposition between popular film and film art. But is any useful purpose served by reversing its polarities?

Works Cited

Collingwood, R. G. *The Principles of Art*. London: Oxford University Press, 1938.
Granger, Stewart. *Sparks Fly Upward*. London: Granada, 1981.
Lejeune, C. A. *Chestnuts in Her Lap, 1936–1946*. London: Phoenix House, 1947a.
———. "A Word in Friendship." In *British Film Yearbook 1947–48*, edited by Peter Noble, 30–32. London: British Yearbooks, 1947b.
Rotha, Paul. *The Film Till Now: A Survey of the Cinema*. Rev. ed. London: Vision, [1930] 1949.
Wolff, Janet. *The Social Production of Art*. London: Macmillan, 1981.

Filmography

Absolute Beginners. Directed by Julien Temple. Palace Pictures (UK), Orion Pictures (US), 1986.
Batman. Directed by Tim Burton. Warner Bros., 1989.
Brief Encounter. Directed by David Lean. Eagle-Lion Distributors, 1945.
The Deer Hunter. Directed by Michael Cimino. EMI (UK), Universal (US), 1978.
Funny Girl. Directed by William Wyler. Columbia Pictures, 1968.

La Grande Illusion. Directed by Jean Renoir. RAC, 1937.
Indiana Jones and the Last Crusade. Directed by Steven Spielberg. Paramount Pictures, 1989.
It Happened One Night. Directed by Frank Capra. Columbia Pictures, 1934.
Liebelei. Directed by Max Ophuls. Metropol-Filmverleih, 1933.
Love Story. Directed by Leslie Arliss. Eagle-Lion Distributors, 1944.
Madonna of the Seven Moons. Directed by Arthur Crabtree. Eagle-Lion Distributors, 1945.
Notorious. Directed by Alfred Hitchcock. RKO Radio Pictures, 1946.
Raise the Titanic. Directed by Jerry Jameson. ITC Film Distributors (UK), Associated Film Distribution (US), 1980.
The Sound of Music. Directed by Robert Wise. Twentieth Century Fox, 1965.
The Wicked Lady. Directed by Leslie Arliss. Eagle-Lion Distributors (UK), Universal (US), 1945.

Notes

1 Given the date of this article, Perkins is likely thinking of the 1989 film *Batman*, directed by Tim Burton, and the 1989 Indiana Jones film, *Indiana Jones and the Last Crusade*, directed by Steven Spielberg. Ed.

2 Quoted from conference brochure, Popular European Cinema Conference, University of Warwick, September 1989. Ed.

WHERE IS THE WORLD?
The Horizon of Events in Movie Fiction

First published in Style and Meaning: Studies in the Detailed Analysis of Film, *edited by John Gibbs and Douglas Pye, 16–41. Manchester: Manchester University Press, 2005.*

Some years ago a distinguished scholar in literature and film advised me that one should consider the idea of the fictional world as no more than a "loose metaphor." The phrase made an impression, and has stayed with me, for two reasons. I took it as the succinct statement of a belief that might well command acceptance within film studies, if the matter were attended to at all. And it seemed to be nearly the opposite of the truth. This essay sets out both to show that the fictional world of a movie is indeed a world and, by means of a few concrete examples, to sketch some of the ways in which it matters that a fictional world is a world.

    I start with an ending, a familiar one. In the final sequence of *Citizen Kane* (Orson Welles, 1941) the journalists pack up and prepare to leave Xanadu, abandoning their quest for the meaning of Kane's last word. At this point two main issues are yet to be resolved: First, what was Rosebud; then, would the identity of Rosebud offer a key to the life and mind of the dead tycoon? When The End title appears, the second question remains unanswered, left open to the speculations both of the on-screen investigators and of the movie's audiences. But before this, in the very last images, the spectator is privileged with a revelation of Rosebud as the name on the child

Kane's sled. This knowledge is emphatically denied to the seekers within the fiction. The separation of viewpoint is developed with a grand rhetoric whose flourishes depend upon extremes of scale from the distended to the abrupt, from the weirdly distant to the impossibly close.

The setting is vast. The Xanadu hallway with its massive staircase is stacked farther than the eye can see with the trophies and detritus of Kane's wealth—everything from an old iron stove to classical statues and, we are told, a dismantled castle and a Burmese temple. In this huge vault voices in conversation are echoing as from distant domes and crevices. His departing colleagues start to quiz the chief reporter, Thompson (William Alland), about his discoveries. To this point the image has tracked their course through the makeshift alleys of monument and keepsake. But now as they stand fixed to listen to Thompson's response the camera detaches itself, craning up and curling away to see them from on high. Thompson's admission of failure tails off with a doubt that one word can explain a man's life, and with his speaking of Rosebud as just a missing piece in a jigsaw puzzle. He leads his group toward the exit, urging haste to catch the evening train, but his sluggish movement suggests a reluctance to leave in defeat. Welles puts a period to this scene of departure by dissolving to a final, speechless, image of the newsmen as they move away through the labyrinth; here the high, static camera is so remote that individual identity is all but erased.

The sound in the scene has been strictly diegetic but now the entry of slow, doom-laden music dictates a mood which is the film's and not that of any of its characters. The declaration of an independent viewpoint is sustained through dissolves across an undefined stretch of time and space to yet another and another image of Kane's treasure-hoard. Now the camera glides high across a further—apparently boundless—expanse of boxed and unboxed stuff, taking a course unrelated to anything human. Its movement is not performable by any wingless being, and it surveys a vista of crates so jumbled and so close-packed as to deny access to man or woman (fig. 14).

The mood of detachment is assisted by contrast, through the disappearance of human comment. Moments ago a disparate chorus of reporters was yelling the inventory of Spanish ceilings and headless statuary; now there is only the whisper of music. In two large ways the image reverses the sense of

Figure 14. A course unrelated to anything human

the crane up from Thompson's group: a movement away has been replaced by a movement of advance; and this traveling camera is not approaching, as the other was drawing back from, a defined object. Nor is it showing interest in any of the articles that its view traverses; its eye is directed across the clutter below and is not seeking in it or sorting it through. The result is that Kane's treasure floats down through the frame in a stream of barely differentiated bits and pieces.

Yet the movement is deliberate. The camera advances in a straight line; portentous musical phrases underscore the fixity of its gaze and the evenness of its pace. Over a terrain without visible limits or shape, this camera knows where it is going. But it is not showing us its goal.

After nearly half a minute, and without having fixed on any singular feature, the camera begins to descend. It maintains its forward momentum as it drops closer and closer to the surface of the junk-ocean. Finally it shifts its angle of vision downward and alters its forward course to veer around as it closes in on a child's sled, brought into view just as a laborer enters the frame to bear it away. A bass chime from the orchestra certifies that with the sled the camera has found its destination. In the memory game that the sequence has encouraged and frustrated we should recognize this object as a relic of Kane's childhood. We just about have time to take it in, lying at the edge of the store and close to a photograph of the boy Kane with his mother, before it is removed from the frame and the image changes.

With the removal of the sled comes a sudden change of pace as the film cuts and we are all at once given a great deal to absorb. For the first time the nature of the space is revealed, together with its difference from the hall where we observed the newsmen's exit. We must be in the cellars of Xanadu, as the new shot reveals the butler, Raymond (Paul Stewart), directing the labors of overalled workmen who are feeding an enormous furnace with flammable scraps from the stockpile—a picture frame, a paddle, a cello case. The camera travels toward the inferno with the laborer who carries the toboggan. It continues its approach as the toy lands in the flames and the workman turns away out of shot, so that now we have a view of the sled that allows us to see, in the last moments of its existence, the inscription "Rosebud."

A new shot enlarges this detail to fill the screen, presenting the impossible image. The camera appears to have entered the furnace. Its view is held and tightened so that it sees only the flames that blast the Rosebud decal, and the paintwork tortured by the heat. A fade to black marks the end of the sled and its emblem. In an exterior shot the camera tilts up to follow the smoke that empties into the night sky from Xanadu's chimney. Repeating the imagery of consumption by fire, the black smoke functions as a sign of oblivion and declares the finality of Rosebud's loss.

Citizen Kane would need very little of this if the only, or overwhelmingly important, point of its finale were the answer to the Rosebud puzzle. For that purpose, it would be necessary only to contrive the disclosure. The method would be optional, and the options would include a new flashback to Kane's childhood. Simplest of all would be to let the journalists make the discovery. Nothing in the enigma-resolution process demanded that the sled be destroyed, or required Welles to stress the completeness of its ruin. Nor was it necessary for the destruction to go, within the world of the film, unremarked. But these are the aspects emphasized in Welles's treatment:

Rosebud is gone forever and a significant moment has passed without notice.

The spectacle of Rosebud's immolation is presented in a context of defeat. Abundance has become clutter and "America's Kubla Khan" has ended as the Ozymandias of his time. While the departure of the journalists could mean no more than that the truth of "Rosebud" is as yet undiscovered, Welles's finale guarantees that nobody will ever find it. The location in the Xanadu vault gives the ironic sense of a near miss to the calling off of the quest. Remember that the reporters are working for a movie newsreel, always taking pictures. Then the image we see of Rosebud's vanishing reverses the process of photographic development and undoes the snapshot that might have been. The presence of know-all Raymond gives the sled's end a further inflection as "what the butler never saw." All these failures of vision are highlighted by contrast since they come at the climax of a movie whose process has been founded on a succession of assigned viewpoints, precisely on what various witnesses had seen and recalled.

Dissonance is crucial to the tone of *Citizen Kane*'s finish, most of all in the clash between the assertiveness of the camera's display and the insistence, within that, on the unseen and ignored. We are at once thrust into knowledge and informed that no one shall ever know. The music adds to this effect by filling our ears with the unheard screams of Rosebud's death throes and by punching out chords certain of their finality over images that refuse to suggest how our knowledge of Rosebud has improved our understanding of Charles Kane, or whether the sled should stand as an instance of the triviality of trivia or of their momentousness. The effect is at its strongest in the shot of the burning decal, where the show of revelation collides most brutally with the erasure of all prospect of discovery.

That we can be present as an audience to witness the absence of witnesses is an index of the separation between our world and the world of the fiction. It climaxes the anomaly that places *Citizen Kane* both in and beyond our world, our 1941 world. Of course this is our world. It shares our economy, our technologies, our architecture, and the legal systems and social forms that yield complex phenomena like slum landlords, divorce scandals, and fame. Its history is our history of wars and slumps and the rise of mass media. Its notorious people (e.g., Adolf Hitler) and its decisive events are the ones we know.

But of course its world is not ours. Kane is famous throughout that world, and we have never heard of him, nor of Jim Geddes, his political rival. Susan Alexander's celebrated fiasco at the Chicago Municipal Opera House involves an occasion and a location without reality for us. Everyone there and nobody here knows about the construction of a new Xanadu (their Xanadu) in Florida (our Florida). These are some of the aspects that mark the world as fictional. They do not thereby negate its worldhood.[1]

The world of *Citizen Kane* is constituted as a world partly because, within it, there are facts known to all, to many, to few, and to none. The phenomena of a world are independent of perception, though in principle and most of the time available to it. To be in a world is to know the partiality of knowledge and the boundedness of vision—to be aware that there is always a bigger picture. To observe a world humanly is to do so from a viewpoint, with angles of vision and points of focus whose selectivity is inflected by the seeing mind. The looking is governed by purposes and expectations, by interests, appetites, hopes, and fears.

The camera's looking escapes some of the restrictions on our sight: those that follow from the fact that, for us, eye and ear always have to go with body. The movie can explore the opportunities of unembodied viewpoint but it can never escape the necessity of viewpoint itself. So one of the arts of the movie is to turn this condition to advantage—for instance, by articulating the condition as a topic within the film—by dramatizing the distinction between the seen and unseen, or the relations between seeing and knowing.

I have begun with these moments from *Citizen Kane* on account of their peculiarly stark display of the connections between narrative, formal device, style, viewpoint, tone, and meaning. My chief concern, however, is with the dependence of all these aspects on the worldhood of the fictional world.

Welles had freedom to choose how and when to reveal Rosebud because there is always more beyond the frame than any image can contain: more in space and more in time. In the first flashback to Kane's boyhood the name on the sled was only one of an infinite number of facets of that world—that world in those moments—that the camera did not display. The camera's selectivity means that the framed image and the (boundless) fictional world create and account for one another. As Bazin told us, on-screen presupposes off-screen.

Selection by the camera, however, asserts significance. The image is displayed not only to relay information but to claim that it matters and to guide us toward the ways in which it matters. Because this is information of and in a world it will be subject to many kinds of attention and assessment, with every shade available from obliviousness to obsession. Rosebud goes ignored. It must have been seen umpteen times. The sled is handled and moved by the laborers in the Xanadu vault but its name escapes notice. It is not seen by those who have been searching for "Rosebud" as the answer to a riddle, and to whom its sight would have significance, would be a discovery.

The music of the scene is interrupted only once, by Raymond's order to "Throw that junk!" Finding junk and treasure in the same object, the film can put it in the context of revered and stockpiled antiquities. So it offers a token of boyhood memory for evaluation against the remnants of lost empires and against a host of objects that evoke ranges of purpose, history, cost, and potentiality. Measured beside a Donatello Nativity or a headless Venus, a child's plaything can pose the issue of what any of these things may represent as achievements or attachments, just as the hungry furnace poses the issue of what is worth preserving. The question of value has been put explicitly into play in the journalists' remarks, among them:

"How much do you think this is all worth?"

"Millions . . . if anybody wants it."

As Rosebud burns, the strident music outlaws an "Is that all?" response to the camera's disclosure. Welles demonstrates here that viewpoint is vastly more than an optical matter. *Citizen Kane* provides a stark instance of something that is always the case: that the material entities of a fictional world are also objects subjectively perceived—as talismanic, say, or intriguing, or negligible.

The movie draws on our ingrained awareness that the things we treasure and the things that haunt us may be odd or unfathomable to our fellows. Reciprocally it invokes the knowledge, born of experience, that our access to the thoughts and feelings of others is uncertain and necessarily partial. None of us can legislate the distinction between the trivial and the momentous for the secret places of another's heart. Against this we know also that there are accepted scales of value, common senses of what matters and how much, in light of which any particular attachment may be seen as normal, individual, eccentric, or outlandish. *Citizen Kane* places itself in a world of recognizable understandings: a *Venus* is valued at twenty-five thousand dollars, but "that's a lot of money to pay for a dame without a head."

The world as inhabited space and the world as communities of understanding come together to underwrite the formal achievement of *Citizen Kane*'s finale. Welles is able to build a grand rhetoric of ruination by emphasizing the distance you have to travel to encompass treasure-hoarding on the Xanadu scale, pitched at the outer limit of what's conceivable in relation to a wealth both real and—for most of us—unimaginable. Within this enormity he can then bring us to a littleness, a trinket not made to endure, remarkable for its survival rather than its fragility. So he can clash the huge against the tiny, the emphatic against the negligible, by sustaining the expansive rhetoric for the burning of a sled. A grand spectacle: flames in a furnace. A climax: smoke from a chimney.

In the moments I have discussed we see Welles making an appropriate style out of gross overemphasis. Still it should be clear that I have chosen to inspect this passage for its representative, not for its freakish, quality. It is representative inasmuch as the film's form and method are incomprehensible outside of a recognition that its story takes place, and its images are both made and found, in a world. I believe this to be true, obviously but importantly, of all movies.[2]

Yet film studies has in the main ignored the fictional world, at best taken it for granted. Lack of attention to the fictional world—what makes it a world rather than what makes it fictional—may be one product of the field's recoil from all that smells of realism. A new engagement with worldhood should be of value, not least in developing our grasp of styles and meanings. An immediate benefit could be to enrich our appreciation of film artistry both in the treatment of space and in the shaping of narrative. The on-screen/off-screen relationship should be opened to explorations that embrace issues far beyond those of spatial continuity. And we should see processes of narrative in more rewarding lights once we break from the narrowness of a concentration on the "cause-and-effect chain."

It seems to be a habit of narratologists, not only in film studies, to reduce a story to a succession of events—or, rather, to the synopsis of a succession of events. Since the synopsis is taken to be an adequate representation of the narrative, it becomes relatively easy to believe that the cause-and-effect account thereby produced is a revelation of the movie's narrative process. But film drama is more than a succession of events, and a cause-and-effect approach can confine us in a mechanistic view not only of human affairs but of narrative as well. It can also distort a movie's time-process since cause and effect are products of the retrospective view (whereby we see the two together) whereas motives and possibilities are among their dynamic counterparts. An event becomes a cause only in its relation to webs of circumstance, together with, say, desires and fears. Why a cause should be understood as a cause, and why an effect should count as an effect, are matters that can be assessed only within a world. It is, after all, a very particularly constituted world in which one man's death can be the occasion for squads of people to set off in an effort to identify the personal meaning of a familiar word.

The world is everything (in space and in time) surrounding and embedding our immediate perceptions. There is always an out-of-sight just as there is always an off-screen. Out of sight cannot be entirely out of mind: we may not know what lies beyond the horizon but we do know that there is a beyond. Fritz Lang can teach us about this. In *You Only Live Once* (1937) the thief Eddie (Henry Fonda) is paroled from jail through the good offices of the priest Dolan (William Gargan) and the lawyer Whitney (Barton MacLane). The day of his release is to be the day of his marriage to naïvely trusting, respectable Joan (Sylvia Sidney), who has been Whitney's secretary and who is the object of her boss's unspoken, unrequited desire. At just over ten minutes into the film, Eddie and Joan pass through the prison gates. They offer thanks to Whitney and Father Dolan, then leave. The camera returns to the two men, tracking them through an outer door where, framed together in mid-shot, they stand to talk. As they do so we hear the sounds of a car's departure—slamming doors, revving engine, and then fading, increasingly distant, motor noise. The combination of sound and image creates in our minds the event of Joan and Eddie's driving off. We have not seen it. The off-screen world is here constructed not only as space but also as action—and not just "background action." All things considered, the departure is more fateful than the Whitney/Dolan exchange.

This occurs in a film designed to provoke awareness of the dangerous power of images by making us repeatedly reassess the conclusions we have drawn from what we have seen and heard.[3] What do we imagine ourselves to have witnessed in these images? How may the camera's power of selection become an agent of misdirection? Here Lang offers an innocent example of our being led to understand more than we have seen. The construction of this one shot enables a variation on the film's themes of perception and prejudice. By watching Dolan and Whitney rather than the car, the camera guides us to observe the different attitudes in which the priest and the disappointed lawyer view this departure. Framed together, their faces and movements offer a study in contrast. Dolan's glance moves back and forth between Whitney and the leaving vehicle, sometimes fixing on Whitney to offer him support and understanding. The lawyer's gaze is entirely held by the car, so that his eyes and head perform one steady movement as he stares after it. Though he is in conversation with the priest, he looks at him not once. At the end, as Whitney remains staring into the distance, the fading car sound becomes emblematic of his vanished hope. Meanwhile priest and lawyer exchange thoughts about the prospects for Joan and Eddie, and their views are inflected by the optimism of the one and the dejection of the other. Issues of individual perception underlie everything that's said, most evidently in Dolan's response to Whitney's declared belief that Joan has made a mistake: "It's only natural you'd think that, feeling the way you do about her." The film has Dolan articulate the bias in Whitney's understanding. But nobody on-screen ever remarks how the priest's vision is skewed by professional cheeriness.

We are placed to observe, not share, the viewpoints of the two men. Lang discovered a vantage point from which to display the relationship between an event and the spirit in which it may be seen. He did this by concentrating on acts of watching, in a way that would not have been available if he had needed also to show us Joan and Eddie on the move. It seems to me important that we do not exactly picture the departing couple, and we do not precisely imagine the manner of their leaving. We assume it. It becomes part of our knowledge of the relevant data. Lang asserts the scale of relevance by a device that declares the unimportance of the particulars of the car journey while dwelling on the split between the two men's ways of observing it. This kind of device is available because there is always more to the world than we need to, or could possibly, see.

The extended world is continually manifest in the ways in which things enter and leave the space of the frame. The fictionality of the world is usually most marked in the characters' relationship to the off-screen zone which is the space forward of the frame—their unawareness of the apparatus through which their actions and images are relayed. Though the performers have to be aware of the camera's needs, their playing most often creates the camera's absence and thereby transforms the nature of the space in front of them.[4] It is not that these characters are oblivious to the camera. There is no camera in their world. Their situation is interestingly contrasted with ours as spectators. We are aware of the mechanisms of presentation and have to be so to make sense of the movie's devices; if we could mistake the screen for a window, the world would have gone mad. There is a projector in our world.[5] The projector is real and present; the absent camera confirms the fictional status of the movie image and the integrity of the movie world.[6]

On location and on the studio floor, the actors' work supports a similar labor by the technicians. A prime objective is to forestall intrusions upon the fictional world by the apparatus, whether in the form of camera shadows, microphone booms, or studio noise. From time to time the image seems designed to demonstrate the camera's annihilation. A mirror shot in *Lady in the Lake* (Robert Montgomery, 1946) shows off the ingenuity that puts the hero's image on screen while the camera is supposedly confined within his point of view. Through trickery, however, the shot is also making a display of the camera's absence. That could well be its most important function.

Performance and framing create a spatial world in our minds that may never—and in some aspects can never—have existed in the studio. In Lang's film it is virtually certain that there was no actual car driven or even present during the performance of the Whitney-Dolan dialogue. However, we should not fall into thinking that the off-screen space is in any special sense fictional or imaginary. That would oblige us to see the on-screen image as nonfictional or real. On-screen and off-screen are equally fictional and imagined; seen/unseen and heard/unheard draw many of the relevant distinctions.

The off-screen world is necessarily a world of time as well as one of space. Movies always take us into the middle of things because the film and its story begin, but the world does not. Joan, Eddie, Whitney, and Dolan all have relevant histories. As the story of a couple, *You Only Live Once* faced its creators with familiar problems in screen dramaturgy: to start before or after the first meeting; if after, to introduce the couple together or separately; if separately, to start with the man or the woman; and, in either case, how to fill in relevant backgrounds (Eddie's criminal past, Joan's having become involved) without loss of momentum.[7]

We are in the middle of things, too, because this is a world without end. It is, crucially, a world of possibilities where an event that comes to count as a cause may have ramifications that we cannot predict. Everything we see, or come to know, has some necessary and innumerable potential consequences. When we see a woman we know she had parents and a childhood, some of whose circumstances may be disclosed to us. It is a safe assumption that Joan grew up in an American, English-speaking, household. She may have a sister (Joan has) who may enter into the action (Bonnie does). She may have cousins or an old boyfriend in Baltimore. (We shall never know.)[8] Her life thus far will have influenced the attitudes that bear on her situation and prospects.

As a zone of fact abutting on zones of possibility, the fictional world poses a relationship between all that we can assume and all that we cannot, or cannot yet, know. Joan and Eddie have driven off. Is the car Joan's? Did she borrow it or rent it? And who is driving? We might take the film's not answering any of these questions as a consequence simply of its power to determine relevance via selection. Then we should look out. Lang has already warned us not to assume the completeness of our knowledge, or its reliability.

The fact that Joan and Eddie are going off by car could become decisive for their fortunes—if, say, the vehicle turned out to have been stolen. We could imagine a Langian turn to the tale that would give crucial significance to the question of the driver's identity: Dolan and Whitney saw—as we did not—who was at the wheel. Five miles along the road a child is knocked down and left for dead. Dolan and Whitney come under pressure—since Joan is not a "two time loser"—to affirm that it was Joan who drove away from the prison. These are among the real, but not to be realized, possibilities ten minutes into the movie.[9]

Since the film's characters are in a world their knowledge of it must be partial, and their perception of it may be, in almost any respect, distorted or deluded. But that applies to us, too, as observers of their world and their understandings. In *You Only Live Once* Lang demonstrates how gullible we may become when we can be persuaded to limit the zone of possibility and so to carry our reading in a preferred direction. Given his skill and ingenuity, Lang can do this because he can rely on our willingness to ignore, by taking for granted, the profound mediation of our access to the fictional world and its events. We may take the mediation for granted; we may be overconfident that we understand its purposes.

We are offered an assembly of bits and pieces from which to compose a world. Fragmentary representation yields an imagined solidity and extensiveness. The malleability of the image is in a reciprocal relationship with the seamlessness and continuity that the image can evoke in our minds. Our imagination of the world is impressively independent of the means of representation; this is most clearly so in flagrantly nonrealistic media like cartoons, opera, or puppet theater.[10] But in the movies too a journey may be conveyed by a car scene, a sound effect, or even an animated diagram. We can take the meaning of an arrow traveling across a map between "Abilene" and "Dallas" as readily as we understand a departure-arrival dissolve. We do not have to see how the action occurs to understand it as taking place in its world, and thereby to know something of its character. There are as many ways of conveying any given thought, fact, or event as creative imagination could devise. Even at our dullest we can see some of the options. That should not suggest that one way is as good as another. Any particular device has aspects and implications unique to itself.

Selective representation creates the stylistically relevant freedoms for the artist. I say this to distinguish expressive choice from the contingencies of production. It does not matter that most likely the set did not exist in which to film the countershot of, say, Joan getting into the car. Since that action did occur in the fictional world, it could have been shown. We might say that the availability of that shot is a dimension of the fiction. The camera's staying with Dolan-Whitney is a choice to which we respond in relation to our understanding of the pictured world, not in relation to the hypothetical economics of the shoot.[11]

A picture from a fictional world brings with it everything that goes without saying. *You Only Live Once* starts with an unpeopled image of the front entrance to a neoclassical building with electric lights and with "Hall of Justice" engraved above its doors. It would be impossible to list all the things that we know from this four-second shot or all the frames of reference that it invokes. Among the most obvious are that we are in a modern town or city, probably in the USA, where recognizable systems are resourced for the proclamation and enforcement of law. We can reasonably suppose a society that erected this building to be in possession also of prisons, police, criminals, banks, armories, transportation, and communications systems. State murder of transgressors, if performed, may be by a number of methods, but boiling in oil will not be among them. There may, though, be some old citizens who claim to recall, with horror or nostalgia, the days when picking a pocket could get you tarred and feathered.

Surrounding all this will be attitudes to law and lawbreaking, some of which will be regarded as ordinary, some aberrant but comprehensible, and some outrageous. (There will be positions, too, on horticulture, music, navigation, and palmistry, but none of these becomes active in Lang's tale.) Concretely the film needs to tell us—because it does not go without saying—that in this jurisdiction a fourth criminal conviction entails life imprisonment and that murder is punished by a death sentence exacted in the electric chair.[12] (It does not need to tell us what is meant by "electric chair.")

The fictional world is a world not only when, and not because, it is *our* world but because it too has an infinity of goes-without-sayings. *The Wizard of Oz* (Victor Fleming, 1939) makes us witnesses to a world of the fantastic with many special rules and properties. Some of them are explained to Dorothy and to us.[13] We have to be told or shown the meaning of a pair of red shoes, instructed to see them as "ruby slippers." We are surprised to discover that a bucket of water can dissolve a witch. On the other hand the film can leave us to assume most of what matters. The physiologies of a man of tin and a man of straw—together with the threats from rust, fire or loss of stuffing—are easy to comprehend; and in Oz, as in Kansas or Coventry, the same things count as evidence of nerve, brain, or heart.

If this were not so, fiction would be impossible. It could never get started if it needed to itemize all the factors of relevance to the actions of its creatures, particularly since these would have to include considerations of the possible as well as of the actual.[14] What the story-maker chooses to articulate is influenced by the needs of exposition to the extent that those needs are not covered by what can be assumed. Beyond that, as Welles and Lang have shown us, articulation is less a route to clarity and more a device of rhetoric. We can take this further with the aid of Douglas Sirk and a moment from his *All I Desire* (1953). Ten years ago, in 1900, Naomi Murdoch (Barbara Stanwyck) left Riverdale, a small town in Wisconsin, deserting her husband and three children in order to avoid a scandal and so as to pursue a career on the stage. Now reduced to performing in low vaudeville, she has received a message from daughter Lily entreating her to return to witness the girl's graduation and her performance in a school play. She believes her husband, Henry, the school principal, to be a party to the invitation. In a tussle with the ambivalence of her feelings she has allowed herself to be persuaded that it would be fun to pay a visit. On the day of the performance, life in Riverdale is sketched for us through its concerns with rectitude and gossip. While Naomi completes the train journey and puts up at the town's one hotel, we are introduced to the members of the Murdoch household. Now, thirteen minutes into the film, it is evening and Naomi approaches the house walking steadily, with controlled apprehension. On the porch she delays, holding back tears. She stands in the shadows to look in on the domestic scene. The film cuts to a head and shoulders shot as she glances about her, hesitating. Her eyes move to a hanging flower basket in the foreground above her head. She reaches up into the top of it to take down a door key that she holds for a long moment in contemplation (fig. 15). She reacts in confusion to the noise of an approach, hurriedly replaces the key, and retreats further into the shadows of the verandah.

Anyone who has experienced this scene through eyes not blinded by snobbery about soap opera will recognize the brilliance with which Sirk has defined a complex of thought and feeling in a great actress's gestures.[15] The richness of the moment depends on the clarity with which the filmmakers have sketched the world of the small town so that its spatial and its social dimensions provide some defining contexts. Design and lighting present an architecture of containment and exclusion that draws on the social, legal, and familial aspects of space as property and privacy. To set foot on this threshold with whatever degree of boldness, anxiety, or carelessness is to enact a sense of one's entitlement and an apprehension of the community's view of it. The

Figure 15. Naomi and the key

meaning of a threshold as an area simultaneously within and beyond the embrace of privacy or intimacy makes Naomi's actions readable.

Again, the film is drawing on information that it has not laid out for us, but that is accessible as required from our knowledge of this world. For a start it is drawing on layered notions of security where the house must be lockable and a key may be kept hidden for emergencies—hidden from the world at large but available for the family so that knowledge of the secret represents inclusion in its community. The hiding place is sufficiently removed and enclosed, on the porch, to be in space marked as private, but it is easy of access to an adult and open enough to public sight to convey a confidence in the law-abiding tenor of the surrounding life. The key is special inasmuch as it has not been used in the family's ordinary coming and going.

Moreover, it has been kept in the same place for a period of years. Naomi reaches up and finds, quite easily, what she thought she might find. The film has discovered the means to dramatize Naomi's familiarity with this environment, and to put it in tension with her knowledge of self-exclusion, her sense of coming back as a stranger. As she looks in upon the family scene it is as separate from her as a lit stage is from a darkened auditorium. There is no occasion for Naomi to use the key. That awareness shades our sense of her motives and feelings in reaching for it. There are degrees of definition, areas of possibility. There was nothing that Naomi was going to *do* with the key. Her motives in looking for it are associated with her emotions rather than her purposes. Given her apprehension in approaching the house, the nervousness in her delaying the moment of entry, she may be seeking reassurance through reperforming an old, old gesture. She seems to find it comforting that the key is still in place: some things don't change even while children are transformed in ways one cannot guess by time and growth. Some of her old knowledge remains reliable.

Note that there are real possibilities that do not seem to be in play. Though it is conceivable that Naomi's response might contain an element of irritation, say, or of contempt, nothing promotes such a notion. Such things remain conceivable rather than visible or to be assumed. But the key in its accustomed place is evidently being seen as an emblem of stability and continuity, the index of an unchanging way of life in a community once abandoned in the search for something more exciting, less predictable.

Today's extraordinary return is experienced in its relation to memories of a once-familiar, even oppressive, routine of homecomings.

What is tentative in the gesture is felt in its pacing and through Naomi's holding the key to dangle at a distance from herself that is shown up by her white, elbow-length gloves. Formality in dress and stealthiness in action conflict to present another register of uncertainty. Then her replacing the key, and doing so hurriedly, enacts her knowledge that she is now excluded from a routine that has been maintained without her participation.

We have not been told, and we could not have been told, all that we draw on to participate in these moments. That comes, we might say, with the territory. We did not need to be informed in advance that there is a key in the flower basket. We did not need this either for clarity or for emphasis.[16] We did not need to be told what it would mean for a key to be secured in this way. Instead, knowing what it would mean, we are able to understand more of the character of the community and to apprehend and enter into the development of Naomi's experience. It is important to the effect that Naomi's knowledge of the world was here larger than ours. Before it caught her eye the basket had featured in the shot only as foreground foliage absorbed by shadow into the surrounding darkness; it was brought to our notice by the movement of her glance. She knew about the key and we did not, so that what was revealed to us was what was confirmed to her.[17]

On the other hand, the film has already taken us inside the house, and has sketched the current situation of each of the members of the family, so that its figures are familiar to us but not to her. We have knowledge of what awaits Naomi whereas she can only speculate. We have been presented with possibilities of development that affect our response to Naomi's hopes and fears.[18] The special nature of our access to the fictional world has the important consequence that we can know things unknown to some, or any, of the characters.[19] It is equally important that each of them has a vast body of knowledge that is not detailed for us. They each have their own store of experiences and memories, just as we have in our world. (This is not a matter of our access to the events of the plot.)

The relation between what is articulated and what goes without saying is vital to the sources of emphasis that enable the assertion of significance, and the grading of significance. We can tell that Naomi knew that a key used to be concealed in the flower basket, so we can tell that she reached up to see if it was still there. The momentary oddity of the gesture gives way to an understanding grounded in our knowledge of what privacy, security, and routine are, and what memories may be. The arc of our comprehension is different from the shape of Naomi's experience but it enables the moment's particular mix of observation and feeling.

The facts that ground our understanding here are sufficiently specific (a flower basket) and sufficiently ordinary (a reserve key) to play tellingly within a modest rhetoric.[20] There is music which, because of our knowledge of the world, we can understand as part of the film and not part of the fiction. It supports the understanding that Naomi's emotions are of an intensity that she must struggle to control and it affirms that we should be moved for her.

Alongside this the camera's gestures are delicately graded. The primary concern with interiority is developed through the pacing, since we are given an extended passage in which the action is stalled on Naomi's indecision. The film turns Naomi's approach to the house into an event, one that it studies when it could move more swiftly to resolve the immediate issues surrounding her arrival and reception. The image dwells on "incidental" aspects of the scene: Naomi's shadow, the movement of her gaze across the exterior of the house. Then, in the mid-shot as she reaches up into the top of the basket, the camera lifts to keep her hand within the frame. It tilts down again, reframing as she lowers the key in contemplation.

A formalist of the more blinkered variety might despise this camera movement as a mere adjustment, a wasteful and unstructured maneuver that subordinates image to performance, and demeans the camera to accommodate the actress. But Hypothetical Formalist would be ignoring the fact that a fractionally withdrawn camera, or a different lens, could have encompassed all the action without adjustment. The initial setup was chosen so as either to allow the hand to go out of shot or to demand the reframing. Sirk made a rhetorical choice that gives a precisely graded emphasis to Naomi's reaching. The gentle, subtle quality of the emphasis is in tune with the reflective tone of this passage. The play with scale is available because the taking of the key is a large matter only in Naomi's consciousness. Within the world of

Riverdale the gesture has a domestic character. Nothing great seems to turn on it—possibilities of embarrassment at most.[21]

Put this instance alongside *Citizen Kane* and I believe it becomes the clearer that the relationship between stylistic gesture and fictional world is crucial for the construction and understanding of tone, hence meaning. The extravagance of Welles's gesture and the modesty of Sirk's are palpable in the context of both the spatial measures and the terms of value obtaining in their worlds. In *Kane* the distance traveled across the Xanadu cellar is huge, and the height of it enormous, relative to what we expect of a cellar; it would be unremarkable in relation to a desert or an ocean, and absurd in relation to a corner grocery store. Sirk's small reframing on the Riverdale porch could be boldly declarative if it brought into view the hiding place of incriminating letters—or a deadly scorpion.

Sirk shifts to encompass Naomi's gesture, and the key, without moving away in the slightest from Barbara Stanwyck's face. A further index of the scale of stress awarded the gesture is found in the musical score. The composer gives the moment hardly any punctuation of its own within the flow of the scene's emotion; no little stinger solicits a special response.

This reticence is maintained as Naomi puts the key back. But here a repetition of the camera's tilt makes an acknowledgment in form that this act is an undoing of her first one. The repetition underscores the difference in mood between the tentative reaching and the hasty replacement. That the camera's moves could be regarded as primarily functional is an aspect of their discreet character (within the overall style of the sequence). Yet they are particularly implicated in the balance of distance and intimacy here, our sharing in and awareness of Naomi's confused, largely unacknowledged emotions in a journey she had portrayed to herself as an amusing adventure.[22] The adjustments of the camera give our eyes a degree of participation in the gestures of taking, inspecting, and giving up the key. They make us sharers in the pacing of the actions as we take the force of the thought-feelings "once mine," "still here, not for me."

Since the character is displaying the key to herself the actress is not required to make a further move to display it to the camera. No special illumination is employed; the key catches the light no more and no less than do Naomi's drop earrings. The moment is not punched up in the editing or by a change of focus. Within the rhythm of the scene the weight of emphasis is assigned simply through the reframings that serve to maintain the visibility of the gestures. The camera's procedures remain within the register of the ordinary. This is a choice of scale that acknowledges the unspectacular nature of a gesture uncomfortably caught between the routine and the transgressive, between what is likely to count, in Riverdale, as Naomi's entitlement and her presumption.

Every world has its own norms. Each world holds to beliefs and practices that place things on scales that stretch from the inevitable through the ordinary to the impermissible or the impossible. There is necessarily a relationship between the import and impact that a thing has in its world and the size of the gestures that display it on the screen. Since this relationship is not fixed, filmcraft can make it telling.

In Riverdale as we are shown it, work and gossip provide the two main points of contact and potential collision between home and the wider community. A place where Naomi's husband, an ambitious conformist, can abjure "progressive nonsense" in his role as school principal, and a place where behind doors and in whispers a prurient fascination attends the new possibilities of scandal offered by Naomi's arrival—this is the same world in different, but related, guises. But of course it is not the whole world, and definitely not the world in all its relevant aspects. By the time of Naomi's arrival we have already been given glimpses of the city with its vaudeville so low that it merges into burlesque, and of Riverdale's gun shop as a forum for dirty talk between men, and we have heard of a zone "out by the lake" that is available, but not secure, for illicit meetings.

Within the larger world, the isolation of any one space or community and its value-system (with its internal conflicts and subsystems) is always far from complete.[23] There are always Elsewheres that may be, for instance and in various mixes, familiar, remote, rumored, desired, feared, imagined, sought, envied, shunned, or demonized. A problem for Naomi, and potentially for her daughter, is whether a move from Riverdale should be welcomed as a liberation or lamented as an exile. Riverdale is not the whole world but it is the world that imposes the immediate context for the characters' actions and prospects. At every moment the film faces stylistic choices over the degree to which it will scale its gestures to the proportions and values of the depicted world.

The movie works for an audience that knows the world always to be larger and larger again than the sector currently in view. This knowledge entails an awareness of selection, hence of the concentrations and emphases that help to determine tone and viewpoint. *All I Desire* stays within the spectrum of domestic emotional turmoil. Within that spectrum the worst that will happen is heartbreak that may or may not be healed, and the best is some occasionally pleasant, more or less tolerable negotiation of conflict.[24]

Of course the film could disrupt the tone it has established. It could have Naomi's distress build to the point of madness or suicide. These are real possibilities of the world, then and there or here and now. But they are not within the movie's zone of choice. This suggests that a picture may define itself generically and tonally—for instance, as romantic melodrama rather than tragedy—partly through the way that it incorporates and excludes aspects necessarily entailed by its setting.[25] *All I Desire* chooses not to introduce material that would put domestic trauma into a withering perspective: destitution, sadistic cruelty, warfare. On the other hand, we see more striving for fulfillment than we see instances of it. Real joy or satisfaction is as little displayed as disease and death.

A contrasting example may be found in [Ernst] Lubitsch's *To Be or Not to Be* (1942), with its extraordinary turns between political melodrama and farce. The horrors of Nazi oppression in Poland are strongly depicted, with the worst of them only just off-screen, though consistently so. A propagandist distribution of good and evil sometimes occupies the foreground of the drama. But the main action of the movie assumes all that as the backdrop to fantastic comedy where theatrical disguise can become effective as a weapon of war and a bit player can think it worthwhile to try to foil the Nazis with his moustache-aided impersonation of the Führer. Meanwhile, with national and individual survival at stake, a troupe of actors finds that however desperate its fix it cannot escape its submission to theatrical values; the petty rivalries and vanities of the performing life repeatedly obtrude upon the immediate crises and threaten to wreck a breath-stoppingly precarious structure of pretenses. The provision of a withering perspective is as crucial for the tone of Lubitsch's film as its absence is to the tone of Sirk's.

The collision of the darkest realities with comic absurdity was assisted by the casting, most obviously of the leading male role. Jack Benny, who was with reason one of the most celebrated of twentieth-century comics, brought his familiar radio persona (unmistakably American) to the part of Josef Tura, an egocentric star of the Warsaw theater longing to play his Hamlet on a larger stage.[26] (A standing feature of Benny's clowning was his striving for cultural prestige through his efforts at the violin.) Seeing Tura as Tura, within the world of the action, alongside seeing Tura as Jack Benny, within our appreciation of the performance, is a main contributor to the success of this film's amazing experiment.

To Be or Not to Be shows us starkly that worldhood is not primarily an issue of realism, and is a concept that should work to illuminate artifice, not to deny it. Further useful provocations could be derived from the end of *Road to Morocco* (David Butler, 1942) and from the brilliant essay in film aesthetics that Max Ophuls offers at the start of *La Ronde* (1950). However, my final example is from Charles Laughton's *The Night of the Hunter* (1955). Another ending, the coda to a tale in which John (Billy Chapin) and Pearl (Sally Jane Bruce), children of the Depression era, have been in flight from a nightmare of betrayal and persecution and, following the defeat of Robert Mitchum's evil preacher, have at last found safety with a fairy-godmother figure, a widow called Rachel and played by Lillian Gish.

It is Christmas day and Rachel is in the kitchen cooking. She receives and praises the simple gifts brought by her orphan brood, then sends them off to find the presents she has left for them. Back at the stove tending to a steaming pan Rachel thinks aloud in the language of one who lives in daily communion with the King James Bible:

> Lord save little children. You'd think the world would be ashamed to name such a day as Christmas for one of them and then go on in the same old way. My soul is humble when I see the way little ones accept their lot. Lord save little children. The wind blows and the rain's cold, yet they abide . . .
>
> They abide and they endure.

At moments the sense of soliloquy is dominant. The camera approaches, not so as to exclude distractions (there are none), but so as to take us closer to the speaker. We are placed both to observe the inwardness of Rachel's rumination and to take its meaning as a homily for us. On the final affirmation, Rachel looks out and faces us with her belief. She smiles, and it may be that her faith gives her contentment; it feels, though, as if this is a smile of reassurance for us. Yet how can it be Rachel smiling at us? Rachel is alone in that 1930s kitchen; she has no audience. Lillian Gish was the one who knew about the camera and who could assume the task of speaking to us through it on the film's behalf.

If we insist too much on reason here we shall divorce criticism from experience. It is normal for a movie to stress and sustain the separation between the fictional world and the world of the viewer. Imagination allows the movie to work within that register. But imagination makes other registers available as well. In one such, a world may be suggested whose beings can respond to our watching. In another, the film may have its actors step aside from their character roles and move apart from the fictional world so as to appear to address or confront us in their own right.

A movie can change registers, or combine them in new ways. It has that power because, in the cinema as in the world at large, there is a constant interplay between background knowledge and immediate perception. Narratives work on the relationship between what we know—what we need to have somewhere in mind in order to follow them—and what takes our attention and engages our concern. The fluidity of that relationship allows us, for instance, to delight in aspects of a movie's style and structure even as we remain involved in the development of its action. It means that we never cease to be aware of performance however little attention we give it and however much we become wrapped up in character and predicament.

One way that fictional worlds match the real world is in the meaningfulness of glance and gesture. It is hard to see how it could be otherwise in a comprehensible movie. As projections or significant withholdings of what the characters have in mind or at heart, perhaps nothing can attract our interest with such ease and force as the actions of their eyes. Movies, as well as our lives, have taught us to be alert to the implications of the glance, boldly declarative, ambiguous, or subtly nuanced as it may be. Our education in this must be constant, and aided by the work we do to control the meanings that our own eyes convey. In film one may understand normal techniques, of cutting in particular, as serving to present clear eyelines that allow interpretation and invite wonder.

Against this background, I am likely to have a strong response to moments when a character's glance appears to be projected forward in my direction. Whatever it seeks on the range between intimacy and confrontation, eye contact ordinarily carries acknowledgment as its fundamental meaning. Yet within the film frame acknowledgment can only be performed, played, because it is without the essential condition for a real acknowledgment, the recognition of my presence and selfhood. When I respond to the invitation of the outward glance I engage in the fiction in a new way, by imagining contact rather than separation between my world and the screen world. By no means all outward glances carry this invitation. Most of the time—in [Yasujirō] Ozu's later films, for instance—such glances are not taken to enact any response either to the camera or to the anticipation of an audience. In *Lady in the Lake* characters regularly project their words and looks in our direction; the effect is certainly odd but it is adequately covered, for the purposes of the fiction, by the claim that we are occupying the eyeline of the gumshoe hero.[27]

We are sufficiently attuned to the minutiae of eye use to make discriminations through such matters as focus and the set of the head, and degrees of tension or relaxation in the surrounding features. At the opening of *The Night of the Hunter* we first encountered the Rachel-to-be as a figure abstracted from time, and framed fantastically within an evocation of the night heavens. Here, too, as she delivered a bible lesson about false prophets, Lillian Gish faced out from the screen. Her words, her appearance, and the tone of her delivery placed her in a dramatic situation that was given no concrete location; we understood her to be an old countrywoman speaking, with kindness and conviction, to a group of children. We also understood her to be delivering the film's epigraph, her words and image deployed to set up for us some of the terms in which we should view the drama to come.

Laughton's film is thus bookended by moments of address from Rachel. The ones at the start prepare the ground for the final ones, to be sure, but in other ways the effects are quite different. At the opening there is an implied audience for Rachel's words within the world that she inhabits, and though she is seen frontally there is very little sense, as she looks up, that her gaze is meeting or challenging ours. Her eyes and her speech project a gentle authority and her manner is fully that of one speaking impromptu to an audience of youngsters.

But at the end there is no audience for Rachel within her world. The setting, in the cottage kitchen, is realistic and familiar but it is shown now in a new way that suggests theater: the "fourth wall" has been removed to give us the view from behind the cooker. The last of the children, John, has left the kitchen before Rachel turns, seeming to shift her attention around to us, for "They abide and they endure." Her movement is matched by one of the camera's that, closing in, amplifies the effect of her turn. Her gaze is now clearly one that seeks to connect with ours. This special effect is placed as an envoi here, almost as clearly as the beginning was a beginning: by the music, by the completion of the main dramatic business, by the departure of the children from the stage of action, and by words that face into the future. The tale is over, the movie is all but over, and the world goes on. Rachel recalls the task in hand and resumes her cooking.

Three points seem equally important here: the special nature of this moment through its adoption of a changed register; its work as a formal device rhyming the picture's end with its start; and the embeddedness of most of its elements in the fictional world. The last of these is what we are most likely to miss. Yet the effect of the break must depend on the degree to which it is a break.

That the matter was of concern to the director is evident in his placing the moment as the climax of a sustained shot that pivots complex interaction and camera movement on the central figure. Most of Rachel's monologue has been spoken while the children are momentarily off-screen; they have run into the next room to open their presents. The reverie is interrupted when the four girls come back to thank her and scurry off upstairs with their gifts. A more weighty interruption, and a key context for the final affirmation, comes when the widow engages John in an exchange about his new watch. The boy's response offers the prospect that Rachel's care can heal the scars of his ordeal.

Other elements of continuity are provided by the words themselves. Rachel has earlier spoken to John about his power of endurance, telling him that "children are man at his strongest; they abide." She remains in character in the final soliloquy, since the children have remarked, and we have witnessed, that in her loneliness she talks to herself all the time.

By emphasis on the forward projection of the closing words as a claim on our consent—our willingness to grant that this figure can speak to us and for us—the film shifts the balance of prominence between the character and the player. What had been constants of our background awareness are now offered for more particular attention. Whether or not we could name the player we had always known that an actress was playing the role of Rachel. Moreover, when delivered to the camera, the role of Lillian Gish is being performed no less than that of Rachel. In bringing the player forward the film moves to invoke Lillian Gish's particular screen history of abused innocence and to remind those who know it that guiltless victims are not always rescued. It presents us with the possibility that she, too, could have an unlikely, lovely faith in benign providence. The particular relevance of these moments to my theme is in the way that they explore some of the possibilities in movement between the fictional world and the means of representation.

Because the world is created in our imaginations it need not suffer damage from any foregrounding of the devices that assist its construction. We can, if we will, glide over inconsistencies and absorb ruptures, or delight in them. It is not difficult to see the image on the screen simultaneously as a world and as a performance. We do it all the time. The degree to which the filmmaker maintains the independence, solidity, and coherence of the fictional world is a matter of choice and a variable. The decisions have great significance for style and meaning but no immediate bearing on achievement. The particular character of this ending depends on Laughton's having been able to hold the actress within her role even while bringing her forward as a spokeswoman. The movements toward and away from soliloquy are seamlessly performed, while the surrounding characters—the children—remain fully within the fiction and Rachel interrupts her musing to talk with them. Throughout, the central gesture of attending to the cooking is sustained. It contributes strongly to a mise-en-scène that keeps the figure of Rachel embedded in the cottage setting and does not seek to isolate her with effects of, for instance, lighting that would compromise the independence of the fictional world.

The result is that the central figure never ceases to be Rachel the cook and housemother (whose faith we may observe) when she presents herself also as Lillian Gish, an actress whose knowledge we must share. That sets up a conflict that I believe is vital for the significance and the emotional impact of this conclusion. "They abide and they endure" might seem to be the film's final message of reassurance, allowing us to believe perhaps that the nightmare was just a bad dream. But that would be to ignore the precarious, all but magical, quality of the children's survival within the fiction. And from our spectating position, whether of 1955 or of the twenty-first century, it would be to disregard our knowledge of the fates of persecuted children in the world that the actress now seems to be addressing. Rachel always had the aspect of a fairy-tale being. When she recounted Herod's slaughter of the innocents her stress was on the survival of the baby Jesus. In her, generosity of feeling and hope for the future of mankind can outweigh knowledge, producing an assessment that we can only long to share. In our world, the world from which we weigh Rachel's words, the endurance of children is too often and too cruelly tested.

Conclusion

Has this essay said anything more than that fictions are made for and by humans and that their strategies necessarily rely on the knowledge that we share? Perhaps not, but it has said nothing less. If, as it seems to me, this has been an exercise in exploring the obvious, then it is an obvious that we have mainly chosen to ignore. My examples demonstrate, to my mind, that understanding the events of a movie as taking place in a world is a prerequisite of the intelligibility not only of plot but also of tone, viewpoint, rhetoric, style, and meaning. If I am right it should be a priority in thinking about cinema—indeed in thinking about narrative more generally—to advance our grasp of what is involved in the worldhood of fictional worlds.

A priority but not an obsession. As a narrowly theoretical pursuit the fictional world is hardly preferable to any other. I would see no benefit in having worlds replace cause/effect, enigma/resolution, or order/disruption/resolution as a formalist distraction. It is an advantage of the fictional world that the concept is too broad to yield a methodology or an interpretive formula. It will not promise critical procedures that can replace attentiveness and dialogue. Not all our interests in film will be furthered by analyzing worldhood. But as the point of convergence between space, community, and the observing self, the fictional world surely earns a place among our central concerns.

Works Cited

Perkins, V. F. *The Magnificent Ambersons*. London: British Film Institute, 1999.
Wilson, George M. *Narration in Light: Studies in Cinematic Point of View*. Baltimore: Johns Hopkins University Press, 1986.

Filmography

All I Desire. Directed by Douglas Sirk. Universal Pictures, 1953.
Citizen Kane. Directed by Orson Welles. RKO Radio Pictures, 1941.
It Happened One Night. Directed by Frank Capra. Columbia Pictures, 1934.
Lady in the Lake. Directed by Robert Montgomery. MGM, 1946.
Late Spring. Directed by Yasujirō Ozu. Shochiku, 1949.
The Lusty Men. Directed by Nicholas Ray. RKO Radio Pictures, 1952.
The Night of the Hunter. Directed by Charles Laughton. United Artists, 1955.
Notorious. Directed by Alfred Hitchcock. RKO Radio Pictures, 1946.
Rebel Without a Cause. Directed by Nicholas Ray. Warner Bros., 1955.
Road to Morocco. Directed by David Butler. Paramount Pictures, 1942.
La Ronde. Directed by Max Ophuls. Films Sacha Gordine/Janus Films, 1950.
Sanshô Dayû. Directed by Kenji Mizoguchi. Daiei, 1954.
Strangers on a Train. Directed by Alfred Hitchcock. Warner Bros., 1951.
To Be or Not to Be. Directed by Ernst Lubitsch. United Artists, 1942.
The Wizard of Oz. Directed by Victor Fleming. MGM, 1939.
Written on the Wind. Directed by Douglas Sirk. Universal Pictures, 1956.
You Only Live Once. Directed by Fritz Lang. United Artists, 1937.

Notes

1   I would be happy if anyone could suggest a better word than this but "worldlikeness" is not a candidate. To describe a fictional world as worldlike is to miss the point; a fictional world *is*, fictionally, a world.

2   By which I mean all motion picture fictions. In fact I think it must be true of all narrative, whatever the medium, but my concern is with the movies.

3   See the brilliant essay in George M. Wilson's *Narration in Light* (1986).

4   Cf. portraiture, where the subject's complicity is often displayed through pose and vital to the picture's meaning. In line with regular usage I shall often use "camera" to stand in for the entire apparatus of filmmaking—lights, microphones, crew, wind machines, and so forth.
    Writing this essay I have been more conscious than ever of some problems attached to our use of the word "camera" to deal with the mobility of frame and viewpoint in movies. There is a gap in our vocabulary here, apparently irreparable since the alternatives to "camera" are all more misleading or more cumbersome. We seem to be stuck with expressions like "looking into the camera" to describe some images where that is not what either the character or the actor can be supposed to be doing.

5   For me, there is a lost magic of cinemagoing, though my lungs are grateful for it, through the removal of the tobacco fog that once gave the projector's beam so strong a presence in the auditorium.

6   Note that the converse does not hold. The actors' occasional acknowledgment of the camera cannot be without effect. But the effect is not necessarily to break the fiction or to detract from the worldhood of the world. In their appeals to our complicity or compassion Oliver Hardy's camera looks seem often to increase the sense of intimacy rather than to produce a new detachment. I shall say more on this point in discussing *The Night of the Hunter*.

7   *It Happened One Night* (Frank Capra, 1934) provides an interesting set of contrasts in its address to these issues.

8   The film can construct zones of relevance beyond which an issue like this one has no reason to arise.

9   A relevant further instance could be *Strangers on a Train* (Alfred Hitchcock, 1951) and the matter of Miriam's shattered glasses. When last seen they are in her husband's keeping and, potentially, damning evidence of Guy's complicity in her murder.

10 For more on this, see Perkins 1999, 40–41.

11 For some critical and scholarly purposes the economics are, of course, vital.

12 The makeup of this "us" is a matter of the constituency for whom the filmmaker has assumed what goes without saying. This huge topic might, for a Western readership, be forwarded by considering the opening shot of *Sanshô Dayû* (Kenji Mizoguchi, 1954) or the matter of Noriko's handbag at the tea ceremony in *Late Spring* (Yasujirō Ozu, 1949).

13 And some of them are not. While the Munchkins can direct Dorothy to the Emerald City, we should wonder why none of them may escort her there.

14 See Sterne, *Tristram Shandy*.

15 This is a scene of homecoming to compare with the equally fine one at the start of Nicholas Ray's *The Lusty Men* (1952).

16 Cf. *Notorious* (Alfred Hitchcock, 1946).

17 Take it the other way around. If she were going to reach into the basket to react to the *absence* of the key then the film (if it wanted immediate understanding rather than to set a puzzle) would have to have found a way to let us know that a key is or was normally stowed there. This illustrates the difference between a created expectation and a possibility inherent in the presented world.

18 For instance, it could become a major issue that Naomi's husband might not be the father of her son, or that she has misrepresented the nature of her work in the theatre.

19 For instance, that the sled called Rosebud has been destroyed.

20 In this world: a key left available to passers-by in Scorsese's New York would have different meanings; one left at the entrance to an igloo would present an enigma and we should have to speculate on its function until we were informed.

21 Cf. *Notorious* again; or replace Naomi with a crook hired to abduct her daughter.

22 Soon she will claim, in the family kitchen, "Now I know I'm really home," where she might say only that she knows herself to be back again.

23 Overtherainbow offers Munchkinland, Oz and the fortress of the Wicked Witch as distinct but adjacent environments, with Kansas as a world away.

24 Cf. the movement toward catastrophe in *Rebel Without a Cause* (Nicholas Ray, 1955) or *Written on the Wind* (Douglas Sirk, 1956). Sirk reflects interestingly on the matter of scale in *All I Desire*, with reference to the choice of school play, in Jon Halliday, *Sirk on Sirk* (London: Secker & Warburg, 1971), 89–90.

25 Here I want to draw attention to the interest and importance of Deborah Thomas's discussion in her book *Beyond Genre: Melodrama, Comedy and Romance in Hollywood Films* (Moffat: Cameron & Hollis, 2000) where—with reference to films that include *All I Desire* and *To Be or Not to Be*—relationships between genre, tone, and world are differently explored.

26 And, as William Rothman reminds me, identifiably Jewish.

27 In its relentlessness the effect soon becomes tedious. *Lady in the Lake* is a useful marker for the contribution that variety of posture and eyeline make elsewhere to the liveliness of film drama.

ACTING ON OBJECTS

First published in The Cine-Files: A Scholarly Journal of Cinema Studies, *no. 4 (Spring 2013): http://www.thecine-files.com/current-issue-2/guest-scholars/v-f-perkins/ (accessed June 1, 2020).*

Stella Dallas (King Vidor, 1937): Stella and the Bow Tie

In the first fifteen minutes of *Stella Dallas*, we are given an effective sketch of the forces, desires, and delusions that propel the abrupt marriage in 1919 between small-town mill-hand's daughter Stella Martin (Barbara Stanwyck) and factory manager Stephen Dallas (John Boles). Then the film whips us forward, past the birth of a daughter, Laurel, for an equally deft account of the resentments and irritations that nag away at the pair now that familiarity has dulled their first hopes and fervors. Stephen, exiled from the wealth and position of his Long Island upbringing, is vexed by his wife's defiant and incorrigible coarseness, while Stella chafes under his pedantic efforts to reform her speech and manners.

All this is dramatized in a scene at Millhampton's country club. To Stephen's disgust, Stella resists those concessions to decorum that would stand in the way of a good time. The sequence ends with Stephen impatient to leave but thwarted, stuck holding his wife's coat while she dallies in unsuitable company.

On the dissolve, the club's dance band music fades into a quiet where our ears pick up even the click of a light switch. It must have been a somber journey that brought the couple back to their apartment. Stephen paces the hallway searching for the words that will express his discontent but contain his fury. Stella breaks the silence and stands at the door of her dressing room.[1] She feigns resignation to the "usual lecture," having asked—disingenuously—"What have I done this time?" Mr. Dallas opens the inventory of his wife's offenses against good taste and his authority. Reproofs and protestations are exchanged until Stella retreats to her dressing table and begins the removal of her jewelry. She takes off trinket after trinket, announcing her indifference with a hostile glance as Stephen advances to stand over her and complete the catalog of his concerns. But her mood changes as she responds to Stephen's challenge to consider the crucial matter: "What's to become of us?" Her hands are arrested at the clasp of her necklace and her eyes lift to meet Stephen's gaze. Her voice softens on the words "Yes, Stephen." Notably it is Stella's attitude that changes here, not Stephen's. He remains fixed in position to ask, "Stella, why did you marry me?"—a question that is fraught with accusation, and a cover for the one that must bother him most.

Stella answers the question in more ways than one. In words: "Because I was crazy about you, silly, and I still am, only . . ." In the tone of her speech: no longer argumentative but conciliatory, even a mite playful. But also in gesture: as she speaks she relaxes into a brief smile and reaches up to undo Stephen's bow tie. A cut to a shot favoring Stephen directs our attention to Stella's hands pulling the tie apart and preparing to deal with his collar.[2] Removing her sparklers, Stella had set about undressing. Releasing his neckwear, she has set about undressing Stephen (fig. 16). The action carries such weight, for Stella and for us, that everything surrounding it is charged with meaning. Most remarkable, by contrast with the mobility of Stella's hands and their effect on his dress, is the rigidity of Stephen's posture and the fixity of his gaze. He has no response at all to Stella's touch, and seems not to notice the invitation that her gesture implies.

The bow tie enables Barbara Stanwyck to declare Stella's sexual availability with intimate indirectness while blocking all suggestion that the move is prompted by the character's own appetite. Her gesture is not extended with any further intimations of desire. We may gather that Stella wishes to dissolve Stephen's annoyance and is relying on the one approach that has always, till

Figure 16. Stella sets about undressing Stephen

now, been effective. We recognize that the failure of her offer marks a turning point. It is certainly, for her, an immediate disappointment. She has rested her arms on Stephen's shoulders (in an answering shot with subtly softened lighting) while beginning a plea for understanding. But Stephen interrupts her, without dilution of his hectoring manner, to resume the declamation of his sorrows and grudges.

Stella's arms sag. "Yes, Stephen," she says, this time in tones of defeat and dejection.[3] She abandons her work on the bow tie and turns away to attend once more to her necklace. Perhaps she has noticed Stephen's repossession of the word "crazy," draining it of erotic meaning. "Once, a long time ago," he charges, "you said you were crazy to learn everything, become someone, didn't you?" The death of Stephen's sexual interest in Stella is definitive. Incapable of being aroused, he is too locked in to his discontents even to observe that an offer has been made. Through all further discussion he stands with the wings of his tie dangling unattended from his collar, the limp remnant of a bid unanswered.[4] His self-righteous protestations of love are rendered hollow. The rest of the sequence presents developments pivotal for the plot: Stephen's (how long withheld?) announcement of his promotion to a post in New York, Stella's refusal to move there with him (on the terms he has laid down), and her lack of concern at the separation thus decreed. But we understand the motives that underlie each turn of these events because we have witnessed the action and inaction centered on a single item of costume.

Johnny Guitar (Nicholas Ray, 1954): Emma and the Chandelier

In the elaborate architecture of *Johnny Guitar* one piece of furniture draws the most particular attention, and may have done most to give the picture its aura of the baroque: the outsized oil-lamp chandelier that illuminates the public area of the gambling saloon erected in the wilderness by the heroine, Vienna (Joan Crawford). More at home in a cathedral (where it would be called a *corona*) than in a barroom, this wonderfully crafted ornament hangs as the symbol of Vienna's most anomalous ambitions and claims.[5] Largely unspecified acts of corruption and self-abasement have financed her rise and the construction of an establishment that she hopes will make her secure and wealthy, if she can survive the hostility of the locals, led by a cattle baron McIvers (Ward Bond), but more determinedly by her antagonist, Emma Small (Mercedes McCambridge).

If Vienna has traded honor, as she laments, for "every board, plank, and beam in the place," then this gorgeous fitment represents quite an investment of shame. But it represents Vienna also in her aim to exchange virtue for splendor. Other articles too—patterned china, a bust of Beethoven, a baby grand piano—offset the liquor barrels, the craps table, and the roulette wheel by providing a dressing of refinement to fill out the spaces and decorate an otherwise gaunt structure. Vienna's is to serve dual functions; it must deliver profit to a saloon-woman capitalist while making a home for one who seeks recognition (her own, most of all) as a lady of culture. The culture will make the lady.

Now chandeliers like this are a familiar item in Western decor, often helping to paint the barroom in the colors of a bordello. Props departments must have been able to offer them in many designs and sizes. What distinguishes *Johnny Guitar* is the prominence the object is given in the image and in the action. (It is not once mentioned in the dialogue.) Its functions have to have been written into the script and it is often cheated into position so as to occupy the upper foreground of the frame (fig. 17).[6] On separate occasions, when lowered on its rope by Johnny and when hauled aloft by Vienna, its weight is displayed to us and made audible in the effortful click of the ratchets. The episode to which it gives a spectacular climax begins with an overhead shot as Vienna circles it, taper in hand, to light each of its six lanterns. The care we see lavished on it gives us the sense that it is an art object particularly cherished as a token of Vienna's achievement and her aspiration.

Having been given so strong a feeling for what the object means to Vienna, we are well placed to apprehend its meaning for her enemy. Emma Small sees Vienna as an intruder who has brought a contagion of vice so potent, so

Figure 17. Vienna and the chandelier

dressed up in glamour, that it cannot be contained and can only be wiped out along with its source. Emma is further convinced that she alone sees this truth with the force and clarity to drive effective opposition. She implicates Vienna in robbery and murder so as to turn a town posse into a lynch mob with Vienna as its main quarry.

Vienna has closed the saloon and redefined it as her private sanctuary, but Emma leads the men to violate its space and drag its owner off to hang. The exit from the saloon is choreographed with power and finesse in a single shot that sweeps everyone out through the building's one entrance, binding many jarring energies into one deadly flow. The momentum is further propelled by the malign thrust of Victor Young's music. But as the last few of the invaders reach the doors the camera ceases to track their movement. It pauses within to observe the last departure. The orchestra holds its breath until Emma trips back in, alone and newly armed with a shotgun almost as big as she is. She smiles inwardly, knowing what to do, as the first thing she sees in the deserted saloon is the chandelier. We are given it from her viewpoint and, for the first time, in close-up.

That image is extended, as are the ones that follow, to capture Emma's savoring the moment. She cocks the shotgun, then grins wide-mouthed and lifts it into firing position. The image teases with readability as Emma discharges her erect, borrowed weapon into the round of Vienna's chandelier. But it is the fulfillment of hatred that brings Emma such joy and wonder. In performance McCambridge identifies Emma first with the chandelier, bowing low with it as it crashes to the floor, then with the awful power of light shattered into flame. A crazy glee enraptures her and she stretches out her arms to urge on the spread of the blaze. She looks with wonder on the fire that will purge her world of saloon-women and everything they stand for. Backing away to rejoin the hanging party, she is glued to the spectacle and holds the swing doors wide apart to feast her eyes as long as she can.

The speechless mania enacted here is a necessary complement to the shrewdly calculated rhetoric with which Emma, the politician, has earlier inflamed the posse. (The duality of her character mirrors the duality of Vienna's.) There's a further marvel of performance a few seconds away, but it projects Emma's delight in the results of her action rather than in the action itself. What about the chandelier?

It gives Emma a violent means to a violent end.[7] It gives the film and the actress the means to display Emma's pleasure in the process of destruction as well as in its outcome. We do not know just how spontaneously she decided on the deed. (Unlike the lynching, it is not something she has advocated.) She may have been nurturing the event in fantasy ever since the first of Vienna's boards, planks, and beams were set in place. Fire is the most promising agent for the ruination of a mainly wooden structure. Setting the blaze allows Emma a part in the eradication of her foe that is hers alone, whereas the gallows work is an essentially communal procedure. But if all that's wanted is a fire, the options are many. A box of matches will do. If the chandelier is to serve, the desired effect may be achieved—we have been shown—by releasing the rope that holds it in place. But that would require effort; the act would be more strenuous than playful. Shooting it down, with one blast, imbues the action with the masculine potency specially attached, in the Western, to gunplay.

But most vital is the way that the assault on the chandelier draws on and sustains the sense that the bond of hatred between Vienna and Emma gives each of them peculiar insight into the other's psyche. (It could be the other way also—that their insights fuel their hatred.) Living delightedly with *Johnny Guitar* over many years I have been persuaded that the unacknowledgeable intimacy of hero[ine] and antagonist is a prime source of the dramatic power that allows extremity of emotion to survive and harmonize with the movie's continuous play with absurdity. Emma has neither seen nor been told anything that suggests what significance the chandelier holds for Vienna. But without this, she knows (and does not have to think about it) that to bring down this chattel is to annihilate Vienna's own emblem of her achievement and her hopes. Not having to think about it goes for us, too. At this crisis we understand the motives that underlie each action and gesture because we have absorbed the meanings invested in a single item of decor.

Filmography

Johnny Guitar. Directed by Nicholas Ray. Republic Pictures, 1954.
Stella Dallas. Directed by King Vidor. United Artists, 1937.

Notes

1. This has also to be the bedroom, though no bed is seen.
2. A striking instance of the way that cutting, as well as visual organization, can define the burden of a movie image. The shot's length is governed by the duration of the gesture. As soon as the action is completed, the shot changes.
3. The repetition here, like the adjacent one on the word "crazy," is one of many gifts bestowed on the actors by expertly crafted dialogue. It is noteworthy that the screenplay was the work of a team who were husband and wife: Sarah Y. Mason and Victor Heerman.
4. Imagine the range of possible meanings of Stephen's action if he were at any point to complete the removal of his tie. When and how he did this would matter greatly, it's clear.
5. For confirmation, see http://www.rouge.com.au/5/perkins.html (accessed June 1, 2020).
6. It is able to be on screen often because Philip Yordan's screenplay locates so much of the drama in the public space of the saloon. The first part of the movie is skillfully constructed to yield thirty minutes of continuous action in this setting.
7. This is a formulation I was delighted to be offered by a student in a long-ago seminar.

DIRECTORS AND MOVIES

LETTER FROM AN UNKNOWN WOMAN (ON THE LINZ SEQUENCE)

First published in Movie, *nos. 29–30 (Summer 1982): 61–72.*

Have you any idea what [a woman's] life is like in a little garrison town?

Letter from an Unknown Woman (1948) is unusual, among the great movies, for the volume and quality of discussion it has received. In particular, Robin Wood's essay in his book *Personal Views* gives a finely argued reading that I would wish to contest in very few matters of substance. Writing in that context, I thought it might be useful to examine one quite brief section of the film in more detail than an overview allows. I chose the Linz sequence partly because it enters very little into the already published discussion.

It seemed also to be characteristic and highly effective without being astonishing. Where other episodes in the film are of immediately striking brilliance, the Linz sequence appeared to be excellent in a straightforward and rather marginal way. That seemed to set up a test case for the impression the film creates of extraordinary unity and coherence. My examination of the sequence is therefore centered on, first, the relevance of its details to the overall structure of the film and, second, the interlock within its mise-en-scène between choices related to filmcraft (that contribute to its dramatic effectiveness) and those which inflect its story material thematically.

For the purposes of my discussion, the sequence consists of two scenes. In the first of them, Lisa (Joan Fontaine) is taken by her mother (Mady Christians) and stepfather (Howard Freeman), the Kastners, to be introduced to a young lieutenant, Leopold (John Good), and his uncle, a colonel. A some-time-later dissolve takes us into the second scene, in which Leopold walks Lisa around the town square during a band concert. The pair are clearly established as a couple, and recognized as such by the parents, whose open-air café table they pass on the way to the public garden, where Leopold begins to propose. The negotiations are broken off when Lisa claims to be engaged to a musician in Vienna.

Synopsis

Vienna, about 1900. Stefan Brandt (Louis Jourdan) returns to his apartment at 2 a.m., three hours before he is due to face—but intends to run away from—a duel. His dumb servant, John (Art Smith), hands him a letter. It tells him that the writer, Lisa, has loved him since her girlhood when she lived with her widowed mother, Frau Berndl, in that same apartment block, and when Stefan was an acclaimed prodigy as a pianist.

A flashback narrated by the "unknown" voice of Lisa shows the girl's romantic obsession, the first glancing encounter and Lisa's subsequent efforts to educate herself so as to feel worthy of her hero. Her devotion survives the dawning awareness that Stefan is a philanderer, so that she is aghast at her mother's plan to marry Herr Kastner, a military tailor from Linz, since that will involve leaving Vienna. She runs away from the railway station minutes before the final departure, believing that she intends to offer Stefan her life. But her resolve is shattered when she sees Stefan returning home with the night's conquest.

In Linz, she is introduced to a young lieutenant, Leopold, whose career is guaranteed, as his uncle is a colonel. She shocks her parents by refusing the offer of marriage, telling Leopold that she has been secretly engaged to a Viennese musician.

She returns to Vienna as a young woman and finds work modeling in the dress shop of Frau Spitzer (Sonja Bryden). Every night she waits in the street by Stefan's apartment until, on a snowy evening, he approaches her and, without recognizing her, rearranges his schedule to take her to dinner and for an evening of pleasure which leads, by way of amusements and dancing in the deserted Prater, to his bedroom. Two days later, he seeks her out at the shop to tell her that a musical engagement has called him away to Milan. He is to be gone for two weeks. But he does not return to Lisa and she refuses to call upon him when their child, whom she names Stefan, is born.

Ten years pass, in which Lisa devotes herself to her son and, at last, marries Johann Stauffer (Marcel Journet), a man of high position. At the opera with her husband, the mature Lisa encounters Stefan again. He is now a middle-aged roué who has all but abandoned music. Despite his failure to remember her, Lisa is convinced that their need is mutual and is determined to offer herself to him, although Stauffer warns of the consequences for herself, her son, and her "seducer." She sends young Stefan away (for "two weeks"), unaware that her action has exposed him to typhus. Her entry to Stefan's apartment is observed by her husband. Disillusioned once more by Stefan's failure to recognize her or the depth of her passion, she leaves to join her son.

Stefan Brandt reads the final lines of the letter, which tell of his son's death and Lisa's mortal illness, as the clock strikes five and the carriage arrives to conduct him to his appointment with Stauffer. Stefan struggles to recall images of Lisa (from his memory or from her letter) but John signals that he has not forgotten the young Lisa Berndl. As he walks out to face the duel, Stefan looks back on the site of his first encounter with the girl and is reassured of the value of his action by a fleeting but "accurate" remembrance of her.

The Linz sequence breaks with one of the main lines of the film's construction: that whereby Lisa's presentation of her life (which "can be measured in the moments I've spent with you and our son") is also a drastic re-presentation, an overhaul, of Stefan's. In reviewing the crucial episodes of her life, Lisa's letter asserts, at last persuasively, that Stefan's life—his, "vivid and real" life—must as well be measured by their moments of meeting, parting, or tantalizing proximity. The film's narrative is shaped by Stefan's presence. But the Linz sequence is defined by his absence.

"There was nothing left for me. I went to Linz." The words which open the sequence contrast bleakly with the promises of renewal, rebirth, in the introductions of the other episodes: Lisa's first contact with Stefan is the second of her "two birthdays ... the beginning of conscious life"; her return to Vienna is "a new beginning"; and the final episode opens as she receives a birthday gift from her husband. The stress on emptiness, lifelessness, is associated with the confinements of provincial life. In the original Stefan Zweig story, the episode is covered in a few paragraphs, generalizing Lisa's state of mind across a period of two years. The burden of the passage is that throughout that time Lisa did nothing of interest, refused to do anything of interest, and retreated from society into a morbid nourishment of her passion. The episode thus presents in miniature the problems of dramatization inherent in the whole project of filming Zweig's tale: apart from its value as an exercise in literary style, its main point of interest, and the thing that distinguishes its plot from the standard saga of unrequited obsession, is the motif of nonrecognition. But that is also, from the filmmaker's viewpoint, its most treacherous feature. It hazards credibility, since the audience, itself performing the act of recognition throughout (of Lisa and of Joan Fontaine), is more likely than the reader to gag on Stefan's failure. Moreover, it gives the plot a negative center. The focus is on an event which (repeatedly) does not occur and which thus threatens to resist expression within the specific times and spaces of the film frame.

At the general, structural level, some of the problems are solved by a double dramatization: first, of the act of narration (writing) through the use of flashback with Lisa's voice-over—a bold move against logic that responds to, but goes beyond, the extreme subjectivism of Zweig's narrative; then of Stefan's act of reading, through the invention of a framing story which makes the time of reading crucial. Thus, the Linz episode is framed by images of Stefan which register not so much the passage of time (no clocks, chimes, or overfilled ashtrays) as the growth of involvement and perhaps commitment. The reading began casually as Stefan stood over his desk, the curiosity roused by the letter's opening not strong enough to absorb him completely; with the pages open at arm's length before him, he could still attend to the lamp, to cigarettes and matches. Now, in counterpoint to "You who have always lived so freely ... ," tightly framed by the image and with a slow minor variant of the Liszt theme to darken the tone, he sits at the desk with the letter held closely and does not notice even his own act of turning the page. At the close of the Linz episode, the camera will react, as he will not, to his servant's arrival with coffee and cognac. The passage of hours in Stefan's night is transferred from the passage of days, months, and years in Lisa's story—whose very deliberate pacing enacts the erosion of the time Stefan needs to make good his flight. But the cognac will speak differently, perhaps of his intention: if time is what is needed to escape the duel, "no more cognac" has been prescribed as a condition of surviving it. But perhaps, too, at that moment, Stefan's main concern will be for his own reappearance at the center of Lisa's tale. For Stefan at this point it may really feel as if "all the clocks in the world have stopped."

Within the Linz sequence, the problem of dramatizing inaction is allied to the problem of creating a distinct character for the episode, so as to evoke Lisa's sense of the absolute separateness of her existence without Stefan from her life with, or within reach of, him. The first problem is one that Howard Koch in a valuable essay published in *The Hollywood Screenwriters* (Corliss 1972, 125–32) characterized as the need to provide actable situations for Joan Fontaine. It is met by dramatizing, not the renunciation of the world that Zweig evokes, but the effort and the failure of Lisa to ignore her "destiny" and take her place in society. The screenplay succeeds in "carrying the emotional progression of Zweig's story" at this point by reversing its specific content: inaction is pictured as action advanced and undone in Lisa's near-submission to Linz and her parents' plans for an advantageous marriage.

That pattern of action yields the elaborated buildup to an abrupt and definitive reversal (culminating in a comic play between parental excitement and the suitor's disappointment) and it shapes the incident as a self-contained, diversionary chapter in Lisa's life. The enclosure is furthered by a presentation that is overtly humorous. At this point alone is the film's irony matched in the phrasing and delivery of Lisa's commentary: "Twice a month that summer we listened, the lieutenant and I."

The isolation of the sequence results, too, from its setting. The most important thing about Linz is that it is not Vienna, but it is given a variety of ways in which not to be Vienna. It is seen only as an exterior, a public setting with none of the delicate (and delicately erotic) play between public and private spaces that characterizes Vienna. Where Lisa's Vienna is mainly nocturnal, Linz is entirely a daylight world, and a summer world. It is enclosed within its season like the spring of Lisa's girlhood, the winter of romance and the autumn of the denouement—a further dimension of the play with time.

It might have been the Mozartian connection of Linz that occasioned the change of locale from Zweig's Innsbruck. At least, to think of Linz as the recipient of the Symphony No. 36 does sharpen the irony in the use of music. Lisa's eager lieutenant is clumsy enough to compare Linz's music with Vienna's; her mocking affirmation of the town's musicality comes after a military band has pumped out four bars of effortful waltz time. Vienna, too, has musicians who can play that way, with the emphatic beat that flattens and unsprings a three-quarter rhythm: most obviously, the disgruntled quintet in the Prater ballroom. But they are marginal elements in the flow of music around the life of the city. The sense that this is Linz's best and only music is given not just by the dialogue and situation but by a use of sound specific to this episode. Apart from Lisa's narration, which exists in a different space, the only sounds we hear are the sounds of Linz itself. They are again insistently public sounds, beginning with the cathedral bells that summon the community to its Sunday obligations. "Background music" is customarily intimate in that its reference is to the interior life of the characters, or to the feelings that we should have about their situation. But there is no intimacy here. The music, like the decor, is entirely exterior and ostentatiously irrelevant to Lisa's emotion. The insistence and the irrelevance are equally important: the music provides backgrounds appropriate to the scenes that society expects Lisa to enact. The slow, wistful waltz could encourage her in a shy exchange of tender sentiment. To these strains she, as well as her lieutenant, might play out the role of respectfully ardent young lover. Then, the razzmatazz of the Radetzky march at the concert's end would supply a perfect, if clichéd, celebration of the outcome. The Radetzky is the ultimate display piece, polka as much as march, and exuberantly ceremonial rather than warlike. This most fitting herald of the general joy sets the wrong pace for the disarrayed return of an offended suitor and his confusedly resistant intended.

The eruption of disharmony at this point has been implicit in Lisa's appearance throughout. For once she is dressed with more effort than success: she carries the costume of a miscast, impossible role (fig. 18). High-waisted

Figure 18. Lisa dressed with more effort than success

and full-bodiced to give an impression of adolescent puppy fat, it engulfs her in ribbons, frills, flowers, and bows, and it suggests (or fails to disguise) that the star has round shoulders. If that makes the design a Hollywood catastrophe, the effect is carefully judged. While the lines and proportions are all wrong, at odds with the human figure caught within and below, they are only just so—enough to enforce Lisa's sense of the ridiculous and the demeaning in her situation without making her a grotesque. The outfit can be read as defining her mother's sense that this is as far as expense and ornament can sensibly go to overcome unpromising material. Lisa's dejected submission is pictured not just in the costume—with a hat that seems to be wearing her—but in the awkwardness of Fontaine's movement. Her parasol is held as an unwieldy prop, endangering the lieutenant, so that they have difficulty in synchronizing their steps to parade as a couple. In the stroll around the town square, Lisa is made to negotiate the hazards of puddles and pigeons as well as the greetings of Leopold's friends, to one side then the other. The camera is set back far enough to show the effort invested in the (only partial) achievement of grace.

In almost every particular, Lisa's introduction to Leopold reverses the characteristic shape of her contacts with Stefan. The Viennese pattern is that Lisa detaches herself from society and hastens to an isolated spot where, as a silent, still, and solitary figure, she can await Stefan's approach. (If he does approach, that will count as Destiny.) While this shape dwells on what is willed and calculated in Lisa's "submission" to her Fate, Stefan's experience of the meeting as fortuitous is marked in the way that Lisa is discovered to one side (in the margin) of his chosen path. Lisa's appearances are diversions from the course of Stefan's life (a life lost in diversion). Like the letter itself, they cut across and distract him from some other action or intention.

By contrast, the rendezvous in Linz is prearranged on both sides and presided over by parents and society. Its movement is into, rather than away from, the flow of surrounding life. Lisa is conducted to the appointed place, flanked by her parents, at a regulated pace which suggests the importance of arriving neither before nor after the appointed time. There is no period of silent waiting before the Colonel is discovered, in charge of his nephew Leopold, facing Lisa's party from immediately in front. The camera pans away from Lisa's group but continues its line of movement to reveal the two soldiers already in place. That they are also above, at the top of a flight of steps, and must descend for the introductions, makes its own comment on the social opportunity in prospect here. The shot develops as a track that charts the progress of Lisa and Leopold in the wake of the parental group until they arrive in the town square and become part of the general stream of movement into the cathedral. The couple's actions are enclosed within parental direction by the way in which shot and scene begin and end with comment from Frau Kastner, begin with parents in the lead and end with parents shepherding from the rear.

The distinctness of the Linz episode is, perhaps, summarized in Ophuls's muting, for this period, of one of the film's most marked visual effects: the presentation of Lisa's face as a globe of radiance, lit from within (because from no material point in the film's world) to shine in the surrounding darkness. The elements that heighten the contrast are removed from Linz by dressing Fontaine all in white and providing a rational source, the sun, to cast light (almost) evenly across the objects and figures around her. The radiance of the Viennese Lisa is one of the main resources through which Ophuls balances the recognition that his heroine, in her stubborn fidelity, is also a fixated adolescent. It images the intensity of the private vision which she asserts against material, psychological, and social reality and makes of it, even or especially in its folly, the source of an extraordinary glamour.

The effect is appropriately muted in Linz because it is there that we see Lisa most nearly accommodating herself to society and suppressing her romantic conviction of the impossibility of a life not centered on Stefan. Indeed, one of the episode's most important functions is to offer a portrait of that life, so as to anticipate the conditions of Lisa's marriage to Johann Stauffer and thus remove the need, at that point, for fresh exposition (or for the more extended presentation of Stauffer that would detract from our awareness of Stefan Jnr as the new center of Lisa's world).

The Linz that is defined by its difference from Vienna, defined as the non-Vienna, is the one seen and experienced by Lisa. The contrasts are with a Vienna perceived, very selectively, as Stefan's world. There is another Linz that she floats through like a sleepwalker, an exigent social world that anticipates the pattern of life in the other, and ultimately more powerful, Vienna. In music, for instance, Lisa measures the sounds of Linz against the private efforts, furtively appropriated, of a soloist. The "music of Vienna" is that music with which she feeds her fantasy of romance. The music of Linz is band music, emphatically regulated by a conductor whose uniform is redolent of the official, the dutiful, and the public. The bandmaster is a military grotesque, one that you could chuckle over all the way to the firing post. What he is grotesque in is a pompous and unyielding propriety that emphasizes hierarchy: his leadership (only ceremonial, yet threatening) consists in ensuring that those under his command are, or adequately pretend to be, as completely responsive to external direction as he is himself. He is a master of uniformity, thus its slave, and the uniformity he imposes is particularly a matter of time and movement.

The power of this public world of enforced regularities is asserted, rather against Lisa, by Ophuls's decision to begin the proposal scene with the bandmaster's image at the moment of his first command, and then to orchestrate the complex movements of characters and camera (and even the delivery of Lisa's narration) to the bandmaster's tempo. Foreshadowed here is that other occasion of public music-making disrupted by Lisa's pursuit of her destiny: the opera. The episodes are similarly structured, and in each case we see society as a performance, a show, with Lisa alone unable to carry through her allotted role. The Linz concert and the Viennese opera are alike musical pretexts for the display of solidarity at the top level of society.

In each of them the dutiful leisure of the upper classes is visibly maintained on the work of others. In Linz the bandmaster drills his cadets in the labor of music-making. His unsmiling grunts of command do not even hint at the possibility of enjoyment. The stiffness of the actor's baton movements emphasizes subjection, as does the framing of the image, which places a faceless horn player in the left foreground so as to present the weight to be lifted as he raises his instrument on the beat of order. Meanly dressed, the players have no share in their leader's splendor and they are marched away, at the scene's end, like a convict squad.

The foregrounding of servitude and menial labor (often explicitly alienated) as the condition and cost of "splendor" is a constant of Ophuls's later work, but it has a particular role in *Letter from an Unknown Woman*. As the disregarded support for an often dazzling way of life, servitude is the skull beneath the skin both of elegance (achieved or attempted) and of romance. For if the bandsmen are conscripted into Leopold's attempt to pass off a parental scheme as his heart's vocation, Lisa, too, will avoid recognizing the mechanics that construct and maintain the fabric of her idyll with Stefan—for example, the tired "railway" workers and, most notably, the bandswomen of the Prater whose mock military garb stresses their correspondence to the Linz cadets. What Lisa cannot see, and this relates to her misreading of Stefan himself, is the substructure of routine on which she elaborates her fantasy of the unique and ordained.

The peasant cart which interrupts our view of the introduction of Leopold to Lisa rumbles across the screen to submerge formality in graceless racket. It is forcibly presented to us as an element in the life of Linz that conducts itself without reference to the schemes and protocols of the bourgeoisie; its direction of travel down the street and across the screen opposes the flow of

Society's movement toward the Cathedral. While its lumbering progress does comment, in bathos, on the effusive attempt at etiquette by Lisa's stepfather (Herr Kastner), its unscheduled eruption in the midst of a carefully drilled ritual is significant largely for the notice it fails to receive from the characters on the screen. They pay it the attention only of avoidance.

The effect here is echoed in that at the end of the sequence, after Lisa's desperate declaration that she is not free to marry Leopold. The couple have to cross the line of the departing bandsmen in order to make their way to their parents' café table. The camera's movement is interrupted so that the image stays on this side of the procession while Leopold and his uncle withdraw from the scene in abrupt propriety. Our access to the action is again restricted by the passage across the foreground not just of the band but also of the following rag-tag of peasants, children, and old people. We hear no word of what is spoken between Leopold, his uncle, and the Kastner family.

Considerations of craft are involved here: for instance, the effort so to deploy limited resources of set and cast as to create the sense of an extensive and fully populated world. More immediately relevant is the avoidance of redundant action. In dumb show, Leopold's exchange with his uncle can be abbreviated; we no more need to be told its content than we needed to hear Leopold's third repetition of "I'm very honored to make your acquaintance." But, beyond that, Ophuls's treatment is a means of telling us that we don't need to be told, of stressing protocol: the curt civilities of renunciation are referred back to the elaborate forms of introduction, while controlled outrage and baffled dismay are set in the frame of exuberance and simple pleasure.

Summarized here is the imperviousness of this world to any but its own orders. Immersed in its performance of itself, the official world of bourgeois propriety—on its journey from Mayerling to Sarajevo—has as little perspective on its goals as Lisa has on hers. Her romantic hallucination is compared with, and preferred to, its social blindness. She is trapped in fantasy: "He writes music," she tells Leopold of Stefan, with a mixture of apology and pride, as if even the Stefan of her inflated vision needed some further push toward grandeur. But Linz is trapped in pretense, the extent of its entrapment being conveyed through the barely containable ecstasy of Frau Kastner at the prospect of her daughter's engagement. Lisa may need to construct the man of her dreams, but the parents have an equal need to see the triumph of young love in the convenient transactions of the marriage market.

Linz is the site, then, for a preliminary confrontation between the strength of inner conviction and the power of social institutions. Everything external is on Leopold's side. The breeze which ruffles Lisa's dress during his monologue opposes the flimsiness of her exterior to the unyielding stiffness of Leopold's, as the hard vertical sheen of his helmet tyrannizes the fruit-salad frivolity of her hat. This stiffness of dress unites Leopold with the bandmaster and with his uncle but also with the nonmilitary figures of Frau Kastner and, later, Johann Stauffer; Herr Kastner's bearing indicates, comically, his aspiration to the same condition. (Compare the looser, softer stuff of which Stefan's clothes and movement are made.) Leopold's uniform, too, is as strikingly "black" as Lisa's is "white"—and this relationship anticipates the distribution of costume tone between Lisa and her husband.

Lisa is trapped by the setting chosen (by Leopold, by Ophuls) for the proposal. The corner of the public garden to which he leads her is encircled by railings, shrubs, benches, and statuary. It is a hard little alcove which offers no means of evasion or convenient distraction, small and private enough to enforce the intimacy that Leopold needs and Lisa fears. Yet its enclosure is not so complete as to put the pair on equal terms. It is under the eye of the parental group: an effect achieved partly in the cutting, against spatial logic, but also produced by their position as distant guardians of the only exit. A couple with a baby carriage is present within the gates to ward off any suggestion that the park is a place of romantic assignations. It is continuously open (through the railings) to the sights and sounds of the surrounding community—sufficiently public, then, to stifle any strong move toward resistance.

Leopold's speech is a juggernaut of long sentences like "It may be unnecessary for me to mention that ever since you came to my attention I have been most favorably impressed." Their cunning accumulation of heavy vocabulary and staggered syntax would not normally be inflicted on an actor, but here the resultant awkwardness in performance can be absorbed into the characterization. The task of holding on to these lines is complicated by

Ophuls's filming the bulk of them within one shot; but the actor's concentration becomes Leopold's effort in delivering himself of a speech to which he has given long and careful, if scarcely inspired, thought. Against the weight of his words, in their continuity and their preparedness, Lisa is given—by the writer and the situation—only frantic spasms of improvisation.

Her sense of being cornered, and Leopold's of having cornered her, are acted out in the use of eyeline. The lieutenant's courtesy obliges Lisa to be the first to sit and so allows him to take up a position that both places her under his inspection and puts a strain on any effort of hers to reciprocate. His scrutiny is interrupted in several moments of anxiety and embarrassment, but his gaze has its point of rest on her face. Conversely Lisa's glance flits up and across to him by moments, in appeal or to acknowledge his presence and her obligations, but her eyes return constantly to look forward and down, away from his stare. To have allowed her to meet his look steadily would have been to offer her in either submission or defiance, and while she is never quite ready to submit, she certainly has not the power to defy.

The effect of Leopold's dominance is amplified by images whose framing takes his height as a pretext to diminish Lisa's presence. The top of the picture consistently crops close to, or across, the lieutenant's helmet but just as consistently it leaves space (and most of the time a lot of it) above Lisa's hat. Even in her close-up, Joan Fontaine's figure does not fill the frame. The effect is particularly pronounced in the matched pair of shots covering the speech and Lisa's intervention. The shot that favors Leopold has Lisa in, but far from dominating, its foreground. In the answering shot of Lisa, Leopold is the foreground.

It would be possible to read these procedures as a registration of male authority as against the natural frailty of women. But such a reading would need to ignore much that Ophuls emphasizes, in particular his pervasive insistence on the playing out of social roles and on the bonding of manners to social structure. (Similarly, interpretation of the motifs of stiffness as phallic should be at least restrained by the recognition that these motifs regularly surround characters who are symbolically impotent and/or sterile. It is as if too firm a devotion to the tokens of male authority were either cause or consequence of emasculation.)

These points are borne out in a further element in the film's gestural vocabulary: the use of hands. It embodies the invisible fact that the power of action has been given to Leopold, leaving to Lisa only the responsibility of reaction. (This might be the gestural correlative of Frau Kastner's injunction: "Let him do the talking—but not all the talking.") From the beginning of the proposal scene, in the progress around the town square, Leopold has free use of his hands to guide, to salute, and to give emphasis to his conversation. Lisa's, meanwhile, are fully engaged in the management of her parasol, handbag, and skirt. On the park bench, Lisa's hands never leave her lap, at most twisting there in resourceless agitation at the neck of her handbag, but Leopold again has command of his gestures, to such an extent that he can silence Lisa's first attempt to arrest the flow of his speech by peremptorily raising his stiffly gloved arm. This abruptly commanding movement is combined with the (albeit reproving) courtesy of "Oh, please allow me to finish." The gesture inflects that apparent request as an order, a reminder—where none should be needed—that it is her place to listen and not, yet, to speak.

The sense of Leopold's having command over her movements is climaxed at the end of the interview, after he has accepted the disintegration of his prospects. He terminates the conversation by rising (in one movement, like a released jack-in-the-box) to salute her and then extending his right arm to her with a disjointed "Oh . . . then . . . please!" as his sense of correct procedure asserts itself over his confusion (fig. 19). Ophuls chooses this moment to cut away to the parental group: misreading, it seems, the distant (and in fact unavailable) sight of Leopold's movement. Herr Kastner predicts that "it won't be long now" and bustles to order the celebratory wine. When we return to the park, the couple are already on the move, with Lisa on the lieutenant's arm, which makes her having risen to his side to accept his support a simple result of his having offered it. They are both, but not equally, prisoners of form.

Leopold need not have offered her his arm; he had not done so for the walk to the park. Gallantry is his to employ for the imposition of his will, even in defeat. He sets an uncomfortable pace that leaves Lisa to grab for her parasol. When their route back to the parental group is obstructed by the band parade, he uses his arm and authority to direct her through the line of

Figure 19. After Lisa's revelation

bandsmen, but chivalry ("Make way for the lady") again covers the pursuit of his own desire, for speedy relief from a now-profitless responsibility.

The sense that the forms of gentlemanliness give access to the structures of male dominance emerges with all the more force because Leopold "in himself" (fresh of face, light of voice and making a youthfully awkward assumption of the role placed upon him) is far from being a commanding figure. Leopold is his uncle's puppet, and the Colonel—in his relaxed and condescending certainty of his place in the social chain and in his sense of crime when thwarted—is what Leopold will become once the authority of his sex and rank has been so internalized as to emerge as "innate" confidence and steely poise. Thus it is the older man (as containing Leopold) rather than Leopold himself that Lisa ends up by marrying in Johann Stauffer. The explicit link between the two figures is the cigarette smoked in the white-gloved hand. But it's worth noting that the Colonel, too, displayed his control over movement, in the scene of introductions, when he signaled the Kastner party to proceed toward the church with a "Shall we walk?" arm gesture. At any rate, this gesture reemerges with Stauffer, in the full strength of its imperiously protective ambiguity, at the Opera, when he summons Lisa back to her place at his side from her contemplation of Stefan. Then, in his surprise appearance in the carriage after the rendezvous on the Opera steps, what might be a considerate reluctance to let Lisa take her "headache" off home alone is quite blatantly a form for the demand that she stay within his sphere of movement.

To this extent, Lisa's disarrayed return to the carriage (the confined space provided for her within the social circuit) is parallel to her return, in Linz, to her parents' café table where—before and after the proposal—we see two chairs reserved for the happy couple. But Lisa's place at the table, unlike her place in the carriage, does not have to be taken up. It can be avoided at only a moderate cost in embarrassment and disapproval: she sinks into the Colonel's vacated chair to meet her mother's demands for explanation. Lisa's crime in Vienna is like but not like her quiet demolition of the schemes of Linz; there, even in resistance, she submitted her will to that of her protector by accepting to be led everywhere at his side. At the Opera, acting "the pursued," she reverses the course laid down for her by Johann. And when Stauffer looks out from the carriage on the act that seals her fate, it is certainly crucial to the intrigue that he has seen her entering the gates of Stefan's apartment, but it is equally important, within the scheme of images, that what he has witnessed is her gentle, reluctant, and inadmissable seizure of the power of independent movement.

The vastly escalated cost of Lisa's pursuit of her destiny in Vienna is pictured in the crossed sabers on the wall behind Johann as he urges her, in effect, to spare him the executioner's role. In Linz, the armory of social power lies in reserve as decoration, posing its sanctions, certainly, but not activating them: thus in the panning shot as Leopold leads his miscreant out of the park they pass between a "cross-fire" of cannon (to the right, then the left of the screen), which have been incidentally visible in the backgrounds of earlier shots but which are now brought to prominence. Their threat is, however, only symbolic, and their ammunition is stacked ornamentally beside them. Lisa may feel that she is being taken to the firing squad, but only blanks will be exploded. It is a lightly humorous effect, almost a gag, in keeping with the mood of the sequence.

The crucial distinction when we get to Stauffer's Vienna (a difference that fissures the continuities of situation, structure, and image and that underwrites the drastic contrast in tone) is that Lisa is now accountable, not to her parents, but to her husband. What alters everything—to a life-and-death matter—is the change in Lisa's social role, brought about by marriage, not in her "nature as a woman"; for instance, neither her natural nor her social role as a mother weighs much in the course of events, however great the surrounding emotion. There is certainly no change in her psychology.

When she tells Johann that she can't help herself, that she's "had no hope but [Stefan's] ever," this Romantic Nonsense is no more than a rephrasing of her statements to Leopold. It is surely by one of the master strokes in the design of the Linz sequence that Lisa is made not to refuse marriage but to declare it impossible, not to reject Leopold but to improvise the truthful lie of her engagement. This presents an exact definition of her feelings and character. It does not occur to her that her will is involved in her inability to accept Leopold. Despite making what from her point of view is every effort to take the place in society desired for her by her parents, she is finally brought up against the desperate fact that she is already and irrevocably spoken for.

Lisa's enslavement is directly contrasted with the subjection to the social order that is evident in Leopold's struggle to comprehend: "You mean you're engaged to a man and your parents don't even know him?" These two kinds of unfreedom, romantic and institutional, are closed around Lisa by marriage. It is Stauffer who emphasizes choice and responsibility, both for Lisa and for himself: committing himself to act out the role of the injured husband, he still sees himself as *deciding* his course. When he says that he will do everything in his power to oppose Lisa's folly, he is deliberately not claiming (as he could readily have been made to claim and as seems to be true) that his actions will be the simple and inevitable consequence of hers. By contrast, Lisa, accepting but not seeking the role of social outcast, shows no more thought of defiance in going to Stefan than in refusing Leopold. Johann can take the initiative simply by acting out the male role; Lisa can take it only by contradicting the female one.

Lisa's tragedy is that being morally the product of Linz and fully a member of Stauffer's world, she has nonetheless fixed her affections on a man who is a stranger to that world's commitments. As a complete daughter of this bourgeoisie, Lisa shows in romance the punctiliousness that Leopold and Johann display toward form.

In both respects, these nicenesses of observance are directly contrasted with the tissue of broken engagements in the life of Stefan who, as he says, almost never gets to the place he starts out for. The Linz sequence is immediately set in the context of that life and of the world which supports it—preceded by a demonstration of the manners of Stefan's promiscuity (witnessed by Lisa from the staircase outside his apartment) and followed by a sketch of the life that revolves around Madame Spitzer's dress shop. It is a world where "Congratulations, my dear" will echo cheerfully around a conquest that promises pleasure and profit, a regime every bit as meticulously constructed and serviced as Johann's for its own purposes of sophisticated hedonism. In that world Stefan is as available to Lisa as he is to any other beautiful woman, and with impunity even from censure. Its particular terms—the terms of its difference from "Linz"—are the acknowledgment of the mutability of appetite and affection. If the bandmaster is Linz's extension into grotesquerie of what Leopold and Johann represent, the equivalent figure in Stefan's Vienna is the drunken soldier who offers to take Lisa "anywhere [because] it makes no difference": his eruption on the scene is so placed, immediately after Lisa's final disillusionment with Stefan, that his words must be taken to represent the most appalling notion that she could be asked to confront. Her recoil from his proposition (as distinct from his somewhat repulsive person) merely confirms that she has only, ever, been as missionary in Stefan's world. Her most un-Spitzerian refusal to tell Stefan of her pregnancy is explicitly the result of her wish to distance herself from all the other women in his life—that is, to enact the most complete rejection of the ways of his world.

Lisa believes in the recklessness of her passion. She believes that she must have Stefan come what may. But she does not, in fact, want him on any terms. She wants him on very strict terms indeed. He must freely recognize their meetings as brought about not under the stars of a particular time and place, but in eternity's grand design.

Herein lies the profundity of the invention which makes reflections on freedom open and close the Linz sequence. "You who have always lived so freely," she addresses Stefan at the start; then, within the action at the end of the sequence, responding to her mother's demand to know what caused the collapse of Leopold's proposal, "I only told him the truth . . . I told him I wasn't free."

Lisa, like her husband, like "responsible" society—but unlike Stefan and his circle—insists on living in a world of binding, life-and-death commitments. She demands a stability that is to be secured not by "such things as honor, decency": not by dutiful submission to social ties, but by the common and spontaneous recognition of asocial romantic destiny. A bond sealed, outside society, by Fate must surely subdue the randomness of appetite and opportunity, uniting Stefan's freedom with the steadfastness of a Stauffer.

But nothing human is ever outside society, as is manifest in the stream of sideline comment, gossip, and inquisitive witness that runs through the film. Lisa's position is quite incoherent. When her letter asserts the inevitability of the encounter at the Opera and says that nothing happens by chance, could she thoughtfully mean that it was Stefan's destiny, to miss his destiny? And what, concretely, does she hope will follow from her visiting Stefan to offer him her life? Its one certain result, after all, must be to make him the target of Johann's fury. (Lisa's devotion here is every bit as murderous as her husband's.) Stefan's forgetfulness, which Lisa represents as the cruelest blow of fate, at least spares her the possibility that he might recognize her, say thanks for the memory, and nonetheless send her packing. The fine irrationality of "If only you could have found what was never lost" shows her at last reduced to using "what might have been" to protect her vision of destiny against the press of reality. Her letter itself, a final attempt at vindication, is pointless except as an invitation to suicide, persuading Stefan to let death prove what life could not.

There is a danger of misrepresenting the film, though, in stressing what is morbid in Lisa's attitude as if this were the (individual, moral) flaw that propelled her tragedy. It is certainly established that Lisa is locked into a particular moment of her adolescence, but if she were broken mainly on her perversity, the film would surely not be entitled to pass her off as a figure of nobility and purity. Also involved, however, is a desperate struggle to live authentically and not to give her life to a convenient denial of her inmost conviction and deepest feeling. It is that which makes the success of her resistance to Linz a kind of triumph, even in its confusion and its comicality. But the struggle dooms her, too, by trapping her in the determined acting out of her role as a woman (in that society) at a point when its conflicting elements have been split apart.

The correspondence of "You who have always lived so freely" and "I told him I wasn't free" is constructed by the film and not observed by Lisa. What the film sees, and she doesn't, is the conflict between a man's freedom and a woman's lack of it. (Lisa sees herself and Stefan as complementary; the film presents them as different.) While the rigidities of Linz are set against the amenability of Madame Spitzer's, the transition offers Lisa no release from the frame of decorative compliance. The price of a woman's entry to Stefan's world of freedom is a place in the higher reaches of prostitution. Already explicit here is the theme developed most fully in *Lola Montès* (1955): that the typical result of a woman's seizure of freedom in matters of the heart is confinement within the role of Woman of Scandal. "The mutability of appetite and affection" has very specific consequences for a woman, and Lisa presumably discovers that offering herself autonomously in the Spitzer market is no more rewarding—as it is certainly not more authentic—than offering herself under contract to Johann Stauffer. Her world has, after all, a less brutal way with aging wives than with aging courtesans. It is important that Lisa does not enter into marriage solely for the sake of her son; it was "as much for his sake as for mine." But Stauffer's Vienna repeats the pattern of Linz in this: that Lisa reacts to Stefan's indifference by embarking on an accommodation with society (arranged marriage/marriage of convenience) only to rediscover the depth of her prior commitment; and it's her passion's *integrity* that disorders the social mechanism, interrupting the musical performance.

Marriage is the given site for the expression of a woman's incorruptibility. When it functions as it's supposed to do, love "covers" the woman's submission to an unequal contract so that the moment of her subjection to a tightly constrained role is dissolved into the moment when she freely acknowledges the choice of her heart. Thus she is invited to believe that her fulfillment and her servitude are the same thing because they are accomplished in the same act of her will. So long as this belief can be sustained, she has a means of reconciling the conflicting imperatives of love (emotional integrity) and duty (subordination). Her unfreedom becomes what she freely desires. But Lisa's role explodes in her face: married to Johann, she comes to see herself as his mistress while society identifies her still as a wife. She is fully persuaded that love and duty go together, and cannot but insist on their unity, even when society is brought to assert the priority of the contract. Lisa's offense is the "excessive" enactment of those qualities which are held out as being woman's nature and woman's glory. It's when she defies marriage that she is being true to the self that her world has offered her, first in the absoluteness of her commitment (her uncompromising fidelity makes her unfaithful) and then in the emotional honesty which refuses the discreet indulgence of an affair.

Here again it might be claimed that the film offers not a *presentation* of Lisa's role, but an indulgence of the stereotyped opposition of emotional woman (a slave to her feelings) and rational man. Yet it is surely clear that Ophuls's irony embraces *all* the film's characters and that the behavior of the men is by no means remarkable for its rationality. More importantly, Lisa is articulated as an *exceptional* figure rather than a typical one: throughout the film she is systematically contrasted with a range of other women. All of them—from the coyly opportunist friend of her girlhood onward—are shown to have made quite different kinds of accommodations to their roles and circumstances. None of them manifests the purity, emotionality, and commitment of "essential womanhood."

Unable to follow their complaisant or resigned acceptance of the best available bargain, Lisa seeks to live out, in purity, the meaning of a woman's life as a thing to be *given*. Her insistence on awaiting Stefan's approach and recognition (like her refusal to exploit her pregnancy) holds her free from the predatory taint on a woman who actively acknowledges her needs and desires. That this leaves her with only her passivity to exploit is articulated in Stefan's hideously acute observation on her flight from the Opera: "Where there is a pursued there must be a pursuer." The letter, after her acceptance of defeat, is the one place where she can tell Stefan of the depth of her need without accusing herself of shamelessness.

Living as a woman, Lisa can dedicate herself to others or she can function for them in a social role which is essentially a thing of gestures and of show.

She is incapacitated from living for herself because no terms are available, beyond these, in which to grasp what that might mean. Her fulfillment is to be discovered in submission; if it can't be, there is something wrong with her (with her soul or with her luck). Her nature—as *that* society has defined it for her—will find its highest expression as a Madonna. But that selflessness produces the cult of sacrifice which makes Lisa obsessive, egocentric, and, ultimately, like Lucia Harper or Madame de . . . , a killer: her stubborn purity is one agent of Stefan's death.

If Ophuls's film is nonetheless in love with her, it thereby acknowledges the madness of a role in which the exercise of her integrity propels her and those around her to catastrophe. Ophuls's delight in Lisa and his sympathy for her surely derive from her construction as a heroine who lives her role, in impossible circumstances, as fully and finely as that role allows. Anything more would require the lucidity that would challenge the role and make her a rebel. It is equally a part of her charm and a source of her deadliness that she is so locked into her role as to preclude her achieving the perspective on her predicament that the film gives us. (We should not pretend that the achievement would necessarily have done her much good.) Her innocence is inseparable from her blindness.

Lisa never sees, never approaches the insight, that her predicament is related to the definitions and constraints that her society imposes on womanhood. Instead she rationalizes her servitude and naturalizes her passivity through her submission to Fate. The myth of destiny is generally available both to give misfortune the comfort of cosmic meaning, and as a magical resolution of the conflict between an experience of unfreedom and the conviction (however derived) of individual liberty: one's fate is one's own, just like one's actions. But the myth has a particular significance for a woman faced, like Lisa, with society's insistence that she must hold herself accountable for her actions and simultaneously accept her subordination to men as a product of her nature. Beyond that, since marriage will be the free act that ratifies her inequality, there is discomfort in any suggestion of contingency in her choice of partner. Destiny romanticizes the contract by presenting submission to Heaven's Plan as the only true freedom. Fulfillment lies in the discovery of "the mate that fate had me created for." Having made the discovery and missed the fulfillment, Lisa has to shift the terms of her commitment. Destiny becomes Malign Fate, through the obscurity—"If only . . ."—of Stefan's vision. Thus when Fortune crushes, it is still someone's fault. Lisa can embrace her unfreedom in its metaphysical guise, she can recognize her misfortune as the product of a moral failure, but (or because) she can never see her predicament in its social dimensions. To do so would be to break the unity between her role and her perceptions. Passivity and blindness are laid down as the terms of her account at its very start: "What happened to us had its own reason beyond our poor understanding." What is at stake is Lisa's attempt to give coherent shape to her experience.

In this sense, the notion of Destiny governs her life, and, perhaps more than anything else, it wrecks her life. To be worthy of her great love, she cannot present herself to it impurely, as a clever deceiver. To enact her conviction of destiny, she has to wait until Stefan's recognition freely responds to hers; she cannot do any of the "practical" things that might break the deadlock without compromising her life's foundation. Thus the same commitment that lets her feel her life's integrity propels it to disintegration. In this she is not typical, but she might be exemplary.

Works Cited

Koch, Howard. "Script to Screen with Max Ophuls." In *The Hollywood Screenwriters*, edited by Richard Corliss, 125–32. New York: Avon, 1972.

Wood, Robin. "Ewig hin der Liebe Glück . . . *Letter from an Unknown Woman*." In Robin Wood, *Personal Views: Explorations in Film*, 115–34. London: Gordon Fraser Gallery, 1976.

Filmography

Letter from an Unknown Woman. Directed by Max Ophuls. Universal-International, 1948.

Lola Montès. Directed by Max Ophuls. Gamma Films, 1955.

IN A LONELY PLACE

First published in The Movie Book of Film Noir, *edited by Ian Cameron,* 222–31. London: Studio Vista, 1992.

Nicholas Ray's *In a Lonely Place* (1950) is a very strange literary adaptation. From Dorothy Hughes's novel it retains the title, the names of some characters, and something of the structure of relationships: the hero, Dixon Steele, has an ex-army buddy called Brub Nicolai who is now a detective working under a Captain Lochner. Nicolai's wife, Sylvia, dislikes Steele, who falls in love with the actress Laurel Gray while becoming involved in Brub's pursuit of a strangler whose victims include Mildred Atkinson. Beyond this, the film's changes and inventions are so extensive that merely cosmetic action—a new title and a new set of names—would have been enough to secure it from any suspicion of plagiarism if Santana Pictures (Humphrey Bogart's production company) had claimed it as an original story.

In the first place, a Los Angeles setting is important to Hughes's novel mainly in its topography. But the film treats Los Angeles, specifically Beverly Hills, primarily as a social environment, subjecting it to a presentation which is both distinctive and mordant. It forgoes all the spectacle of moviemaking and all the glamour of movie promotion. We never see the inside—or even so much as the gates—of a studio, we meet no tycoons, and we are taken to no extravagant premieres or anxious previews. In doing without the familiar facades of the Hollywood picture, *In a Lonely Place* also deprives itself of occasions to bounce expressively between glittering display and the sad or sordid realities below. Nicholas Ray directs the film without reference to the splurged mascara school of movie rhetoric, holding it to a scale that avoids narrative and thematic inflation so as to pursue intimacy and detail.

Modesty and the commitment to chamber drama underlie the film's most drastic switch from the novel's content. Dorothy Hughes's hero is the killer, a serial killer at that, and the tension of her tale is in the tightening of the police net that catches Dix Steele. The film has only one murder victim, Mildred Atkinson, and it is clear that Humphrey Bogart's Dix did not kill her. If Dix had been produced as her murderer at the end of the movie, *In a Lonely Place* would have gone beyond the acceptable deviousness of the murder mystery to indulge in outrageous and probably futile cheating. The film is interested neither in creating mystery nor in following a process of detection. It is but mildly concerned, for reasons of its own, to identify Mildred's killer. Above plot it promotes character and both psychological and social portraiture, using the suspicion of murder as a pressure to dramatize the course of a romance from the discovery of love to its disintegration.

The twists of conspiracy and revelation that convolute so many noir narratives and produce the hero as fall guy are not among the pleasures this picture offers. There is no femme fatale, and there are no monsters of greed and perversity. The book works much more in the mainstream of noir fiction, immersing the reader in the sick consciousness of its haunted hero. A faithful translation to the screen (but please don't bother) would be likely to involve privileging the antihero's perspective by means of voice-over. Ray's movie is shaped as, in the first place, the story of Dixon Steele, but its viewpoint is independent of Dix's; it assesses his responses as well as reflecting them. The film conveys the texture and rhythm of his experience while offering us an understanding larger than Dix's own. Far from locking us into Dix's perceptions, the film gives us much information that is deliberately withheld from him and, as a surprising result, presents a world that in many respects validates rather than offsets his paranoia. He disrupts a nightclub performance by walking out when a cop turns up, unreasonably and perhaps incorrectly supposing that the cop has come to spy on him and to keep his relationship with Laurel under surveillance. However inappropriate Dix's reaction—its violence consists in the noticeable crushing of a cigarette—we have been made aware that he is indeed being spied on, by people representing themselves as his friends, and that the police are taking a covert but intrusive interest in his relationship with Laurel. While paranoia can show itself in a conviction of hostile conspiracy, Dix is also right when he comes to fear that he is being deceived and that he is the subject of others' attempts at manipulation.

Lochner, the chief cop, is played (brilliantly) by Carl Benton Reid so as to evoke the image of the studio boss, secure in the corruptibility of his underlings, as free with an insult as with a purely formal apology, yet puritanically quick to take offense and intolerant of detachment from his definitions of necessity and decorum. As a cop, Captain Lochner from the outset treats Dix and Laurel with a disdain that can be supposed to reflect an impatience with the motion-picture crowd; he much prefers people who work in banks (like Kesler, the killer).

A sneaky identification of the cops with the film industry establishment is surely involved when Dix tells his friend and agent Mel Lippman (Art Smith) not to worry about the news reports that Mildred Atkinson, a checkroom girl from Paul's Restaurant, was in his apartment to tell him the story of bestseller *Althea Bruce*. Mel thinks that Brodie, the producer, will be outraged by this affront to his property and that Dix will lose a much-needed screenwriting job. Dix thinks not, as there is a way for Mel to appease Brodie. He can say that the motive Dix claimed for taking Mildred home was just an excuse for the police. It was more certainly an excuse for the Breen Office: what Dix offers as a convenient lie about Hollywood prostitution, the Production Code Administration would have vetoed for its discomforting frankness on the same subject. The front office/detective squad parallel is reinforced through the documentation of Dix's misdemeanors that Lochner, giving dictation, intones with such zealous distaste; it looks like a cuttings file and it consists largely of the scandal queens' gossip and commissary tittle-tattle that studios compiled to control the employability of the talent. The Frances Randolph that Lochner and others adduce as their only instance of a female victim of Dix's violence is the same Fran (Alix Talton) who twice shows herself happy to recall and eager to renew her one-time affair with Dix. Lochner's note on Dix's fist fight with a producer ("Fired. No charges preferred") indicates a free exchange of information between the studios and the investigative apparatus of the state. The relevance to the blacklist is clear, and we are invited, though not compelled, to see *In a Lonely Place* as reflecting on suspicion, deceit, and hysteria in personal relations under a threat which, of course, it cannot name: that of the Hollywood witch-hunt.

Making Dixon Steele a screenwriter, in the other most significant change from Hughes's novel, gives ironic access to a metaphor of following the book as a measure of conformism. The film echoes the erratic personality of its hero in its own erratic processes, notable among which is the establishment of the murder victim not as an ingratiating figure of pathos but as a figure of grating comedy. Mildred's enthusiastic synopsis of *Althea Bruce* is part of what extinguishes Dix's sexual interest (more important is his first sight of Laurel), and hastening Mildred's exit from his apartment is an expression of his desire for release from the romance's grotesque narrative. It is an insider's joke that "what Brodie wants—a faithful adaptation" should be at issue in a film which is itself unconstrained by respect for its literary source. The boldly nonsensical synopsis delivered by Mildred points up the despair that haunts Dix's efforts to do well in a job that it is demeaning to do at all. Dix's ambivalence about his work and its context emerges in the vulnerability not just of his material prospects but also of his self-esteem to the opinions of those for whose judgment he has an intelligent contempt. It is one dimension of conflict in Dix that he is alert to the hollowness of success and tormented by the fear of failure.

That aspect of the character embodies a tension widely remarked as a feature of Hollywood life. Beyond this, the film draws on Hollywood lore for detail like the jibe thrown at a loud-mouthed producer; according to Ray, "You have put the son-in-law business back fifty years" was a crack famously directed at Milton Sperling (father-in-law, Harry Warner). The character of Dix, the trouble-seeking alcoholic screenwriter who has not written a hit since before the war, seems to owe much to the character and legend of Herman J. Mankiewicz, writer of *Citizen Kane* (1941), but also of *A Woman's Secret* (1949), which was derived from a Vicki Baum novel and became, two years before *In a Lonely Place*, the silliest of Nicholas Ray's directorial assignments. In his autobiography, the producer John Houseman gave an account of a car journey across America shared with Mankiewicz and Ray: "Two of the most violently self-destructive men I have ever known—both drinkers and gamblers on different curves of their respective roller-coasters. Herman was on the downslope ... and his great wild days were behind him.... Behind a truculent front he was worrying about jobs.... His teeth were still sharp but the appetite was gone" (1979, 177). Like Dix again, Mankiewicz was a victim of the gossip columns, with the Hearst press taking regular revenge for *Citizen Kane*.

Many aspects of Dix's character connect him also to the heroes of other Ray movies like *On Dangerous Ground* (1951), *The Lusty Men* (1952), *Johnny Guitar* (1954), and *Rebel Without a Cause* (1955)—tortured male romantics looking for redemption from their own ferocities and riven by the contradiction between what they knowingly desire and what they, in fact, pursue or provoke. Confirmation of autobiographical relevance here can be found in some further snippets from Houseman's account: "Nick was a difficult and sometimes disturbing companion.... The chance to save him from his own self-destructive habits proved an irresistible attraction [to women] of which Nick took full advantage and for which he rarely forgave them.... [He had] a perfectionism and sense of commitment to his work which were rare in the theatre and even more rare in the film business. But in his personal life he was the victim of irresistible impulses that, finally, left his career and his personal relationships in ruins" (178).

Repeatedly, Ray's hero gives, receives, and gives himself one simple piece of advice which also sets a goal beyond price or power: "Take it easy." Like several of Ray's best pictures, *In a Lonely Place* explores the results of casting a woman in the role of "warrior's rest" as a figure whose clear sight, calm, and commitment are valued to the extent that they seem to enable relaxation and to promise refuge from the stresses in the male world of public competition. This film offers a rebuff to Hollywood's, and most likely Ray's own, desire to believe in romance as a solution rather than a combination of lovers' problems.

The investment in love, doomed here because on both sides excessive, relates the character of Dix to the persona of Bogart, whose public image had become that of a hell-raiser brought to a late mellowing, after his notoriously violent marriage to Mayo Methot, through the happy chance that had united him with Lauren Bacall. Ray claimed credit as the director who took the gun out of Bogart's hand, and that is achieved partly by setting contexts of tenderness and sentiment in which Bogart's still guarded, mainly indirect acknowledgment of need and affection can be felt to express a sensitivity and warmth less rigidly encased in smartness than is the case with his regular tough-guy roles. A key instance here is the scene in which his friends collude in "preparing him for repose," making him the sleepy dedicatee of a Shakespearean avowal of love. It is a prime example of reaction-shot stardom, relieved of the burdens of exposition to become the art of charismatic passivity. The Bogart role had developed as one in which his character knew what he was after and pursued it directly. Hero or villain, his status was guaranteed by his effectiveness in violence. It is here that *In a Lonely Place* marks so impressive an extension of Bogart's range. Dix is introduced to us as a character preoccupied, locked into his own evidently painful turmoil as he drives through the Los Angeles evening traffic. The first words spoken in the film are his own name, called out to him at a traffic light to summon him back into a public world where recognition is a prime concern. ("Dix Steele! . . . Don't you remember me?") The image is cut to show the delay in his reaction, as if he is waking to consciousness but also as if his own name is as obscure to him as the identity of the woman calling it. Showbiz is, of course, a world where unfamiliarity with one's name may be a fact as well as a metaphor.

If Bogart did not like *In a Lonely Place*—his biographer Joe Hyams says so—that may have been through embarrassment at its evocation of witch-hunt Hollywood; he believed himself to have been duped by the victims of the blacklist and he certainly was humbled by its perpetrators, who maneuvered him into billboarding his "Americanism" as if he were a friendly witness. It is also possible that he was uneasy with the exposure in Dix of the pain, anxiety, and clumsiness that make this role unique in his career. Yet one of his and the film's triumphs is to render the violence in his instability of mood and purpose with full force, taking it to the edge of absurdity without loss of conviction. For instance, it is almost funny—a risk boldly run—that Dix's attack on Laurel in the final scene occurs when he has come to her apartment to declare his regret for an earlier outburst, and closely follows his contrite vow that such things will never happen again.

The reorientation of the Bogart persona is, though, as much a matter of perspective as of performance. The film aligns him with other Ray heroes by making his violence the index of weakness rather than of strength. When he lashes out at "Junior" (Lewis Howard), the son-in-law producer, his pretext is outrage at the abuse of his friend, the one-time matinée idol Charles Waterman (Robert Warwick). But the image has displayed Dix's growing rage at the meanings for himself in Junior's trumpeted contempt for a drunk and has-been. It is Dix that Junior leans on while addressing the onlookers at Paul's Restaurant; when Junior responds to the son-in-law crack by tapping his cigar ash into Waterman's brandy, this final provocation (the drink was Dix's gift to Charlie) triggers a release of anger that reflects Dix's identification with failure and his vulnerability to a fool's contempt even more clearly than it shows his carelessness of self-interest in defense of a friend.

The truly frightening aspect of Dix is not so much his volatility or his capacity for violence as his almost complete blindness to his own actions, either in their impact on others or in their meanings for himself. He seems never to face the implications of his own feelings or fantasies. Sylvia Nicolai (Jeff Donnell) is repelled by the intensity of his involvement in the imagined motives of a woman-strangler, and that's a reflection of her small-mindedness. But Dix does not pause to think anything about it, which seems to indicate a panic flight from self-knowledge (fig. 20).

The event that dramatizes Laurel's recoil from Dix is his attack on a young motorist whose car he crashes into while driving furiously away from what he has read, correctly, as a scene of betrayal. Diverted by Laurel at a moment when he might, rock in hand, have become a murderer, Dix does his best to repair the damage without appreciating what the damage is. He allows Laurel to demolish his attempts at self-justification but once more evades inspection of the sources and likely consequences of his action. In particular, he shows no awareness of the impact on Laurel; he recognizes no shock and he offers no apology. His recovery of calm is as abrupt as his swing into rage. When he reaches his arm out to draw her toward him, the image registers Laurel's recognition and Dix's unconsciousness of the similarity between this embrace and the imagined stranglehold of Mildred's killer. Bogart's facility in irony and mockery is redirected to portray Dix's defense against useful introspection.

Figure 20. The intensity of Dix's involvement in the imagined motives of a woman-strangler

The casting of Gloria Grahame as Laurel points up one dimension of correspondence between Dix and Bogart which may have been calculated to provoke the actor into drawing on his experience as much as he relied on his skill. Grahame was just a little younger than Lauren Bacall, but older at the time of filming than Bacall had been when she married Bogart. Just as the word "starlet" is never explicitly attached to Laurel, so the twenty-five-year gap in age is not mentioned in the film, though it opens Laurel to Lochner's sarcasm and makes her vulnerable to the sneers embedded in questions like "Were you interested in Mr. Steele because he's a celebrity?" and "Do you receive a salary for your work?"

While the casting of Grahame has resonance in relation to the star, it is startling in relation to the director. According to Ray (who admitted to being a liar, though not on the John Ford scale), Harry Cohn and Columbia Pictures wanted Ginger Rogers as Laurel. Ray held out for Grahame, his wife, although their brief marriage was in active disintegration. From a director who encouraged actors to make use of their own experiences and emotions, such a role was not only a generous farewell gift but also—as farewell gifts are apt to be—sharply barbed in its reflections on character and motive. Laurel Gray is constructed as a woman well equipped, under the relevant pressures, to confirm the fears that underlie and follow from Dix's misogyny. The role draws on those aspects of the player that gave unaffected conviction in *The Big Heat* (Fritz Lang, 1953) to "I've been rich and I've been poor. Believe me, rich is better."

In many accounts of the film, a romance that otherwise promises redemption and fulfillment is destroyed by the pressures of the police investigation and/or as a result of Dix's neurosis. These versions underrate the picture's depth and originality by either imposing the notion that someone has to be at fault when a love affair ends or perceiving it within stock molds for the "if only" love story where star-crossed lovers are threatened by external circumstance. They conventionalize it, too, by making Laurel a passive, only reactive figure. The film's insistence on Laurel's active role is marked by a shot worthy of its place in the Nicholas Ray gallery of strange inserts: the viewpoint into the coffee cup tilted in Laurel's hand when she is first brought to Lochner's office. That image signals the definitive entry into the narrative of a new subjectivity.

Before this, she has been seen only in relation to Dix's perspectives. On her first appearance, her indirectness is apparent as well as her pronounced investment in poise. She walks between Dix and Mildred in the courtyard of the apartments where both she and Dix are tenants with an "Excuse me" that commands attention but also positions her to claim that she was only minding her own business and being polite. Here and later, she is skillfully dressed in costumes so well supplied with edges and angles as to construct the space for movements simultaneously elegant, erotically promising (she passes close enough for Dix to catch her perfume) and—hands pushed forward inside the pockets of her overcoat—held off from any risk of contact. The stiffness that possesses Dix at climaxes of anxiety is always more or less a feature of Laurel's bearing. She is ever so neat. Finding her way through without being touched is one of her prime objectives. She is visibly a woman who hates to be taken by surprise and not to have her performance under control. The strains to which this subjects her are pictured in the close-up of her shoes pressing against the floor of the car during Dix's enraged drive from the beach, all her terror held with great effort out of sight. But once Dix picks up the rock in his attack on the young driver, Laurel's panic can no longer be contained. The image of her distraught face leaning into camera to shriek at Dix contradicts the earlier shot to mark the discovery that attachment to Dix makes it impossible for her to inhabit her preferred posture.

Life with Dix offers excitement at the cost of security, and Laurel's priorities are the opposite. She brings Dix the priceless gift of relaxation, quieting his turmoil and enabling him to direct his energies creatively. But we should not ignore the darker implications of the sequence that characterizes the couple's happiness: in it we learn that Laurel is delighted to have Dix "kind of dopey this morning. I love him that way," she tells Mel. (By contrast, Dix is unsettled by Laurel's dopiness when he discovers her in drug-assisted sleep.) Her avowal of love at the scene's end is spoken in twice-relayed words, from Shakespeare via Charlie Waterman, in the process of putting Dix to sleep. I note the strategy for getting a bedroom scene past the censors, but I take it seriously that it's an inactive, semiconscious Dix in whose love Laurel scorns to change her state with kings.

It is illuminatingly credible that she turns out to have a lot in common with Mrs. Nicolai, the Sylvia who is glad that her husband is not like Dix but "attractive and average." Visiting Sylvia, ostensibly for reassurance about Dix—immediately after a scene in which Dix has said that if you want information about him you should ask him directly—Laurel states her aspiration to a life like the Nicolais: "This is what I'd like to have some day [pause, stands], a small cozy house, near the ocean."

That? With Dix? Laurel is not sure. Known around town as the mistress of "the real-estate Baker," she has been lucky on the run from that affair ("We were thinking of getting married. It wouldn't have worked") to find employment with Dix. Laurel's is the ambition of the tender-hearted gold digger; there is no scheme to sacrifice desire to calculation but a reasonable hope, when love is found, to find it advantageously. That creates room for a deal of self-deception and uncertainty.

We have to wonder why Laurel puts such a convenient gloss on the role in her life of Martha, the masseuse, explaining her to Dix as the last remnant of a movie career, but suppressing her function as a pipeline to Mr. Baker. So long as Martha is on hand, Baker can be avoided without being discarded or lost. Laurel is conspicuously economical with the truth here. She makes a point of describing Martha, when she is still only a name spoken into the telephone, as a married woman with a grown-up son. That is an alternative to mentioning what will turn out to be her most striking aspect. The film casts Martha within the butch lesbian stereotype and thereby reflects on Laurel's nervous opportunism; she finds comfort in the knowledge that her glamour will keep Martha at her disposal and eager to be of service.

Laurel is upset when Martha relays the gossip about Dix and Frances Randolph; she tells Martha to leave. Martha's response runs: "I'll get out, angel. But you'll beg me to come back when you're in trouble. You will, angel, because you don't have anybody else." That is accurate as a summary of Laurel's position and as a prediction. It also confirms (and announces to us) the knowledge that the break can be enacted without cost to Laurel since it has no effect on Martha's availability—"You haven't anybody else" contains "You still have me, and you know it." Chucking Martha out gives Laurel a way of refusing to listen to insinuations against Dix, after having listened to them.

It is a measure of Laurel's uncertainty, well before the car incident and at a time when she claims to have found happiness, that here and in her interview with Lochner she can manage only a stiffly formal assertion of her belief in Dix. She cannot produce what would really count—a quick and spontaneous rejoinder, along the lines of "Don't be silly," either to Martha or to Lochner's "He's our most logical suspect." Inasmuch as Martha speaks the voices in Laurel's mind, throwing her out is an effort at suppression.

Laurel's problem is that it is not enough to know that Dix is innocent of murder. She needs to feel able to deny that he is, in Lochner's words, an erratic, violent man, or that killing has a fascination for him; and these are simple truths. With Dix, Laurel is incapable of sustaining the irrational trust and reckless commitment that would be love. In Ray's work the ready contrast is with Keechie, the heroine of *They Live by Night* (1948): "Some say he's bad, but I say he's bonny." Keechie's counterpart in *In a Lonely Place* is not Laurel but Mel, whose first concern, when he imagines Dix to be the murderer, is how to fix his escape across the border. In this role, Art Smith offers a wry and touching portrait of a friendship (no more platonic, surely, than Martha's for Laurel) that, unlike the lovers' love, is without conditions or reservations.

Mel makes Laurel feel ashamed, appropriately, since the route to her betrayal of Dix is prepared largely by her own lies and evasions. Her first really important deception comes when Dix mentions a picnic invitation from the Nicolais and asks if she remembers Brub. Dix does not know that Laurel has been talking to Lochner again and that Brub played a major role in the interview. Not knowing that Laurel is lying when she claims only vaguely to recall the cop in Lochner's office, Dix does not have our reasons for wondering why Laurel is concealing the fact of the interview and withholding the knowledge that she gained there, which any friend would think it important to pass on. Dix is entitled to know that he is under surveillance as Lochner's prime suspect and that any contact with the Nicolais, who are never going to sacrifice Brub's prospects to friendship, is less a social occasion than an extension of the investigative process.

If Laurel is unable to be open about a meeting which of itself threatened no disloyalty, we have to conclude that her unease has a different source, in doubts that the interview has created in her own mind about the security of her relationship with Dix. At the very least, Laurel's commitment to Dix does not outweigh the authority of Lochner. When, at the beach, Laurel tries to excuse her silence with "We didn't want to tell you because it would only have upset you," the thinness of the explanation is evident, but no more striking than the identification that makes Laurel present herself as part of a "we" with Brub Nicolai. For both Laurel and Dix, friendship with the Nicolais represents an attempted accommodation with the Lochner world, in which you are supposed to affect concern as to whether a cop reckons your behavior to be that of a gentleman (or, of course, a lady). One side of Laurel is anxiously responsive to any indication of her acceptability in the established world of official decorum—an escape from her identity as "Baker's girl."

Laurel's need for security is at odds with her keenness to keep her options open. The conflict makes her unable to leave Dix and it makes her in staying unable to offer him the reassurance that *his* insecurity constantly demands. So it builds the pressure that pushes Laurel by stages into hysterical deviousness and treachery. First, she visits Sylvia Nicolai, the woman who, at the beach, could not fathom her own motives in breaking the secret of Laurel's meeting with Lochner: "I don't know why I said it. Brub especially asked me not to." While at the Nicolais' house, ostensibly to seek persuasion of Dix's innocence, she gives Sylvia information that is sure to be passed on to a grateful Lochner, of Dix's assault on the young motorist. Then she accepts Dix's proposal of marriage while intending to leave him in the lurch. In this way, she embarks on a course of attempted manipulation that is certain to enrage Dix and to construct the circumstances which, directing the Nicolais' enactment of the Atkinson murder, he has imagined as the ones in which a man would kill the woman he loved: "She's telling you she's done nothing wrong. . . . You love her and she's deceived you . . . she wants to get rid of you."

Finally, she uses Mel as an intermediary to deliver Dix's *Althea Bruce* script to Brodie, gambling that it will be greeted with the warmth to divert Dix from her desertion. The scale of this betrayal, and Laurel's awareness of it, is pictured in the two-handed gesture with which Laurel passes the script into Mel's keeping. The script is what she and Dix have made together out of their love—Dix as writer, Laurel as inspiration and typist—and using it to cheat Dix is poignantly shown to be like giving their baby away. A chairback between Laurel and Mel constructs space across which Laurel has to stretch to pass the script, enlarging the gesture to emphasize the responsibility that Laurel is imposing on Mel. The act and the gesture join the several instances in Ray's work of disastrous efforts at disarmament where a well-intentioned deception (like Jim's of Plato in *Rebel Without a Cause*) is experienced as a lacerating betrayal.

At this point, the relationship is over. "I wanted it to last so much, for my own sake," Laurel tells Mel, recognizing the fact. The film is now concerned with the consequences of this way of making the break from a man with an anguished fear of manipulation and abandonment. Dix's attack on Laurel, interrupted by the telephone call from Lochner that concedes his innocence, is not the cause of the rupture. "Yesterday," Laurel tells Lochner, "this would have meant so much to us. Now it doesn't matter at all." Yesterday, not an hour ago—that is, before Dix's proposal rather than before his assault.

It is probably more unusual in the movies than elsewhere that the marriage proposal is a sign of the relationship's decay rather than of its prosperity. A marriage contract is a poor substitute for the easy warmth and commitment that Dix wants of Laurel. But, failing that, he wants to rush into marriage, which suggests a desire to avoid having time for thought. It seems that the prospect of marriage panics him to different effect but almost as much as it does Laurel. The marriage project is repeatedly advanced by others (Lochner, Sylvia, Effie the housekeeper), and it is in the contemplation of marriage that Dix's behavior becomes most bizarre. Consider the beach scene and its consequences. Sylvia's gaffe is to tell Laurel to marry Dix and to remind her that she promised Lochner an invitation to the wedding. Dix's immediate response picks up the issue of marriage: "She promised Lochner what?"—not "Promised who?" Dix's fury and the reassertion of control implied by his wild drive up the canyon are responses to a context that includes, alongside Brub's treachery and Laurel's lack of candor, the articulation of the marriage prospect. I give this some weight because, in the aftermath of Dix's attack on the crash victim, the topic of marriage remains unmentioned, and, where we might expect it to reemerge in the apparent restoration of calm and intimacy, Dix's mind instead turns to divorce. He presents his thoughts for the farewell note in the screenplay, where ("I lived a few weeks while she loved me") the focus is on suffering the loss of a woman's love as a kind of death.

Marriage is on his mind again (put there by Effie) when he starts to prepare breakfast in Laurel's kitchen. The celebrated gesture in which he straightens the grapefruit knife betrays his unfamiliarity with domestic routine. By contrast with his earlier readiness to accept or demand Laurel's mothering, his taking the housekeeping role in itself suggests an anxious desire to be of service. But we should not go too far with these common-sense readings: after all, he has picked the utensil correctly. Removing its curve, while thinking about marriage and a dopily distraught Laurel, he turns the tool into a weapon, the knife into something more like a dagger (fig. 21).

Figure 21. Dix and the grapefruit knife

In its reconciliation of clarity with depth of suggestion, in its extraordinary mixture of charm, humor, and violence, this moment is representative of the film's achievement. Throughout, we find an eloquence and spontaneity of gesture unsurpassed in Ray's work. In the final scene, Dix's fury in his long-avoided recognition of Laurel's betrayal implodes as an attempt to crush and subdue her, a terrible counterfeit of a loving embrace. After this, the parting, echoing the courtship, is performed with Lochner as a relay. But where the courtship was a conspiracy to make something else out of a police interrogation, the parting disguises itself as a conversation with the cops. Dix leaves the telephone for Laurel instead of handing it to her; he acknowledges her recoil from contact, and the fact that their space cannot now be shared, by putting the receiver down on a chairback and moving to the door. There he pauses with his hand on the doorknob and makes a tentative turn into the room, looking at Laurel to submit himself to her decision. That means that Dix feels a possibility of forgiving Laurel's deceit and is concerned to know whether she might forgive his violence. Speaking to Lochner but looking at Dix, Laurel affirms with "Now it doesn't matter" what Dix still needs to be told: that their love has ended in mutual and mutually justified mistrust.

The film's depth and its modesty are both manifest in an ending which is sad and oddly unresolved rather than tragic. Dix and Laurel are left more or less where we found them at the start; only their relationship has reached a conclusion. Even here, inflation is avoided: what has come to an end is not the finest of romances but a briefly creative respite from looking at the world with anger and receiving its glance with shame.

Works Cited

Houseman, John. *Front and Center*. New York: Simon & Schuster, 1979.
Hughes, Dorothy. *In a Lonely Place*. New York: Duell, Sloan & Pearce, 1947.

Filmography

The Big Heat. Directed by Fritz Lang. Columbia Pictures, 1953.
Citizen Kane. Directed by Orson Welles. RKO Radio Pictures, 1941.
In a Lonely Place. Directed by Nicholas Ray. Columbia Pictures, 1950.
Johnny Guitar. Directed by Nicholas Ray. Republic Pictures, 1954.
The Lusty Men. Directed by Nicholas Ray. RKO Radio Pictures, 1952.
On Dangerous Ground. Directed by Nicholas Ray. RKO Pictures, 1951.
Rebel Without a Cause. Directed by Nicholas Ray. Warner Bros., 1955.
They Live by Night. Directed by Nicholas Ray. RKO Radio Pictures, 1948.
A Woman's Secret. Directed by Nicholas Ray. RKO Radio Pictures, 1949.

JOHNNY GUITAR

First published in The Movie Book of the Western, *edited by Ian Cameron and Douglas Pye, 221–28. London: Studio Vista, 1996.*

"Play it again, Johnny Guitar." These words do not occur in Nicholas Ray's film, and they echo those which notoriously do not quite occur in *Casablanca* (Michael Curtiz, 1942). Still, the echo is not all that distant. The words are heard in Peggy Lee's lyrics for the title song that she sang on a record whose popularity did much to promote *Johnny Guitar* (1954). She recorded them for use in the film (behind the opening titles, presumably) but they were dropped at some stage in the editing so that her vocal version of Victor Young's romantic theme is heard only for one verse over the finale.

"Play it again" in the lyric refers to the scene in which Johnny (Sterling Hayden) answers a request from his employer, saloon keeper Vienna (Joan Crawford), to play a tune with a lot of love in it. His choice brings the soundtrack's romance theme for the first time into the world of the characters and turns out, as time has gone by, to stir fine and painful memories for Vienna. When she tells Johnny to play something else, it is not just the tune she is rejecting but also his invitation to revisit an undefined scene of shared ecstasy and anguish. The status of the longed-for and forbidden melody in *Johnny Guitar*, and its relationship to "As Time Goes By," are one element of the film's negotiation with popular culture and what was possible in the Western in Hollywood in 1953/54. A barefaced lift from a successful model, it is as much a contemplation and a subversion as it is a theft.

The most immediate precedent for the Western title song was the Ned Washington/Dmitri Tiomkin Oscar winner from *High Noon* (1952). "Do Not Forsake Me, Oh My Darling" gestures toward romance ("on this our wedding day") but is preoccupied with the shoot-out and the chivalric test of courage. It sold hugely in two competing versions featuring the manly voices of Tex Ritter and Frankie Laine. The hard and massive male sound was successful again, in the year of *Johnny Guitar*, when Tennessee Ernie Ford sang the title number for *River of No Return* (1954). By contrast, Peggy Lee did not make a big noise, and her voice was anything but hard-edged. She was renowned for the subtlety of her musicianship rather than her force; her way with a song was soft, warm, and delicate. "Johnny Guitar" refuses the familiar yeehaw! dimension of the Western anthem, its celebration of strenuous and rugged action. The refrain of "Johnny Guitar" could be the slogan for a Western poster: "There was never a man like . . . the one they call Johnny Guitar." Indeed, it recalls Paramount's claim in 1953 that "there never was a picture like *Shane*." Yet the mention of the guitar is the ballad's nearest approach to generic definition. Above all, it is a reproachful song of adoration, addressed by a woman to a man, and focused on the anxiety and pain of her attachment.

The choice of Peggy Lee as *Johnny Guitar*'s vocalist amounted to an advertisement of the film's claim to offer something new, a difference focused on the matter of gender. It confirmed what was plain to the filmgoers of the day. The title was *Johnny Guitar*, but the name above it was Joan Crawford's. As one of the tiny number of Westerns where the crucial casting was that of the leading woman, *Johnny Guitar* set itself problems about the kind of Western drama that could be centered on a female character. But the range of answers that it could explore was crucially conditioned by its construction as a vehicle for Joan Crawford. The casting links the three terms Western, Woman, and Star to another that has marked the picture ever since its first release: Weird.

By 1953, Crawford's stardom was peculiar and desperate. No other star was comparably menaced by the shade of Norma Desmond in *Sunset Boulevard* (1950). Battling to hold her audience while the cinema business itself was in crisis, Crawford was making, from film to film, the changes that she had relied on to renew her image and her career once a decade since her start in 1925. Switches of genre from thriller (*Sudden Fear*, David Miller, 1952) to musical (*Torch Song*, Charles Walters, 1953) and now to Western gave each movie the air of a comeback. *Torch Song*'s trailer had splashed "Crawford as you've always remembered her. Crawford as you'll never forget her. . . . The New Joan Crawford in her first Technicolor triumph." The Republic Pictures press book for *Johnny Guitar* followed with "a new Joan Crawford in the most startling role of her colorful screen history." These were uncomfortable efforts to exploit familiarity without quite evoking age. (Another *Torch Song* slogan proclaimed Crawford the Eternal Female!) Through a play on expectation, they promoted the old as the new—reliably the same yet surprisingly different. The Crawford brand identified a movie subgenre now suffering the same strains of generic renewal as the Western itself at a time when the singing cowboys, a recent staple of Republic's output, had already moved into series television. In both instances, expanding the scale of proven effects to tender them newly spectacular carried the risk of broadening them to the point of grotesquerie.

In one respect, the threat to Crawford was greater than that to the Western. She had more to lose from the move into color. There was no other star so identified with a makeup. In black and white, the Crawford image used the planes of the face as the ground for an elegant and expressive design with poised exaggerations uniting the willful with the stylish. The bold lines given to the mouth and eyebrows were gestures of confidence, bringing them up to scale with her large eyes, but the matching depended on monochrome to unify these features as closely related shades of grey. In color, the different elements of the design threatened to riot as the red gash of the lips became less convincingly a complement to the blackened arches of eyebrow. This threat had been fully realized in *Torch Song* where the problem of hair color, too, had been variously approached but at no point pleasingly resolved. Loaded with color stock, the camera, for so long Crawford's adoring ally, was beginning to see her face differently; it became less enchanted by the magnificence of the bones, less dazzled by the play of light across the contours, and disrespectfully inquisitive about the tone and texture of the skin. In black and white, the face was an achieved product of the will; translation into color, with the foundation displayed, upset its balance and turned the Crawford makeup into a mask—more a covering than a projection of identity. In any case, makeup it brazenly was, a product of the Max Factor era and a glaring anachronism in any depiction of the West that aspired to realism. There was no question of developing the story as a representative exploration of women's lives on the frontier. A Crawford Western in color had to accommodate the movie star as a distinctly perceptible presence alongside that of her fictional character. *Torch Song* had skirted some of the difficulties through its theatrical setting and its all-studio shooting. Somehow *Johnny Guitar* had to make the whiff of the studio compatible with the outdoor action of an oater.

These difficulties arose from the requirement of glamour for a figure late in her forties. Crawford lacked the range and flexibility of technique to support a transition to character roles. Glamour demanded her presentation as the focus of desire, which in turn depended on her being seen to be desired by the desirable. But she faced a costar crisis. She had maintained her stardom beyond that of most of her contemporaries, and the remaining male stars of her generation were being paired with much younger women. In the years around 1953 Clark Gable (b. 1901) appeared with Ava Gardner, Grace Kelly, Gene Tierney, and Lana Turner—the oldest of whom was twenty years his junior. Most often now Crawford's name stood alone above the title. That tribute to her eminence was also a sign of her predicament. It was 1962 when Crawford next shared the screen with a star whose celebrity matched her own, and that was in the special circumstances of Robert Aldrich's *What Ever Happened to Baby Jane? Johnny Guitar* provided her with two leading men, dramatizing her allure by having them compete for her affections, but neither Sterling Hayden in the name part nor Scott Brady as his rival, the Dancing Kid, was a major star.

Crawford's isolation had unavoidably entered into the dramatic fabric of her movies. Her character was regularly brought to crisis by the emotional costs of keeping others in awe—in admiration and terror—of her force. *Johnny Guitar* addresses the problem of integrating this figure into a Western by combining two of the genre's three most isolated roles: the gunman hero and the saloon woman. More precisely, it gives Crawford the role of the saloon woman while fitting her out with some of the gunman's iconography and fitting her into the gunman's place in the narrative structure. She receives the initial unresolved challenge, and she faces her antagonist in the climactic duel.

Making the saloon woman the hero was almost as big a twist as making the gunfighter female. The saloon woman's regular role was to offer a sexual option not based on community and family, one that could sustain the hero in his unattached and nomadic state by holding out the hotel—the place where beds are paid for—as a thinkable erotic alternative to the home. Removing the saloon woman from her marginal, oppositional place in the structure—the place that typically she would at last vacate and all but renounce in stopping a bullet for the hero—could not be only a structural change. It entailed an upheaval in the system of values which was furthered, in a move that accommodated Crawford's gifts of command as well as her age, by promoting her to be the owner rather than an employee of the saloon. We are first shown Vienna's place as an isolated building remote from any community. Its interior is large, amply furnished and staffed. Everything is in place to service a boom in drinking and gambling, but it is echoingly empty of patrons. Organized for a prosperity that has yet to arrive, it is unwelcoming to a lone stranger. No cordiality informs the barman's rasped demand, "What's your pleasure?" It turns out that Vienna has erected her place on land that she knows (she has come by the knowledge corruptly) to be the site of a railroad development. She is doubly a speculator since she aims to get rich on a multiplication of land values as well as an influx of spenders. Her pioneering has a mercenary end. Her property stands in contradiction to the traditional icons of benign development: the home, the school, the church.

Vienna's capital has been built on the sale of her virtue and is now invested in an enterprise that lacks the moral prestige of farming or indeed of villain-targeted gun slinging. She is unapologetic about her greed. The film neither announces nor ultimately constructs a scheme to dramatize her moral education or reform. (None of her supporters is shown to deplore her venality.) But with neither her goals nor her methods offered for admiration, and given a troubling vehemence in her pursuit of them, the protagonist is an antiheroine whose hold on our sympathy results first from the glamour of stardom and then from the character's fortitude in opposing more numerous and more disreputable foes.

When it assigns the hero's position to the saloon woman—and through ownership makes her presence in the saloon a form of settlement rather than an accessory to the wanderer's life—the film sets up an ideological turmoil that affects the genre's other woman. That figure of chastity, dedicated to the puritan values of toil, thrift, and endurance, is called into question at the same time as she is propelled into prominence. If Vienna is the hero and not, in the received terms, virtuous, her counterpart becomes the female villain, with the attributes of the good woman damagingly inflected. In Emma Small (Mercedes McCambridge), maidenhood and decorous sexual reticence become appetite unacknowledged and distorted by denial; temperance and rectitude become killjoy bigotry, a persecuting fervor directed with hypocrisy at the sinfulness of others. In dress and manner, she is a close relation of the hellfire Bible-basher; McCambridge herself has referred to her costume as a "slightly modified nun's habit."

Constructing the villain in this way is partly a matter of creating an interesting and worthily formidable antagonist for the star. The film's narrative pattern is that of the siege; the objectives of staying put and surviving—ordinarily undramatic—gain force in face of the threat from an enemy set on penetrating and destroying the citadel.

A gambling house is an odd kind of citadel, but the design of Vienna's place is eloquent. It brings together aspects of a shack, a mansion, and a fortress. In its fortress dimension, it is made to endure and to withstand attack. Though formed of wood, its sides are sunk into the cliff-face behind so that the rear wall is solid stone, rough and earth-colored. The resulting image embodies Vienna's boast that she has built her house upon the rock. The red glow of the exposed stone is so pronounced whenever the back wall is in shot that we are kept aware of Vienna's defiant assertion that she is here to stay. The dust storm that blows outside during the opening sequences characterizes Vienna's as a place of refuge but also stresses its stability; the gusts enter its rooms only as noise and have not the power to make its fabric shake or creak. While the rock secures the rear of the building, the window of Vienna's private quarters surmounts the front entrance like a castle lookout. It is the product and a token of her concern never to be taken by surprise, the architectural expression of wariness. So the building declares what it cannot satisfy: its owner's hunger for security.

By constructing Vienna as a woman desperate to defend the position she has won, and by constructing the plot so that she is under virulent attack, the film draws on the reality of Joan Crawford's situation, exploits the resonances of her screen persona, and works with the actress's peculiar powers. A Crawford role had glamorously to combine authority and pathos, a difficult trick. To establish her strength of will and her command was not the hard part; she had learned to stand her ground with conviction, and she could use her eyes and voice masterfully to govern the tone of any exchange. The price for her command was stiffness, the steel that informed her assumptions of graciousness, the control of manner—most evident in her careful speech and the deliberate pace of her movements and responses—that could block the suggestion of spontaneous (tender) feeling and betray the calculation in her projections of vulnerability and need.

One of the film's strategies for dealing with these problems is to frame Crawford's performance as a spectacle and almost never to seem to seek intimacy. It causes Vienna herself to do a lot of acting, and it stresses the masking of her private self in the interests of her performed authority. The movie's famous love scene plays on her control. Johnny's "Tell me something nice. . . . Lie to me" is a demeaning request for a performance: "Anything nice you might say to me would be a lie." Vienna counters first by demanding that Johnny give her the lines—"What do you want to hear?"—and then by reading them back flatly so as to seem to accept rather than to contest Johnny's accusations. She turns the tables by demonstrating that Johnny's lack of trust, his protection of his right to feel betrayed, means that it makes little difference what she says or how she says it. When she recites "All these years I've waited," her tone says, "I am doing what you asked, telling you a lie." She throws back to Johnny the task of deciding whether he will hear the lie in the words or in the tone. At the same time, her caustic performance accuses Johnny of handing her a rotten script, one that raises false issues and can as a result only be rendered badly, without energy or conviction.

The risk in the film's fascination with the spectacle of performance is of ending up with a flatly posturing figure devoid of interior life. The obvious way to counter that danger might be to create moments where Vienna's control is broken and to require the actress to relax her command so as to let herself and the character be found off guard. That may have been outside the range of Crawford's abilities and certainly it is not Nicholas Ray's method here. He stresses and exaggerates Vienna/Crawford's command, but frames it precariously (as in the construction of the decor) so that it emerges not as the authority of confidence or vanity—in which case the exterior and the interior would be without tension—but as an insistence born of terror. Command is what Vienna clings to (fig. 22).

The film is able to use the undertow of panic in Crawford's self-assertion, producing a character that the star can inhabit as well as perform by making Vienna carry with her an ineradicable conviction and fear of the world's contempt. She is trying to reach a height from which she will be unassailable, but she is afflicted with doubt as to whether eminence secures her from censure or creates a larger exposure to it. The character is driven by knowledge of

Figure 22. Command is what Vienna clings to

the ugliness from which she has come, and Crawford has only to play the exterior—the effortful poise and authority, the investment in the perfected mask—for it to be palpable how violent is her process of concealment and denial, how deep her sense of taint. The relevant contrast is with Barbara Stanwyck, who retains and cherishes her capacity for coarseness in no matter what sphere of prosperity or elegance. For Stanwyck, a wretched past can be a source of useful knowledge rather than of shame, to be drawn on rather than erased; her *Stella Dallas* (1937) is made to pay for her inability wholly to regret or despise the life she has left behind. With Crawford, the sense of herself as victim, and the feeling that the position won has continuously and strenuously to be held, persist through any degree of achievement. They produce the ferocity for which the later Crawford was noted. That collision of authority with panic meant that her intensity was always at the edge of the grotesque and needed only an element of play to become parodic.

Johnny Guitar builds its style on an understanding of Crawford's stardom by combining a precisely graded exaggeration of effects with an unusual overtness of construction. Victor Young's music is masterly in its comprehension of and contribution to the film's peculiar idiom. A grandly symphonic score employing a large orchestra, it is very high-toned in its deployment of leitmotif, its melodic use of percussion and drums, and its provision of concertino opportunities for piano and guitar. But in the scenes of action and confrontation, it regularly goes to the limit of seemingly naïve pictorialism by duplicating the image or mickey-mousing its movement. Characters struggle uphill to a background of effortlessly stepped rising chords. Falls to earth are marked with tumbling or crashing descents into the bass. Qualities of movement are closely described and thus boldly displayed by an accompaniment that exerts itself to turn action into choreography. But it is not just events in the film's world that Young seeks to annotate. He can seem to be counting off the shot changes, as if on the fingers of one hand, with jabbing chimes to greet the arrival of each new image. The music often repeats and at times takes over from diegetic sound effects, submerging the noise of a waterfall with harp glissandi or ousting the hiss and crackle of spreading flame with wavering wind figures that also evoke the crazy glee of an arsonist. In a literal spirit, too, it takes upon itself to echo processes of thought with stinging shifts in the musical line to signal each fresh realization: there is a lovely one when a floored and cornered Vienna spots a possibly handy gun lying nearby. There are moments when the music declares its burnout and invites us to share a joke with figures on-screen. For the most part, however, an ironic attitude informs but does not undermine the construction of effects.

The star is drawn into complicity with the film's musical devices, exposing them within the world of the fiction, when the vigilantes invade Vienna's for the second time, now to denounce her as an accomplice to the bank robbery committed by the Kid's gang. They are not aware that she has seconds ago made herself an accessory to the crime by hiding one of the robbers on her premises. They enter the saloon to find her alone, playing the piano; the tune she has just started is, of course, "Johnny Guitar." Her assumption of calm and her attempt to demean the posse by seeming untroubled in its presence are conveyed by having her continue to play the melody as she started, in the reflective vein of a nocturne: Vienna declares that the posse is intruding on a private space (the saloon has now become her home). She plays, softly and slowly, a rather naïve arrangement with small elaborations that she treats with more care than finesse. She is musing over this intimate melody in what could be a ruminative improvisation or an effort to recall how it used to go. A lack of evenness in her touch carries a hint of distraction but confirms that this is a personal communion, not offered for the benefit or to the judgment of others. When spoken to, Vienna speaks over the notes with a controlled show of indifference so that the music becomes a supportive counterpoint to her mood. (The sense that this is background music as well as Vienna's music is constructed by a sound balance that never lets the piano compromise the audibility of speech, and heightened by camera angles that mask Crawford's hands so that we never see them touch the keyboard.) Her playing develops through the interrogation as an emotional commentary. Its hesitations and resumptions, its changes of key and dynamic, inflect what is said and articulate what is unspoken. Vienna's second playing of the refrain reflects a point of deadlock in the negotiation. When she rises from the piano, abandoning the tune in the middle of a bar, a final discord with both hands slammed into the keys results from but also announces, rhetorically, the exhaustion of her patience.

The use of the piano here can stand as an emblem of the movie's way with music. The hyperbolic quality of Young's score is appreciated even as it contributes to the urgency of conflict and the vividness of emotional depiction. Intensification is calculated to arrive at, but not to pass, the edge of absurdity. The daring in this process constructs an aesthetic suspense that defines the film's special thrill.

In this regard, the musical strategy is in harmony with visual design that uses blocks of color, strong line, and a bold separation of foreground from background—aided by costumes made up from one-fabric, one-color elements—to evoke a comic-book approach to composition. That inspiration inflects but does not contradict the film's quest for eloquence and beauty.

More evidently bizarre is a use of the camera to construct characters' remarks as soliloquies and their private gestures as asides. The most glaring instance occurs at the start of the film, just after Vienna's introduction, and it sets a frame of reference for later, more sober, uses of the device. Vienna has overridden the reasoned objections of one of her staff, Sam (Robert Osterloh), and ordered him to fetch a lamp to hang outside. Osterloh walks straight toward the camera smirking, then says, as if confiding in us, "I never saw a woman who was more a man. She thinks like one, acts like one and sometimes makes me feel like I'm not." After "acts like one," a cut to a fresh setup rescues his action, reinserting it into the fictional world by showing that the character is speaking through a hatchway to the kitchen hand, Tom (John Carradine). The shock of the effect could have been muted if the viewpoint had been prepared as Tom's eyeline. But such a marking is not merely withheld, it is contradicted. To have the actor head for and speak into the camera is to compromise the integrity of the fictional world and to unsettle our confidence in the identity of performer and role. Since there is no camera in the world of the characters, the actor (who can be aware of the camera) is distinguished from his character (who cannot). The camera's interception of the moment produces this effect by exploiting the modes of presence and absence specific to cinema. But it does so without having the actor step out of his role or break his performance.

To address remarks or gestures to the camera is a device used more in comedy than in melodrama and most frequent in a special subgenre of comedy, the spoof. Bob Hope, for instance, celebrated a spectacularly implausible twist in events by turning to the audience with the challenge "Let's see them top this on television." That was at the end of *Son of Paleface* (1952), one of a pair of pictures that had burlesqued the genre by taking the familiar Hope figure of the cowardly and incompetent braggart out West and having him gulled and outgunned by a cross-dressed Jane Russell, whose friends call her Mike. (Oddly enough, Roy Rogers appeared as an undercover gunman with the alias of "The Guitar Player." It is pleasantly credible that the Paleface movies may have been at the back of Roy Chanslor's mind when he plotted the original novel of *Johnny Guitar* and that the figure of Jane Russell in gunfighter garb may have influenced the look designed for Joan Crawford.)

Where the spoof performs a relatively straightforward reversal of Western formulas, particularly by making jokes out of the lead male's failures of courage, integrity, and competence, *Johnny Guitar*'s play with the genre involves a more intricate and challenging pattern in which established expectations are in some respects maintained, in some varied or reversed, and in some exposed through overfulfillment.

Ray's movie was made at a time when A-feature Westerns were aspiring to treat serious themes and to stress their solemnity by means of a weighty style; George Stevens pronounced his concern to "aggrandize the Western legend" in *Shane* (1953). With its contemporary reference, its themes of persecution and demagoguery, and its insistence on obscurities of psychological motivation, *Johnny Guitar* was part of the general trend. But it was wildly aberrant in obliging these elements to coexist with Z-feature and serial-movie plot devices that point up its attachment to the most extravagant traditions of blood-and-thunder melodrama.

There is a proliferation of aliases: the pacific Johnny Guitar is in reality the gunfighter Johnny Logan, while Vienna (no surname) and the Dancing Kid are evidently assumed identities. Correspondingly, we have an underground escape by hidden mineshaft and a secret lair reached through a cave whose entrance is screened by a curtain of water. At crucial points, outlandish coincidence propels the plot. When Emma leads the posse to Vienna's to carry her off for lynching, two obstacles stand in her way—the marshal

(Frank Ferguson), who demands an orderly trial, and Vienna's old retainer, Tom, who pulls a gun to drive the posse out. Emma shoots Tom, and his falling spasm sets off his pistol to fire a bullet that fells the marshal.

The lynching follows the familiar pattern of the serials in which the apparently final catastrophe at the end of one episode would be amazingly averted at the start of the next. Vienna's hands are tied. She is mounted on a horse that stands in a gully. The noose around her neck is slung from a beam of the bridge overhead. Emma takes a whip to strike the horse whose bolting will plunge Vienna to her death. But at just that moment, Johnny, concealed on top of the bridge, cuts the rope; the horse carries Vienna off, giving her a start on the confounded lynchers. A fresh chapter opens. Such brazen moments are not safely hived off into special sectors of the film. Vienna's remarkable escape comes only seconds after the hanging of the adolescent Turkey (Ben Cooper), when terror and pitiless brutality were strongly conveyed.

In *Son of Paleface*, Bob Hope is on his way to an assignation with Jane Russell when he receives an old sidekick's advice: "Don't forget, this is the West where men are men." "That's what she likes about me," he replies. "I'm a novelty." The spoof's way with Western manhood is to turn it on its head. But *Johnny Guitar* acts on the perception that, so long as it stays within the genre, a Western cannot lose its preoccupation with masculinity even when it has women in its leading roles. It tells us this at the moment that it first presents Vienna. Old Tom has been constructed as the housemaid; he has emerged from his place in the kitchen to fetch a broom from the bar, and he welcomes Johnny with these words: "That's a lot of man you're carrying in those boots, stranger. You know, there's something about a tall man that makes people sit up and take notice." Although addressed to Johnny, and intriguingly so, the words play over the image of Vienna alone, seen from below as the camera looks up to her position of advantage on the landing above the saloon. It is Joan Crawford in trousers and riding boots with a tie at the neck of her dark shirt. Though she is not (yet) wearing a gun belt, she stands erect, silent and challenging, as if poised for the draw. Her figure is not entirely masculinized. The trousers are closely tailored—shaped more like tights than denims—and belted to show off her waist. But the image is definite enough for Tom's words to adhere as a first description of this woman: "That's a lot of man . . ."

Johnny Guitar makes its closest approaches to overt parody in its overfulfillment of the expectation that a Western will dramatize myths of masculinity. When the adolescent Turkey sets out to prove his manhood to Vienna by showing off with his gun, Johnny blazes into action and shoots the pistol out of Turkey's hand. In the aftermath, Turkey's crisis of self-doubt is shown in his abashed and speechless withdrawal. His attention is divided between contemplation of the man who bested him and anxiety over the abused weapon, which is returned to its holster and then taken out again for further unhappy inspection. The symbolic function of the gun and of gunplay is glaringly at issue here. (For Johnny, too, since his need to assert his prowess has been shown as psychotic.)

The articulation of desires and worries around the phallic value of weaponry extends to Emma. "That's big talk for a little gun," she says when Vienna tries to expel the posse on its first visit. It is through its presentation of Emma that the film insists most on the inspection of subtext and the exposure of unacknowledged motives. Vienna makes a number of notably anachronistic attempts at reading Emma's subconscious in order to explain her enmity. They all center on Emma's feeling for the Dancing Kid, as in, "You want the Kid and you're so ashamed of it you want him dead." What this ignores or represses is that Emma allows no distinction between the Kid and Vienna: "I say they are [the same]. They both cast the same shadow." Emma's words repeatedly couple Vienna and the Kid, but since we have been so strongly directed to ponder her hidden motives, we can hardly fail to see that the goal of her actions is the annihilation of Vienna and that the Kid is a relatively insignificant accessory to that desire.

Emma is fascinated by Vienna and the *filth* that she represents. The bond between the two women is such that each can claim, with justice, to see through the other. The challenges that pass between them are exploratory and teasing:

Emma: You don't have the nerve.
Vienna: Try me!

and

Emma: I'm coming up, Vienna.
Vienna: I'm waiting.

Their words balance and mesh, sounding their entanglement. At the dissolution of their first public confrontation, Emma approaches Vienna to speak to her in intimacy. Vienna steps down the stairs toward her and stops to hear what she has to say. Excitement chokes Emma's speech at first, until she is able to get out, "I'm going to kill you." The words emerge with a coaxing softness that makes them as much inviting as threatening, and her eyes hold Vienna with a kind of awe. Vienna's return—"I know. If I don't kill you first"—accepts the fatality of their mutual involvement but refuses the intimacy. She cuts off further exchange by striding away from Emma; she is not going to any particular spot, and her gaze is rigidly fixed ahead to deny contact.

A vital constituent of the film's weirdness is its flaunting of the erotic dimension of hatred. The embittered exchanges between Johnny and Vienna are germane here. But it is in the conflict of the women that the theme achieves its freest expression. Since these women are in evident ways performing the roles usually taken by men, the effect is to bring erotic subtexts of the Western so near the surface as to display them in their intensity and their confusion.

Filmography

Casablanca. Directed by Michael Curtiz. Warner Bros., 1942.
High Noon. Directed by Fred Zinnemann. United Artists, 1952.
Johnny Guitar. Directed by Nicholas Ray. Republic Pictures, 1954.
River of No Return. Directed by Otto Preminger. Twentieth Century Fox, 1954.
Shane. Directed by George Stevens. Paramount Pictures, 1953.
Son of Paleface. Directed by Frank Tashlin. Paramount Pictures, 1952.
Stella Dallas. Directed by King Vidor. United Artists, 1937.
Sudden Fear. Directed by David Miller. RKO Pictures, 1952.
Sunset Boulevard. Directed by Billy Wilder. Paramount Pictures, 1950.
Torch Song. Directed by Charles Walters. MGM, 1953.
What Ever Happened to Baby Jane? Directed by Robert Aldrich. Warner Bros., 1962.

I CONFESS
Photographs of People Speaking

First published in CineAction, *no. 52 (June 2000): 28–39.*

> We were to consider . . . some cases and senses . . . in which to *say* something is to *do* something; or in which *by* saying or *in* saying something we are doing something. This topic is one development . . . in the recent movement towards questioning an age-old assumption in philosophy . . . that to say something . . . is always and simply to *state* something. (Austin 1975, 12)

In the Truffaut book (1968), various reasons are proposed for the failure of *I Confess* (1953). Hitchcock suggests that there was a lack of humor and subtlety in the screenplay that gave an effect of heaviness. He identifies some local difficulties, too: the linguistic contrivances involved in setting an English-speaking movie in French Canada, and the problems arising from Warner Bros.' last-minute insistence on putting Anne Baxter into the female lead in place of the Swedish actress Anita Bjork. Those of us who enjoy and admire Anne Baxter, here and elsewhere, may be inclined to dispute the justice of comparing an actual performance with an imagined one, but we should also bear in mind the habitual precision of Hitchcock's casting.

Truffaut and Hitchcock seem agreed that the film suffered because non-Catholic audiences were unsympathetic to the plot's founding conceit—that the sanctity of the confessional would bind a priest to silence even when he found himself suspected of killing and at risk of execution in place of a murderer known to him through confession. I am not a Christian but I do not experience the difficulty suggested, and I know of no evidence that *I Confess* fared better in Catholic than in other territories. Hitchcock and Truffaut are here falling into the same error as those who suppose that male spectators are unable to sympathize with female characters or that the feelings and experiences of white actors must be inaccessible to the imaginations of black filmgoers.

Very early in the film we are with Father Michael Logan (Montgomery Clift) as he hears the confession of the sacristan Otto Keller (O. E. Hasse); Keller says that he has killed the lawyer Villette (Ovila Légaré), who had surprised him in the act of burglary. Since we know of Logan's innocence and Keller's guilt, the film has a difficulty in making it seem that Logan is in danger. Moreover—and this is an aspect that Hitchcock could have altered—the world does not talk about Logan with suspicion, or treat him like a murderer. It is only late in the picture, when we reach the theater of the courtroom, that anyone makes a show of believing him guilty.

Complacency is disturbed, however, by presenting the villain as an increasingly demonic figure. Starting in a sniveling, shifty kind of pathos Keller develops a mirthlessly teasing fascination with Logan's ordeal and begins to savor the knowledge of his own power. We see the results of his glimpsing the desperate hope that he may enjoy providential protection. He becomes a cousin to Bruno, Robert Walker's wonderful creation in Hitchcock's previous film, *Strangers on a Train* (1951). He has the same appalling flirtatiousness and moral sadism but none of the glamour. Failing to subdue his terror and surmount his cowardice, he remains a colorless lump of corruption; there is little of Bruno's dreadful zest to enliven his malevolence. Keller is interesting to the extent that he is vile. He is very interesting.

We might regret that Hitchcock and his writers did not trust more to the potency of their villain. A greater respect for Keller's satanic command might have relieved them of the concern to secure each link in the circumstantial chain connecting Father Logan to the crime. The story starts like a murder mystery, with the disclosure of the corpse. It then moves almost directly to the identification of the murderer, giving us the confession that usually concludes a detective story. Nonetheless the narrative continues to be shaped as a mystery, where each step forward is also a step back that brings a new revelation about the events in the past leading up to the victim's death. In the normal way this course would be followed in order to fill out the motivation of the murder, but Hitchcock does not go the normal way. Keller gives reasons for killing Villette that are tricked out with sentiment and more evidently self-serving than they are plausible. It would be easier to believe that Keller was driven to homicide as one of Villette's blackmail victims—since extortion will turn out to have been Villette's business—than it is to credit his tale of money stolen in order to free his wife, Alma (Dolly Haas), from a life of drudgery.[1] But while the film's imagery and its characterization of Keller encourage speculation, its dramatic action offers no challenge to Keller's repeated claim. Instead the pasts that come into question are those of Father Logan and Ruth Grandfort (Anne Baxter), the wife of a prominent politician.

This procedure was necessary because of the problem latent within the alluring premise of the movie's action. It is wonderful to have the hero menaced and immobilized by the very knowledge that should guarantee his freedom; but in order to bring him into danger it is necessary to construct another strand of plot to trace a history that will cause him to be accused of just that crime of which he has received the killer's confession. The priest has to have had a connection not with the killer alone but with the victim, too, and the connection needs to have been such as to provide a colorable incentive to murder. Beyond that he must be without other means of establishing his innocence (such as an alibi) while the police investigation must encounter nothing that directs it to the real killer. All this while satisfying the requirements of the Production Code Administration, which was professionally touchy in its protection of Catholic interests. A tall order.

The writers (Hitchcock of course included) are remarkably successful in drawing the noose that snares the priest. The middle section of the film is constructed as the gradual exposure of the connection between Logan and Ruth Grandfort. Their relationship is presented to us as a puzzle as soon as

Ruth enters the movie. On the morning after the murder and Keller's confession to Logan, the detective on the case, Inspector Larue (Karl Malden), catches sight of a meeting on the pavement outside Villette's house. He is curious to see Logan hurry Mme Grandfort away from the scene (figs. 23 and 24) but he is too distant to hear her response to the news of the murder: "He's dead? I can't believe it. We're free." Thereafter the circumstances that make this woman think of herself and the priest as jointly liberated by Villette's death are unraveled in tandem with the development of the police case against Michael Logan.

Although the management of the narration involves a fair number of supplementary contrivances (whereby, for instance, Mme Grandfort can keep abreast of Inspector Larue's enquiries) it is a mark of the ingenuity with which the action is plotted and of the precision with which viewpoint is controlled that the film avoids troubling us with its implausibilities until a late stage, when the case comes to trial. Unfortunately, so much effort is

Figure 23.

368 • V. F. Perkins on Movies

Figure 24. Inspector Larue watches Logan hurrying Mme Grandfort away from the scene

invested in nailing down the plot and disguising its improbabilities that narrative economy and propulsion are sacrificed. Credibility is maintained but sometimes at the expense of interest. No doubt because of the centrality of religion, the movie cannot embrace the extravagance of invention that energizes, for instance, *Notorious* (1946) and *Vertigo* (1958). A work of genius and a fine picture, *I Confess* has—like many other fine pictures, including some masterpieces—feeble moments and some passages when it plods and it bores. Brief as they are, they do a lot of damage.

While second-rank Hitchcock is treasurable in its own right, it also has the great value of showing us what an unlikely achievement first-rank Hitchcock is, how delicate are the balances and fine the intuitions on which it depends. The Hitchcock movie is a genre impossible for anyone but Hitchcock and extremely hard to bring off even for him. The weaknesses of *I Confess* are primarily dramatic, and they are incurred largely in pursuit of ambitions in the realm of character and theme.

The screenplay seeks to make a virtue of a necessarily complex plot by developing, within the constraints of a ninety-minute span, a large range of secondary roles. These are not the highly colored bits that appear briefly and delightfully in such films as *North by Northwest* (1959) and *The Birds* (1963), but characters whose fates depend on the unwinding of the Logan-Keller affair and who appear throughout the picture with attitudes and aims, frustrations and perplexities of their own. This widening of perspective seems designed to balance the central role, a figure whose interior life could not be articulated, but it also serves to compose an eloquent image of ramification, and an informing sense of the uncontrollable consequentiality not only of deeds—a murder is, after all, predictably laden with consequence for others beside the victim—but also of speech.

If Hitchcock had been working with writers of the caliber of Ben Hecht (*Notorious*), Thornton Wilder (*Shadow of a Doubt* [1943]), or Samuel Raphaelson (*Suspicion* [1941]), his success might have been more consistent. He might have avoided those flatly explicit moments that turn characters into diagrams, muffling the resonance that is elsewhere achieved through the allusive power of presence and imagery. Willie Robertson, the crown prosecutor (Brian Aherne), is the figure who links the Grandforts to the Larue investigation. In his early appearances he is interestingly loathsome—and one of those many figures through whom Hitchcock expresses his ambivalence toward a familiar model of Englishness. Robertson's vanity far outruns his accomplishments; party tricks are his forté; his arrogance and lack of imagination keep him at his ease even as they display the dullness of his mind. At the trial he becomes the converse of Father Logan, as well as his antagonist, since these traits preserve him from discomfort when professional obligation goes against personal interest, requiring him to harangue his friend Ruth Grandfort as an adulteress. Unfortunately his part in the trial is not (perhaps could not have been) well enough written to make Robertson's opportunism interesting. He seems merely foolish, ineffectually blustering. Since that is not an effect that we can suppose to be intended, it is the actor rather than the character that we turn against.

The problem is in the relation between characterization and plot. The film cannot afford to recognize how feeble is the case against Logan because its denouement—the exposure of Keller—depends on the jury's reaching a "not proven" verdict and the judge's expressing a conviction of Logan's guilt. Symptomatically, defense procedures hardly exist in the trial as presented. None of the witnesses is cross-examined; Logan's attorney is scarcely heard, seen, or mentioned. It may be that Hitchcock's distrust of the machinery of the law went so deep that he saw no conflict between the trial's being a farce and its producing a general execration of the accused. But that viewpoint does not achieve dramatic expression. There are high spots in the trial scenes, some of Logan's evidence and all of Keller's, but elsewhere the action is by moments turgid and unconvincing.

That is because one central point has got muffled in the construction: Logan is striving to protect Ruth Grandfort's secrets as well as Otto Keller's. His silences and equivocations about Ruth are not necessitated by his priestly obligations, since they do not cover information obtained in the confessional, but they crucially extend his vulnerability. It is in relation to Ruth, and not in relation to Keller, that the world believes he has something to hide. Logan knows this, but he will not declare the facts that would expose Ruth as (in wish if not in deed) an adulteress. This dramatically vital matter never reaches articulation with the necessary force or clarity, partly because throughout its first half the film treats the relationship between Ruth and Michael as a mystery. Perhaps we have in *I Confess* a vindication of Hitchcock's regularly stated belief that mystery is hostile to drama.

The weaknesses of the plot create difficulties for our understanding of Hitchcock's design. At the outset we are instructed to accept that a man wearing a cassock will be understood to be a priest. That should stand untroubled as a premise of the action, and it might do if the cassock were then forgotten. However, it comes back in a big way when Keller decides to plant it with its unwashed bloodstains in Logan's trunk, and it features largely in the trial. We can place this in the film's scheme to the extent that we can accept that the world about him is so thrilled by the prospect of seeing a priest guilty of murder that it blocks out other possibilities. Part of the film's aim does seem to be to chart the varieties of temperament, role, and desire through which the convenience of a disparate group can come to be served by the identification of Logan as Ruth Grandfort's lover and Villette's killer.

Inspector Larue presents himself as meticulously concerned with every shred of evidence. We can take the film to reflect on the vanity of this self-image in offering us a detective self-esteemed as a model of thoroughness and rationality to whom it never occurs that a man in a cassock could be a man in disguise. Perhaps it is Larue's passion for neatness that ensnares him. Hitchcock's imagery defines the moment when his attention is diverted from Keller and fixed onto Logan. The detective is in the middle of questioning Keller, listening to his tale of having discovered Villette's corpse, when there is a cut—stressed by a chime in Dimitri Tiomkin's score—to a shot that places the back of Keller's head in the foreground and shows that Larue has ceased to look at him. The camera is placed close enough to make a large movement across the screen out of a slight sideways shift of Karl Malden's head. Showing less than half his face, the image is effectively a close-up of his right eye, agleam as its gaze is drawn to the distance. The answering shot gives us his view through a window as Logan paces back and forth on the pavement beyond Villette's house. With Keller excluded from its foreground the frame defines Larue's concentration rather than his field of vision. Over this we hear Larue distractedly dismiss Keller, and we cut back to see the murderer move away out of shot while Larue's gaze, trained on the action outside, ignores his departure. Further inserts break with Larue's eyeline to give us the meeting that he can see but not hear, between Logan and Ruth Grandfort. The sequence ends by returning, through a repetition of the POV shot as Logan and Ruth move off together, to the image of Larue fixed in thought as if holding the picture of the meeting in his mind to see what it might yield. We must take it that he has been impressed by its two most visible aspects: the radiance of the woman (in what was his, as well as our, first sight of the Anne Baxter character) and Logan's action as he interrupted her movement. He reached out to touch her arm in a gesture of what could seem unpriestly intimacy.

The choice of location contributes subtly to visual expression. The pavement has a slope, not very pronounced but enough that the quality of movement downhill is distinct from that going the other way. As a result it is made palpable that Logan has intervened to reverse Ruth's action, that he knew where she would be going and has turned her away. That is visible to Larue, of course, and is further fuel for his speculations. Larue's concern with Logan is established here, well before grounds are discovered to place a priest at the scene of the crime. From this point his curiosity is directed only to Logan and the woman; it is as if the Villette investigation becomes the pretext that allows him to pursue his fascination with their relationship. Keller disappears from the case because nothing about him excites the inspector's interest.

The mainspring of the plot that brings Logan under suspicion is the relationship between Ruth Grandfort and her husband. In all that is unspoken it is eloquently staged. Pierre Grandfort is played by Roger Dann. In a weakly written part that needs any help performance can give it, his acting betrays (and may explain) his lack of screen experience. Yet, assisted by his unfamiliarity, he creates telling images of a husband who is successful in the world of public affairs but passes almost unnoticed within his marriage. He has access to his wife's social and sexual services but not to her desire. Lit by cameraman Robert Burks so as to subdue his presence, he hovers in the middle distance offering his help in a soft mutter and commanding the frame no more than he commands the situation. The annoyances and frustrations of finding himself cuckolded by his wife's imagination produce a finely suggestive moment in the scene where he breaks the news to Ruth that her efforts to supply the priest with an alibi have backfired and will result in his being charged with murder. As he leaves her bedroom offering to have her breakfast brought up, he reaches out to close the door on her. It is a gesture that we have seen before, but performed this time with a fresh strength. The camera, catching it as a jailer's move, notices his sense of a new power to keep her in her place.

Ruth Grandfort fuels her romantic fantasy with a range of supposedly desperate or well-meaning notions that serve to cause trouble for Michael Logan and to bind him within her sphere of action. It seems possible that Hitchcock wanted us to understand that Villette's blackmail had no particular force, except insofar as it was conferred by Ruth's hysteria and her eagerness to make use of his threats as a pretext for involving Logan. It seems quite an exaggeration when she claims, "Pierre's career would be finished; Michael might be unfrocked"; in any case, she indicates elsewhere that neither of these prospects is unthinkable to her. When the priest is about to be accused she goes so far as to trail the idea that they might run away and become fugitive lovers. ("You must do something, they're going to arrest you. Michael, what can we do? . . . You're not going to let them bring you to trial? . . . You can't let that happen.")

Hitchcock's direction and Anne Baxter's performance construct Ruth Grandfort as a melodramatist, an emotional arsonist desperate to set a fire or two under passionless men who inflame her the more by their reluctance to become inflamed. She is a cousin to Lisa in *Letter from an Unknown Woman* (1948)—the motives, manner, and effects of their confessions are interesting to compare—and, like Lisa, a figure observed with critical sympathy. Her scenes with Logan, where her offers are repeatedly refused or evaded, are notably better written than those with her husband. The film has committed itself to exploring this marriage but not found the means, or given itself the space, to do so with subtlety. It feels as if material filling out its character may have been dropped at the cutting stage. The relationship is developed too much for interest and too little for depth. In the dialogue exchanges we are brought close to the "photographs of people talking" that compose Hitchcock's own definition of cinematic vacancy.

We can indulge any film in patches when it has to plod us through a stretch of data (as in a montage tour of the rectories following the police investigation) in order to set up the terms of its big scenes. Serious trouble comes when the big scenes are themselves afflicted with plodding. Story problems may again be at the root of the matter. The crucial link between Logan, the Grandforts, and Villette is going to be forged with the news that Ruth Grandfort was under blackmail for adultery as a result of a night spent with the priest. Ruth's eagerness for adultery is made plain. But nothing we are shown or told gives Villette the exploitable evidence (letters, a photograph, an item of clothing, a witness, anything) that would support his threats.

It is presumably the Breen Office that we should blame—either the one in Los Angeles or the one in Hitchcock's mind. If it had been possible to build a secret affair between the priest and the politician's wife of sufficient length and passion, however far in the past, the film would have had everything required to peg its net of circumstance. And if Pierre Grandfort had tolerated the affair, that would be enough to jeopardize his career in government. Intriguingly, it was during their discussion of *I Confess* that Hitchcock thought to tell Truffaut the tale of a cleric who was involved in a ménage à trois with a married couple: "I wanted to shoot a scene showing the parson making violent love to the young woman while the husband . . . looked on." But if Hitch is here trailing a hint about the story behind the story, the film itself allows only that there may have been a night of love when Logan was in ignorance of Ruth's marriage, and before he entered the priesthood. Other suggestions are so comprehensively blocked that there seems to be no basis either for Villette's blackmail or for the prosecutor's effort to construct a long-standing illicit connection. Since this circumstance is not plausibly established, there is a weak foundation to the scenes that depend on it, and the screenplay is constrained in its efforts to develop them.

Most interesting stories are to some degree implausible. Part of the critical interest of *I Confess* is due to the ways in which its implausibilities, unlike those of, say, *Vertigo* or *Shadow of a Doubt*, work to compromise its achievement. (Imagine a *Vertigo* obliged to give us scenes that plotted Gavin Elster's relationship with his wife, or his recruitment of Judy into the murder scheme.) In *I Confess* some confusion arises from our not knowing which of its implausibilities we are meant to notice and therefore interpret and which are meant to be left undisturbed as the given material of its tale. This difficulty particularly affects the claims, and our understanding of the motives, of Ruth Grandfort and Otto Keller.

It would be interesting to know whether Hitchcock at any point contemplated the other available development of the narrative premise, where the one who hears the confession is never himself under suspicion but is fated to observe in torment as another innocent is carried toward the scaffold. He might have called it *The Priest Who Knew Too Much*. Maybe the bloodstained cassock is too much of a MacGuffin to sustain a serious tone. Or perhaps the narrative themes of imposture and mistaken identity are better suited to comic than to melodramatic exploration. Their ideal vehicle may not be the story of an anguished priest suffering the obligations of confession, but that of a glib adman mistaken for a nonexistent spy.

But if the narrative of *I Confess* can let us down, Hitchcock's treatment is a great compensation, since it achieves a power of suggestion and a coherence that is not always evident in the drama.

The opening, behind the credits, presents imagery that is stronger in thematic suggestion than in atmosphere or story content. It is true that for some part of the audience—I have no idea how large a part—the first shot would establish the location in Quebec. It presents a view across the St. Lawrence of the landmark Château Frontenac. But what it shows is less important than how it looks. It uses the peculiarities of day-for-night filtering to picture the looming mass of a national monument silhouetted to display its strict lines and sharp angles—an architecture of civic debate and judicial arbitration through which the state sets out its claims to authority, permanence, and grandeur. Below this rigid presence, there is water; above it, the indeterminate, drifting form of a silvery cloudscape. The shot works with the cloudiness and against the rigidity, as the camera floats forward and up, without apparent goal, to give the clouds more and more of the frame.

Meanwhile we are hearing perhaps the strangest of all movie theme songs. It sounds like a song. Its tune laments with falling measures and yearns with rising ones. It is delivered as a solo by a high soprano of impressive gifts, and she certainly is singing a lyric—which seems to be in English. But we cannot make out her words. The odd phrase seems to emerge, though never quite into clarity—was that "Lost in one another's arms"?—only to be swallowed again into an acoustic fog. Heartfelt words are being declaimed, and yet our understanding cannot reach them.

We can suspect a touch of malice here, as Hitchcock enjoyed spoiling the composer Dmitri Tiomkin's occasion for a title song, the like of "I Confess (The Love I Feel for You)." *I Confess* came the year after Tiomkin won an Oscar and a fortune, and changed the nature of film scoring, with the ballad "Do Not Forsake Me, Oh My Darling" in *High Noon*. It came the year before, it is said, he offered to write another title number, "Dial M for Me." But if there was a tease it was compatible with serious purpose. The lyric we can hear but not apprehend, whose moods are strong but whose statements remain obscure, this complements and shades the meeting in the image of the crisply defined, the publicly asserted, and the intangible.

The solo singer's projection of longing and anguish prepares the centrality of romance and of a woman's feelings to a story ostensibly centered on a priest. It backs the presentation of a title that puts the stress on making rather than receiving confession. *I Confess* gives us confession as an act and as a voicing not as a moral or theological abstraction. The title is a declaration, catching the confessor at the moment of speech, rather than preparing a procedure ("Confession"), a site ("The Confessional"), or, as in the French title, an issue ("The Law of Silence").

That choice yields the peculiar form of the title card that follows the Warner Bros logo: *Alfred Hitchcock's "I Confess."* The first living person we see, once the credits are over, is the director himself. Remote, outlined as a distant but recognizable, solitary and uncommunicative figure at the top of a flight of steps, he crosses the screen in a straight line from right to left. As soon as he has completed his passage there is a cut to a shot that features a Quebec sign but also, and more prominently, an arrow pointing across the screen from left to right, bearing the word DIRECTION. The story is starting with a (or with yet another) play on words; we in the anglophone audience can understand that this is a place where direction means a one-way street. Here in French Canada and here on this screen. The point is insisted upon through a firm pattern of alternation between characteristic views of the night city and four different shots of direction arrows, closer and more centered with each repetition, and stressed each time by a stinger in the music.

Having displayed himself in his independence as the director, Hitchcock proceeds to show us what it means to be the directed. At the fourth assertion of the arrow image, his camera seems to decide to obey the direction indicated. The effect of decision is created by beginning this shot as if it is to be a plain repetition of the third one, with a static camera that offers a new angle on the sign yet adds no new information. But then the pattern is broken. Instead of cutting again to a fresh location the shot runs on as the camera slides across the sign and turns to push forward into the space ahead of the pointer.

Hitchcock is famously a master of the eyeline shot, where the camera sometimes reports and sometimes transmits the perceptions of a character. No less eloquent, though, is his use of a camera that goes out of its way to declare its independence of human vision. One of many startling examples (and perhaps the most gorgeous) is the crane shot down onto the purloined key concealed in Ingrid Bergman's hand at the beginning of the big party scene in *Notorious*. At its start it mixes human and nonhuman aspects. It looks down onto a gallery from ceiling height; the remoteness of its view is stressed by placing a grand chandelier in the foreground. The camera sees across the top of this as it takes in a stream of guests descending the curve of a marble staircase. The focus is deep, unselective. But the camera's motion, in its direction and its pace, suggests the view of a human observer. It pans around and down as if to survey the action on the stairs, and it seems to fix its attention on one guest in particular as she crosses from the bottom step. Then it changes. Discovering the figure of Bergman, the hostess, in the hallway below it edges out and probes down across the space of the foyer, tracing a course and performing a movement unavailable to any human observer. It is vital that the shifting frame can no longer appear to be caused by or to respond to developments within the characters' world. The responsibility for the changing viewpoint is not now discharged in any way onto the events of the fiction. The camera's vision has taken on a goal not evident to us and not shared by any of the actors. Its movement enacts the knowledge of a secret, displayed only at the last when Bergman's hand drops to the center of the frame, fidgeting open for a moment so that we glimpse its freight. The shot started by announcing its interest in what was on show to all—the performance of guests at a high society reception. It has become an exposure of what is visible to none.

The possibility of declaring the camera's intent, using a change in apparent motivation to give the declaration force, is exploited in the opening of *I Confess*. Offered three ways to go, by the most pointedly pointed arrows there could be, the camera refuses two of them before choosing to follow the third. It traces a course, higher above the roadway than any human eye, determined only by the chain of inference it constructs. It tips in through the open window of an office to reveal a corpse spread-eagled on the floor beside a metal bar, in a diagrammatic image of a crime scene. It tilts up to show the doorway at the far side of the room, with its bead curtain swinging from recent disturbance. It sweeps to the right across the corner of the building and in apparent continuity it presents the sidewalk, and the back view of an already distant, hurriedly retreating figure in a cassock.

In other words it tells us that this priest is in flight from that murder. There is a cut to a more distant shot from across the street. As the priest figure exits the frame on the right two girls stroll in from the left. Through a dissolve with continuity strongly asserted on the soundtrack we see the man who will come to be named as Keller hurrying down another, an empty, street. He checks behind him furtively then, in a closer shot lit to display his features for the first time, he removes and folds the cassock. The light reveals, too, the rest of his attire. It is not clerical. He may be a killer but he is no priest.

Evidently this sequence sets down some of the premises of the drama, but it also sets forth the methods and concerns of the direction. It leads us along a chain of inference through which, on the evidence of our eyes (little is given to our ears) we are drawn to three main conclusions: that x has been murdered; that he has been murdered by y; and that y is a priest. It then lets us see that the priest figure is seen (by the girls) and that he does not see this. Here it reports acts of perception and unawareness, seeming to give the full picture not grasped by any of the actors. Finally it overturns a key fact of the story it has just been telling, and so demonstrates its capacity to delude us.

None of the events has been falsified in the manner of *Stage Fright* (1950). Images accurate to the fiction have been strung together so as both to deceive and undeceive the viewer. Direction, we have been shown, has the power to lead us. Of necessity it also has the power to mislead us—to make us jump to conclusions. Finally it asserts its power to inform us about the ways in which we may be misled. In demonstrating that as a vehicle of truth film language must also be capable of falsehood—and of the demonstration—I *Confess* prepares its ground for what is virtually an inventory of deceptions and concealments within quests for truth and for self-disclosure.

The film takes its cue, thematically, from the strange symmetry in the main device of its plot—confession as an act of speech that binds to silence, an act that conveys at the same time knowledge and paralysis. It is concerned with words and the powers of words spoken and withheld. Hitchcock's ongoing engagement with what can be hidden and exposed—in the image, in the world—is here extended in a particularly systematic way to the operations of speech as the "visible" dimension of thought. The dramatic progression is from the closed spaces of the murder scene and the confessional to spaces increasingly open and apt for public declaration—the courtroom, the streets, and at the denouement an auditorium where everything spoken has to be shouted. With Keller it moves from the murder of Villette, unseen and unheard within the walls of a small chamber, to the shooting of his wife in a public place crowded with witnesses at a moment when all eyes have been directed to him by her gesture of denunciation.

This moment and this deed are parts of a pattern that compares the secrets of the confessional to the secrets within marriage—two kinds of intimacy. Keller's confession to Father Logan is immediately followed by his unburdening himself to Alma, and the comparison is stressed through the film's repetition of his words, each side of the dissolve, that Villette had been "going to call the police." The irony is that Keller has complete confidence in Alma. After he has told her about the murder he can say that he is safe because, Logan apart, "No one knows." Yet it is Alma who finally cannot bear the secret and betrays him. Her hand performs the deed anticipated in her husband's words to Logan: "Perhaps you will point your finger at me. Perhaps you will say 'It's Keller.'" Conversely, he is never at ease in Logan's knowledge of his crime; he gives himself away to Larue through his assumption that "the priest talked."

Both Otto and Alma die asking Logan for words of forgiveness. There is ambiguity in the asking and in the response. Is it the forgiveness of Michael Logan or the church's absolution that they most keenly desire, and do they receive the first as well as the second? Alma dies in the arms of Logan's superior and with no answer to a plea that Logan translates in a flat tone, using the public facts—the meaning of her German words—as a veil for his private thought: "She says 'Forgive me.'" Otto Keller dies in Logan's embrace, his eyes gently closed by the priest's hand, with Logan saying the words he needs to hear, but only in their official, impersonal version—the Latin words of absolution.

Hitchcock must have weighed the option of centering the story of I Confess on the figure of Otto Keller. In some ways his predicament is more interesting than Logan's; he is able to clear an innocent man only at the cost of his own life. Certainly within the regime of fifties Hollywood his mind and motives are more available to inspection than a priest's. But, staying with the priest as the central figure, Hitchcock's choice was to split the Keller character so as to dramatize alternative responses to guilty knowledge and silence by taking Otto along the path of tormenting glee while developing the figure of Alma as the sharer of his secret to embody the burden of remorse and dread.

The decision to make the couple German follows no dramatic necessity but serves to draw additional attention to matters of language. (One might also cast a Swedish actress as Ruth with this in mind.) A film that begins by punning French against English around the word "direction" ends by contrasting Alma's plea in German with Otto's "Father, forgive me" in English that then receives its answer in Latin. Plays on words are made explicit for us at two key moments: first, when Ruth Grandfort meets Larue's interrogation with "You only want everything clear, and I want to clear Father Logan"; then, when under oath in the witness box, Logan finds in "I can't say" a form of words which both precisely defines his situation and misleads all who hear him. He combines perfect truthfulness with dutiful evasion of the truth he may not speak. Earlier the film has set out innocent, trivial instances of the dependence of speech on the context of understanding by showing us Keller's bafflement at a remark about a bicycle tire—he needed to have received an earlier message—and a detective's inability to follow a cleric's joke about the moral properties of paint; he needed the habit of talking in parables. The thematic ambition is further marked in the picturing of Pierre Grandfort's profession. Our first view of him is as a public speaker, debating across the spaces of the Parliament chamber. The image is patterned against scenes on either side where we see Ruth withholding and guarded in private conversation.

Another interesting coincidence in the Hitchcock-Truffaut discussion of *I Confess* is that it provides the setting for Hitchcock's remarks on the productive tension between picture and sound: "You mean the sound-track says one thing while the image says something else? That's a fundamental of film direction" (Truffaut 1969, 251). The particular twist in this film is that the image is often used to point up the fact that the soundtrack is saying *more* than one thing. "Good morning" is several times a case in point. These words of polite greeting do not take the form of a statement, but they can say much and they can tell a lie. We see this when the words are exchanged between

Ruth and Logan to display the sense of a chance encounter to any who may witness their prearranged assignation on the Levis ferry. In contrast, when Logan is ushered into the prosecutor's office where Ruth is about to give her evidence, she uses the words "Good evening, Father Logan" to challenge Larue's pretense that he is introducing them as strangers, to acknowledge a relationship that she had previously used "Good morning, Father Logan" to falsify.

This is at the start of a sequence in which it is demonstrated that not only words but silence as well may be used to deceive, may have the intent and effect of a lie. In her evidence Ruth reveals that she had several years before made a date with Logan and spent the night with him without letting him know of her marriage. But to invite intercourse was to present herself as (still) single. Her sexual availability amounted to a declaration of her moral availability, in the terms that she knew Logan would take for granted. Since those terms went without saying, their abrogation needed to be spoken.

There is a relationship between the deliberateness of the silence and the calculation implied by the act that Ruth does not acknowledge and that the flashback image does not show her performing—the removal of her wedding ring. Her ringless left hand is most clearly visible in two shots: first when she seeks Michael's kiss and then as she reacts to the words that unmask her as Grandfort's wife. When she later reflects on her history of deception ("I lied before, I should have lied last night") it seems, since we have not heard her say anything untrue, that she recognizes the practice of silent withholding as her particular form of perjury. Ruth's neglect of her obligation to declare herself matches her to Keller. Her inaction, deceitful and self-serving, enters into the film's pattern as the moral inverse of Logan's silence.

One of the challenges that Hitchcock set himself in *I Confess* was to invent ways of filming events that do not happen, and the particular case of speech acts not performed. Ruth's concealment of her marriage occurs throughout the day and night of her tryst with Michael and there is no one moment at which it is available to the camera. Its eye can absorb anything she does, but it cannot make distinctions and priorities between the things it does not record. Negatives that are easily expressed in language, such as "He did not go to the bank," are almost impossible to film because it is difficult to put us in mind of one particular item among the infinity of things that we are not seeing. A limited solution of the problem is available through construction, by building an expectation so that it may be visibly unfulfilled—the gun does not go off. But to give us the expectation that Ruth will speak of her marriage would create the sense of her attending to that possibility. The voice-over flashback allows Hitchcock to move into a different time register, that of highly selective memory, and to place Ruth's admission ("I had not told him I was married") in the aftermath of Michael's discovery. Even now, in recalling the events, her impulse is to avoid the issue until it is forced upon her from outside.

The sequence of Ruth's police statement is astonishing; it earns a distinguished place in the distinguished history of voice-over narration. The editing floats us in and out of flashback through a panning wipe/dissolve effect that shades Ruth's recounting of her past with the sense of ecstasy in the release of a long-pent sorrow. What she says has different meaning for each of her hearers—the detective, the public prosecutor, her husband, and the priest, her one-time sweetheart. She is at the same time giving evidence, telling her story, remembering, reproaching, and confessing. On her entry in the first flashback her image is voluptuously distorted by slow motion and gauze effects. Hyperbolic depiction unites with the dislocated voice and the floating transitions to mark the episode with the devices of a dream sequence. The regular returns to Ruth's narrating present are necessary reminders that what she is speaking is ostensibly memory rather than hallucination. It is still clear that her need to proclaim her vision outruns the official purpose of her testimony.

Completely absent is any suggestion of remorse. The content and the manner of her narration convey Ruth's blindness to her own actions. "Pierre, why must you hear what I'm going to say?" she asks, of a story that she insists on detailing in his presence. The parallel with confession is in many ways overt but is also drawn through subtle formal invention whereby Ruth's speech, like Keller's in church, deprives Logan of his voice.

Her tale covers several years in a few minutes. Like Lisa's in *Letter from an Unknown Woman* it reformulates the events of a man's life by isolating as its key moments the few occasions of his contact with the teller. But there is no equivalent for the ellipses which in Ophuls's film make flashbacks stand for unheard passages in Lisa's letter. There is no dot-dot-dot effect parallel to "Night after night I returned to the same spot but you never noticed me until one evening." While the events of Ruth's account are presented in images and some of these enacted segments make pauses in her narration of—if we were attending to them as pauses—unlikely duration, her verbal account exists in apparent continuity. There are no gaps that the pictures fill. In fact much of what Ruth tells is repeated in what we are shown. The repetitions make her selectivity the more evident—for example, in the way she dwells on the early stages of her romance with Logan, giving detail superfluous to the Villette story. The stress on the partiality of Ruth's view of events has special relevance to the presentation of Villette because he appears in the film, other than as a corpse, only here in the version of him constructed by Ruth.

A peculiar form of emphasis is created when Ruth's commentary duplicates the content of the image so that a single fact is stated twice. The device is most strikingly used in the account of Villette's intrusion on the compromising scene. Michael and Ruth have sheltered through the night in a summer house when Villette approaches. Michael goes to speak to him: "I was still in the summer house. I didn't know who it was but apparently he knew I was a woman, because he made some remark to Michael." At this point we cut from a shot of Villette and Logan outside the gazebo to Ruth within, recumbent and hidden. She gets up and moves out into the light, and we see her taking evident pleasure in a fracas between the two men. In the wake of this Ruth's narrating voice tells us, "I came out and stood on the steps of the summer house and looked down at him." This is the moment when Villette recognizes her as Madame Grandfort. The repetition, with the commentary coming after the event, makes it forcefully clear that Ruth chose to present herself to the stranger's view. Her self-display is set in direct contrast both with the concealment of her marriage and with her later insistence that the world must not know of these events. We have been directed to see how she empowers Villette by exposing the secret whose suppression she later urges, and whose existence serves to keep Logan on call.

Duplication on the soundtrack of information conveyed visually draws attention to the substitution of Ruth's voice for any other. The effect is prepared at the start when we see, but only see, the young Michael Logan cup his hands to shout up to his sweetheart from the street below. Thereafter the events are strategically noisy, with a consistent emphasis on acts of speech—none of which we hear. When Pierre Grandfort is seen for the first time he is giving dictation to Ruth as his secretary. Reunited with Ruth after wartime service, "Michael talked and talked." A storm blows up but it is heard only in music that subjectivizes the wind and rain as projections of feeling. Most remarkably it is Ruth's voice that speaks the words "Good morning, Madame Grandfort," taking over from Villette's mouthing image, when she tells how Villette recognized her and revealed her to Logan as a married woman.

Apart from Ruth's voice, music supplies the only sound during the flashbacks. At the start the word-veiled song returns, and it floods each moment of romance between Ruth and Michael. In one episode it emerges from its role as emotive background to become the diegetic sound of a girl singer with a band playing as the couple dance on their last night before Michael's departure for battle. The change in its function is marked by the sharpening of aural focus on the voice, so that the lyric becomes more distinctly audible. When the tune is interrupted by the summons to embarkation, the strangely fogged singing we have heard since the film's opening is given a point of origin in Ruth's fragmentary but rhapsodic memory of this time of love and parting. (The song is last heard just before Villette makes his appearance, and I do not hear any trace of it in the rest of the film; it is as if exorcized by Ruth's confession.)

There was another use of flashback earlier in the film. When the two girl witnesses told of having seen a priest leaving Villette's house on the night of the murder the flashback imagery added nothing significant—despite some new viewpoints—to what had already been shown. But the relatively detached nature of their account was indicated by the repetition of detail, including detail of sound with the noise of footsteps given a realistic presence in the sound mix. That fullness of representation is offered as the sound of memory when the facts recalled are without emotional significance for the rememberers. It sets down a marker against which we may the more immediately hear Ruth's need to validate her own version of a shared history by asserting her own voice, her own sound world, over any other.

As Ruth's narrative ends we see again, from entirely different viewpoints, her meeting with Logan on the morning after the murder. Earlier we heard her greet the news of Villette's death with "I can't believe it. We're free." Now she reports, "I couldn't believe it. I was free." The change seems to suggest that, for this moment, in this company, she is giving up her claim to exist in a "we" with Michael Logan. But the whole of her statement has offered him a song of love and longing, more clearly an offering of shared pain than of shared joy.

That is one of the deeper aspects in which Ruth's confession parallels Otto Keller's. At the point in Ruth's relation which elides her adultery (sought and probably achieved) we return to the present on the words "It had stopped raining in the morning" to find her face aglow and her gaze trained on Logan, inviting him to join her in the memory. But he has one hand raised to his face to shield his downcast eyes, in a gesture we recognize. We saw it earlier when he was hearing Keller's confession. For both Otto and Ruth the declaration of guilt offers the means to assert and to further an emotional connection that Logan denies. One of the first things Keller says to the priest, before claiming his right to make confession, is "You will hate me now."

Thereafter both Otto and Ruth are insistent in their demands on Logan. They hound him to acknowledge the bonds of intimate knowledge, preferring his reproach or his hatred to his silence and indifferent charity. The interchangeability of their demands is finely pictured in the moments that follow Logan's last rebuff to Ruth when he has met her call for action ("You must do something") with an affirmation of impotence ("There is nothing we can do"). As Ruth leaves the church she collides at the door with Keller, entering with flowers for the altar, and Keller takes her place in the frame. The camera, having followed Ruth to the door, follows Keller from it in a virtually palindromic arrangement that is bracketed by the genuflections of each of them. Then Logan walks past Keller and Keller pursues him, hectoring him with questions and speculations. The continuities and exchanges are extended at the end of this encounter when Logan leaves, and his place in the frame is immediately assumed, in silence and without motion, by Alma. It is as if the priest is seen as an alternative equally to Ruth's husband and Keller's wife.

The casting of Montgomery Clift is central to these effects. There is a potent anomaly in putting a method actor of such intense inner turbulence into a role whose interior world is to remain hidden and whose motives the film will not expose. The Clift of 1953 also represents glamour—to my eye the most remarkable male object of the camera's rapture since the young Gary Cooper, one on whose features monochrome settles in bliss. Anne Baxter's beauty, though considerable, does not have the dazzle of Clift's, and the rest of the cast seems to have been chosen to offset his allure. Truffaut was very acute in pointing to the appeal of the figure's momentum, and the way Hitchcock's camera responds to its surging penetration of space (Truffaut 1969, 251). Some credit for this should go to the costume designer, Orry-Kelly, for providing gowns that enhance the force and beauty of Clift's movement. But where Truffaut sees Logan's constant forward motion as an index of his integrity it is possible to respond to it differently, as an emblem of his elusiveness. The camera displays the unapproachability of this man who makes himself available to all. His private quarters are never seen, and we observe him in no conversation that he has sought for himself. The film offers us an experience of Logan as impossibly attractive and frustratingly distant, the two qualities being interdependent.

Keller's implication of Logan in his crime (by stowing the bloodstained cassock in Logan's trunk) has little practical purpose. It does not serve Keller's material interest that Logan should come under suspicion. But it does strengthen the bond between them and give Keller the prospect of drawing Logan into his experience of society's hostility and suspicion. A scene that establishes this motivation comes early in the picture when Keller returns to the rectory from police questioning to find Father Logan up a stepladder painting the walls of the library. He receives no satisfaction of his demand that the priest relax the prescribed mode of expiation—"I can't give myself up. You must tell me some other way." Logan withholds contact by continuing to paint. Keller moves to force him to meet his gaze; he steps up onto the wrong side of the ladder to pull himself toward Logan's height and stares into his eyes. "Aren't you human? Haven't you ever been afraid? You are so good. It's easy for you to be good. Have you no pity for me?"[2] On this last question he reaches out his free hand to touch Logan's breast in a gesture unmistakable though obscured—one might think censored—by the paint tin in the foreground. Logan remains fixed and responds neither to the words nor to the gesture. Then Otto jumps away, startled, as an off-screen call announces the approach of his wife. Logan resumes his painting as if nothing has happened.

This scene seems, more clearly than any in *Strangers on a Train*, to show the villain either exploiting his crime or driven by it to seek physical contact with the hero. If I am not concerned to advance a "gay reading" (of the scene or of the film), that is because it is unclear how our understanding improves if we think of either character as pursuing or repressing desires for sexual intimacy. It is beyond dispute that Keller seeks and Logan withholds emotional involvement and an acknowledgment of complicity. Keller and Ruth are alike in constantly approaching Logan but in managing to draw him to them only in his priestly role. They share in frustration at his eagerness to help and his indifference to touch.

It turns out that Keller can kill his wife ("my Alma") but not the priest. Finally it is his own death that he uses to bring Logan close. The point is strongly presented both acoustically and by the camera. Keller is caught as a tiny, distant figure in front of a proscenium, seen and heard from afar with a wide-angle lens stressing the depth of the space and the length of the ballroom floor that separates him from Logan and the detectives. This image is repeated ten times and cut against much closer shots of his pursuers—group shots and close-ups in shallower perspective that include five of Larue and five of Logan in which Clift is seen at his most glowingly photogenic, his face lovingly molded by the light. Only when—in response to Logan's "Don't make them do it, Keller"—the trapped man provokes a wounding gunshot by firing at the police, only then do we get a closer view. Immediately, the picture cuts back to the police group, then presents the distant perspective on Keller again as Logan enters the frame in the foreground to stride directly toward him. The shrinking of the distance between them is measured by traveling a close shot in front of Logan as he advances and intercutting it with deep-focus viewpoint shots that track in onto Keller. Logan's final approach—ending a pause that threatened to become a standoff—is caused by Keller's suicidal pretense of preparing to fire at him. The stalemate is broken as Keller is hit by a police bullet and Logan rushes forward to catch him in his arms.

The drama ends with Logan stilled in mournful contemplation of the corpse he holds, possibly—but how can we know?—turning in his mind the portrait that Keller has drawn of his friendless, isolated state. Perhaps he is weighing his own role in the film's events. Perhaps, but if he is we cannot tell what kind of responsibility he assumes. Logan remains as perfectly masked at the end as he was at the beginning, when nothing suggested a man who had just come from a meeting, with Ruth, that had roused his fury and had landed him with an awkward assignment, confronting her blackmailer. The film fades to black on a lovely, unrevealing close-up with music subdued and inconclusive. This nonending seems a recognition that the film cannot tell Logan's story, or that Logan does not have one.

We might expect "The End" to come up over the dark screen but instead the music surges into a change of mood and we are returned to that same floating image of the defined and the cloudy with which we started. (It is not, this time, backed by the woman's song.)

To restate that image is to refer us back to the opening, to DIRECTION and the display of the distant figure of Alfred Hitchcock. One of the notable features of this personal appearance was that the author presented himself in profile. The peculiarities of the profile shot, most often in close-up, have been exploited by no one more eloquently than by Hitchcock. It is the shot that allows inspection without creating contact or offering intimacy. At the start of *Alfred Hitchcock's "I Confess"* it allows him to display himself without revealing or, say, exposing himself. And of course he says nothing. Then what was the confession? One who parades in public may have to balance hope and terror over the way he will be seen and judged: the hope of the world's approval with the terror of the world's contempt. This is particularly the case for one who parades in front of a camera knowing that he cannot command the camera's awe in the manner of a movie star. "Look at me!" is a dangerous cry for a man so aware of insecurity and of the mortal agony of public humiliation. Yet it is a cry issued in every one of Hitchcock's films.

In its movement through confession from the closed and contained to the open and exposed, the movie tries to work out the problem of the secret and the prices of silence. Against a range of declarations variously volunteered and extracted, it patterns the mute seclusion of Michael Logan, who guards the secrets of others and remains unreadable in respect of his own. Relief from the terror of guilty knowledge may be imagined in two directions: by hiding everything perfectly—the silent route—or by complete self-exposure so that one has nothing to hide. But if the dread of being immured is equal to the horror of being unmasked, and if these emotions are always stronger than the enjoyment of solitude, or pleasure in community, you are caught in a suspense of which you will not reliably be the Master. If, as I believe, Hitchcock's ambition was to shape this film as his own confession he was making an avowal of his riven nature, his inability to find a point of rest between the desire for recognition and the terror of being known.

So he was one of us, after all.

Works Cited

Austin, J. L. *How to Do Things with Words: The William James Lectures Delivered at Harvard University in 1955.* 2nd ed. Edited by J. O. Urmson and Marina Sbisà. Oxford: Oxford University Press, [1962] 1975.

Sloan, Jane E. *Alfred Hitchcock: The Definitive Filmography.* Berkeley: University of California Press, 1995.

Spoto, Donald. *The Dark Side of Genius: The Life of Alfred Hitchcock.* Boston: Da Capo, 1983.

Thomas, Deborah. "Confession as Betrayal: Hitchcock's *I Confess* as Enigmatic Text." *CineAction* 40 (May 1996): 32–37.

Truffaut, François. *Hitchcock.* London: Panther, [1968] 1969.

Filmography

The Birds. Directed by Alfred Hitchcock. Universal Pictures, 1963.
High Noon. Directed by Fred Zinnemann. United Artists, 1952.
I Confess. Directed by Alfred Hitchcock. Warner Bros., 1953.
Letter from an Unknown Woman. Directed by Max Ophuls. Universal-International, 1948.
North by Northwest. Directed by Alfred Hitchcock. MGM, 1959.
Notorious. Directed by Alfred Hitchcock. RKO Radio Pictures, 1946.

Shadow of a Doubt. Directed by Alfred Hitchcock. Universal Pictures, 1943.
Stage Fright. Directed by Alfred Hitchcock. Warner Bros., 1950.
Strangers on a Train. Directed by Alfred Hitchcock. Warner Bros., 1951.
Suspicion. Directed by Alfred Hitchcock. RKO Radio Pictures, 1941.
Vertigo. Directed by Alfred Hitchcock. Paramount Pictures, 1958.

Notes

1 Donald Spoto says that the name Alma was chosen in the final stages of scripting. We can hardly be expected to ignore Hitchcock's giving his own wife's name to the killer's wife (Spoto 1983, 337). Deborah Thomas offers interesting reflections on the name, and much else, in her essay on *I Confess* (1996, 32–37).

2 One writer reports this as "You're so cold" (Sloan 1995, 246). O. E. Hasse's German inflections make it hard to distinguish, but it is an interesting possibility that would only strengthen the reading I offer.

OPHULS CONTRA WAGNER AND OTHERS

First published in Movie, *no. 36 (January 2000): 73–79.*

This article extends the one written for *Movie* 29–30 (Summer 1982) in which I discussed *Letter from an Unknown Woman* and offered an analysis of the Linz sequence, the single episode in the film not set in Vienna and the one in which the heroine (Lisa, played by Joan Fontaine) frustrates her parents' scheme of marrying her to a young lieutenant, Leopold (John Good).

The parallel passage in Stefan Zweig's original novella was set in Innsbruck. The change is odd. Speculating on the reasons for it, I focused on the film's pattern of contrasts between Linz and Vienna. I suggested that the satire directed against Linz, with its pretensions to musicality, might be sharpened by the fact that one of Mozart's most celebrated symphonies bears the town's name. I had discounted contingent explanations: that Universal's back-lot German town set might represent one better than the other (if Innsbruck demands an Alpine background, Linz is hardly Linz without the Danube) or that Linz would better match the film's description of "a little garrison town" (Innsbruck, guarding the Brenner Pass, would suit those terms more straightforwardly than Linz).

In any case, the garrison setting was the film's invention; there is no trace of a military theme in Zweig's story. Its insertion balances the most noticeable of the film's alterations, that which converts the leading male from a novelist into a concert pianist. One effect of these changes is to create a link between the uniformed figures who in Linz (her suitor) and in Vienna (her husband) represent the forces ranged against Lisa's pursuit of her romantic destiny, and to construct the link in terms that stress hierarchy and coercive power under the exclusive control of men.

That understanding may be extended by reopening the Linz question and taking into account a point that I have to thank Mark Furstenberg for bringing to my attention: that for Max Ophuls and screenwriter Howard Koch, working in 1947, the most immediate associations of Linz would have been with Adolf Hitler and the rise of Nazism. Hitler (b. 1889) went to school in Linz from 1900 and proclaimed it as his hometown: he "repeatedly called the years in Linz the happiest time of his life, 'a lovely dream.' Only the memory of his failure at school somewhat darkened its brightness" (Fest 1974, 23).

Moreover, the people of Linz offered him one of his decisive political triumphs. Historians dispute the schemes and intentions with which he launched the invasion of Austria in 1938, but it is clear that an ill-prepared and accident-prone excursion was redeemed for the Nazis by the enthusiasm of the Austrian welcome. The first and most significant expression of that welcome was offered by the people of Linz: more than a hundred thousand turned out on March 12 to display their rapture in the streets as Hitler's procession passed and as he prepared to address them from the balcony of the town hall. The adulation prompted a response from Hitler that would make Linz notorious. In A. J. P. Taylor's account: "As he went on to the balcony ... he made a sudden, unexpected decision: instead of setting up a tame government in Vienna, he would incorporate Austria in the Reich. Seyss-Inquart, Chancellor for a day, was told to issue a law, ordering himself and Austria out of existence. He did so on 13th March" (1964, 188).

Hitler's speech gave Linz a special role: "If Providence once called me from this city to assume the leadership of the Reich, it must have charged me with a mission, and that mission can only have been to restore my dear homeland to the German Reich. I have believed in this mission, have lived and fought for it, and I believe I have now fulfilled it" (Fest 1974, 548). The next evening in Linz's Hotel Weinzinger, Hitler was able to affirm his triumph by signing the law that declared *Anschluss*. The Viennese Stefan Zweig was among those who in the immediate aftermath became refugees, as the German Ophuls had already been for five years, and he wrote a vivid account of the terror in which "all the sickly unclean fantasies of hate that had been conceived in many orgiastic nights found raging expression in bright daylight" (1943, 305).

The events of March 1938 signaled a new turn in which conquest replaced diplomatic pressure as the chief instrument of German policy. It was the infamy of Linz to have been the site of the policy's first success: "The belief soon became established that Hitler's seizure of Austria was a deliberate plot, devised long in advance, and the first step towards the domination of Europe.... By the *Anschluss*—or rather by the way in which it was accomplished—Hitler took the first step in the policy which was to brand him as the greatest of war criminals" (Taylor 1964, 189).

The fervor of its welcome increased the town's hold on Hitler's affections. He became famously grateful and generous, endowing it with a large orchestra. On the third anniversary of the *Anschluss*, Josef Goebbels flew to Linz for the celebrations; his diary for March 12, 1941, records: "I stand with the Führer on the balcony of his hotel room, and we look out over his home town. He loves this city very much, and this is understandable. He intends to establish a new center of culture here. As a counterweight to Vienna, which will have to be gradually phased out of the picture. He does not like Vienna, basically for political reasons.... But Linz is his darling.... We spend a long time chatting with people from Linz. Real German men. Not like those Viennese mongrels" (F. Taylor 1982, 266).

If Linz held out the lovely dream, still cherished in the final weeks and hours of Hitler's destruction, Vienna was well known as the site of his youthful shame. There, the Academy of Fine Arts having twice turned him down for training as a painter and architect, he had lived on his wits for seven years of demeaning odd-jobbery until 1913, when, at the age of twenty-four, he left Austria to avoid conscription. "He hated the city ever after for the rejection and insults he had suffered there.... It is not far-fetched to suspect that Hitler's subsequent plans [for Linz] ... were inspired by resentment toward Vienna" (Fest 1974, 56).

Within a year of the *Anschluss*, Hitler had set up a special commission, the *Sonderauftrag Linz*, charged with planning new museums that would "convert [his] stuffy provincial birthplace into the world's greatest treasure house of (looted) art" (Grunberger 1971, 431). The town was to become his memorial and a shrine to Aryan civilization. Jewish property and the occupied countries were pillaged for treasures of art and antiquity, the choicest of which—Hitler's pickings—were set aside for Linz.

With his plan encompassing libraries as well as an observatory and an opera house, Hitler was set on rescuing Linz from its inferiority to the Austrian capital: "Ten years after the end of the war Linz must have become the new metropolis of the Danube. I become daily more enthusiastic about this beautifying of Linz, and I think it is the reaction of the artistic sense in me. . . . Far be it from me to lessen the importance of Vienna. . . . But when one thinks of the truly unique position of Linz, it is impossible . . . to give up the idea. . . . It would be a crime." (Trevor-Roper 1973, 446, entry for April 28, 1942).

Letter from an Unknown Woman picks up scathingly on two aspects of Hitler's attachment to Linz: his partisanship in its imagined rivalry with Vienna, and his ambitions for the vindication of Linz in the sphere of culture. Like Hitler, the film plays off Linz against Vienna; it constructs an intricate system of contrasts and reversals (traced in my article in *Movie* 29/30), through which Linz becomes defined as the non-Vienna. But, against Hitler, the system's negative terms are all assigned to Linz. The movie's shooting script prescribed a "stiff primness about the people, their clothes and manner—which suggests the town's narrow, almost ludicrously bourgeois character" (Bacher 1996, 477).

Mockery of Linz seems like a small revenge, on the town and on the Nazis, and perhaps a special gesture to the memory of Stefan Zweig, whose forename the film borrowed for its hero. Zweig's last book, *The World of Yesterday*, was published after his suicide in exile in 1942. These memoirs are a fascinating source on Viennese life around 1900 and surely informed the writing of Koch's screenplay. In them, Zweig also gives a proud and gleeful account of the embarrassment that he caused Hitler when state cultural policy was challenged by the collaboration between him, a Jew whose writings were proscribed, and Germany's most eminent artist, the composer Richard Strauss. That, I take it, was the spirit in which Ophuls constructed a sequence to realize, with spite, Hitler's ambition that "Linz should become the personification of the Reich" (Trevor-Roper 1973, 710, entry for June 24, 1943).

While these speculations are mainly directed at Ophuls's off-screen motives for making Linz the butt of the film's sarcasm, the awareness of Linz's Hitlerian connotation might also warn us against making too clean a division between what is in and what lies behind the film. To use Linz as the site of the marriage market on which Lisa is touted is—for a 1948 movie—to place the forces that oppose Lisa's romantic vision in a world that already contains the seeds of the Third Reich.

On that account, the switch from Innsbruck to Linz is related in complex ways to another little-remarked-upon change to Zweig's tale, the shift of period from the era of political and economic turmoil after World War I to the apparently stable imperial order of turn-of-the-century Vienna. Zweig's novella was published in 1922, and while its trappings clearly set it in the contemporary world, its narration is almost entirely given over to the chronicle of romantic obsession constructed in the woman's letter. The social world is noticed only in passing, and the political world not at all. A film, with a vision that cannot be confined to the heroine's perceptions, would necessarily incorporate more of the historical world. This can be seen in Universal's earlier version of the tale, John Stahl's *Only Yesterday* (1933), which shifts the locales from Austria to the United States while keeping the period modern: America's entry into World War I and the Wall Street Crash of 1929 are defining events in Stahl's narrative.

Ophuls's operation is much more complex. The Austrian setting is retained, but transformed by the change of period: Vienna circa 1900 is a world away from Vienna circa 1920. The film moves the romance into a setting which, as no historical events receive attention, seems timeless. It then stresses, by elaboration, the markers of time: hours of the clock, days and nights, fortnights, youth and age, sunlight and darkness, seasons, birthdays, fixations on past and future, questions of memory and hope—all these proliferate within the action and dialogue. The characters express acute awareness of passages in biographical time, yet they regard their social world as permanent and, for better or worse, immutable. The peculiarity of the film's operation is announced right at the start with the title "Vienna About 1900," approximate as to time, superimposed over an image which articulates several kinds of time and in which clock time is specified both in conversation and through the striking of the hour on the soundtrack; "About 1900," with its evocation of a turning point, is positioned against "2 a.m. precisely" and, in relation to the hero's appointment to fight a duel with a superior opponent, "only three hours left."

In a film whose strategy depends so much on drawing our attention to what its characters are not noticing, and which so regularly makes us aware of their failures of vision, the choice of period has thematic bearing. "About 1900" becomes "only fourteen years left." The whole society is seen in relation to, and in its unawareness of, imminent catastrophe. Ophuls's autobiography makes clear that he had no temperamental attachment to a city he had experienced in 1926 as moribund and backward-looking. But it is a standing possibility of "Vienna Before 1914" to encourage the audience's perception of the human capacity for delusions of permanence and for moral investments in the stability of the social order. In that context, the reference to Hitler via Linz should be seen as part of a design to locate a complacently oppressive society in relation to the violence of the twentieth century, so to reassert history in our perception of a world where all the clocks might seem to have stopped.

In Ophuls's film his heroine and her soldier suitor are alike in making an opposition between Linz and Vienna, except that the lieutenant anticipates Hitler by making the contrast in favor of Linz. For Lisa, the town hardly has an identity of its own; it is just "away"; her letter will declare that all the time she was away she thought longingly of Vienna, as Stefan's city. But Leopold is hard put to imagine what there might be to like about Vienna. As for the music, "we also have good music here. Every other Saturday afternoon they have a concert on the Courso. . . . I must say I'm glad we both like music." I believe now that when they put these words into Leopold's mouth, Koch and Ophuls intended to sound a derisive echo of Hitlerian cultural presumption. My confidence in this belief is supported by the music that exemplifies the lieutenant's Linzian taste and which plays throughout his courtship of Lisa. In Vienna we hear, among others, Liszt, Mozart, Schubert, two Strausses, and Ziehrer. The music of Linz that will rival Vienna's turns out to be Wagner, in a vein that reflects Leopold's jejune pomposity. It is a (skillfully subversive) arrangement for military band of the "Song to the Evening Star" from the opera *Tannhäuser*, in which it is sung by Wolfram, who, in the competition for the heroine's love and the audience's sympathy, plays the Ralph Bellamy role.

There was in 1947 no more certain way of affirming the identity of Linz as Hitler's town than by associating it simultaneously with a grotesque version of military pomp and with Wagner. Hitler consistently proclaimed his worship of Wagner; he named the composer, a vicious and noisy anti-Semite, as his only forerunner. The Führer's regular visits to—and enthusiastic welcome at—Wahnfried, the home of the Wagner family, were well publicized, and his "pilgrimages to the Wagner shrine of Bayreuth became as much a part of the public scene as the Royal Opening of Parliament in Britain . . . The festival became an annual highlight in the calendar of the Third Reich" (Grunberger 25, 411). By 1947, Wagner's racist political and musical works were commonly seen as major intellectual and cultural sources of Nazism. Even Thomas Mann now tempered his admiration for the music dramas with recognition of "too much that is repellent, too much 'Hitler,' really too much latent and even manifest Nazism" (Windell 1962–63, 482).

Tannhäuser offers the perfect musical representation of the Hitler whose "taste reflected his late-Victorian small-town origins . . . He wanted pride of place at his Linz museum to be accorded to . . . saccharine fantasies of a serenely intact world" (Grunberger 1971, 431). Of all Wagner's operas—although it was not in fact the one most prized by Hitler—*Tannhäuser* is most vulnerable to derisive parody. It is the best suited to characterizing an immersion in sanctimonious kitsch and so offers the most likely choice to evoke, with scorn, the aesthetics of Schicklgruber. Wolfram's song is a big crowd-grabbing number, plausibly a staple for a band recital of Gems from the Masters. It is also, in its dramatic context, redolent of bad-faith romanticism where the avowal of love is corrupted for post-Freudian ears by a denial of appetite: the purity of Wolfram's attachment to the heroine Elisabeth is sung as distant worship, safe from even the thought of bodily contact. Wagner's horrid brilliance here contrived the love song as a dirge, anticipating the beloved's death: the evening star is called upon not to bless Wolfram's desire but to light Elisabeth's path to heaven.

Ophuls delighted in offering insults to Wagner. In *Lola Montès* the king's ear doctor agrees that it would be a fine thing to overcome deafness so as to be able once more to listen to music, especially Mozart's, where everything is tender and light, but scarcely worthwhile for Wagner—"His stuff you could hear from the bottom of the sea." That recalls a passage in Ophuls's 1946 autobiography where he referred to the noise of military exercises that had disrupted location work for *Werther* (*Le Roman de Werther* [*The Novel of Werther*], 1938) as a Wagnerian intrusion upon Goethe's charming exchanges (1963, 197). In *Letter from an Unknown Woman*, in the sequence where the young Lisa goes to the library to study the lives of the great musicians, the set design improbably fits the Wagner shelf between the Mozart above and the Schumann below. That allows the action to begin with Lisa dismissively thumping a Wagner folio back into its place before reaching up to take a volume from the Mozart shelf and carrying it, raptly, back to her seat; meanwhile, the soundtrack quotes the slow movement of the 39th Symphony to endorse her preference.

The practice of setting Wagner in damaging relation to Mozart may be seen to inform the selection and performance of the "Song to the Evening Star." My 1982 article pointed out how systematically the pattern of the Linz sequence is reworked in the scene that takes place ten years later at the Vienna Opera during a performance of Mozart's *Die Zauberflöte (The Magic Flute)*. In both cases, Lisa has been escorted to a public musical occasion by a partner of convenience who wears military dress: Leopold in Linz; at the Vienna Opera, the rich and powerful, elderly husband Johann Stauffer who has offered a home to young Stefan, the son Lisa has named after his father. Both times Lisa abandons her socially legitimated partner to seek reunion with her forgetful lover (fig. 25).

The comparison between Linz and Vienna should now acknowledge the operatic contrast and embrace the siting of Linz's military Wagner against Vienna's sung Mozart, of Tannhäuser against *The Magic Flute* and of Wolfram's song against Papageno's "Ein Mädchen oder Weibchen." (It is a neat coincidence that Wolfram and Papageno are in both operas roles for

Figure 25. At the Vienna Opera

the baritone. I have no explanation for the film's use of the Italian text: *Il flauto magico* was widely performed, but not in Vienna where even Mozart's Italian operas were given in German until the reforms of the Karajan era in the 1950s.)

Like Stefan, the bird catcher Papageno looks to the future for the discovery of his mate (and shortly after this number he is deprived of his Papagena, having shown himself unworthy of her—in part through a failure of recognition). Unlike Stefan, Papageno wants a real woman, not a goddess. Papageno's song is of frank and blameless desire, at ease with its own carnality, declaring appetites that are emphatically those of the body. In all this, the music indulges him with tender playfulness, offering him the support of one of Mozart's most delightful melodies. Of course, Papageno is not the hero of the piece, and it is important to the uses which the film can make of the reference that within Mozart's terms he is a comic rather than an elevated figure—the tune derives from popular song—and not fully an adult. The image of Papageno reflects on Stefan but does not mirror him. Where the strenuous presence of the military hand makes Wagner an intrusive participant in the Linz proposal scene, the sources of music at the Vienna Opera remain unshown and the sound perspective renders the playing of Papageno's tune as distant, lost music. *The Magic Flute*, product of the composer's last months, haunts the scene while Stefan, who as a young prodigy had earned comparison with Mozart, shows himself to be a man of wasted talents. The dissonance created here by the use of "Ein Mädchen" matches the irony in the earlier calls of "Second Act. Curtain going up"—off-screen in the Opera foyer—as a comment on the structure of Lisa's encounters with Stefan. With his usual tact, Ophuls avoids the reference that the Mozart/ Vienna pairing most obviously invites—to the figure of Don Juan. An evocation of libertinage via Mozart's *Don Giovanni* would repeat what we can readily observe of Stefan; it would fit the character with a reductive tightness. But Papageno's aria alludes to the ordinary and potentially joyful dimensions of lust; its hopeful tone offsets what is soured in the feeling and obscured in the vision of the hero. It contributes to the devices through which the film observes, penetrates, but does not submit to the attitudes and understandings of its characters.

Tannhäuser by contrast, presents a tale whose elements, especially the climactic ones, can be found reworked in the film. In the last act, the devout heroine Elisabeth believes that Tannhäuser is lost to her in dissipation; she dies begging heaven's forgiveness for his sins. The recollection of her name, the evidence of her devotion, and the knowledge of her self-sacrifice finally lead Tannhäuser to redemption and, sinking across her funeral bier, he joins her in death.

Although it now appears an essential component of the movie's design, the framing story of the duel and Stefan's implied death was probably devised in the first place to placate the censors by compensating for the many objectionable aspects of Zweig's novella. Even without the intrusions of the Breen Office, some development of the man's story would have been required. A result of dramatization is that the man becomes a figure in the film's world independent of the woman's perception and narrative. The more presence his character is given, the greater the pressure to resolve his situation, most of all by giving expression—through his decisions and actions—to the impact on him of the woman's tale. Thus, in *Only Yesterday*, the hero is introduced to us as a man intent on suicide, and the effect of the letter is to give him something to live for. But Stahl's film was made before the enforcement of the Production Code became effective; in its contrasts with the Ophuls, it is a salutary demonstration of the impact of the Code on story content. By 1945 the Breen Office was branding the material "thoroughly and completely unacceptable under the provisions of the Production Code." (This and most of the information on the film's production that follows was derived from Lutz Bacher's doctoral thesis for Wayne State University, which became part of his invaluable book, *Max Ophuls in the Hollywood Studios* [1996].)

The particular form of the framing story in *Letter from an Unknown Woman* can be seen as an attempt to meet the Breen Office's objections to a narrative constructed around the pursuit of sexual experience outside marriage. The duel with Lisa's husband which, before reading the letter, Stefan intends to evade and which, after, he decides to face is an invention that could be represented to the censors as both Stefan's acknowledgment of wrongdoing and his punishment for it. This concession is deftly calculated in that its events can be held open in the filming to viewpoints detached from or opposed to Breen Office hypocrisy. Stefan's experiences of realization and redemption can be conveyed as aspects of his subjectivity observed but not endorsed by the film: he has been persuaded by Lisa's fantasy of fated love and commits himself to enact its suitably sacrificial conclusion; or, with Lisa safely dead, Stefan becomes free to acknowledge her and the waste of his life while disguising his suicide as an act of honor. Maintaining ambiguity allows Lisa's dying declaration—"I love you now as I've always loved you"—to react with the knowledge that attending to the letter has used up the time Stefan needed to make good his flight and so to trouble us with the feeling that there may always have been something murderous—in Stanley Cavell's term, "death-dealing"—about Lisa's way of loving (Cavell 1996, 171).

Keeping the film open to ranges of philosophical and psychological possibility was, though, a matter of the greatest delicacy; note, for instance, how few and inconclusive are the words spoken after the "If only . . ." that suspends Lisa's narration. The balances of suggestion were so fine that they could not withstand the emphatic clarifications of "morality" that tended to result from deals done between the studios and the Breen Office. Ophuls had, in fact, every reason for concern. The final shooting script was declared unacceptable shortly before filming began, and throughout production the matter remained to be resolved. Breen himself had written to the studio to stress the need for changes that would "punch up the compensating moral values . . . [and] the flavor of condemnation" (Vizzard 1970, 142).

But Ophuls, with his uniquely tender respect for his literary sources, was barely reconciled to some departures from Zweig that had been conceded before he had been assigned to the production—for instance, that the woman would not, as she had in *Only Yesterday*, give herself to the man in their final encounter. So it would have been vital for him to multiply and protect those elements of mise-en-scène that could in all apparent innocence inflect viewpoint and, in the specific area of sexual morality, ward off a damaging precision. One matter of strong concern was the music track. Consider the end of the opera scene. It is important here that Lisa does not know what she is doing and is racked with indecision; Joan Fontaine conveys this exquisitely by turning her gaze back to Stefan as she walks away from him to her carriage. (It takes her husband, with his talk of honor, decency, and will, to provoke her declaration that she "can't help" going to Stefan.) And while we see Stefan as a roué, in whom the urge to pursue has scarcely the strength to overcome the boredom of routine, it was evidently also part of the design that the character should at this point evoke old hopes perhaps not yet beyond recall. As Stefan speaks of his feeling that Lisa may be able to help him, and thus suggests a memory holding itself just the other side of thought, Papageno's tune ends and is followed by the orchestral "March of the Priests," the solemnity of which shadows the rest of the scene with nobility and grave mystery.

I have no evidence that Ophuls specified this number. But any number from *The Magic Flute* was preferable to any contribution from the film's composer, Daniele Amfitheatrof, though not mainly on grounds of musical quality: sounds represented as coming, distantly, from within the opera house—represented, that is, as contingencies of the world of the film—have a weakly determined bearing on the dramatic events and can have an obliqueness of relevance to its emotional line. An original film score, on the other hand, is necessarily appropriate. As background music, a score that stopped then started again in an entirely different tone would declare a marked turn in the issues of the drama and, with no such turn visible, would be anomalous. Background music, unmistakably editorial, would have committed the film to a view of Lisa's crisis. Predictably, in working for pathos and urgency, an Amfitheatrof theme would have threatened to surround Stefan's reappearance with the sense of temptation, of scandal.

Something like this I believe to be the artistic logic behind what we do know about Ophuls's involvement with the music of the sequence. He wrote to his (at this point) absentee producer John Houseman to report on the trials and conflicts of post-production: "I am in the midst of dubbing, and . . . in the midst of trouble. . . . The score is not as bad as we thought it would be but it is by far not as good as we had hoped for. . . . Whenever I turn away, they take the great masters out and put some original music in. . . . Imagine, John, the following: Lisa leaves the box in the opera. . . . She is outside the opera house waiting for her carriage. Stefan comes out. Presto! The music from inside the opera house changes in [the] Amfitheatrof score [to a] love motif. It took me two days to let them allow only Mozart to be heard during this scene" (Wright Wexman and Hollinger 1986, 206).

Ophuls did not shrink from deploying arguments based on—of all things—realism in his fight to preserve and extend the role of Mozart's music in this scene. Bacher's dissertation (456) reveals that it was Ophuls, too, who decided to build up the role of the military band in the Linz sequence. On the morning of filming, he overturned plans based on a shooting script that used the bandsmen only at the start of the scene, marching them off before the lieutenant began to propose. He decided instead to keep the band playing in the Courso throughout the proposal. In so doing, he protected this scene, too, from Amfitheatrof, but he also prepared a musical parallel between the Linz sequence and the scene at the Vienna Opera that joined these episodes much more strongly into the film's—all but palindromic—patterns of repetition and reversal.

The paired reference to *Tannhäuser* and *The Magic Flute* enabled an ironic undercutting of the Breen Office's moral certainties. It was Wagner who took a Breen Office perspective on the tale of the redeemed reprobate. *Tannhäuser* wallows in prurient masochism; through a series of revisions

Wagner directed its energies to an ever more gaudy elaboration of desire as sickness. His hero is torn between carnal and spiritual impulses, and these are presented with a starkness both lurid and crass. Self-denial is offered as the only alternative to the "delights of hell" on the Venusberg—yes, the Mount of Venus. The opera presents a world with no place for a decent sensuality; everything in it depends on the virgin/whore polarity that Ophuls both evokes and rejects when he places Lisa under the sign of the Madonna at just the point—waiting alone after dark on a snowblown corner—when she most risks being seen as a streetwalker.

Tannhäuser's heroine prays for death and boasts that "if ever earthly longing rose within me I strove with untold anguish to stifle it in my heart." This should alert us to the absence of remorse in Lisa who, remarkably, is so far from reproaching Stefan for having taken advantage of her that it does not occur to her to characterize their brief union as a seduction. She declares her joy in motherhood and claims that Stefan, too, would have been proud of their son. Her letter's final passage is careless of sin or guilt in loving Stefan "now as I have always loved you." And if Stefan goes to his death with many regrets, it is not suggested that he includes among them a regret at having made love to Lisa. The required recognition of error is located with the Sister-in-Charge of St Catherine's Hospital; her note, tagged to the end of a letter that she has evidently read with distaste, is placed under the sign of the cross to assert the couple's need for divine mercy. (I have thought of this as standing for a note from the Breen Office attached to a copy of the screenplay.) Ophuls's treatment, with the news of Lisa's death presented in cold typescript, dramatizes a recoil from joylessly dutiful, censorious charity (and, I take it, from the institutions of Christianity) as strongly here as in the eerie and brutal images of young Stefan's birthplace.

Prominent among the institutions of Christianity in Ophuls's Hollywood were the Catholic-dominated Breen Office and its yet uglier friend, the Legion of Decency. It is a matter for celebration that the film was never sufficiently compromised to render it acceptable to those bodies. Possibly because Joan Fontaine's husband was a vice president of the studio, Universal stood firm against the rejection of the completed picture. In the end, the studio bosses faced the censors down.

I hope to have traced a confluence of factors that plausibly motivated some broad and some detailed features of *Letter from an Unknown Woman*. In particular I have wanted to explore the bearing of Linz/Hitler/Wagner on the structures of viewpoint that Ophuls composed. I now see the film as wishing to treat—and to be open about treating—a Wagner subject from a Mozart perspective. If the deaths of Lisa and Stefan both have a suicidal aspect, the movie's climax is nevertheless no Wagnerian love death, since the values that inform the presentation—in constant movement and at the same time sympathetic and critical, humorous and appalled—have much more of Mozart about them than of Wagner. Most of all, the meanings of Linz and the Wagner/Mozart opposition serve to evaluate the forces that stand against and finally defeat Lisa and Stefan. For all the clarity with which the film exposes the complementary follies and blindnesses of its central pair, its moral preference is affirmed by placing both of them—pursued and pursuer alike—on the side of the scale marked "Mozart."

Works Cited

Bacher, Lutz. *Max Ophuls in the Hollywood Studios*. New Brunswick, NJ: Rutgers University Press, 1996.

Cavell, Stanley. *Contesting Tears: The Melodrama of the Unknown Woman*. Chicago: University of Chicago Press, 1996.

Fest, Joachim. *Hitler*. London: Weidenfeld & Nicolson, 1974.

Goebbels, Joseph. *The Goebbels Diaries: 1939–1941*. Translated and edited by Fred Taylor. London: Hamish Hamilton, 1982.

Grunberger, Richard. *A Social History of the Third Reich*. London: Weidenfeld & Nicolson, 1971.

Ophüls, Max. *Max Ophüls par Max Ophüls*. Paris: Robert Laffont, 1963.

Taylor A. J. P. *The Origins of the Second World War*. Harmondsworth: Penguin, 1964.

Trevor-Roper, H. R., ed. *Hitler's Table Talk 1941–1944*. London: Weidenfeld & Nicolson, 1973.

Vizzard, Jack. *See No Evil: Life Inside a Hollywood Censor*. New York: Simon & Schuster, 1970.

Windell, George G. "Hitler, National Socialism, and Richard Wagner." *Journal of Central European Affairs* 22, no. 4 (1963): 479–97.

Wright Wexman, Virginia, and Karen Hollinger, eds. *Letter from an Unknown Woman—Max Ophuls, Director*. New Brunswick, NJ: Rutgers University Press, 1986.

Zweig, Stefan. *The World of Yesterday*. London: Cassell, 1943.

Filmography

Letter from an Unknown Woman. Directed by Max Ophuls. Universal-International, 1948.

Lola Montès. Directed by Max Ophuls. Gamma Films, 1955.

Only Yesterday. Directed by John M. Stahl. Universal Pictures, 1933.

Le Roman de Werther (*The Novel of Werther*). Directed by Max Ophuls. Monopol Film, 1938.

"SAME TUNE AGAIN!"

Repetition and Framing in *Letter from an Unknown Woman*

First published in CineAction, *no. 52 (June 2000): 40–48.*

Toward the end of *The Reckless Moment* (1949), at a point when it seems the heroine's problems have been resolved, there is a scene in a bar. The camera foregrounds an attractive young woman, dissolute-looking and most likely drunk, as she leans across a jukebox to berate the mechanism: "No, no, no, no! Just play the same tune again. Same tune again!" This is in the course of a rapid movement tracing Martin Donnelly's (James Mason) agitated quest, so the woman is held in the frame only for a moment as he pauses. But the soundtrack retains her words beyond the passing of her image. "Same tune again!" marks a stage where what seemed settled is about to be cast back into jeopardy, and Donnelly is about to be given a reason to renew his efforts to be of service to the heroine, along with the opportunity to resume their strange, unacknowledged courtship.

An equivalent moment in *Letter from an Unknown Woman* (1948) comes at the opera, with the repeated calls of "Second act. Curtain going up" just when Stefan (Louis Jourdan) is about to reenter Lisa's (Joan Fontaine) life.[1] In each case the device marks the shape of the story, marks the story as being shaped and not just unwinding with the course of events or the process of memory. Both devices articulate a relationship between the pattern of the story and the pattern of the film. They do this, in part, through their stress on things not starting but starting again. They incorporate processes independent of the protagonists' aims and actions—the mechanism of the jukebox, the conventions of operatic performance—so as to invoke the routine quality of the world's repetitions and the possibility of being habituated or inured to its ways of going on going around.

These emphases are in permanent tension with another possibility, that of the decisive, the crucial, where every moment may be the one to be measured, and every step may count. Each of the characters experiences time differently because for each of them any given moment has its own, and their own, blend between the mundane and the special. Emblematic here is the film's use of the idea of the birthday as on the one hand an occasion that comes around year on year, advancing us stealthily from cradle to grave, and on the other as marking a beginning, or a new beginning. The film is at pains to specify whether a repetition is acknowledged or ignored or vaguely apprehended, and to discriminate between repetition lived as boredom or servitude or disappointment and repetition embraced or desired as renewal and affirmation.

Such shadings are not easy to achieve. They require both boldness and delicacy. As a ground the film builds a careful discrimination between its own processes and those in the lives and world of its characters, insisting on its own ability both to observe and to produce patterns of repetition and variation. Crucially, the marked returns to Stefan at various stages in his reading of Lisa's letter pronounce the film's paragraphing of her story by making a formal repetition out of what could be mere continuation, more of the same. Once the film has established its devices—Joan Fontaine's narrating voice as representing the words of Lisa's letter, the moves out of and into focus as transitions from the reading present to the recounted past—it uses them with freedom and refuses to be governed by any simple understanding that would dictate a strict system of equivalences. So the focus-blur that most often marks a move between past and present, and is most often bridged by a resumption of narration, can function also to make the ellipse that covers the birth of young Stefan without any return to the moment of reading.

The challenge to the film is to arrive at order and comprehensibility without falling into an impoverishing neatness. It is vital to its effect that it should not solicit a literal reading of its devices, and that it should arrive at a persuasive form while blocking any coherent understanding of the relations between the words of the letter, the speaking voice and the movie's images. No rational timescale or system of subjectivities holds the key elements in harmony. Lisa cannot be reading the letter, since Lisa is dead. Stefan cannot be imagining the reading in Lisa's voice, since he does not know who sent it. The images we see are not explicable as projections of the letter's content, since we are so often shown events and transactions of which Lisa was unaware. Of course a loose convention is in play, one that allows us to understand the voice-over as speaking (some of) the words of the letter, and the images as constituting an internal movie that offers an independent version of the letter's events. But Ophuls and [Howard] Koch push very hard against the limits of this convention and expose—where others would seek to naturalize—its artifice.

A relevant contrast is with *Brief Encounter* (David Lean/Noël Coward, 1945) and it would be interesting to know how consciously it was a model for Ophuls and Koch. One could imagine Ophuls, a director generous to the work of fellow artists, as an admirer of the British film and one impressed—as so many were—by its restraint and its refusal of glamour and gloss. Equally it would be unsurprising to find that his artistic conscience was affronted by the Lean film's mixture of schematism and inconsistency in, for instance, its opportunistic use of Rachmaninov's music. In *Brief Encounter* the flashback story is narrated by a voice representing the unspoken thoughts of the Celia Johnson character (Laura). The film stays carefully within the constraints of its narrative premise until near its end but then makes one very large deviation (in the scene that Billy Wilder claims as the inspiration for *The Apartment*). Laura scurries away down the fire escape when an assignation with her passionate friend Alec (Trevor Howard) is interrupted by the surprise return of the apartment's owner. We are then given a scene between the two men—the dialogue that famously climaxes in "No, Alec—not angry—just disappointed." The scene defies the logic of the flashbacks as Laura's memories (which may be her fantasies). When it is finished we rejoin Laura; her voice-over resumes to tell us that she spent the next three hours wandering alone to overcome her humiliation and shame.[2] Nothing has given her access to the men's exchange, and nothing legitimizes their scene as, say, a product of Laura's imagination.

Brief Encounter's mapping of viewpoint is insistently tidy, with concealments at the start that have no other value than to prepare the ground for clarifications at the end. The governing contrivance jars against the film's unwillingness or inability to sustain its narrative premise. Neatness without formal rigor reduces to fussiness. Whether or not in reaction to *Brief Encounter* Ophuls's strategy is just the reverse. Where Lean's Laura is silent about the men's conversation, and the film is seemingly embarrassed by the break in its narrative logic, *Letter from an Unknown Woman* frequently and systematically displays the mismatch between conflicting narrative assumptions, most particularly by stressing Lisa's absence from, or obliviousness to, scenes and incidents pictured in the flashbacks.

Much comment has for good reason centered on those elements that undercut her enraptured view of the romance. Representative here are Stefan's negotiations with the old couple who run the scenic train in the Prater. Both times attention is drawn to Stefan's leaving Lisa in the compartment and so leaving Lisa in ignorance of his transaction. There is in each case a cut to the exterior of the closed compartment, a cut emphatic in its refusal of the fluid continuity that was at Ophuls's command. Then the camera tracks and pans with Stefan so as to measure the length of his walk from the compartment to the ticket kiosk when he goes to "talk to the engineer." Finally, in each instance, after Stefan's return toward the compartment the camera stays with the mechanics to detail the labor of illusion-making in a process from which Stefan, too, is excluded.

This scene stays within the relatively easy convention whereby the film, being bound to show more than a narrator can describe, is also free to show us more of the world than the narrator could have observed, and to point to the significance of aspects ignored by the protagonists. The film's emphases can be more or less striking in their divergence from those of the narrator—variables that Ophuls keeps under finely nuanced control. The convention is stretched to its limits perhaps in those moments where within the flashbacks we are given sights which could have fallen within Lisa's consciousness and which, if they had done so, would have required her to make a response. The starkest instance of this comes when the married Lisa, Frau Stauffer, is standing at the gates of Stefan's apartment. In an abrupt break from the continuity that has carried us smoothly to a close shot of Lisa from within the gates, the film cuts to a long view of her from the far end of the street, and a rapid pan reveals Johann Stauffer (Marcel Journet) at the window of his carriage observing the action which is, for him, definitive of Lisa's infidelity. If the continuity has shown Lisa to be revisiting the scenes of her youth, through a process of sound and image that recalls earlier passages, the break in the flow is equally emphatic that a married woman in this society incurs radically changed consequences for herself and her beloved when she attempts to renew the romantic pursuits of an unattached young woman. Here, in a shot which is all about seeing, being seen, and their opposites, it is vivid that Lisa is unaware of her husband's presence.

It is in those devices that bear on the relationship between the letter and the flashbacks that Ophuls and Koch are boldest in their defiance of narrative logic. The design is, I take it, to ensure that we cannot come to feel that there is a real world within the fiction where Lisa's writing of the letter can merge with Stefan's reading. Their coming together occurs only in and through the artifice of the film. Beyond that we are blocked from giving them the responsibility for the information and viewpoints that the film presents. Fictionality extends from the story to the narrative method with the film's flaunting of impossibility, at its most overt in the scene that depicts Lisa's life once she has left Linz to make her own way in Vienna, and to seek reunion with Stefan. As soon as we are taken into the dress shop to find Lisa modeling garments for Mme Spitzer (Sonja Bryden) Ophuls embarks on a swift delineation of its various spaces, levels, and barriers, emphasizing the separation between areas in terms of function and protocol as well as of space and structure. With smoothness and economy he establishes a stage for Lisa's display in relation to a range of backstages and offstages. Action and camera movement then show the quest for privacy as an old lecher in an officer's uniform crosses the room away from his wife to engage in a sly consultation with Mme Spitzer, who is seated at her desk on the other side of a railing at a level below Lisa's stage. More could hardly be done to stress that theirs is an intimate and furtive conversation as the officer, with his back turned from Lisa, hears the disappointing news that "she is not like that.... Every evening as soon as the shutters are closed, off she goes—straight home."

The next words are Lisa's, delivered in the narration: "Madame Spitzer spoke the truth. I was not like the others..." The lines are written to disturb our understanding. Lisa seems to have heard the words that were so conspicuously withheld from her. But if she could not have heard them then, where is she that she can comment on them now? Boldness is balanced with delicacy in the achievement of this impossible continuity. No words intervene between Mme Spitzer's and Lisa's, but their lines are spaced by a dissolve through time and a move from inside to out. A new action has begun with the women's departure from work into the snow-strewn evening streets before we hear Lisa's comment. Through his pacing Ophuls ensures that the effect is not to explode the narrative into absurdity with a gag, but subtly to position it beyond any real time and space.

We should ask ourselves what is performed by Joan Fontaine in her delivery of the narration. She is not enacting the composition of the letter; she does not pause or correct herself in the effort to find the right words. Although she suggests at the start that she may be dying, her voice is not fevered or enfeebled. The film does without one of Stefan Zweig's key literary effects, the adoption of a stilted manner that displays the woman's straining after the weight and depth that she wants her words to attain. In Zweig's tale the letter opens with a blunt statement of the death of the writer's child. Then the fact of it is obsessively restated so that the whole account is governed by one mood of heartbreak at the edge of hysteria. But in the film both the narration and the performance vary their tone in response to the events immediately under description. The moods of the words and of the voice carry the sense that Lisa is speaking to Stefan, reliving the feelings and thoughts of the moments as she retraces them. The fiction is almost of Lisa's seeing the past now as Stefan reads about it, and offering her response to its sights and statements—responding *now*, for instance, to Mme Spitzer's description. So the impression of presence, of an impossible presence, is reinforced.

The effect is reversed in Stefan's reading of the letter. At its completion his mute servant, John (Art Smith), does him the service of writing down the name of Lisa Berndl. He responds to this as if to new information. Yet the name has been extensively used throughout the flashbacks. It could hardly be otherwise, one might think.³ But here, too, *Letter from an Unknown Woman* aggravates a difficulty that other films would avoid. The first word spoken within the first flashback is Lisa's name. It is not spoken but shouted, three times, as Lisa's mother summons her indoors from her dreamy contemplation of the delivery van with Stefan's "beautiful things." Thereafter the name is frequently used, often with peremptory emphasis to command Lisa's movement, notably right at the start of three of the four major flashback sequences—in close juxtaposition, then, with Stefan's reading image.⁴ It should at least trouble us to find Stefan at the end still without the knowledge of Lisa's name that we seem to have obtained through his reading.

We could understand the intention coherently as a design to maintain the subjectivity of the narrative in the letter's text (where Lisa is only—like the heroine in *Rebecca*—a nameless "I") and to stress the independence of the much broader perspective taken in the film's enactments: the film knows her name, though the letter does not tell it. Yet we must understand the drama of the flashbacks to be closely derived from the letter's account; its shape is determined by Lisa's experience and we see nothing of Stefan's past life or career (for instance, in Milan or America or in the concert hall) that does not immediately bear upon Lisa's story as Lisa has told it.

It is, on the face of it, odder that the letter is unaddressed than that it is unsigned. Lisa was never going to reach the end of what she had to tell because she was never going, in the circumstances of her writing, to arrive at the one point that could satisfy her: Stefan's recognition. So her writing would stop only as her strength failed, at the start of yet another "If only . . ."

At the opening there is no "Dear Stefan" to specify the "you" in "By the time you read this letter I may be dead." There is a play with the names here whereby the writer has omitted Stefan's name and withheld her own, only for the film to have it shouted by her mother on the break as narration yields to enactment in the flashback that takes us to Lisa's girlhood. On this day—which she speaks of as her birthday—Lisa's mother names her for us, performing the introduction that Lisa consistently evades. One aspect of the deadlock between Lisa and Stefan, reflecting their different orientations to time and memory and hope, is that Lisa is unwilling to sully the authenticity and spontaneity of Stefan's recognition by identifying herself while Stefan in his narcissism wants to hear his own name on Lisa's lips more than he wants to learn hers.

His "Who are you?" outside the opera is hardly a request for her name. It is quite probable that he knows her as Stauffer's wife. What would be involved in his remembering her name is a world away from what it would mean to be told it.

Stefan would at last be preferring knowledge to mystery. His "Who are you?" is not only "Where have I seen you before?" but "Why does it matter?" He is asking Lisa to tell him her role in his life—a question which it will take Lisa the whole of her letter to define and which Lisa can present only from Lisa's point of view. Stefan's "Who are you?" believes that the answer on this woman's significance for him must come from outside himself. It requires notions of perfection and romantic destiny—"that one face among all others"—at least as powerful as those that govern Lisa. (And it requires unattainability, which means that Lisa's presenting herself as a married woman available for seduction can only make her one of the "usual things.")

If Lisa neither addresses nor signs her letter, these functions are performed for her—both of them—by John. In their essays on *Letter from an Unknown Woman* Stanley Cavell and George M. Wilson have drawn attention to his role as signatory, seeing it as Ophuls's acknowledgment of authorship (Cavell 1996, 109; Wilson 1986, 125). But John's role in recalling Lisa's name—effectively, for Stefan, giving her a name—continues his role as the bearer of her letter (which can also be seen as his delivery of the screenplay). When Stefan arrives home at the start of the film he is intending to make a quick departure from Vienna to avoid a duel. He has given his orders and is walking away, almost out of shot, when John summons him back into the corridor with a touch (as if to remind him of something he has forgotten) and goes to fetch a silver salver on which the letter sits unopened. Making the delivery of the letter an interruption in Stefan's movement and a reversal of its direction anticipates the pattern of his encounters with Lisa. The action of fetching and offering the letter is elaborated to stress John's role as intermediary. This elaboration stands in contrast with the absence of attention to the writing on the envelope, and is a stylistic decision in line with the definition of the letter as an object that sits unattended in the hallway, waiting for Stefan. It is placed near the center of the frame and given quite a glow by Franz Planer's lighting. Among the rejected options were to have the letter delivered after Stefan's return, to have it offered to him as one of several (Zweig's way), or to have him find it on his desk without John's aid.

The transmission of the letter allows for a strengthening of John's part in the palindromic patterns of the film's start and finish. Palindrome is a special case of repetition and variation where the elements of the first part are repeated in reverse order in the second so that the approach to the end is also a return to the start. The clear reversal of the opening image in the closing one, as the departing carriages mirror Stefan's arrival, articulates the framing of Lisa's story by Stefan's. Matched sets of gestures, immediately before and straight after Stefan's reading of the letter, help to mark the palindromic pattern because the gestures are more striking and less in the flow of the action than, say, John's holding the door open for Stefan at the start and closing it on him at the end. I refer to the gestures in which Stefan attends to his eyes. Having thrown the letter onto his desk, Stefan pinches the corners of his eyes in a gesture of tiredness; he then walks to the bathroom, removing the letter from its packet, and sluices his eyes with water at the washstand. At that moment his attention is caught by the letter's first statement. A close-up of the writing is answered by a close-up of Stefan, his face wet with beads of water. He picks up the letter and takes a towel to dab at the drops as he goes to begin his reading.

At the close of the final flashback, Stefan completes his reading on Lisa's last "If only . . . ," and we move from the letter's end page to a close shot of Stefan, tracking in to glimpse the tears in his eyes. Then, in the wake of the fragmentary, misted images that suggest his effort to grasp a memory of Lisa—scenes from the past that haunt but that cannot be held—we see in close-up the gesture that Stanley Cavell takes as the starting-point for his discussion: "His response . . . is to cover his eyes with the out-spread fingers of both hands in a melodramatic gesture of horror and exhaustion" (1996, 81).

My suggestion is that both the tears and the blocking of the eyes have been anticipated palindromically in the imagery of the opening.

I want to avoid imposing on the film a more precise patterning than that offered by Ophuls. An inventory of sights and sounds in the opening and closing sequences would yield more unmatched than matched elements. (Strict palindrome could only be absurd in a fiction movie.) But there is a sufficiently pronounced matching in the content and order of some major moments to give a suggestion of palindrome. The effect is to lend weight to the containment of Lisa's story within Stefan's, and so to balance our sense of Lisa's letter as the frame within which the events of the past are accessed. Viewpoint is important in Stefan's reading as well as in Lisa's writing. (If we share Stefan's reading, learning about the past at the same time as he does and within similar limits, our involvement is of a different order since only Stefan is reading, perhaps seeing, himself within Lisa's account and is experiencing its impact both as a revision of his life story and as a challenge to his memory.)

A major distinction between Stefan's story and Lisa's—against Lisa's desire to insist that the two stories are one—is that Stefan's story is ongoing and unresolved whereas Lisa's is at an end. Hence the emphasis on the delivery of Lisa's letter as a sealed packet of a certain bulk and weight. It is from another place. It is the past; there is no more to come. So Stefan's reading is of a narrative already concluded. There was an evident opportunity, refused by the film, to develop the symmetry in the framing of Lisa's tale. When Stefan started to read, and the voice of Joan Fontaine repeated the opening sentences, we could have been taken to Lisa as she began to write the letter in the hospital, adding another layer to the flashback sequence. That would have naturalized the use of the voice (which many filmmakers would have thought useful) at the cost of bringing the moment of Lisa's narrative into a present and uniting it with the moment of Stefan's reading. The film's "irrational" procedure prevents these moments from merging and allows them to approach one another only in the letter's end at Lisa's death, imaged in the black blot that halted her script. The new discovery here, revising the sense of the sealed packet, is that the letter's story is not complete. It is instead no more than over, because the reading is finished though the writing could not be.

There is a significant advantage in the refusal to balance the flashback structure, showing us the end of the writing but not its beginning: the film can present Lisa's life in strict chronology, taking her by stages from her "second birthday" to her maturity and death. That makes it less difficult for Joan Fontaine to convince us as the schoolgirl Lisa of the early sequences.[5] The corresponding problem for Louis Jourdan is eased by delaying his appearance in each of the flashback sections so that he is not immediately juxtaposed with his reading image. Still, the alternation is eloquent: we see various stages of Stefan's life in relation to the recurrent framing image of the middle-aged roué. The alternation in Stefan's image, as against the steady development of Lisa's, gives formal expression to the dissonance between their stories and their attitudes.

Whereas the structure of the flashbacks would tend to depict Stefan's life as a series of incidents in Lisa's, the framing scenes insist on his having immediate and urgent predicaments of his own. To observe symmetries here as elsewhere is not to resolve the question of their function and effect, since patterning can serve both to create or reinforce order and to give the emphasis of contrast to the unmatched aspects.

The opening shot instructs us on the relationship between the stylistic patterns created by the film and the events portrayed within its world. In "Vienna About 1900" the horse-drawn carriage is driven toward the camera through the rain of a gaslit street. The shot displays the precision of its framing, since it turns out that the camera, panning to hold the vehicle in view, is in place to approach the side window as it comes to a halt, neatly encompassing a centered view of the occupants and of Stefan's head when he dismounts, within the further frame of the far side window. The convergence of the camera's view with the carriage's point of arrest holds the movements of the fictional Vienna within an elegantly ordered continuity. Not everything, though, fits within its pattern. The film is telling a story that it knows. It is not telling a story about automata. As the carriage approaches from the distance, a running figure enters the frame from the left foreground, a man with an umbrella hurrying away down the street to avoid the rain. The direction of his movement counters the flow of the shot to sketch a world that proceeds in indifference to the motions and concerns of *this* telling. He is placed at the start of the film as an emblem of the ordinary. The figure prepares an immediate contrast with Stefan, whose bearing is of one who does not greatly care whether he lives or dies; he stands shamefaced in the rain, avoiding the gaze of his companions but doing nothing to propel their conversation to a close while the water streams from the brim of his top hat as if from a gutter.[6]

At the end the rain has cleared so that although the street is still wet with puddles the scene looks and sounds quite different. The elements of style do not determine for us, though, how we shall balance the significance of the completion of the film's opening image against that of change in key aspects of tone: the disappearance of the rain, the replacement of darkness by dawning light. Louis Jourdan's bearing is eloquent that Stefan faces death in better spirit than he faced running off and living on. But how far his vision has cleared and how far he has been drawn into a delusion—a "romantic nonsense" that colludes with the morbid rituals of the duel—these are questions that the film is concerned not to resolve.

Ophuls unites precision of form with openness to possibility rather than making it serve the definition of a thesis. His precision shows in the preparation of the material that will be the subject of repetition, variation, or inversion in the film's development. The boldness of presence and the strength of shape given to the repeated features determines whereabout the later references fall on a scale between faint allusion and bold statement. In a film so concerned with the significance of memory it is appropriate that the eloquence of its effects should depend on its capacity to stir our recall, with varying degrees of definition, of moments and patterns that we have seen before. One danger—that *Brief Encounter* seems to me not to avoid—is that the material being set up for repetition will be inert on its first presentation.

These are the considerations that I want to hold in mind in revisiting a pair of shots that has already received extensive discussion—the matched camera movements over the staircase as first the adolescent Lisa watches Stefan's return from a night on the town in the company of a giggling mistress and then, years later, as he is seen to lead Lisa herself up the same stairs. Much comment has dwelt, appropriately, on the removal of Lisa's watching presence. The sense is that she has entered as a dream something which on her earlier witnessing of it had more the force of a nightmare, and that she is oblivious to the particular aspects of repetition that are so strongly presented to us (figs. 26 and 27).

Directors and Movies • 419

Figures 26 and 27. The two staircase scenes

Strength in the repetition partly depends on the boldness with which the image is shaped in its first instance. Since very many of the film's images involve the staircase, the structure that is to be particularly invoked in repetition needs to be highly distinctive. Its extremities are marked at the left by the gaslit globes of the hallway chandelier—an unusual sight because we are looking down into the jets of flame—and at the right by the expanse of bare wall that shields Lisa. The lines of the composition take added force from the curved patterns of metalwork and shadow constructed from the steel banisters. The extraordinary nature of the camera movement is determined by the effort to encompass the action on the staircase while keeping Lisa continuously in frame in the foreground, and showing her attempts to go on seeing without being seen. That produces the twisting camera movement, pivoted over Lisa's head at the right as she shrinks back against the wall of the stairwell. It also produces a pattern of repeated appearance and disappearance in the figures on the staircase. We see them enter from the vestibule; they go out of sight as they approach the stairs. They reemerge as they reach the top and pause near the landing, only to disappear again behind the wall that masks the approach to Stefan's door. Their invisibility is stressed by the sound of furtive giggles and whispers at the bottom of the stairs and at the top by renewed giggling and the rattle as Stefan fumbles with his door key.

The main features of this image, including the pattern of appearance and disappearance at the bottom of the stairs, are duplicated in the second instance. The repetition is pronounced because the cut to the overhead view is much more shocking as it has become a cut from exterior to interior, from a close view to a distant one, and because it is no longer in continuity with Lisa's waiting and watching by the landing. The position and movement of the camera lack the motivation that justified their contortions in the earlier instance since there is no longer a foreground figure to be held in frame. The crane out over the stairwell has become more vertiginous now that it is not shadowing the viewpoint of a human observer.

The visual repetition is cued by repetition on the soundtrack. The closing of the outer gates and of the hall door are sounds bracketing the familiar exchange that begins with "Who is it?" from the concierge (Otto Waldis).

After these reminders, however, the pattern of sound is crucial to a radical change of tone and the sense of difference between this occasion and the one that its images repeat. When Lisa and Stefan go out of view at the bottom of the stairs the emptiness of the image is matched by their silence; their soft, slow footfall is quite unlike the frivolous clatter and chatter we heard before. Then the suggestion was of tipsiness, and of an awareness of behaving disreputably. Those tones were amplified by the styleless flounces and frills of the woman's white gown and headdress and by the way that Stefan, in searching for his key, was encumbered by his evening dress, awkward in his management of a bulky cloak, his top hat and gloves. At the top of the stairs the haste in his leading of the woman, almost pulling her and hardly giving her a glance, together with his fumbling to remove his hat as they approach his door, carried the feeling (within the terms available in 1948) of his eagerness to get out of his clothes. Everything had a clumsy physicality. Since the event had a context for us only in Lisa's life, and none in the lives of Stefan or his woman, we saw his partner distantly as a nameless stranger—truly an unknown woman. She had the identity only of a floozy.

That has all changed in the repeated shot. It comes as the culmination not of Lisa's watching and waiting but of her, shall we say, courtship of Stefan. All that was sordid has become sacramental. There is no rush. The movements have a solemn, considerate grace. Lisa's hesitation at the top of the stairs is grave rather than coy, a moment of commitment with no demand to be coaxed. Her dress and hat are in undecorated black with a chaste simplicity of line. Stefan's clothing, too, has been softened and simplified so that clumsy urgency may be the more visibly replaced by attentiveness.

And noise has given way to music. The Ziehrer waltz played by the bandswomen and then by Stefan in the Prater ballroom ("Wiener Mad'ln") has been sustained on the soundtrack to become the fragrantly romantic accompaniment to this ascent. The calm and quiet of the sequence from ballroom and carriage to staircase stand in place of any moment of invitation or persuasion. We know that the return with Stefan is a matter of unspoken agreement, of desires mutually acknowledged from the outset.

So the assertion of similarity is put in tension with the sense of transformation.

We know that Lisa longs to give herself to Stefan. We do not know how fully she recognizes the role of appetite and the body in this sacrament, or whether she recognizes anything that unites her with Stefan's, and the film's, other women. "I wanted," she will later write, "to be one woman . . . who asked you for nothing."

The purposes of her ascent would, then, from her own viewpoint be utterly unlike those involved in Stefan's routines of pleasure. Here it becomes relevant to consider the culminations of the staircase shots and their sharp differences.

When Stefan and his woman disappeared from view for the second time they did so behind a flat, blank expanse of whitewashed wall at screen right that censored their activity. The shot was held while sound filled the blankness with suggestions of the flighty and illicit. Lisa was fixed near the center of the frame but we could not see what, apart from her exclusion, the sounds meant to her. At the start we could see that she was watching; at the end we could not tell if she was listening.

In the reprise the pattern of appearance and disappearance is repeated, but the shot changes as soon as Stefan and Lisa go out of sight for the second time. We cut to the inside of Stefan's apartment for the couple's entrance and Lisa's immediate surrender to Stefan's embrace. There is a direct sense in which this action fills in the earlier blankness, so it is doubly striking that it yields straightaway to blankness reasserted. The conventional kiss fade-out is followed at the fade-in by an image of remarkable emptiness, reinforced by the disappearance of music. It turns out that we are looking at closed draperies sealing off an area of the dress shop, but indecipherable silence is what we first encounter.

In the pattern of repetition and variation the emptiness here replaces the extended diminuendo in which the disillusioned Lisa had made her lonely way back down the stairs, the camera holding its position until she had exited at the bottom of the frame: "And so there was nothing left for me. I went to Linz." That was the point at which music came in, as an expression of anguished disappointment. When this shot is repeated it comes again in strikingly abbreviated form. It cuts off at the point where, earlier, it had developed as a sorrowing reflection on Stefan's infidelity. We may see frustration replaced by fulfillment. But it is an equal part of the pattern that an extended assessment of events is replaced by silence.

Staircase One was embedded in one of the letter's most extended, almost garrulous passages of commentary in which the words spoken by Lisa became something close to an interior monologue accompanying her exploration of the now empty rooms of the home she had had to leave.[7] It was part of a lengthy passage in which the only significant, dramatically salient, words were those of the commentary that culminated in the first return to the present and Stefan's reading image on "You who have always lived so freely . . ." The shot's vital context, then, included its context in Lisa's reflections.

Such a context is entirely absent from Staircase Two. In the sequences depicting the love affair the commentary tails off at the moment when Stefan is at last about to notice Lisa waiting in the snow outside the apartment building. It yields to the music of the street singers here, and it does not return until Stefan's departure for Milan and the letter's thoughts about his promise to return in two weeks: "How little you knew yourself. That train was taking you out of my life."[8] It is as if Lisa is overflowing with words to express disappointment and regret. She can never come to the end of "If only . . ." But she has nothing to say about fulfillment.[9] We may choose to understand her speechlessness as an expression of the sense that rapture is beyond words. But it is one of the functions of the pattern of repetition and reversal to open up other ways of responding.

Lisa's silence goes with the absence of her witnessing foreground presence. It is a silence about her place in the stream of Stefan's lovers as well as about the consummation of her passion. We may relate it to her presentation of her first disillusionment. What had Lisa learned from the sight of Stefan's mistress to persuade her that there was "nothing left for me"? She already knew that many of his friends—most of them—were women. Staircase One already condensed some significant repetitions, of the staircase itself as the central emblem of the routines of Stefan's life, of Lisa's overhead view of adult sexuality (when she emerged at the top of the stairs to surprise her mother in embrace with Herr Kastner), and of Lisa's spying from above on Stefan's nocturnal activity. This last was in continuity with the instances of the illicit (stealing, hiding) in Lisa's appropriation of Stefan's music into her fantasies when "though [because?] you didn't know it, you were giving me some of the happiest hours of my life." Happiness in fantasy prepares the misery of disillusion not because Lisa finds out that Stefan is a sexual being, but because his timing is catastrophic for her. The perfection of Lisa's romantic fantasy required Stefan to be ready for her at precisely the moment when she was ready for him, ready "to throw myself at your feet, and cling to you and never leave you." For Lisa, as for Stefan, the pursuit of perfection means a life defined by disappointment.

What is it that encourages me to talk of the absence of commentary on the scenes of romantic fulfillment as Lisa's silence? We have to understand that the events of the past, insofar as Stefan is told of them, are recounted in the text of the letter ("Night after night I returned to the same spot, but you never noticed me until one evening"). This must be a sentence that continues in the letter, whose continuation the film has replaced with images. Sensibly, then, Lisa is *not* silent about the events of Staircase Two—only unheard. But here I want to return to my start. Ophuls and Koch devised a form that baffles the attempt at a sensible reading. My argument is that the intention, and certainly the effect, was to create an unstable set of frames so that while a story is told, with events whose occurrence is not to be doubted, the definition of their significance is never pursued at the cost of suggestion. The film's lucidity is a lucidity in presenting ranges of possibility, through what it can omit to specify as well as through what it can show.

The refusal to confine flashback and voice-over within a coherent convention gave the film access to the metaphorical possibilities of these devices, allowing the passages of speech and silence, explicitness and reticence, to register expressively. At the same time there was a partial submission to limitations of viewpoint that seemed to assign Lisa a role in determining what was to be seen of her life and of Stefan's, so that opportunities were created for veiling motivations and for leaving thoughts, feelings, and attitudes open to speculation. For instance, when Stefan comes to the photographs that Lisa has enclosed to stand as his son's biography, it is clear that he is moved by these glimpses of a child he will never meet; his use of a magnifying glass speaks of a hunger for knowledge that the snapshots cannot satisfy. But nothing tells us how far Stefan attends to Lisa's presence in one of these images. And when Lisa tells of her marriage and says that Stefan knows who her husband is, we are without guidance about the extent of Stefan's appreciation that this letter is from that woman whose husband has challenged him to a duel—the woman who, we shall shortly discover, came calling a few days ago after an encounter at the Opera.

The masking of Stefan within Lisa's viewpoints is particularly powerful in Staircase Two, for Stefan's attitude here is perhaps the most crucial issue in our sense of what is being repeated and what has been transformed. We are shown that Lisa *could* be seen as just one in the succession of Stefan's women. We are not told whether Stefan sees her in that way. As a result we are given no hint about what Stefan's response might have been if Lisa had been able to seek him out with the news of her pregnancy after his return from Milan.

Stefan's leaving is able to be read by Lisa as a confirmation of her prophecy (in the Prater ballroom, when Stefan had asked for her promise) "I won't be the one to vanish." This terrible form of words predicted betrayal while recognizing itself only as a loving vow of fidelity. Unacknowledged in the letter, but confirmed by what we see as clearly as the repetition in Staircase Two, is that Lisa is each time the one who vanishes—to Linz, into the charity hospital, and away in flight from the final sad encounter. Stefan's reaction to the last disappearance is withheld from us, and is something to which Lisa gives no apparent thought, but it is an issue brought to mind by the reaction that we do see: the servant John's witnessing her departure as she crosses him on the stairs.

The patterns of revelation and masking enabled by the film's structure allow Lisa to speak as if her actions and inactions are perfectly explained by her love for Stefan and his son. Other possibilities are built into the picture's fabric but not enforced—for instance, an element of revenge in Lisa's presentation of the photographs of young Stefan and her reflections on the happiness he brought her. It becomes a possibility, too, but not a dogmatic assertion, that Lisa's Ideal was by her definition a man who would disappoint her, and that Stefan's Ideal was by his definition a woman he would never find. Ophuls and Koch discovered a form that avoided sentimentality while negotiating the danger of a merely cynical denial of romance—one that would only have sneered at yearnings for love and transcendence. The film's unique blending of strength of pattern with openness results in our being shown the failures of Lisa's vision and of Stefan's without being made complacent about the perfection of our own.

Works Cited

Cavell, Stanley. *Contesting Tears: The Melodrama of the Unknown Woman*. Chicago: University of Chicago Press, 1996.

White, Susan M. *The Cinema of Max Ophuls: Magisterial Vision and the Figure of Woman*. New York: Columbia University Press, 1995.

Wilson, George M. *Narration in Light: Studies in Cinematic Point of View*. Baltimore: Johns Hopkins University Press, 1986.

Wright Wexman, Virginia. "The Transfiguration of History: Ophuls, Vienna, and *Letter from an Unknown Woman*." In *Letter from an Unknown Woman—Max Ophuls, Director*, edited by Virginia Wright Wexman and Karen Hollinger, 3–14. New Brunswick, NJ: Rutgers University Press, 1986.

———, and Karen Hollinger, eds. *Letter from an Unknown Woman—Max Ophuls, Director*. New Brunswick, NJ: Rutgers University Press, 1986.

Filmography

Brief Encounter. Directed by David Lean. Eagle-Lion Distributors, 1945.
Letter from an Unknown Woman. Directed by Max Ophuls. Universal-International, 1948.
The Reckless Moment. Directed by Max Ophuls. Columbia Pictures, 1949.

Notes

1 There's also, more elliptically, "We'll revisit the scenes of our youth."

2 In the course of this sequence there occurs an image which does seem to be taken up by Ophuls in the parallel passage after the married Lisa's flight from Stefan's apartment. An overhead shot that sees Laura walking to a park bench beneath the statuary of a war memorial finds an echo (minus some grotesquely phallic elements) in Ophuls's high angle on Lisa as she walks across a deserted square beneath a fountain. The prominence of railway scenes in *Letter from an Unknown Woman* might also be thought to owe something to Lean's film. The shooting script envisaged a scene in that crucial *Brief Encounter* setting, the station buffet, when Lisa has seen her son onto the train but has not yet made the move to set out in search of Stefan (Wright Wexman and Hollinger 1986, 148).

3   Wrongly, but understandably—since it is so easy to underestimate the inventiveness of filmmakers.

4   It is not used in the same way at the start of the final flashback. By then, Lisa has become Frau Stauffer; she has that name because "you know who my husband is."

5   Ophuls's brilliance of craft shows in the way he gives us our first sight of Lisa, dwarfing the actress's height by framing her face at the bottom of the window through which she gazes into the removals van.

6   And attempting to manage a cigarette. This opening shot establishes smoking as a motif. Throughout the dialogue the foreground of the image is dominated by the white-gloved hand in which the one of Stefan's friends nearest the camera holds a cigarette. Thereafter few of the men of the film are without something to smoke in their hands or in their mouths. (John the manservant and Lisa's young lieutenant in Linz are the notable exceptions.) Cigarettes recur through the film as emblems of enslavement and unfulfilled appetite. At the start Stefan is a chain-smoker. By the end he seems to have found something to displace the habit. It is possible that the smoking motif was Ophuls's way of implicating himself with the men of the film and specially with Stefan. To judge from photographs Ophuls was quite a smoker and according to a number of reports he was quite a womanizer.

7   I am adopting "Staircase One" and "Staircase Two" to identify the first and second of the repeated pair because it would be a distorting inaccuracy to describe them as the first and second of the staircase shots. It is a vital fact that Staircase One is already the repetition of a familiar setting.

8   For the record, their song is "Nur für Natur" from the operetta *Der lustige Krieg* (*The Merry War*) by Johann Strauss II—worth specifying in order to correct a misunderstanding propounded by Virginia Wright Wexman and taken up by Susan M. White in her book *The Cinema of Max Ophuls* (1995), that the film "contains not a single word of German" (Wright Wexman 1986, 14). Both writers give a lot of weight to this strange assertion. The film presents a riotous patchwork of languages and accents, and it incorporates plenty of German words. There may be food for thought in the choice of a German word for fire—"brand"—as the surname for Lisa's Stefan.

9   Of course it would have been a formidable task to find something for her to say that would not have caused an explosion at the Breen Office, but Ophuls and Koch were equal to formidable tasks.

LE PLAISIR
"The Mask" and "The Model"

First published in Film Quarterly *63, no. 1 (2009): 15–22. © 2009 by the Regents of the University of California. Published by the University of California Press.*

Max Ophuls's *Le Plaisir* (1952) has been out of circulation for much too long. It has at last reemerged on DVD, a fine release from Criterion now joining Second Sight's UK edition. Its appearance ends a deprivation and is an occasion of joy.

Inspired by three stories by Guy de Maupassant, *Le Plaisir* belongs to a genre that was still new in 1952. The anthology picture had been invented in 1948 in England by the producer Sydney Box of Gainsborough Pictures when *Quartet* presented a sequence of four short stories by W. Somerset Maugham. *Quartet* knew such success that it was followed, to Maugham's great profit, by *Trio* (1950) and *Encore* (1951). Elsewhere Fox assembled five tales to make up *O. Henry's Full House* (1952). Maupassant's work was so inviting that in the year of *Le Plaisir* France saw also *Trois Femmes*, a film directed by André Michel presenting "Mouche" alongside two less celebrated stories.

The portmanteau movie that juggled a number of narratives was something else. Dating back at latest to 1916, with *Intolerance*, it was neither new nor done with in 1948. *Tales of Manhattan* (1942) and *Dead of Night* (1945) were recent examples. The novelty with *Quartet* and its followers was that the common authorship of the original stories provided the one, loudly asserted, connection between self-contained dramas. The Maugham pictures all start by having the aged writer address the camera about the methods and aims of his work. As the series progressed the on-screen Maugham associated himself ever more closely with the films, speaking as one of the "we" of the production company.

André Hakim at Fox evidently wished to copy the format of *Quartet* in producing the O. Henry picture, but was faced with the unavailability of the author (d. 1910). As the next best thing, John Steinbeck was filmed in a library setting to pay tribute to a fellow storyteller and to be seen as if choosing for us five from O. Henry's 270 tales. When Steinbeck begins by declaring O. Henry "the real star of this picture" he borrows the thought from the start of *Quartet*. Claiming the status of tributes to great writers, these movies ascribe authorship to Maugham and O. Henry. In sum the Maugham trilogy credited six screenwriters and seven directors. The five segments of *O. Henry's Full House* seem to have been made by five quite distinct units.

Le Plaisir is offered differently, as "Un Film de Max Ophüls." The filmmaker's name comes before and Maupassant's after the main title. It is not "Guy de Maupassant's *Le Plaisir*," only "based on three tales by . . . ," but the writer's name comes back in surprising form when the final credit reads: "And the voice of Guy de Maupassant: Jean Servais." An iris effect darkens the screen, music ends, and from the silence speaks the soft, confiding voice. It tells of the various options that have been considered "for bringing you three of my tales" and claims to have reached the view that "it would be simplest if I tell them to you myself." This author, then, is a movie character—not the film's creator but its creation.

He does not present himself as a ghost, which would be an identity of sorts, but his words are backed by the gentle strains of a harp, and he does recognize his difference from us in the audience who, being alive, may have a modern disdain for his old stories. He says how much he has always liked the dark, and suggests that he might be sitting alongside us in the cinema. With this suggestion the voice makes a claim upon our talent for fantasy, placing itself as completely a figure of the imagination. Ophuls refuses the solidity that the template movies sought.[1] He pictures no source for the voice from the blackness. Nowhere does Servais claim the name of Maupassant, but he makes us hear an author's savoring of language and his relish for storytelling. The voice falls on our ears as the spirit of the writing, not as a phantom but as what lives on in the work of fiction after the death of its creator.

It undertakes to tell us the stories. Tell, not read. Maupassant's prose is not always the source for the words spoken or even of the thoughts expressed. A further mark of Ophuls's originality is that the texts are never presented to our eyes. Elsewhere a familiar formula served to boost the literary prestige of a movie's source: a library edition of the book, never some well-thumbed paperback, would be brought into close-up as pages turned to reveal the start of the story just before an off-screen voice pronounced the title and began reading the first lines. The black screen that follows *Le Plaisir*'s opening titles serves to put a space between our reading of the credits and the start of the narration, having us sit in the dark with nothing to look at as Servais speaks. (This effect, vital at key moments in the film, is weakened when one's eyes are engaged with subtitles. It is worth getting to know the movie well enough to do without them.)

Withholding the words on the page is a further move against solidity, implying that Maupassant's work transcends the material form of printed merchandise. That is a deeper mark of respect than the conventional tropes can yield, and it is very Max to have paid tribute with an absence rather than a flourish. Asking us to listen, only to listen, the film begins by establishing the overspoken word and the overspeaking voice as elements vital to its form. In the template movies narration is a convenience. Once it has nodded to Maugham's opening lines and done a little setting of scene or character it fades out, to return—if at all—only between sequences as an aid to continuity. *Le Plaisir* gives us Servais's voice and the narrator's words throughout, within scenes as well as between them and at the completion of each tale as well as at its start. It invites us to delight in the language of the stories no less than their invention of character and incident.

The first tale is "The Mask." At its start the scene-setting is shared between narration, image, and sound so that each element complements and punctuates the others. As the darkness of the screen gives way to the darkness of depicted night, the first image is of a word. Servais begins the description of a Montmartre dance hall and hits the word *bal*. At the same moment the camera holds its glance up to the shining letters "BAL," vertical on-screen, before dipping and drawing back to present an intricate survey of the life, human and animal, drawn up to and into the palais. The music of the dance band within, its rhythms brashly beaten out, becomes the constant background to the sounds of other comings and goings in the street. The camera discovers so much of fascination that it cannot rest for more than a few beats on any one group or action, but must keep changing the direction of its gaze and movement as it falls upon a new aspect of the human spectacle.

In these first moments the film embraces a range of relationships between literary modes of depiction and those of the cinema. As soon as we cut to the inside of the dance hall, the shots are timed to the rhythm of the narrator's account, a new image entering—young beauties, rich women of a certain age, tailcoated gallants—as each new phrase begins. A cut for each comma. Information from the camera and information from the storyteller can be brought like this into marked coincidence. But the doubling stops well short of the point where the human figures might become puppets of the description. They have not been made to show in their action the roles and purposes that the teller asserts: we see no pimping, for instance, from the men described as pimps.

The rush of activity and the surfeit of detail in the image offset the calmly itemized description and the dry delivery that asserts detachment while it hints at distaste. The speaker develops a metaphor of rainstorms and floodwaters, likening the flow of pleasure-seekers into the palais to a torrent pouring through a sluice. In scripting the storyteller's role Ophuls and Jacques Natanson strategically retain prose imagery that both repeats and counterpoints the sights and sounds of the film.

They do this most expansively in the second story, "La Maison Tellier," in the passage which depicts a journey in a hay cart along country lanes by a group of prostitutes on an excursion from their small-town Normandy brothel. Ophuls's camera occupies the fixed vantage point of the narrator to show us, in time with the description, how "the cart rolled along behind the white horse . . . disappeared behind tall trees . . . reappeared beyond the foliage . . . and continued on its sunlit way." The emphatic matching here forms the ground for pronounced and repeated contrast. In the tobacco-saturated picture palace we are teased over and over with remarks on the smells of the countryside—as wholesome, strong, penetrating, sweet—and a verbal rainbow plays against our monochrome image: "Green pastures . . . yellow rape . . . green and gold crops, speckled with red and blue."

Through doubling and difference *Le Plaisir* becomes an essay on the shared and unique values of telling and showing. The overspeech both describes what is in plain view and incorporates what resists translation. It puts on display the peculiar ways in which language deals with time, and its subjection to sequence, as well as its freedom to articulate the invisible—meanings, thoughts, emotions, concepts. Weaving these elaborately crafted threads into the film's texture Ophuls pays homage to Maupassant and to the literary tradition that his work adorns.

All the sadder, then, that *Le Plaisir* was reviled on its French premiere as a Germanic travesty of a great national writer. André Bazin was particularly obtuse. Preferring competence to genius, he used the appearance of *Trois Femmes* as an occasion to restate his disapproval for the extravagant intricacy of Ophuls's approach. More sensitive appreciations came later, from Claude Beylie, François Truffaut, and, most notably, Jean-Luc Godard, who lost no occasion to laud the film and in 1963 offered an elegant rebuff to cultural chauvinism by placing *Le Plaisir* at the head of his nominations for "Best French Film since the Liberation." Ophuls himself made an answer to his critics in a letter to Jean-Jacques Gautier. This document is sadly omitted from Criterion's otherwise splendid array of extras. With its clear and impassioned unfolding of a complex design it proclaims Ophuls's pride in the film's achievement.

One aspect of his ambition is declared in the title. *Le Plaisir* uniquely announces a theme, and says that it is all one movie where *Quartet* and its fellows insist on variety rather than unity. Ophuls's three tales are "The Mask," "La Maison Tellier," and "The Model," in that order, but the titles are withheld, the better for us to receive each as a variation on the central theme—*Pleasure: Parts One, Two, and Three*. A triptych structure, defying convention, puts the longest and most fully dramatized narrative in the middle, flanked by two much slighter anecdotes, each less than twenty minutes long.

Le Plaisir's unlikely triumph is to develop a formal design that spans its three sections while realizing to the full the particularities of mood and incident that give each story its own completeness as well as its place in the triptych. The recurrence of Servais's voice throughout is a major resource brilliantly deployed. Hardly less vital are the musical themes, limited in number and not originating with the film, that weave through the tales, their repetitions sometimes startling but always eloquent. In architecture, Ophuls and his designer Jean d'Eaubonne contrived without forcing to have bridge-like structures return to govern the composition of image and action. Sets and locations allow stagings that repeatedly carry the action upward, across, and down again, providing also for a change of register with rarer but marked movements along the level.

These patterns of movement carry thematic weight and are linked to motifs in performance of running, rushing, chasing, and (by contrast) steadiness and stillness. The motif is established with the appearance of the key figure in the first story, the masked dancer at the ball (Jean Galland). He enters the image in a high-stepping run which already has a dance aspect, his momentum scarcely checked by the crowd as he hastens to the palais up the steps at its entrance, and up the stairs and across the galleries within, to descend onto the dance floor at a speed only a little broken by the shedding of his cane, scarf, and tailcoat. The camera shares in the delirium of his ungainly movement, and thereby keeps us from fixed scrutiny of his strange features until the moment when he collapses in the middle of the floor.

What a gamble it was to begin with this story, a parable of regret for lost youth and beauty—a man's lost youth and beauty, and lost prowess. Behind the mask is an old man clinging to his place in the dance, obsessively performing the remembered motions of display and seduction. It's an unlikely tale, with more than a hint of doppelgänger Gothic. Catastrophe threatens if this figure looks too much or too little like the others at the ball. Ophuls doubled the risk with the decision not to make it, as in Maupassant, a fancy-dress ball, with all the dancers masked. The visual impact of the contrast he sought could have been lost in absurdity if the mask itself had let him down.

Georges Annenkov was responsible for the design of costume and makeup. If you want an easy check on the brilliance of his art, just survey the hats in any of the crowd scenes. The particular touch of genius in the construction of the mask is to have fixed a Charlie McCarthy monocle in its eye, a token of dandyism that also betrays the inhuman rigidity of its features (fig. 28). The skin, too, is beardlessly smooth, shining waxy. With a wiry moustache and coal-black curls, the face models that of a youth aspiring to pass for a grown-up. Double dislocation: the fake youth is also a fake adult.

The masked dancer is the pivotal figure but not the main character in the story. The active principals are the doctor (Claude Dauphin) who releases him from the disguise and the wife (Gaby Morlay) who is discovered when curiosity about the wizened creature beneath the mask pushes the medic to escort the old man back to his cramped and shabby apartment. What the doctor learns about the dancer's past as a Lothario, he learns from the wife. She is something like the widow of her husband's obsession, though complicit in his masquerade. Her words tell of the misery she has endured first as the victim of his promiscuities, and lately as the witness and aide to his haunting the sites of others' pleasure. But her actions and her manner tell him something else—of a lifetime of tender and generous devotion to an

Figure 28. The mask

object that we are not allowed to see as worthy, a life of service rewarded only if tenderness and devotion are their own rewards.

The doctor seems to see the wife's lot as preferable to the husband's; she is less driven, more clear-sighted. He laments his own enslavement to a chase that will carry him, unable to act upon the precious lesson he has been offered, back to the exertions of the palais. As the witness to a drama of betrayals and constancy the doctor here foreshadows the role of the third figure in the final tale, that of "The Model" and her artist lover.

Foreshadows but also contrasts. Ophuls always destabilizes the position of his narrator figures. The voice that has come to us from no location enters at last into the body of an elderly bystander, played by Jean Servais, a man wasted by his own cynicism. He claims to know the truth of the relationship between a married couple approaching along a wind-swept promenade. We do not see them, but we see that he cannot take his eyes off them. He sucks on a spit-soaked cigar and begins his account with remarks upon the folly of marriage (for a man) and the unfathomability (to all men) of the actions and motives of women. This is the introduction to a tale about a young man certain that life is unbearable without and, after less than a summer, unbearable with the woman that he has taken as his model and mistress.

The nameless "chronicler" tells how he witnessed the first meeting between the artist, Jean (Daniel Gélin) and the model Josephine (Simone Simon). On this we dissolve to a flashback in which on a sudden whim Jean quits his work and his friend to chase up a steep flight of steps (at the École des Beaux Arts) in a pursuit which is revealed to be that of a young woman, seen only distantly from below and behind. It is an image that is all about Jean's appetite and his abandonment of his friend. It does nothing to particularize the woman and her attractions.

As the tale develops the chronicler plays an active and troubling but never acknowledged part in the events that propel Josephine to disaster. She will remark that he has always loathed her, and this insight gains support from one of Ophuls's boldest devices. In something like a present-tense flashback-within-a-flashback, the voice-over passes to Jean as he contemplates the beauties and graces of his beloved. Matching Jean's words to a run of visual fragments—a gesture, a movement, a pose—Ophuls takes us to share a vision informed rather than blinded by desire. The words of enchantment pronounced here (over scenes unwitnessed by our witness) challenge the surrounding dry commentary on infatuation's quick decay.

At the denouement Jean has abandoned his mistress and gone back to share his crony's garret lodgings. When she bursts in upon the pair, refusing to be paid off like a tart, Jean feigns to concentrate on hammering out a woodcut, defies her threat of suicide. He derides fidelity and offers a bitter parody of marriage vows by demanding to know if she intends to stick to him until he dies. Does he take his cue from his chum? He hands her over to his friend, who mocks the drama of love forsaken and strums the piano all through the final argument, beating out the themes of dance and gaiety to bolster Jean's callous challenge to the woman's pleas. The playing persists as the background to the climactic instance of the film's pattern of ascents and descents, an amazing image which shares in the momentum of Josephine's run upstairs to throw herself through a window and plunge down to crash through a glass roof below.

On the sight and sound of the crash a direct cut raps us back to the narrating present, and now we see the prospect that the chronicler was contemplating at the start. From the deserted end of the wintry beach, Jean—it must be Jean, much older—is walking steadily forward, pushing his crippled wife in a wheelchair. The camera glides with them up to and past, without acknowledging, the erstwhile friend whose voice continues the attempt to account for the stupidity of Jean's marriage (fig. 29).

A simple shot can be just as intricately structured as a complex one. The flatness of the scene and the evenness of the camera's motion reverse the frenzy of the climb and crash. The calm horizontality of the beachscape is echoed in the camera's lateral process, but the groundedness of the action is offset by the background play of kids with kites as well as by the upright shapes of beach chairs, lampposts, and bathing huts. These mark out the stages of the couple's direct and steady progress up to the moment when, beyond sight of the chronicler, Jean stops to remove the mantle from his own shoulders and place it protectively around those of his wife before continuing on their way.

Figure 29. The unacknowledged former friend

Again and finally we see what the storyteller does not. The film's variations on word and image climax here.

The chronicler's vision is of frustration and enslavement. When he recalls his own "intervention," and laments Jean's refusal to pardon it, he seems at the edge of an acknowledgment of the homosexual rivalry that is a subtext of Ophuls's but not Maupassant's treatment of the anecdote. In "The Model" the writer had the invalid chair pushed by a servant, with Jean walking alongside unresponsively. The change that removed the manservant has allowed a physical connection between Jean and his wife, and created an image of the responsibility he now accepts. Then the gesture of care for Josephine's comfort, showing intuitive concern for her warmth, takes us beyond obligation into a zone of more generous feeling.

Another salient change put a thirty-year gap between the framing story and the flashback. Converting the end couple into figures of lost youth and agility heightens the correspondence between the film's first and final episodes. In "The Mask" a long marriage makes the wife the pained but loving servant of her man's obsession. In "The Model" a husband devotes himself through the years to the service of a woman he had loved and wronged. *Amour fou*? Or simply *amour*? Or something else altogether? The film leaves these questions with us. It refuses the insert shot closing in on the couple to show their faces that could so easily have resolved matters: devotion (eye contact, words, smiles) or bondage (none of those). It is Ophuls's way to create possibilities, not to close them down. Keeping his distance, he leaves it open to us to see the wife and the artist as having found rest from strenuous submission to appetite, and a measure of fulfillment in companionship.

A film organized around topics of pleasure culminates in a question about happiness. The chronicler comments acidly that Jean, his life over, has buried himself in his work and so found love, glory, and wealth. (He spares no thought for Josephine and his tongue passes over the word "love," giving it no greater weight than fame or riches.) He asks if that doesn't mean happiness. He finishes with the now famous and almost untranslatable observation that "le bonheur n'est pas gai." The Criterion subtitle offers "There's no joy in happiness," but that really won't do. English offers happiness as an emotion and has difficulty with the sense that the "bonheur" that matters would not be a feeling made visible by merriment, but a condition of the soul too inward for display.

That such a state of being is attainable is nowhere proclaimed. That it is imaginable is brought before us in another breathtaking gesture. As Jean's cry of horror and the sound of shattering glass put an end to the noises of strife—the tinkling piano, the hammer blows on Jean's chisel merged with the clatter of Josephine's heels on the stairs—the soundtrack is calmed and uplifted by the music with which the film began. It is an arrangement of the melody, without words, of Mozart's KV618 *Ave verum corpus*, and it is timed to reach its completion after the fade-out on the receding image of Jean and Josephine and the bleak world that surrounds them. This music, grave and tender, brings a beauty that puts pleasure and the merely pleasurable into relief.

Mozart's is the one composition that has no point of origin within the world of the stories. It frames the whole film and it occurs at the dramatic center of the middle episode. At the start, having made its impression, it gives way to a potpourri of the themes of song and dance that will lace through the stories. These themes can charm and seduce—tribute should be paid to Joe Hayos's fine arrangements—but they can also become insistent to the point of riot. Music can become noise. Movement, which some commentators see as an unqualified value in Ophuls's work, can become frenzy and futile agitation. The enslaved movement of exploited puppets is often put before us. In "The Mask" the energy and athleticism of the quadrille is seen behind later action to have given way to a joyless, near grotesque, routine of bobbing up and down. Josephine's leap into destruction is shared by the camera as horror, not as exhilaration.

Her paralysis at the end is a dreadful price to pay for a marriage, and it can be seen as a savage fate's extension of her role as a model—fixed in place to serve the urges of an artist's image-making. We could also share the chronicler's view that, on the man's side, a lifelong commitment is a dreadful price to pay for a brief romance, or for two broken legs. But in the first story the doctor was hoping to find with marriage a relief from the compulsions of the sex chase. And in this final one Mozart works with the calm that the image has at last discovered to indicate the possibility—not more—of a progress from servitude to service.

Filmography

Dead of Night. Directed by Alberto Cavalcanti, Charles Crichton, Basil Dearden, and Robert Hamer. Eagle-Lion Distributors, 1945.

Encore. Directed by Pat Jackson, Anthony Pelissier, and Harold French. General Film Distributors, 1951.

Intolerance. Directed by D. W. Griffith. Triangle Distributing Corporation, 1916.

O. Henry's Full House. Directed by Henry Hathaway, Howard Hawks, Henry King, Henry Koster, and Jean Negulesco. Twentieth Century Fox, 1952.

Le Plaisir. Directed by Max Ophuls. Columbia Pictures, 1952.

Quartet. Directed by Ken Annakin, Arthur Crabtree, Harold French, and Ralph Smart. General Film Distributors, 1948.

Tales of Manhattan. Directed by Julien Duvivier. Twentieth Century Fox, 1942.

Trio. Directed by Ken Annakin and Harold French. General Film Distributors (UK), Paramount Pictures (US), 1950.

Trois Femmes. Directed by André Michel. Les Films Corona, 1952.

Note

1. Ophuls would certainly have known of, and probably seen, *Quartet* and *Trio*. He could not have seen *Full House*. As inspiration or influence are more welcome than coincidence, it is a sadness for criticism that Ophuls could not have seen *Encore*; that film's final story, like *Le Plaisir*'s, climaxes in a woman's fall from a great height, subjectively filmed. But where Simone Simon in "The Model" ends her days in a wheelchair, Glynis Johns's high diver in "Gigolo and Gigolette" is like Ophuls's Lola Montès; she survives to jump another day.

LE PLAISIR
"La Maison Tellier"

First published in Film Quarterly *63, no. 2 (2009): 66–71. © 2009 by the Regents of the University of California. Published by the University of California Press.*

Set by Maupassant in Fécamp, "La Maison Tellier" is the tale of a brothel, its clients, and its workers. This middle episode of Max Ophuls's *Le Plaisir* is longer and more fully dramatized than the two sketches that come before and after. No doubt the story appealed to Ophuls (and even more to producers impressed by the international career of his carnival of copulation, *La Ronde*) because it promised a space of laughter and bawdry between two somber anecdotes.

Maupassant supplied a witty collision between institutions serving bodily and religious appetites—between pleasure and purity, as the film's narrator puts it—by taking the prostitutes on a weekend trip to a Normandy village to go to church and witness the first communion of the madam's little niece. Perhaps most attractive was the tale's clear and eloquent three-part structure, with the narrative moving from town to country and back again. It allowed Ophuls to place a central triptych within the triptych of *Le Plaisir*.

With his cowriter Jacques Natanson, Ophuls honored Maupassant by holding to the shape of the story and its key events, retaining also many of its minor incidents and allowing us to savor passages of the descriptive prose in the voice-over narration. Of dialogue there was little, and since most of the events were related in general terms the author had supplied few of the specific words, gestures, and images that a performing version demands. The filmmakers had a need—which was also a space—to fill out the detail and bring their own inventions to the drama.

In *Le Plaisir* "La Maison Tellier" becomes both a largely faithful translation of the original and a radical transformation of it. The difference is above all one of tone and viewpoint. Wry humor, and a few belly laughs, are found in both places. But it is as unlikely that a reader was ever moved to tears by the story as it is difficult to imagine any audience being unmoved by the film. Where Maupassant is hard and sarcastic, glad to shock, Ophuls is tactful and humane, his irony deepened by subtlety.

No director has a finer appreciation than Ophuls of the difference between visibility and display. "La Maison Tellier" shows how film, which offers so many ways of bringing a sight or sound to our particular attention, offers as a result tuneable scales from the starkly emphasized to the passingly present. On-screen, since nothing is insignificant, details can work like background sound, informing our vision without demanding to be noticed or read or remembered. Everything we see stands as well in a relationship with what it implies but is unshown. In film after film Ophuls experimented with the play between what is put before our eyes and ears and what remains out of sight or unheard. Most boldly, he worked with the narrated image so as to find a new power of suggestion in the harmonies and tensions between the spoken and the seen.

As the Tellier House is first presented, the film's Voice of Maupassant is almost garrulous in describing its layout and customs; it introduces the personnel one by one, and goes into some detail about Madame Tellier's role, history, and status. But this effusiveness offsets a reticence in other areas, so that the unspoken becomes as telling as what's declared. No reference is made to the primary purpose of the establishment, and the plain words "brothel" and "prostitute" are never pronounced.

Ophuls's camera takes its cue from silences whose discretion hints at a context in social hypocrisy. The image is restricted to the glimpses of the action within the house that it can obtain as it roves across the outside walls and windows. We catch no gestures or spaces with an evidently erotic purpose, and no character is seen at a before or after moment. Leaving explanation to the storyteller, Ophuls counts on our awareness of the basics of the sex trade while he renders the Tellier house with a pervasive air of fellowship and innocence. He creates a tone appropriate to the "fairy tale for grown-ups" that the narrator has promised, but also pictures the incompleteness of our view: the walls, shutters, and blinds that veil the image are continuously before us, whereas we have only intermittent access to the rooms beyond. The camera's impressive mobility lets us see and feel, even if we do not tell ourselves, that we have been both held off and protected from an available penetration.

This exposition is offered in a passage marked as a prologue, and as it ends Mme Tellier (Madeleine Renaud) is one of two characters who have been brought to prominence. The other is the prostitute Rosa (Danielle Darrieux). But whereas the narrator was free with his account of the madam's situation and attitudes, he has fallen into silence since Rosa appeared. We learn nothing of her past and what we gather of her inner self we derive entirely from the way she looks, sounds, acts, and is seen. No comment is made, for instance, about the gestures which complete the prologue. Rosa escorts her client to the bordello's front door, where payment is made and received as a matter of course, without embarrassment. The man is on his way out when Rosa calls him back, using nothing more familiar than his surname. "Monsieur Dupuis," she says, "don't take cold," and she reaches to pull a scarf from his pocket and tie it around his neck, saying a fond "There, now" as she releases him. Their smiles suggest that they recognize the motherliness of the gesture and that they conspire to leave its ironies unprobed.

Rosa's character is developed, and made to matter to us, through passing moments like these where we sense depths ignored by her world and largely by herself. Not one of them will be observed or defined by a narrator who addresses only general and shared circumstance, never the movements of an individual consciousness. The tale began as an account of the brothel's everyday social and economic function but it evolves, with the move to the countryside, to chart the women's experience of a rare departure from routine and of an encounter that could, but does not, transform their lives. While never shedding her identity with the group, Rosa is the woman brought to the center as the one most gravely stirred by the sight of a different world.

There are two climactic moments. In each of them a vital role is played by Joseph Rivet (Jean Gabin). He is Julia Tellier's brother, a carpenter, and it is his only child whose first communion is the occasion for the break from Fécamp's routine. Rivet's relationship with the group is familial rather than erotic. He comes on the scene as a brother and a host, not with the identity of an actual or potential client. As contacts between Rosa and Rivet gather, Ophuls develops their relationship through a balance between invention and restraint: invention in bringing forward brief exchanges whose warmth goes beyond that displayed between Joseph and any other of the Tellier women: restraint in having these moments occur across public space, involving neither touch nor any signal of appetite. What is not done, or is unshown, colors our understanding. We comprehend, without observing, that Rosa never calls Rivet by name. When Joseph bids his guest goodnight after directing her toward her bedroom, it is with no thought that he might follow her there. He smiles as he heads off alone in the opposite direction, happy with just that degree of contact. The film bars a too-readily-available reaction, that this is a missed opportunity.

That, then, is the background against which we witness Rivet's involvement in the crisis that overtakes Rosa in church on the following day. During the service she breaks down in tears. Her emotions infect her fellows and spread through the whole congregation. The power of the scene depends upon playing reticence against profusion and density of detail. The approach to the church and the negotiation of seating arrangements within are delightfully charted. But all the fuss subsides, and detailed depiction ceases once the little communicants have paraded down the aisle. While the pacing becomes reverential, we are given no more than an impression of the service. None of the key moments in the ritual is set before us. No word, no sight, sound, or occasion, is singled out as the cause of Rosa's tears, or our own.

Although he has plenty to say about the public aspects of the event, the storyteller is silent about Rosa. Where Maupassant's text is expansive about her thoughts and feelings, the film avoids the limiting clarity of what can be named. Where Maupassant put explanation, Ophuls puts music. Strings take over from the choir with the sacred strains of Mozart's *Ave verum corpus* but this harmony comes from nowhere within the space of the church. The music is vital to the feeling of the scene. It offers an emotional understanding but, wordless, it deepens the mystery of the events.

As the contagion spreads there are people weeping all around and on either side of him, but Rivet singles out Rosa for an attempt at comfort, as if he senses a sorrow uniquely deep. That choice, and the need that drives it, are dramatized by his having to fumble along the pew as quietly as he can manage, changing places to sit next to Rosa and whisper unavailingly that she should not be crying. His sympathy seems the more genuine and tender because it does not come in a context of flirtation or courtship.

But what follows makes an odd and uncomfortable connection between protective compassion and brute desire. There is an ellipse to postcommunion celebrations back at the Rivet house, where Joseph is garrulous with drink. The moment of Rosa's passion is left completely behind. While the women are preparing themselves for departure, Rivet stumbles at speed toward Rosa's room and makes—behind its closed door—an advance of some kind. It is repelled by the women as a squad. Their rebukes tell us that the approach was more undignified than alarming; evidently it involved the removal of Joseph's waistcoat. Rosa is out of sight and the timing is such that we are not invited, while we laugh, to imagine her reaction. Once Joseph's wagon is on its way back toward the railway station the incident seems to have been forgotten.

We have almost forgotten it ourselves when the women interrupt the journey to spend a few minutes picking wildflowers in a laneside meadow. Mozart has been left behind long since. Scattered about the field, the women are in chorus with the popular song whose tune harks back to the life of the brothel and whose words put the delights of the body, and regret for their passing, in defiance of religious obligation.

In what follows, the stillness of the camera is just as telling as its mobility elsewhere. Nearest, but held off from us by a foreground of greenery, are Rivet and Rosa. She is doing the same as her more distantly seen companions, gathering flowers and singing. Joseph is sitting to the right of her, only a couple of feet away. How this nearness came about, we were not shown. If Joseph sought it, Rosa is doing nothing to escape it. Adding to her collection of blooms, she bobs up and down, turns this way and that, but stays close to him. Joseph, a dark figure fixed low in the frame, is not hearing the song. His few movements are small and slow. He fiddles, with a straw, with his hat, with a flower, and darts glances at Rosa while her eyes are turned away. When at last speech comes to him—gentle, hesitant—its tone freezes Rosa's movement and her song, leaving her bowed as she grasps the seriousness of his mood.

Joseph finds the words to beg Rosa's pardon. Under an open sky, with the others in view though removed from earshot, he summons a confessional intimacy to seek an absolution that is Rosa's alone to grant (fig. 30). He wants her to know that only the drink made him forget himself back there. His posture speaks his mind: he is looking up to her, humbled. For us, his misdemeanor was a laughing matter, and Rosa has not acted as if anything unusual was involved. His apology pierces her, chokes her voice. She can manage only a nod to set him at ease. Then she turns away, whispering a single word. She thanks him.

Gratitude lies far outside anything Joseph looked for. But we have no time to work through the meanings of Rosa's response. We have just felt the depth of it when Rosa's moment—one that needed to be dwelt upon—is swept

Figure 30. Rosa and Joseph in the field

away. The real world breaks in, the world whose urgencies leave little room for what is important. Madame Tellier recalls everyone to roles, routines, and commerce. More than ever the schoolmarm, she rushes the whole flock back to the cart so as not to risk missing the afternoon train. The break is enforced by a cut from the whispering stillness of Rivet and Rosa to a panning shot that shares the shrill momentum of Julia's stride down the hillside. What goes unmarked, here as elsewhere, is Rosa's reentering the group. When next seen she is simply one of the half-dozen women who make up a cartful.

Rosa's encounters—with Joseph, with solitude, with her god, with herself—stir feelings that ought surely to have consequence in the world. They should change something. But Rosa like everyone else will catch the 3.55, leaving behind the countryside, the church and Rivet. No other possibility is so much as glimpsed. When Joseph singles her out for a special farewell, any chance that they may meet again depends upon his making a visit to the brothel and finding her back at work there.

The episode of the Tellier women's country visit ends here, but not with the women. The climax of what has become Rosa's tale is played on Joseph Rivet. In the imagery of departure Ophuls lets us know how strong a feeling can be that brings no alteration to the course of people's lives. The camera tracks Rivet as he runs through fields beside the train until he reaches a gap in the hedge where he may call a last "À bientôt, Madame Rosa." He stares after the train as it gathers speed and disappears from view, until he is left waving his hat at just the last wisp of its white steam dissolving in the sunlight. The shot—a technician's nightmare and a viewer's wonder—continues to trace Rivet in his new solitude, walking off with just the slope of the terrain to propel his gait.

In a remarkable displacement all the emotion that has built up across Rosa's encounters is released in a long anticlimax, an extended treatment of Rivet's saddened journey back toward his daily life. No close-ups, no commentary, only a gentle panning shot, and a wistful reprise of Rosa's tune, as the horse and cart carry his sagging figure into the distance back along the tree-lined lane. Closing the country interlude, this passage answers the one at the start that brought the women all excited on the train from Fécamp; it stands in, then, for scenes of their return. Its mood is of loss, and regret for promise unfulfilled, though the days in the country, we knew, were just an excursion. There was never a likely future for Rosa and Rivet. Through the picture of these imagined lives, Ophuls grieves with us that the world is as it is.

The final sequence plunges us back into night and the town. Words come easily now. The film smiles indulgently, implicating itself in delight and deceit as the brothel's regulars celebrate the women's return. Champagne is ordered. Madame Tellier—Joseph's sister—is swept up in the mood. She concedes a reduction in price, and orders flowers everywhere. In an image of abandon, the barman straddles above the front door and kicks it open for each new arrival. He is up there to place a floral wreath around the outside lantern whose brightness declares the resumption of normal services.

The story of the whorehouse and its role in society was promised to bring a mood of gaiety. It cannot find its end in melodrama or tragedy, not even in pathos. So a humming chorus on the soundtrack voices a rising excitement. A raucous crescendo in the music of the dance refuses all recognition to the bitterness of human potential wasted and ignored. Only an edge of frenzy in the celebration could worry us about what we know but are not seeing.

The more seductive the jollity of these images, the stronger the paradox of merriment as the endnote and the successor to Rivet's lonely moments. Coming back to the Tellier House we come back to the outside view, manifestly partial, incomplete. The formal repetition embraces the lack of change, and brings to climax the mode of ironic euphemism that has prevailed ever since the storyteller promised us a fairy tale and introduced Mme Tellier's with elaborate reticence as an establishment to be named only as a "house." Where Rivet's departure was marked with sorrow, the film enacts Rosa's fate by losing her from view. She is neither heard from nor mentioned again, and she is glimpsed just enough to affirm that she is back at work—once more dancing, cigarette in mouth, with M Dupuis. The clients and the madam carry all the prominent action. Rosa is simply there, not brought forward as she was at the start, not brought forward now like her companions or even the barman, and for all we can tell swept up as much as the others, and as much as we are in the "gale of naive and careless joy" that blows through the company. It was generous of Ophuls, as well as brilliant, to wrap the sadness of this outcome in a scene of riot and revel. We are allowed, if we will, to mistake gaiety for happiness.

Filmography

Le Plaisir. Directed by Max Ophuls. Columbia Pictures, 1952.

SCARLET, NO EMPRESS

First published in Film Quarterly *65, no. 2 (2011): 28–31. © 2011 by the Regents of the University of California. Published by the University of California Press.*

Alongside the wonders of the film itself, Criterion's edition of the restored *Lola Montès* (1955) offers unusually rewarding extras. They include the 1965 edition of *Cinéastes de notre temps* from French television, in which Martine Carol is one of the many technicians and actors to pay tribute to Ophuls, who died in 1957. She recalls a director whose brilliance and charm had helped her out in the starring role, which was "not really a part for me," and who had enabled her to extend herself beyond anything she had previously attempted. Her warmth, ten years after the event, is all the more remarkable because the film's reception had been just as disastrous for her as it was for its creator. Fifty years on, the reassessment of *Lola Montès* as a manifest of the genius of Ophuls has not been, and I think could not be, echoed in acclaim for a performance that seldom rises much above—and does not consistently reach—adequacy. The critical question is how far its character and shortcomings are absorbed into the themes and textures of the movie, how far they contribute to or detract from its achievement.

Carol's generosity is touching. As it testifies to the intimacy of the collaboration between director and star it adds vitally to our understanding of the picture's fraught production history. Other witnesses fill out the portrait of a filmmaker without rest or mercy in the search for the essential detail that could inflect the atmosphere, hence significance, of a scene or a moment. They add to the record assembled by the late Claude Beylie in his treasurable 1963 monograph on Ophuls. There, Jean Valère, an assistant on *Le Plaisir*

(1952), remembered him as "as exceptional improviser and, for all that, one who left nothing to chance.... It was extremely difficult to predict what out of the way prop he was going to send me to find at the very last moment—some unexpected something that might be invisible in the shot, or even set down yards away from the camera, but that found its place wonderfully in the ensemble."

The vitality of detail was a matter on which Ophuls himself was eloquent, detail in performance and detail in the image, the detail of persons through casting and the detail of objects through selection and design. Some of this could be, had to be, planned ahead and was only enhanced in the frenzy of improvisation. Take as an instance Lola's coach. It is her only home and it is her assertion, as much as the director's image, of her demand for freedom. She claims mobility on her own terms. As we first see it the coach supports her resolve always to be able to choose when to end a love affair, to leave rather than to be left. It is bedded into a main theme and strategy of the movie whereby the circus show's gaudy celebration of Lola's triumphs is set in contrast with enacted fragments of memory returning time after time to the act of moving on, to endings, failures, and losses.

The theme is boldly presented in a first sketch that defies chronology and expectation to show the composer Franz Liszt (Will Quadflieg) and the mature, already notorious Lola negotiating the end of their liaison. Our first glimpse, or hallucination, of reality brings an extended scene of farewell. Regret for the passing of appetite and obsession is in contest with impatience to be freed from the tedium of a deadlocked affair whose early ecstasies are now awkward to recall. Liszt and Lola are traveling through Italy in the musician's sumptuously furnished carriage. He raises the prospect of separation by twice going to the window to observe, without occasion to doubt, that their progress is distantly trailed by Lola's much more modest vehicle, drawn by a pair of horses as against his own team of four.

Thereafter the coach makes occasional appearances in the flashback scenes. Its color declares Lola's intention never to go unnoticed, but, cramped and shabby, the transport also betrays the reality of her status as showgirl-courtesan and the uncertainty of her earning power. The coach is unseen for long stretches of time, the better to emphasize its primary quality: constant readiness and availability. Thus it carries Lola into Bavaria and is with her for her entry into Munich, but it is out of sight throughout her romance with the king. Ludwig (Anton Walbrook) builds her a palace in his attempt to provide a gilded cage, a home without wheels, that will hold her in place at his side. But when revolution threatens and the two of them must abandon their pretense of domesticity, the coach can be brought out of store dust-caked but good for a quick getaway.

The coach's aspect as something that is always there in support of Lola's needs and choices has its human counterparts in the coach driver, Maurice (Henri Guisol) and Lola's maid, Joséphine. They are husband and wife. The role of Joséphine is played by the late Paulette Dubost, whose place in posterity is guaranteed by her performance as the maid, Lisette, in Renoir's *La Règle du jeu* (*The Rules of the Game*, 1939). Ophuls had already worked with her in 1951 when he cast her as one of the prostitutes in "La Maison Tellier," the episode of his *Le Plaisir* which pays clear tribute to the Renoir of *Partie de campagne* (1936). Dubost's role alongside Martine Carol is truly a "supporting part," and in a double sense.

In the first place Ophuls relied on Dubost's support, even when she was not required as Joséphine. She was called to the set on days when no scene of hers was scheduled because the director found her, amid the pressures and turmoil of the shoot, a reassuring presence. She reflected on this in her autobiography and to Beylie: "With others one would have rebelled and slammed the door in their face. It has to be that it was impossible with Ophuls, because nobody ever did it.... He had such charm.... You could not refuse him anything."

In the more obvious sense Joséphine is a supporting role because the character is presented as part of the furniture of Lola's life. She is one of those props of which Valère spoke, "set down yards away from the camera... that found its place wonderfully in the ensemble." On her first appearance neither the camera nor the screenplay gives her an introduction. She is just one element in a traveling long shot as Liszt's coach arrives at a countryside inn in Italy. Dressed for dullness all in brown, she is standing beside the driver and straining to see back the way they have come (fig. 31). The walls of the inn are much more colorful than Dubost's costume. When the coach slows to a

Figure 31. Josephine's first appearance

halt she has been all but lost to sight. On the cut Liszt, in the foreground, helps Lola down. Hardly visible in the background his driver performs the same service for the woman who will be named as Joséphine when Lola calls then gives her some instructions withheld from us as from Liszt. We do not hear the maid's responses—her voicelessness is a further reduction of presence—but she is evidently obeying her mistress's command when she runs back to greet Lola's carriage and speak to its driver.

Their embrace tells us that Joséphine and Maurice are a couple. Their gestures and talk give us the flavor of their marriage. They are happy to take one another, and this reunion, for granted. Their undemonstrative pleasure at being together again is a contrast (that we are not urged to notice) with the reflections on passing fancy in Lola's scenes with Liszt. After this, Joséphine is always on hand, as concerned for and constant with Lola as she is with her husband.

So much is apparent on the return from flashback to the circus present. Backstage, while the ringmaster (Peter Ustinov) spins his lies about Lola's happy childhood, Joséphine is in attendance with Maurice, dispensing medicine and readying Lola for her return to the ring. Here as elsewhere Dubost often has her back to the camera and is ignored by the lighting. Through all the changes of Lola's life we never have a scene in which Joséphine decides whether to continue in her service. At the forced end of the Ludwig idyll, for instance, Joséphine has evidently followed her mistress across the Atlantic, acquiescing in Lola's submission to the American freak show. The decision to do so does not enter into the drama. It is as if no decision was involved. Lola did not have to ask—or so we might conclude if we gave the matter any thought at all.

Joséphine is a character without a story, an unpresented presence—"bien effacé," in Dubost's words (documented by Beylie). The film gives her no biography. We do not learn how or when she entered Lola's service, for example, or how she met and married Maurice. Though a vital support to Lola's career, sharing good times and bad, she goes without mention in the ringmaster's narration and is seen by us only in the slipstream of scandal, seduction, and display. But seen by us enough to observe how she is relied upon and ignored. It is her job to be unobtrusive. The temptation for the actress playing her is to act unobtrusiveness, to solicit our attention to busy gestures in the background. Dubost is better than that, better directed, more intelligent and more accomplished, so less visible.

Like the servant John played by Art Smith in *Letter from an Unknown Woman* (1948), she "makes life possible" for the figures who structure the story. And in her thematic relevance to Lola's life of spectacle in the world and in the circus, she recalls a living prop in another Ophuls work, the greyhound Harras in *La Ronde* (1950). That movie is a suite of episodes, each of which is a variation on the pursuit of sexual gratification, none of which is complete until penetration is achieved. It is all about coming and going. The last sequences of its carnival of lust and infidelity concern the spaced-out aristocrat so handsomely embodied by Gérard Philipe. Everywhere he goes he takes his dog. Everywhere he goes Harras settles down to wait for him, and when the latest stupidity is over, Harras follows. The greyhound was an invention, nowhere to be found in Arthur Schnitzler's original theater piece, and only seen—never remarked upon—in the film. As elegant as the count, almost an extension of the count's fine wardrobe, Harras shows a constancy that stands in final, quiet contrast with the fickleness of the humans.

Constancy and service are prime values for Ophuls, an underscore to the self-seeking betrayals, delusions, and lusts so often in the foreground. On several occasions, at least one in *Lola Montès*, care for another's warmth is the dramatic emblem of these ideals. In 1953 Ophuls wrote of his work in Europe and Hollywood as "a kind of international service for poets and literature" (n.p.). His life was the more difficult on account of his feeling duty-bound to serve the audience by offering the best that his talent could create. In the case of *Lola Montès* that meant constructing the film as a repudiation, scene by scene, of the saucy bodice-ripper that his producers had bargained for.

It meant that our first view of the scandalous Lola would be as a frail mannequin wheeled here and there to cater to the fantasies of a prurient crowd, and that the first insight into Lola's history would present not a romantic conquest and not the melodrama of love turned to hatred, but sexual desire so wilted that Lola needs to solicit *un bel adieu* to check whether her techniques of seduction still have effect. (The seduction then exposes not a millimeter of Lola's skin, but involves only an invitation to make-believe and the gentle displacement of Liszt's top hat, cane, and cravat.)

The movie's end, similarly, is in defiance of the blockbuster convention that sends the audience out on a loud assertion of the magnificence it has witnessed. Ophuls contrives a dying fall with a bronchial hurdy-gurdy for accompaniment as the camera draws back, back, and back from a caged Lola, dressed in sackcloth to allow the loan of her hands at a dollar a kiss to the stream of male punters buying themselves an illusion of stage-door homage. Lola is ambiguously a goddess in her temple and a fallen woman in the stocks. The cage completes the ringmaster's equation of her with a dangerous beast. In design and color the cage mimics her coach to relate her place in the menagerie to her quest for a life of mobility and self-determination (fig. 32).

Figure 32. Lola in the cage

"The countess has chosen," the ringmaster declared, having manipulated her into the death-seeking leap without which his show would lack a climax. But the claim refers us back to their first meeting, when she rejected his offer of a circus contract and boasted of acting always as she pleased. He responded with a parable from the ring, the absurdity of which poured scorn on her assertion of free choice. He trained an elephant, he said, to play the piano: "Nowadays it has a passion for music." Does he finally recognize that the allegory has meaning for himself? He stands alongside Lola's cage, his whip at the ready, pimping out the price of her degradation—a mere dollar for "an unforgettable souvenir." The concern to realize every last cent of Lola's market value holds him in place and is at odds with the love he avows. When he murmurs that he was terrified by the jump and could not live without her, we have no reason to doubt him.

The whip is the emblem of the ringmaster's claim to be in control of the show and the starkest token of the abusiveness that haunts his desire and his devotion. The last words we hear are the litany of his abject commerce ("One dollar, that's nothing. . . . You'll never miss it. . . . One dollar . . ."). We might think that no relationship escapes this corruption. We would have failed to see how Joséphine's presence behind Lola and the ringmaster finds its place in the ensemble.

Joséphine is the antiringmaster. Her first reaction to this figure, announcing him to Lola back on the Riviera, was "He's weird. He gives me the creeps." Those were the most surprising, therefore arresting, words anywhere in her dialogue. Now at the end, not seeking the public eye or ear, abjuring a starring role, Joséphine is coming and going in attendance upon Lola. The ringmaster gives her Lola's coffee cup to deal with. We cannot miss her presence but we are not told to think about it. We must regard it as normal—as normal as prostitution, exploitation, bad faith, vanity, and so forth. Joséphine's devotion, longer-lasting than the nameless ringmaster's, is not compromised for us by avarice and contorted desire. There is nothing that she wants to seem. While it cannot be without an economic aspect, her form of service is untainted by villainy and nothing like an enslavement. Relatively speaking, in an endlessly corrupted world, it has nobility.

This unexpected something may not be highly visible in the shot but it balances the irony, anger, and sadness of the ending and holds tragedy back from despair. My title wanted to point up Ophuls's debt to Josef von Sternberg. But *The Scarlet Empress* (1934) ends with the triumph of monstrosity bitterly celebrated. Joséphine, as played by Paulette Dubost, is a key element in the unique and more humane mixture of tones on which *Lola Montès* so movingly fades away.

Ophuls via Beylie: "Details, details, details! The most insignificant, the least observed of them are often the most evocative, characteristic and even decisive."

Works Cited

Beylie, Claude. *Max Ophuls*. Paris: Editions Seghers, 1963.
Ophüls, Max. "Dichter und Film." *Theater und Zeit: Monatsblätter der Städtischen Bühnen Wuppertal-Solingen* 1, no. 2 (1953): n.p.

Filmography

Letter from an Unknown Woman. Directed by Max Ophuls. Universal-International, 1948.
Lola Montès. Directed by Max Ophuls. Gamma Films, 1955.
Partie de campagne. Directed by Jean Renoir. Panthéon Productions, 1936.
Le Plaisir. Directed by Max Ophuls. Columbia Pictures, 1952.
La Règle du jeu (*The Rules of the Game*). Directed by Jean Renoir. Gaumont, 1939.
La Ronde. Directed by Max Ophuls. Films Sacha Gordine/Janus Films, 1950.
The Scarlet Empress. Directed by Josef von Sternberg. Paramount Pictures, 1934.

YOU ONLY LIVE ONCE

First published in Movie: A Journal of Film Criticism, *no. 3 (January 2012): 12–21. https://warwick.ac.uk/fac/arts/film/movie/contents/you_only_live_ once_final_3.pdf (accessed June 1, 2020).*

The criminal careers of Clyde Barrow and Bonnie Parker ended in a police ambush in 1934. *You Only Live Once* (1937) is a version of their story. Screenwriters Graham Baker and Gene Towne had already derived one script from this material in 1935, an earlier Walter Wanger production with Sylvia Sidney in the lead as *Mary Burns, Fugitive.* Lang is known to have directed the revision of their first screenplay ("Three Time Loser") for *You Only Live Once*, so he was very possibly responsible for its debt to Ferenc Molnar's play *Liliom*, which he had filmed in France with Charles Boyer in 1933. However Molnar's work would have been extremely well known in Hollywood. Its first Budapest production in 1909 had been poorly received, but since then the play as well as its author had built a great, entirely deserved, international reputation. Success on Broadway in 1920 led to a Hollywood version directed for Fox by Frank Borzage ten years later. The movie that Lang made in France is very remarkable and insufficiently known. It remained, as Patrick McGilligan reports (1997, 201), one of Lang's own favorites. What *Liliom* seems to feed into the outlaw lovers story is a viewpoint that inflects it as the tale of a weak, corrupted man confused by love, struggling and mainly failing to become worthy of the faith of a steadfast woman. Through *You Only Live Once* this theme comes to inform a vital strand of film noir whose finest instance may be [Nicholas] Ray's *They Live by Night* (1948).

Anyone who wants to write usefully about *You Only Live Once* has to build on the work of George M. Wilson. A chapter in *Narration in Light* makes a systematic presentation of the movie's narrative strategies, and a detailed reading of key images (1986, 16–38). Wilson shows how Lang's picture is designed to educate its viewers in the manipulability of the image, and to demonstrate the power of the film sequence to deceive us by obscuring key points in its story and by soliciting preferred readings that the content of the images may not in fact guarantee. The achievement that Wilson uncovers is the more remarkable in that it occurs not in an illustrated lecture but in a fiction movie, one that works to powerful effect within its genre of social protest melodrama.

Wilson's essay opened my eyes to *You Only Live Once*, a movie that I had previously found opaque because, apart from its evident social project, I had not seen a purpose in its meticulous design beyond that of giving power and plausibility to a noticeably contrived tale. In what follows I take for granted the main lines of Wilson's argument in order to develop some remarks on Lang's mise-en-scène in two representative sequences.

I start with the honeymoon episode. One odd feature seems to have passed unremarked. In this rightly celebrated passage a great deal of romantic pathos is generated around the supposed obedience of frogs to ideals of heterosexual monogamy. The husband Eddie Taylor (Henry Fonda) draws his bride, Joan (Sylvia Sidney), into a fantasy of fidelity whereby a frog pair will stay together for life. "When one dies the other dies," he tells her. She reads the image that this makes for her not in the Darby-and-Joan terms of a couple growing old together but in the perspective of doomed young love "like Romeo and Juliet." When she asks how he has come to be an expert on frogs Eddie replies, "I've always known that. I thought everybody did" (fig. 33).

Well, what everybody knows about frogs, or should know, is that their mating sees the nearest thing in nature to a gang bang. At the season's prompt they assemble at the ponds where successful males clamber wetly aboard the available females to fertilize the spawn. They then go their separate ways and have no further contact either with their mates or with the eggs/tadpoles/froglets that develop from their coupling.

Figure 33. "Like Romeo and Juliet"

Lang's film elaborates the frog reference aurally as well as visually—through the croaking that makes Eddie and Joan hear them as crooners. Imagination is here taking freedom to roam transformatively over any of the world's ordinary phenomena, touching them with a beauty soft-focused by tears. Perhaps Eddie is more knowingly exploiting this freedom than Joan. After all, his tale of frog fidelity follows on from his first frog story, and Joan's warm response to it. Eddie is a convict just released from his third stretch in jail. The sight of the frogs draws from him, if it does not suggest to him, a backstory where his descent into criminality began with a gallant attempt to prevent cruelty to the croaky critters:

> When I was a kid we used to catch them in the sewer-drains. . . . I got my first rap protecting a frog's life. It's the truth! I caught a kid [torturing] a frog once. I beat him up and his mother sent me to reform school.

Directors and Movies • 461

A detached listener might suppose that it would have taken a good deal more than one blacked eye to get the young Eddie locked up. But Joan is too full of sympathy and desire to probe the darker aspects of his tale. She does not hear its hints that Eddie leans toward both violence and self-justification. She accepts Eddie's attitude along with his account of the facts, just as she will accept and embellish his information about star-crossed amphibians. Eddie's "It's the truth" here anticipates "I thought everybody knew that"; both claims have the potential to alert us to other possibilities.

But only the potential. Eddie may be telling the truth in the first instance. In the second he could simply be mistaken. It is not unusual for people to be convinced by pure nonsense. Nothing either confirms or contradicts Eddie's hard-luck story, but the film has not put us in a mood to ask ourselves whether he is being truthful or merely plausible. *You Only Live Once* is meticulously constructed to make us prefer the most indulgent view of Joan and Eddie, while it also puts in plain sight much detail that could carry us in a different direction. For instance, when Joan meets Eddie at the jail, she is prompted to ask if he had not believed her promises to be there to greet his release. Eddie replies, "I do now," speaking the words with joyful warmth. Joan is reassured and the moment is lost in the swirl of succeeding action. One has to be very sharp to catch that "I do now" is an alternative form for "That's right. I did not believe you." Keeping sharp would involve reading against the dominant tones of the scene.

Similarly here. So much supports an emotional investment in—particularly—Joan's happiness. We are guided this way by narrative structure, by genre, by performance and star-power, by aspects of visual style and, most blatantly, by a musical score that follows Tchaikovsky to evoke the beauty of sadness and the sadness of beauty. This film about prejudiced vision, and its consequences in action, works hard to prejudice its viewers in favor of the newlyweds. They are young, attractive, and in love. In these respects the film makes them unique. It offsets them against a drab world in which the reigning passions are greed and self-righteousness; and it makes them the victims of that world.

The film's time process colludes in the victimization. The honeymoon scene has barely started before we are taken away from Joan and Eddie to meet the proprietors of the Valley Tavern. All the earnest talk of love and fidelity will be heard under the shadow of the knowledge that Hester Parmenter (Margaret Hamilton) has challenged her husband, Ethan (Chic Sale), to find the mug shot of Eddie that he is convinced he has seen somewhere in his stockpile of true crime magazines. "I'll find it," Ethan has vowed, "if I have to sit up all night." The success of his mission will provide the movie's first instance of the fatality of Eddie's image.

When Ethan speaks of his grim pursuit as his way of spending the night we can hardly fail to register the contrast with a honeymooning couple who have waited three years to be together. Lang does everything to make the differences between the two couples work in favor of the threatened lovers. Their softly confiding voices bracket a scene where the Parmenters shout their hostilities in the language and tones of a backwoods Punch and Judy. In the role of Hester, Margaret Hamilton could almost be reading for her most celebrated appearance as Miss Gulch/the Wicked Witch in *The Wizard of Oz* (1939). She is dressed in widow's black, with her hair lying flat on her head to heighten the severity of her features. Her looks are designed to ward off tender words and intimate approaches. They suggest a strategy to keep Ethan well away on his side of the room, his side of the bed. But then, looking at Ethan, we can see Hester's point. He is servile. His thin frame is dowdily dressed in a shrunken waistcoat and saggy cardigan as if he seeks a cheap escape from chill. A bow tie droops from his neck like the souvenir of a long-defeated aspiration to style.

The first words we hear from him are "You know, Hester, I've seen that fellow's face somewhere before—and I don't like it." (The face in question is Henry Fonda's.) To give emphasis to his declaration Ethan holds aloft the match that he has just struck on the seat of his pants, tightening the trouser fabric by jerking up his right knee as if to fire off a fart. His wife glowers fixedly, making no reaction to these gestures; she seems wearily familiar with such displays and not at all entertained by them. "Land of pity, Ethan . . ." she replies, getting in a reference to neglected chores in the manner of an exasperated grandmother. She is sitting upright in an armchair with an unyielding wooden frame and she interrupts her reproof to attend to an itching ankle. She rubs at it with the heel of the other foot. These gestures of Hester's and Ethan's entail contact only with their own bodies. Through them the actors construct a version of intimacy far removed from Joan and Eddie's. It is the intimacy of people who know each other all too well and who no longer wish or think to present themselves to one another with the decorum that they observe in public. There's more of the same gross physicality when Ethan lets his match fall to the parlor floor and sticks his unlit cheroot back in his mouth as a tacky comforter.

Lang's images give a graphic extension to the aspects of caricature in the performances. The space is hard edged, cramped, and comfortless. There are none of the softening curves of flower and leaf so effective in the images of Joan and Eddie. The stiff lines of the decor are stressed by hard lighting that casts a grotesque shadow of Hester's profile onto the wall beside her. After an opening image that shows them as far apart as the space permits, Ethan and Hester are seen in separate shots or heard in voice-over as the camera presents first the shelves stacked with back numbers of Ethan's favorite reading, and finally the magazine pages turning under his determined inspection.

It is from this image that the film dissolves back to Joan and Eddie. The turning pages reinforce Ethan's "up all night" as a projection forward into the time of the lovers' conversation. Throughout this Joan and Eddie are always in the same frame and always close when not touching. Their talk fills in the background to their relationship, but it does so entirely in terms of Joan's experience and feelings. So it glides over, even as it states, the awkward fact that Eddie's third crime was committed after Joan had become his sweetheart. At its end Eddie sweeps Joan into his arms and carries her up the steps toward their room.

From this action, with its across-the-threshold implication, a dissolve returns us to the pages of Ethan's magazine, open and stilled under the weight of a reading glass. The clearest picture in a four-convict spread is a mug shot of Eddie Taylor. This dissolves to a shot that looks down on the Parmenters and pans with them as they climb the stairs to confront the honeymooners. Ethan has loosened his tie and Hester is now wearing, over a nightdress, what looks like a man's dressing gown. Eddie's criminal record, represented photographically, has supplied the bridge between Joan and Eddie's ascent to the wedding chamber and an ascent that aims at their ejection.

The construction of the sequence is characteristic of Lang's method in the alternation of detailed realization with ellipsis. Typically the elided material is resumed in a single, concentrated image. So the whole process between Eddie's arrest for murder, his trial, his conviction, and the judge's sentence will be compressed into one vignette in the editorial room of a newspaper where the verdict is awaited. Lang retains the option of leaving gaps in the story unfilled; for example, as Eddie's misfortunes pile up, the movie will keep a veil over the circumstances of his reunion with Monk, an old partner in crime. In the Valley Tavern sequence the static magazine image resumes the lengthy fulfillment of Ethan's quest, adding via the reading glass a mocking reflection on his self-image as Sherlock Holmes. The following dissolve covers Ethan's rousing Hester from her bed and their joint decision to expel their guests.

Compressed in one way, the sequence is also extended in another. There was no need to introduce the Parmenters as an interruption of the foreplay between Eddie and Joan. The honeymoon conversation could simply have been completed before we were taken to witness events in the parlor. But this tidier continuity would have sacrificed the menace projected over Joan and Eddie's love scene, and it would have weakened the contrasts not only between the two couples but also between the two warring modes of romance and grotesque comedy.

Going back and forth between the Taylors and the Parmenters constructs a parallel that foregrounds contrast but conceals a comparison. Against Joan's enraptured prospect of lifelong devotion, Ethan and Hester present a bitter portrait of what may become of marriages. Locked together, clearly, till death do them part, the pair are able to make contact only in warfare that vents Hester's contempt and affirms Ethan's servility. This first scene of the world's persecution of Joan and Eddie did not demand a husband and wife as the antagonists. The field was free for the film to characterize the Valley Tavern's management. By opting for a couple embittered by a stale marriage *You Only Live Once* makes the intimacy of Eddie and Joan the more precious but also the less secure.

The shot where Eddie carries Joan up the outside staircase is interrupted by an image of two frogs apparently staring up at them from the surface of the pond below. Where the frogs have become the Taylors' emblem of ecstatic fidelity, this pair pose a resemblance rather to Ethan and Hester. Their beady stare has much more in common with a glare of accusation than with the tender lovers' glances. The insert coincides with a turn in the music, from romance to menace, that supports this alternative response.

At the start of the honeymoon sequence, before we discovered Joan and Eddie taking the night air, Lang presented three more of the signpost images that summarize vital developments. He dissolved from a scene at the prison gates to the hotel sign for the Valley Tavern, through the open pages of the hotel register signed for "Mr. and Mrs. Edward Taylor," to a marriage license fondly displayed in a frame of foliage and roses. (No doubt the censors wanted everything clear and legitimate.) These images fill in for another large ellipsis but they do much more than the routine work of exposition.

The hanging sign is backlit—by clouded moonlight, it's implied. It appears as a silhouette that stresses the two-dimensional aspect of its pressed-metal emblem. The sign is held within a hard iron frame whose rigid lines are decorated by glistening dew and a leafy surround. Beside and below the words "Valley Tavern"—displayed in ornamented lettering—is represented a jolly scene of olde-tyme travel, a stagecoach drawn by a team of horses. At the left, the outline of a tree certifies the setting as away from town. A top-hatted driver and footman complete a nostalgically Dickensian scene—one suitable for, if not derived from, a greeting card. Since the sign is as much as we see of the hotel's exterior, the scene that follows is played in an uncertain, abstracted, space. All we can know is that the place is not a bit like the one that the name and the sign evoke.

The image from the sign is repeated at the top of the hotel register in the next shot. The Valley Tavern has been self-consciously branded as a retreat from such realities of the contemporary world as motor transport—or convicts and penal systems, or gutter journalism. What the sign does for a guesthouse has a lot in common with what Joan has done to the marriage license by adorning a civil document as a shrine to true love. The pretty fantasies are brought together in Eddie's first remark: "What a nest for a honeymoon," he says dreamily.

In a response whose double edge Eddie cannot ignore, Joan says that she had three years to seek out such a nest. The idealization evident in the hotel sign is what has drawn the lovers to this place, but it is also what will get them expelled from it, since Ethan and Hester prove determined not to allow unacceptable realities to upset the vision. Under the pressure of Lang's mise-en-scène, Ethan's self-righteous vow that "no jail-bird's going to spend the night in Valley Tavern" gains new meaning. The casting out of Joan and Eddie becomes a measure in defense of the glamorized image that first brought them there.

The diagrammatic shots that begin the honeymoon scene echo those at the start of the film. Here, too, we have a sequence of three static images; they take us from an establishing shot of a Hall of Justice building, through to an angle from a corridor onto the closed door of the Public Defender's office, and on through to a close view onto a desktop on which are arranged two piles of apples modeled as matching pyramids. The journey from outside to inside is moderated by no human agency. Lang refuses the convention whereby a succession of this kind could be measured and bridged by having the shots trace the progress of a messenger, or newspaper boy, or mailman. The disembodied sense of the images is the stronger on account of the absence of sound from the first of them; out in the city street we hear no trace of traffic on highway or sidewalk, no shriek or murmur of urban life. One door of the Hall of Justice stands a little ajar, and that is the sole immediate trace of human activity. The image is completely void of people and motion.

These abstractions mean that the film begins by displaying its control over the sequence of information. It is as much the movie's choice to bring in a voice over the "Public Defender" sign, before we can identify its source, as it is to present a daylight street image in complete silence. A mailman's progress could have made the succession of images appear to be determined by action in the movie's world. With no human process traced by his shots and without movement to bridge his cuts, Lang composes and deploys the opening images in a design that we can only observe and work to follow. The first pair begins a sequence which should culminate in penetration of the office space, specially since number two has ("My dear lady . . .") the start of a speech that we can expect to hear continued—but surely also to see spoken. Then the apple piles are completely removed from anything we might have anticipated within. Their impact of surprise can bolster awareness of our submission to choices imposed upon us both negatively (no general view of the office, no introduction of the man who speaks or of anyone listening) and positively (displaying the unprepared and bizarre image of the desktop).

The uncertain continuity of the exposition plays oddly against a clear, indeed emphatic, continuity of visual design. The three images carry a single basic shape. In each of them the camera displays a symmetrical structure whose lines could easily be matched to the screen's rectangular format. However, the viewpoint is repeatedly angled so that the lines of the composition, the horizontals in particular, are tilted within the frame. The symmetry of the objects is marked in an image that displays them asymmetrically. The repetition of the linear structure is stressed by a variation that places the tilt from right to left, left to right, right to left. This zig-zag-zig gives emphasis to a visual metaphor of tilted scales. Prepared in shot one by the lamp globes set on either side of the main entrance, the design climaxes in the two apple piles where the left one seems to outweigh the one on the right.

In this context it is worth taking note of Matthew Bernstein's report that "the most interesting element of *Mary Burns, Fugitive* is [director] William K. Howard's deployment of the iconography of justice. Under the film's titles is etched the familiar woman blindfolded and holding up scales" (1994, 121). Lang would almost certainly have seen the earlier film, and it may well have prompted him to open *You Only Live Once* on an inversion of its imagery. In any case, the graphic allusion to a tilted scale seems strategic. In the first shot Lang is able at the same time to display the pretensions of civic architecture, by foregrounding the mass of a neoclassical column, and to embed in the composition an ironic motif that casts doubt on all that boasting.

This opening sequence has received little discussion, despite Lang's known stress on the crucial importance of the way a film starts. The rest of this essay will focus on the first minutes of *You Only Live Once* and present an understanding of their determinedly eccentric process.

The surface drama is presented by the run of the monologue that began in voice-over. A heavily accented voice is heard protesting injustice and claiming the law's protection:

> My dear lady, each day for the last couple of months, this policeman he's walk right past my fruit-stand, then he's turned around and . . . pfffpph . . . he's taken the apple and . . . hmph! And when I tell him to leave my apple alone he's telling me go chase himself! So, I think to myself I will have him put in a jail for stealing an apple. But . . . ahhh-sttt! . . . this idea is no good, you know, because all the policemen have a union. And one cop is not going to arrest other one. . . . Now, Miss, I have come here for to have your boss sue this cop for stealing my apple.

The dissolve through to the office interior is completed on the words "This policeman . . ." and straightaway a hand enters right of frame in close-up, with two fingers extended to strut the space between the apple piles. The mystery of the transition is clarified as we witness a complex act of representation. The narrator is working his fingers to mimic the walk of a beat-pounding cop. Thereby he transforms the desktop into an image of a city sidewalk, which in turn makes sense of the apple pyramids as marking out the space of his fruit stand. The movement of the fingers is synchronized with the separate enunciation of each word—"right . . . past . . . my . . . fruit-stand." The teller is insisting, then, on the deliberate accuracy of his enactment, an insistence maintained when—on "he's turned around"—the hand performs a balletic twistabout with one finger bent at the knuckle-knee.

> . . . he's turned around . . . AND

On this the hand abruptly reverts to its off-stage function as the real hand, here and now, of the complainant. The index finger points across to the right to assert its call on the attention of the off-screen listener. Then another change. The hand remains a hand but, as it swoops to grab the apple from the top of the left pyramid, it ceases to be *this* hand and becomes the represented hand of the thieving policeman. This gesture transforms the apple also: no longer an emblem of the fruit stand's presence it becomes a real, edible apple—yet not *this* apple but one of the several lost before now to the cop's delinquency.

Here the camera pulls back to reveal, first, the speaker as he continues his performance by rubbing the apple vigorously on his forearm, taking it to his mouth and making as if to munch it. We see a pale, middle-aged, balding man with a moustache. He wears work clothes and carries a pencil behind his ear; the urgency of his grievance, to him, is marked by his evidently having snatched this time away from his stall to seek remedy. At the same time, through his gestures, he has transformed his whole body to represent the cop in the act of biting the fruit: his hand is the cop's hand, his mouth is the cop's mouth. All this is confined to the mime, of course, since in his words the stallholder is speaking on his own behalf and maintaining the cop as a "he," an other.

The camera's movement continues, drawing back to frame in mid-shot the speaker on the left and, seated behind the office desk, his listener—a smiling young woman who divides her time between hearing the complaint and attending to the papers in front of her. (She is not yet "Joan.") The funny foreigner extends the range of his graphic gestures as the protest goes on. For instance, on "I think to myself" he points to his head to show where the thinking occurred; on "put in a jail" his hand plunges down to the desktop to locate the jail, imaging it as a dungeon and celebrating the power and finality of the desired retribution; and when speaking of the coppers' union he makes a spreading and squeezing motion with both hands to picture the scale, tightness, and ferocity of the hostile syndicate.

The demands on the actor here are extraordinary, and it is disgraceful that he is not named in the closing credits. (He is Henry Taylor; some filmographies name the character "Kozderonas.") Reading his performance in the light of the film's first emphasis on the claims of official Justice we could understand it to be offering an initial statement, in comic vein, of the themes of fair play in conflict with the institutions of the law, individual humanity versus the system. This might be considered as the meaning of the scene if what we are seeking is an abstraction that we can draw from the scene's particularity. We might be tempted, then, to regard the scene as significant mainly for what it illustrates rather than for what it shows.

What it shows is, first of all, the excess of signification displayed in the profuse and exaggerated readability of the complainant's gestures. Everything he does pictures something else, something not actually present and visible. The relations of sound to image constructed by Lang's framings make the spoken words the narration to a sequence of visual drama; the voice functions as a commentary that controls the meanings of the images within Lang's image and imposes a particular sense on configurations that would otherwise be baffling.

Our understanding of the scene should include, then, its work as an explication of the act of storytelling in words and pictures, where the two combine to construct mental images that stand in no fixed relationship to the material content of what we see and what we hear. (Note how gesture fills in for gaps in the spoken account on the acts of polishing and chomping the apple.) The episode demonstrates some of the powers of the audiovisual storyteller both on-screen and behind the camera. Most strongly, perhaps, it should impress on us how ready we are to let vividness of representation stand in for verisimilitude in the telling, and the showing, of a tale.

So far my account has ignored the figure of the secretary that the film's audience would have recognized as the star as soon as she appeared on screen. But this is in accord with the priorities that Lang establishes. Sylvia Sidney is not awarded a star entrance. The camera merely discovers her as it draws back, and she is given no activity likely to compete for our attention with the colorful performance of the man standing over her. Nevertheless, by the end of this episode we shall have derived, without apparent effort, a strong impression of her character. The scene is as demanding for Sylvia Sidney as for Henry Taylor. While she remains sitting at the desk and mainly silent, her activity requires a multitude of small gestures so that she can display appropriate attention to the complainant, listening to his tale with an amusement that is kindly rather than contemptuous or dismissive, while nonetheless dealing with a range of competing obligations. She makes notes, assembles a clutch of papers and files them, takes a message on the phone, meanwhile receiving a packet from a mailman, signing for it and finding a coin to give him a tip; finally she responds to a voice on the intercom by excusing herself to answer her boss's call.

Giving Joan so many things to deal with, and having her do so with a continuous—even excessive—cheerfulness, establishes her as competent and a bit hyperactive. The discreet nameplate on her desk contributes to our sense of a young woman in command of a secure job with middle-class status. That puts her at a height against which her fall will come to be measured. The scene has been constructed with great skill to suggest that we are seeing something like Joan's customary working environment; it would have been all too easy to distract us from the characterization by making us wonder why the office is having such an unusually busy day. All this is an alternative to starting with the key narrative information: that today is Joan's wedding day and that she will be leaving to marry a convicted robber.

The exposition is decidedly offbeat. We start with a setting, necessarily, but we start also with a figure who will not appear again and whose business, expansively introduced, will have no impact on the course of events. The complainant explains himself, tells his story. We learn about Joan only from apparently incidental actions and reactions within what looks like a daily routine. It is only at the end of this section, as the camera moves away with Joan, that Lang's treatment acknowledges her as the center of attention.

You Only Live Once presents the story of a couple and does so (with one remarkable deviation) chronologically. The concern for narrative compression is shown in the scenario by the move that gave Eddie's lover a job to tie her into the justice system. Further weighty choices are entailed by the decision to begin at this point in the story and to begin with Joan. We have yet to be told about the couple's meeting, courtship, and current situation. Eddie remains to be introduced and his character is in need of exposition.

The film could delay our view of Eddie until Joan is reunited with him. Instead it opts to introduce Eddie separately, in action connected with his discharge from prison. This choice is one that balances the two characters by giving each of them a life and a context that is independent of their partnership. The balance is the more pronounced in that each of them has a surround of supporters and commentators, most prominently Joan's sister Bonnie (Jean Dixon) and her boss, Stephen Whitney (Barton MacLane), and Eddie's prison chaplain, Father Dolan (William Gargan). This structure allows Whitney and Dolan to be positioned in complementary roles, as differently prejudiced observers of the couple. The risk the picture runs is of halting the momentum achieved in the exposition of Joan's story while it catches up the essential details both about Eddie and about the couple's shared past. Apart from their significance in relation to themes of prejudice and fatality, Ethan and Hester also serve to maintain dramatic urgency in the honeymoon episode, allowing the lovers' conversation to serve as the conduit for the (quite sparse) backstory of their relationship.

Lang films the action in Joan's office so that it has the feeling of a single long take with one interruption. With the camera at mid-shot framing both Joan and her visitor, he makes a cutaway to the office door—seen from something like Joan's viewpoint—as the mailman enters with a packet. It could be argued that this is a strictly practical device, allowing a discreet change of setup so that the shot that comes after can appear to be continuous with the shot that came before. However, that would not account for the design that implies the single take and thereby creates what would not otherwise be felt—the sense of an interruption.

This moment should be considered in relation to the staging of Joan's departure from the office. As she goes to speak to her boss in the inner office, carrying her notepad and the recently received packet, the camera tracks across to the right with her. In its movement it passes behind another seated figure in the lower foreground, a stenographer, ending with her framed in the bottom left corner of the screen. She would be all but unnoticeable if Joan did not stop at Whitney's door and surprise us by turning to speak to her (fig. 34). The image gives her no identity beyond that of a dark-haired female typist and the recipient of Joan's instructions. She says nothing and we do not see her face. Joan's action alerts us to the presence of a figure that the camera appears to have regarded as perfectly negligible. (She will no longer be there when the camera returns to the office with Joan.)

The strategic oddity here is the momentary, punctuating, emphasis on a presence that has so far been systematically ignored—one might say erased. Ordinary procedure is for the establishing shot in any setting, however achieved, to give us a complete inventory of the significant, especially the human, components. Yet not only has the camera treated Joan and her visitor as if they were the sole presences in the office, but the soundtrack has omitted to report any off-screen activity—for instance, at the typewriter.

Figure 34. The stenographer

Coming at this point of punctuation, before the move into a new space, the small surprise can have the effect of alerting us to the completeness of the film's control over the sequence of information. (We might not think of this as *Lang's* control, but we should.) By flaunting an eccentricity the device advertises the director's command over the mediation of everything the film will recount. It warns us not to suppose that we shall always—or can ever—receive a complete and uninflected report of events in the movie's world. Right at the start it demonstrates (with a tiny, no-account instance) that control over the camera's selectivity gives the film artist the power to deceive us and the power to choose whether and when to give us the whole picture. This sets up some of the terms for the film's presentation of the bank robbery sequence. Is Eddie Taylor involved or not? Since vital issues will turn on the number of people in on the crime, we ought to be concerned whether we have received a complete or a deceptive account of the occupancy of the getaway van.

Given its work of concealing and revealing the stenographer's presence, the film's insistence on detailing the arrival of the mailman should be seen as a complementary demonstration. It is asserting its freedom to follow its own course, whether that involves defying or adhering to, or feinting to follow, normal procedures. I had this in mind when I spoke of the abolition of human presence from the opening images. Agree that a mailman is typically a figure who can humanize the continuity of such a sequence. Then we see Lang developing an oddly convoluted gag, and a germane point, by making a big issue out of the mailman's entry now. He has, in formal terms, put together the same kind of jack-in-the-box by withholding and flourishing the mailman as he is in the process of constructing with the hidden stenographer.

In the first ninety seconds of his movie, the director brought together three distinct strands of exposition: a concealed character sketch of his leading woman, a first statement of the film's social themes, and a complex articulation of problems in the authorship and perception of movie fiction. We have seen similar concentration at work in the treatment of the honeymoon scenes, and a similar blend between overt, recognizably generic features and embedded structures. There is a malicious humor in the way that these embedded structures develop a secret movie in tension, if not at odds, with the genre piece that *You Only Live Once* so powerfully delivers. The humor is all the more strange as it serves purposes beyond those of comic relief within a tale of injustice and the defeat of hope, yet it may be less surprising if we recall how many laughs Lang managed to find in *M*, the story of a psychopathic killer of children. If Lang's style can often seem glacial, that may be in large part because its humor is not of the more familiar kind that invites us into complicity and warmth.

Works Cited

Bernstein, Matthew. *Walter Wanger, Hollywood Independent*. Berkeley: University of California Press, 1994.

McGilligan, Patrick. *Fritz Lang: The Nature of the Beast*. London: Faber & Faber, 1997.

Wilson, George M. *Narration in Light: Studies in Cinematic Point of View*. Baltimore: Johns Hopkins University Press, 1986.

Filmography

Liliom. Directed by Frank Borzage. Fox Film Corporation, 1930.
Liliom. Directed by Fritz Lang. Société Anonyme Française Fox Film, 1934.
M. Directed by Fritz Lang. Vereinigte Star-Film GmbH, 1931.
Mary Burns, Fugitive. Directed by William K. Howard. Paramount Pictures, 1935.
They Live by Night. Directed by Nicholas Ray. RKO Radio Pictures, 1948.
The Wizard of Oz. Directed by Victor Fleming. MGM, 1939.
You Only Live Once. Directed by Fritz Lang. United Artists, 1937.

OMISSION AND OVERSIGHT IN CLOSE READING

The Final Moments of Frederick Wiseman's *High School*

First published in The Philosophy of Documentary Film, *edited by David LaRocca, 381–94. Lanham, MD: Rowman & Littlefield, 2017.*

In the early days of film studies, Frederick Wiseman's 1968 documentary *High School* was choice teaching material. It was much studied and discussed for two particular reasons over and above its own achievement: first because it would reliably connect with students' recent experience, and then because it gave ready access to key issues of realism and viewpoint.

It was the second film that Wiseman completed, developing a strongly individual approach to the opportunities presented by developments in technology: lightweight gear had become available that needed only two operators to record synchronized sound and image under available light conditions. By reducing the scale of the filmmakers' presence, the equipment encouraged observational-fly-on-the-wall-moviemaking. Wiseman's approach to these opportunities was strikingly fresh because it excluded voice-over narration and made no use of on-camera interviews. There was no attempt to construct a narrative by following a person, a group, or a process.

Instead the camera observed events in the routines of an institution—in this case, Northeast High School in Philadelphia. Around forty hours of film was shot over a period of weeks and the resulting material was pruned and shaped in the editing room to yield a seventy-five-minute movie.

Wiseman refused the usual labels—documentary, cinema verité, or direct cinema. He described his film as "reality fiction." With this tag he emphasized the freedom with which he assembled sound and image—for instance, the freedom to disregard the actual chronology of the filmed material. The sequence of events and images in the film was constructed independently in pursuit of formal and expressive aims. In an interview in *Sight and Sound* he gave a useful summary of his editing approach. "The structure of the film," he said, "is a theory about the events that are in the film" (Sutherland 1978, 82). He more than once illustrated that approach to structure by citing the final shot of *High School*.

In it we see and hear the principal, Dr. Haller, speaking to a faculty meeting. She reads a letter she has received from a recent graduate. The letter comes from Vietnam. The sender is about to be flown on a dangerous mission, and he recognizes the possibility that he may be killed. He expresses commitment to the American cause, has pledged his GI insurance money to support a scholarship fund at the school, and thanks his teachers for all that they did for him. As she ends the reading, the principal offers the letter as proof of the school's success.

Although this sequence was in fact filmed on the final day of shooting, that is not the reason why it comes last in the movie. Wiseman put it this way: "The placement of the letter at the end of *High School* makes it a different film than if the letter hadn't been used or if the letter started the film. When you hear the letter at the end of the film I hope you read the film into the letter. It connects the major themes I think I've been dealing with and hopefully enlarges the context of the film" (Ellsworth 1979, 3).

Wiseman's design achieved its purpose. So much is evident from the large body of critical and scholarly comment on the film. Pauline Kael set the trend in an influential column in the *New Yorker*. She greeted Wiseman as "probably the most sophisticated intelligence to enter the documentary field in recent years," and she climaxed her review by transcribing very nearly the whole text of the final sequence (1976, 101).

Like most of those to follow, Kael related the principal's verdict of success to one particular phrase in the letter—the writer's self-description in his role as a soldier: "I am only a body doing a job." In academic studies of *High School* a consensus developed that saw the institution as a machine for producing subservience and conformity. That interpretation was supported by taking the end sequence as the completion of a pattern, and relating it back to an image in the opening scene where the camera's approach to the school has it looking much like a factory.

Part of the ground for this reading, clearly, is a dissident response to US involvement in Vietnam. An audience on the other side of the political divide would most likely revere the soldier's self-sacrificial commitment to the victory of the "free world." The success claimed by the principal could then be endorsed without irony. This is not a position taken up in any of the scholarly literature.

Here is the text of the final sequence, complete. Only Dr. Haller is heard. I have marked with square brackets her interjections in the reading:

> Now let me read you this one, if I'm able to get through it. This is written from, and I might say that the letter that I'm about to read is from Bob Walters. Bob Walters, as Fran could tell you—she could write his biography—was a boy without parents who might have been a nobody. He certainly was not a high academic student. He was most average or sub-average in many ways. But a few teachers who cared made a great difference in this boy's life. His letter comes on, uuh . . . stationery marked *USS Okinawa*. I hope I can get through it. If I don't, Hy will have to go on.
>
> Dear Dr. Haller, I have only a few hours before I go. Today I will take a plane trip from this ship. I pray that I'll make it back, but it is all in God's hands now. You see, I am going with three other men. We are going to be dropped behind the DMZ (the demiliarize [demilitarized] zone). The reason for telling you this is that all my insurance money will be given for that scholarship I once started but never finished, if I don't make it back.

I am only insured for ten thousand dollars. Maybe it could help someone. I have been trying to become a Big Brother in Vietnam but it is very hard to do. I have to write back and forth to San Diego, California and that takes time. I only hope that I am good enough to become one. God only knows. I really pray that the young men in your cooking classes will use this change of learning very well. Thank you Dr. Haller for helping these men become good, very fine cooks. [He should have said "Thank you, Mrs. C."] My personal family usually doesn't understand me. They don't see, they don't understand why I have to do what I do do. They say that I'm a real nut to do such work, but . . . thus they say: "Don't you value life? Are you crazy?" My answer is "Yes, but I value all the lives of South Vietnam and the free world, so that they and all of us can live in peace." Am I wrong Dr. Haller? If I do my best all the time and believe in what I do, believe that what I do is right, that is all I can do. Dr. Haller, if anything happens to me, James C. Heckwicker [I think it is] will send you a telegram and in time he will send you the money. Please don't say anything to Mrs. C. [but I did] she would only worry over me. I am not worth it. I am only a bo . . . a body doing a job. In closing I thank everyone for what they all have done for me. Yours truly, Bob Walters. Thank you all again very much. Please forgive my handwriting, I am a little jumpy. Please understand.

Now when you get a letter like this, to me it means that we are very successful at Northeast High School. I think you will agree with me.

The full text gives a sense of the scene's duration, I hope, because its length and its concentration are important for its effect. The scene lasts around four minutes. Once the reading has begun, the camera remains fixed on the reader, Dr. Haller. Her head is framed tightly but insecurely in a low-angle telephoto shot that magnifies the smallest shifts of face and eyeline (fig. 35). Scrutiny only a little less probing, a slight retreat easily achieved, would have

Figure 35. From the final shot of *High School*

given space for the movements of Dr. Hailer's head within a steady frame. We do not need to think these matters through to feel the insistence of the camera's gaze. It imposes close attention to both the words of the writer and the performance of the reader.

It is notable that most of the *High School* criticism follows Kael in relating the principal's assertion of success directly to the letter's words about "a body doing a job," and, in this juxtaposition of selected spoken matter, few writers mention other aspects or indeed other words. One point that escapes notice is the proficiency of the recital; its inflections convey at the same time understanding of the writer's emotions and the reader's feelings in response. It is forgotten, too, that Dr. Haller introduces the letter as an instance of the achievement of "teachers who cared"; she prepares a context within which we, as well as her real-life audience, attend to the text: the whole reading will be a celebration. Another context is given by the last words of introduction, where she repeats the warning that emotion may make her unable to complete the reading. By its end we understand that she is moved, but it is clear that her feelings of pride and pleasure outweigh distress that the young man may have been about to kill or be killed. "I hope I can get through it" alerts us to the stresses of performance, and the difficulty of balancing the professional values of control and empathy. The threat of breakdown could make us sensitive to the reader's stumble when she comes to the words "just a body." If the words carry weight (and I agree that they do) the stumble must also speak. After all, the word "body" does not present the hazards to enunciation offered by "demilitarized." Finally, much could be said about Dr. Hailer's declaring, with an evident sense of her colleagues' approval, her entitlement to disregard the writer's most emphatic request: that she keep the letter to herself so as to save a fondly remembered teacher from distress.

Critics worth reading support their understandings and their evaluations with material verifiably present in the sights and sounds of movies. But no criticism, detailed as it may reckon to be, will ever encompass all that might be observed about a passage of film, or even a moment. Needing to select, I could choose to ignore the stumble on "body," for instance, as I do not claim for it the weight of relevance carried by Dr. Haller's pride in the achievement of the institution that she heads and speaks for. When some salient detail escapes comment, the omission may as soon result from a writer's decision and priorities as from a failure of observation. Inevitably though, we do fall victim to failures of observation. I am going to present two cases that I believe qualify as oversights, rather than strategic omissions, since they concern features that, once observed, could hardly be left unremarked.

The first is a lapse not over fact but over significance. All accounts concur that the film has time and again highlighted gender issues, yet none applies this insight to the movie's climactic episode. Nobody seems to ask how it matters for the effect of the sequence that it fixes at length on the figure and actions of a woman, a mature woman of polished appearance who judged it suitable to her role and the occasion that her silver hair be neatly styled. Nobody fails, or can fail, to see that the principal is female. Everyone acknowledges the fact simply through use of the personal pronoun. But Kael comes nearest to recognizing how much that matters in her parenthetical description of Dr. Haller as "a fine-looking woman" (1976, 100). Discussion elsewhere treats Dr. Haller as no more than a relay of the letter's words and the institution's judgment, yet her appearance, voice, and manner are prominent features of the scene, not dissociable from her gender, that vitally inform our response to the finale. (For a start, they enable us to recognize her status as principal.) The sequence falls into a pattern that suggests a gendered division of labor: it's a woman who carries the work of memory and emotion. Aware that it may be his last farewell, a young man has chosen to write home not to the "personal family [that] usually doesn't understand" but to the institution whose moral authority he respects and whose approval he seeks. It is specifically the women there that he remembers and addresses. (In Dr. Haller's preamble, Wiseman responds to "teachers who cared" with cutaways that single out only women among the listeners.) It feels appropriate, then, that Bob Walters's words are spoken with acknowledged emotion by this female reader. As a result we sense the more strongly one of the prime sources of the writer's attachment and thankfulness to the school: he found there—it seems, uniquely—a motherly concern whose memory stays with him and is cherished.

It is important that we feel this, little as we may examine the feeling, because the strength of the sentiment usefully confuses the factory image of the school. If the letter's text might tip us toward a hostile verdict on an educational machine, wider possibilities are brought into play by a presence and a bearing that evoke the maternal. To observe only the mechanical and oppressive, then, would do poor justice to Wiseman's subtlety and the breadth of his vision.

Perhaps the principal's sex is too obvious to be taken note of. But I suspect there's a further reason why its significance escapes comment: it was a factor outside the filmmaker's control. Wiseman chose to include the letter in the film, and to place it as the finale. He did not choose the sex or manner of the letter's reader. In documentary, criticism is rightly alert for the editorial decisions that give shape to the material, embodying the director's attitude and intention. But this concentration can mislead when it isolates what the artist constructs from what the camera discloses.

Film aesthetics has wanted to celebrate the malleability of the moving image, to erect a filmmaker who enjoys freedom of artistic choice of the kind that is attributed to the composer or the painter. Pursuing that desire, it has exaggerated the selectivity of the cinema apparatus. The film frame selects by exclusion. Within the frame, few means exist to distinguish the vital information from the incidentals that come with it. In standard film technique the issue is addressed largely by constructing a line of continuity to carry us from key point to key point. But Wiseman's editing between episodes most often forgoes this means of distinguishing the essential from the secondary. An action cannot be captured minus the features of the actor, nor can microphones detach the spoken word from the character of a voice or the rhythm of an utterance. Wiseman's camera could not ignore Dr. Hailer's discreetly showy earrings or evade the look of her dark, oval spectacle frames. While observing the authority of the speaker's position the lens had also to observe the little tics and hesitations that may suggest anxieties imperfectly controlled. But criticism, mine included, has chosen to neglect these incidentals even though they must be relevant to our impression of the principal, and must inform the context in which we hear her address.

In speaking of the film Wiseman shares the critics' emphasis, dwelling on the content of the letter, taking less account of what belongs to the reading. No doubt that reflects his priorities. But in a film prepared for presentation to an audience "unintended consequences" cannot be simply unintended. Collateral effects are effects nonetheless. Wiseman made his choice knowing that the letter brought with it *this* reader with *these* attributes. He would have had to look for a different way of ending the movie if he had judged that the lady's presence and her performance were ruinous, confusing, or even unhelpful for his design.

When choice is equated with invention, nostalgia for unconstrained freedom may deceive us. It may obscure the relationship between intention and contingency, distract us from the role that the incidental plays in the expressive. Since the apparatus seizes all it is allowed to see and hear, skilled film artists know abundance of detail for a resource rather than a limitation. In the movie—a fiction rehearsed and refined—the detail can be highly controlled. Witness Max Ophuls: "Details, details, details! The most insignificant, the least observed of them are often the most evocative, characteristic and even decisive" (Beylie 1963, 120). Or witness Vincente

Minnelli: "A picture that stays with you is made up of more than a hundred hidden things" (2010, xiv).

These "hidden things" are most often, like the principal's features, hidden in plain sight. We take them in without taking them up. That remains true even in a "reality fiction" that forgoes the metteur en scene's freedom to invent and control. However, I now turn to consider a different case, where what escapes notice is an editorial intervention that was clearly a matter of choice. At the very end of *High School*, Wiseman closes the movie with a device of great rhetorical weight, and it is remarkable that it goes unmentioned even in those studies that offer themselves as close reading, or transcripts, or analysis.

In a book-length study of Wiseman's cinema, Barry Keith Grant is one of those who draw attention to the last words we hear: "I think you will agree with me." He comments that in its place the remark "functions like a rhetorical question, addressed as much to the viewer as to the assembled teachers.... The fact that the film ends abruptly as she concludes her reading leaves the viewer to contemplate the extent to which one agrees with her" (1992, 58).

It is not part of my purpose to challenge the consensus reading of *High School*, which gains support from more than one of Wiseman's published remarks about his design. Indeed it is because the film leaves me too at a distance from the principal's assessment that I see particular relevance in one aspect to which none of the scholarly literature attends: how the abrupt ending noted by Grant splits image from sound. A rapid fade-out on the soundtrack occurs moments before the image fades to black and we lose sight of Dr. Haller. The silent image is very brief, but long enough for us to take in the speaker's gestures as she looks down to her right then jerks her head up and across to the left and begins to smile. We have time to feel that the smile asserts a mood close to triumph. The silence behind it is palpable because our ears have been used to listening through a background of hall noise and incidental sound, like the rustling of the sheets of paper between the reader's fingers. The effect is the effect of a change, a loss, not just of an absence.

Dropping the sound out is, I believe, a key element in Wiseman's strategy. So it is remarkable that it escapes notice in studies whose main concern is with the means through which the artist shapes his film to carry a personal viewpoint on events which he recorded but did not control.

In early editions of the textbook *Film Art: An Introduction* (1986) by David Bordwell and Kristin Thompson, *High School* is discussed at some length in a chapter headed "Film Criticism: Sample Analyses." The account is alert and helpful in tracing patterns built into the movie's form; it witnesses "the film's development from educational discipline to military regimentation" (320). Like others, it ends by juxtaposing "a body doing a job" with "we are very successful" but also without mentioning Wiseman's intervention on the soundtrack. The oversight is the more surprising in view of the context: the discussion is introduced as one of several "models of short critical analyses" (286), the declared purpose in this case being to illustrate "how the film-maker's formal and stylistic choices can create a coherent impression, strong spectator effects, and a particular range of explicit and implicit meanings" (287).

We should note that the sample analysis is of the whole film, not just of its end sequence. Inevitably, then, the treatment is highly selective. Nevertheless, Wiseman's formal and stylistic choice to end by divorcing sound from image is a strong spectator effect, and we might expect it to gain acknowledgment. The problem is, I think, that the device escapes accommodation to the interpretive process favored by *Film Art*. The book offers itself as a guide to the skills of film appreciation. However, those skills turn out to consist of the ability to determine, for any given film, the ways in which it can be accommodated to some prescribed categories. In the present instance that entails requiring interpretation to work with meanings conceived as "formal entities" (1986, 31) and divided into four types. Of these the two most forcefully applied are, as above, the explicit and the implicit.

I have argued elsewhere against this conception (Perkins 1990, 1–6), and George Wilson has set out convincing reasons to distrust the application to cinema of the implicit/explicit divide (1999, 221–26). It's enough here to note the confusions that follow when the analysis of *High School* is subjected to the given categories. We were promised a range of explicit meanings but we are offered only one: "We are very successful" (Bordwell and Thompson 1986, 320). That single specimen, undoubtedly explicit, is not a meaning of the film. As a view expressed within the movie, and placed at the end in relation to everything we have seen and heard, the principal's claim is her own, and it stands to be weighed against, for instance, an equally clear assertion by one student: "Morally, socially, this school is a garbage can."

There are damaging consequences when a unique but specious instance of explicit meaning forms the basis for a contrast with whatever may be identified as implicit. Perceptions of irony and ambiguity are coarsened when made dependent on that clash. Under this regime, ambiguity loses all richness and complexity; it emerges as a flat contradiction between mutually exclusive readings—the film celebrates (explicit) or the film condemns (implicit). The scheme has no place for the ambiguity that holds conflicting or mutually qualifying possibilities in suspension. Likewise, with irony, a literary definition is invoked with no recognition of the muddles that arise when it is applied to a motion picture. The film is more generous, and its ironies are deeper, than can be recognized within a scheme that pitches the principal's assertion of success against a view of the institution as "an oppressive bureaucracy." If the institution succeeds in operating an oppressive bureaucracy and in hiding the recognition from itself, that is in part because it sees no reason to doubt its own good intentions. The ironies accumulated by the film do not depend on our being led to deny the school's success. (The two sequences preceding Dr. Haller's address, though carrying a taint of the grotesque, are essentially celebratory.) We are likely to have witnessed the successes, but often with alarm. Wiseman's approach leaves open to scrutiny the terms in which success is defined and pursued.

At the editing stage a great deal of thought must have been given to the precise timing of the final moments. It was a significant decision to go on beyond the principal's boast and to offer "I think you will agree with me" as the last words to be heard. With this extension, as Grant suggests, the issue of agreement lingers and becomes shaded as a question for the movie audience. The case for this reading is strengthened when we take into account Wiseman's play with the sound level. The effect of the cutoff is to withhold any reaction from the hall that the microphone had picked up. The context is such that even an audible lack of response from the faculty would weigh as heavily as any other reactions. The plea for agreement would then be answered from within the film. The challenge to the audience in the cinema would be muffled.

Still, if nothing more were at issue, it would have been possible to preserve synchronization and fade the picture out along with the sound. In making his editing choice, Wiseman must have thought that there was a particular value in the half second of muted image. My sense of it is that it impresses on us the last thing that we see and that persists into the fade-out: the smile. Without the context that the sound would have supplied, no new information is given to us that would define the source of Dr. Haller's satisfaction. As a result we are encouraged to refer the expression of pleasure back to the context of the letter, the celebration of success, and the asserted confidence in the quest for validation. Joy lights the principal's face, and triumph powers the swing of her head. But joy and triumph are not the inevitably appropriate responses to the news that the letter has conveyed, or to the doubt that it leaves about the fate of the soldier. The enthusiasm of the soundless image is tinged—but only tinged—with frenzy.

Wiseman's device reminds me of the vernacular use of "No comment" when the words withhold an invited gesture of assent. When I try to articulate the significance of this ending I have to resort to verbal imagery. The principal is left high and dry, I say, or "stranded" or "out on a limb." Or I say that the image is "hollowed out." These attempts to evoke feeling by reliance on metaphors seem to serve the case better than any words that would decipher a meaning in Wiseman's device. In a case like this, and very often, I think we are wise to avoid the word "meaning": it prompts us always to search for a proposition, or a set of them, that the film can he said to advance; it pulls us away from complexity and nuance in a way that "significance," for instance, does not.

The dropout of sound works against the sustained big close-up of the principal. The final shot lasts a deal longer than any other in the film where the camera holds on a single talking head. (In the whole film there's only one shot of longer duration.) Its uninterrupted continuity contributes to the sense that the film has reached its culmination. In a place where, for the first time, the institution offers its verdict on itself, the camera hangs on the subject's every word. These are factors that contribute to the ability of the sound loss to affect us while escaping notice—in other words, to inflect our response subtly, with a rhetoric that is all the more effective for not being blatant.

Maybe this becomes more apparent if we imagine other possibilities. What if the silent close-up on the principal were held for another three seconds before the fade-out? In that case, the absence of sound could not fail to strike us, and would have us wondering about its purpose. Or reverse the procedure: fade the image out before the sound and have "I think you will agree with me" echoing under a blank screen. Either of these alternatives would keep many, not all, of the film's effects, and enable many of the familiar readings, but with a much blunter, more overt, rhetoric.

By contrast it is surely the case that Wiseman's device not only—as the record shows—escapes notice, but is calculated to do so. We can hardly doubt that the film would have failed in its purpose if the viewer's first reaction to the final moments became "Wow, they dropped the sound out." Working stealthily, Wiseman is able to color our response to the principal and her claims within an overall viewpoint that can encompass complexity. The film can identify and at moments satirize a trend in the school's operation without demonizing its staff and while allowing us to observe, as Kael's review remarked, "genuine benevolence behind the cant" (1976, 100).[1] Why have I chosen to bring to light a device in a nearly fifty-year-old movie? The first reason is that I have not come across a clearer instance where a much studied and intelligently analyzed sequence has so successfully guarded one of its secrets. An interest in the "possibilities of the medium" entails an interest in the discoveries that filmmakers have made in opening up routes to eloquence.

Two discoveries are of special interest here. The first lies in the possibilities in the separation between image and soundtrack. We should keep it in mind that the talking picture addresses the distinct perceptual activities of the eye and ear, which are served by the outputs of two completely separate technologies—those of the projector and those of the loudspeaker. (Lens and microphone are equally separate, which is why Wiseman's work required a two-man crew.) Moreover, what we hear is more amenable to covert manipulation than what we see. I have highlighted a climactic instance where Wiseman's editing makes the formal separation of sound and image serve the purposes of expression. The film's viewpoint is embedded in an effect of technique.

The second discovery lies precisely in the grading of a formal intervention such that it escapes notice. The possibilities of depth and nuance in the movies depend largely on the filmmakers' ability to scale sights and sounds so that they can register with us at every level of force and prominence. "Every level" has to include passing unobserved. This medium—by which I mean the medium of the movie—depends on our ability to absorb the significance of objects, gestures, images, and sounds without paying attention to them, or pausing to articulate their significance. Films play on the differences between seeing-and-hearing, on the one hand, and noticing on the other. There is no room for doubt that all of us hear what happens on the soundtrack in *High School*. We could say, though, that the film does not prompt us, or give us time, to register it in consciousness.

Only a medium with the resources to grade its effects can allow both clarity and subtlety, and encourage what is plainly shown to submit to qualification by what is delicately suggested. That is why I see harm in a system of categories that will draw away from the recognition of degree and variousness. A stark opposition between the explicit and the implicit obscures the ranges of emphasis where some implications are blatant, others plain but unemphatic, and a host of them gently atmospheric and undertonal. Filmmakers face a constant challenge to arrive at stresses that enrich our understanding, and achieve a weight of expression appropriate to the weight of significance that a moment can bear. The flows of response, of feeling, thought, and observation can gain or suffer, be blocked or enhanced, by judgments of balance between force and tact. Wiseman faces issues of the appropriate at every moment, and in our appreciation of his work we face them too.

Earlier in my discussion I referred to Wiseman's "stealth" in the construction of an unnoticed effect. I wrote this way in order to slide in the sense that the "possibilities of the medium" include possibilities of dishonesty, falsification, bad faith—all the potential for duplicity extended by any form of communication. That is one basis for the role of close reading in criticism.

Whether in the fiction film or the documentary, the movie medium presents a standing opportunity and a standing problem in the relationship between recording and viewpoint. When Wiseman says that "the structure of the film is a theory about the events that are in the film," he is reflecting on the tension between the demands of reportage, and his concern to mold the recorded material according to his own sense of form and truth. Examining moments of eloquence in film, however minute, can be a way of illuminating structure by relating part and whole. The practice can be motivated by simple curiosity, sometimes by hostility, but its larger justification lies in the way that it relates the achievements of a movie and its maker to a discovery of the medium and its possibilities.

Missing the significance of Dr. Haller's gender is like and unlike missing the fact of the sound cut. The oversights might in both cases be described as gaps in realization or articulation. It does not follow that there are corresponding gaps in the experience of *High School*. But both oversights are relevant to the relationship between close reading and appreciation or criticism. In both respects, too, these final remarks should begin with an acknowledgment. My own awareness did not come punctually and was not prompted by seeing the film under ordinary viewing conditions. The sound effect is observed in notes that I took in preparation for a lecture-seminar in the late 1980s, more than a decade after first seeing the film. I was working with a 16 mm print, evidently on an analyzing projector or an editing table. The technology enabled me to stop and start, pause and rewind so that reflection and note-taking could proceed at a pace no longer governed by the film's own continuity. The rewind lever freed the work from dependence on the hazards of memory, allowing me to check data and at least to try to trace in the detail of scenes the sources of impressions I had formed. Then, it was only recently the impact of the principal's personality came to consciousness. I had already given the conference paper from which this chapter derives. That presentation made no mention of gender. It was only in the course of writing this, running and rerunning the final sequence on DVD in order to check details of the camera's response to Dr. Haller's gestures, that I came to see what was hidden in plain sight.

The technologies that enable these kinds of work can be seen to have something in common with those employed by filmmakers at the editing stage. What is more certain is that they involve a radical interference with the film and the way in which it was intended to play. In the predigital era movies were made to be seen under what we may call cinema conditions. That is, crucially, with no possibility of audience impact on the process of exhibition. As a result the use of time, pace, continuity, was the work of the movie alone. Extracurricular enjoyments apart, the spectator surrendered to the run of the film and, particularly, had no sense that it could be slowed to the pace of thought or the requirements of analysis. Films were not seen in isolated fragments; nobody mistook a trailer for a movie. In the case of *High School* the viewer would arrive at Dr. Haller's scene, and then discover it to be Wiseman's finale, having ceded control over the duration and the succession of sights, sounds, and events.

It makes for an experience distinct from that of any ordinary viewing when one acquires the ability to pause, start, freeze, skip forward, or back. We should ask what safeguards should be put on our close readings when the control of time has been stolen from the artist in the interests of study. The temptations are many, and not the least of them is the temptation of cleverness. Distortion threatens when an aspect is isolated from its context to take on perhaps disproportionate weight or implausible significance.

When analysis serves a critical purpose—one that goes beyond cataloging to touch on the significance of a work or the achievement of its makers—it must be held answerable to a true experience of the movie. The analyst must ask what case can be advanced with sincerity and conviction. Readiness for conversation and correction is a vital discipline. Still, we cannot say that the reference point must always be past viewings, or the memory of them, as that would contradict a large part of the motivation for close work (either by scholars or by enthusiasts). It would rule out new discoveries and fresh realizations. When accurate analysis opens our eyes to new possibilities, or to new data that challenges our understanding, it is a future, better-informed encounter with the movie that we have in prospect. Quite often a further viewing will be both possible and enriching. We may then see an offered reading as convincing, revelatory, merely credible, or not even that. The question will need to be addressed through lively interrogation of our renewed experience. In this process of introspection we shall, at our best, be alert for what we can truthfully say and mean.

Sincerity and introspection have not been terms privileged in the philosophy of film, but close reading cannot prosper without them.

Works Cited

Beylie, Claude. *Max Ophuls*. Paris: Editions Seghers, 1963.
Bordwell, David, and Kristin Thompson. *Film Art: An Introduction*. 2nd ed. New York, [1979] 1986.
Ellsworth, Liz. *Frederick Wiseman: A Guide to References and Resources*. Boston: G. K. Hall, 1979.
Grant, Barry Keith. *Voyages of Discovery: The Cinema of Frederick Wiseman*. Chicago: University of Illinois Press, 1992.
Griffin, Mark. *A Hundred and One Hidden Things: The Life and Films of Vincente Minnelli*. Cambridge, MA: Da Capo, 2010.
Kael, Pauline. "Review of *High School*" (1969). In *Frederick Wiseman*, edited by Thomas R. Atkins, 95–101. New York: Monarch, 1976.
Perkins, V. F. "Must We Say What They Mean?: Film Criticism and Interpretation." *Movie*, nos. 34–35 (Winter 1990): 1–6.
Sutherland, Allan T. "Wiseman on Polemic." *Sight and Sound* 47, no. 2 (1978): 82.
Wilson, George M. "On Film Narrative and Narrative Meaning." In *Film Theory and Philosophy*, edited by Richard Allen and Murray Smith, 221–26. Oxford: Oxford University Press, 1999.

Filmography

High School. Directed by Frederick Wiseman. Osti Productions, 1968.

Note

1 Again, it is notable that Kael's review, with no pretensions to offer analysis, responds to aspects of the movie unremarked in the scholarly literature.

INDEX

Italicised entries are film titles except where stated.
Film titles that are shared with other films have the relevant year in brackets.
Extended discussions of individual films are indexed as part of the director's entry as well as under the film title, where the complete list of references to the film will be found.

ABC (Associated British Cinemas), 65–71 passim, 81
À Bout de souffle (*Breathless*), 35, 45, 46, 193
Above Us the Waves, 3, 34
Absolute Beginners, 260
Actress, The (1953), 103
Adam's Rib (1949), 103
À Double Tour, 45
Advise and Consent, 113n1, 126
Aherne, Brian, 370
Air Force, 146
Akins, Claude, 123
Aldrich, Robert, 3, 37, 72, 353
Alland, William, 271
Allen, Corey, 91, 93
Allen, Elizabeth, 188
Allen, Fred, 139
All I Desire, 13, 284, 291, 300nn24–25
Alligator Named Daisy, An, 3, 34
All Night Long (1962), 39
All Quiet on the Western Front (1930), 210
Alphaville, 193, 194
America America (*The Anatolian Smile*), 8, 197–204

Amfitheatrof, Daniele, 403, 404
amiche, Le, 45
Anatomy of a Murder, 37, 45, 113n1, 120, 126
Anderson, Judith, 215
Anderson, Lindsay, 31n1, 32n2
Andrews, David, 54
Angel Face (1953), 193
Angry Hills, The, 3, 37
Angry Silence, The, 35, 38, 45
Annenkov, Georges, 434
Archibald, James, 52
Arrangement, The, 203
Ashes and Diamonds (*Popiól i diament*), 34–35
Asian, Gregoire, 107
Austin, J. L., 365
avventura, L', 36, 46
Awful Truth, The (1937), 232

Bacall, Lauren, 338, 341
Bacher, Lutz, 395, 402, 404
Backus, Jim, 91, 163, 165
Bacon, Francis, 134
Baim, Harold, 82, 83n4

Baker, Graham, 459
Baker, Stanley, 36
Ball of Fire, 146
Balsam, Martin, 98
Barabbas (1961), 178, 180
Barrow, Clyde, 459
Batman (1989), 257, 269n1
Baum, Vicki, 337
Baxter, Anne, 225, 238n4, 365, 367, 372, 374, 387
Bazin, André, 154, 155, 276, 433
Bazlen, Brigid, 107
BBFC (British Board of Film Censors), 4–5, 61–63
Bel Geddes, Barbara, 240, 243
Bellamy, Ralph, 398
Ben-Hur (1959), 28
Bennett, Joan, 211
Benny, Jack, 292
Bergman, Ingmar, 35
Bergman, Ingrid, 228, 378
Berkshire College of Education, 8. *See also* Bulmershe College of Higher Education
Berle, Milton, 105
Bernstein, Matthew, 468
Best Years of Our Lives, The, 155
Beylie, Claude, 433, 451, 453, 455, 458, 484
Beyond the Time Barrier, 42
BFI (British Film Institute), 2, 26–28, 31n1, 32n6, 78
Big Country, The, 92, 127
Bigger than Life, 108, 143, 162, 165, 166, 167, 174, 176
Big Heat, The (1953), 342
Big Sky, The, 145
Birds, The, 370
Birth of a Nation, The (1915), 28
Bitter Victory, 162, 163, 170, 172, 175, 176, 179, 214
Bjork, Anita, 365
Blackmail (1929), 29
Blain, Gerard, 145, 149
Blind Date (1959), 43, 46, 61

Blood and Roses (*Et Mourir de plaisir*), 61
Blow-Up, 79
Blue Murder at St. Trinian's, 50n3
Board of Trade, 64
Bogarde, Dirk, 103, 104
Bogart, Humphrey, 90, 92, 163, 334, 335, 338–39, 340, 341
Bogdanovich, Peter, 139, 146
Boles, John, 301
Bond, Ward, 148, 304
Bonjour Tristesse, 193
Bonnie and Clyde, 76, 79
Bordwell, David, 10, 11, 243–51, 254, 486
Born Yesterday (1950), 103, 104, 139
Borzage, Frank, 459
Bowen, Peter, 20n11
Box, Betty, 67
Box, Sydney, 429
Boyer, Charles, 459
Brady, Ruth, 253
Brady, Scott, 167, 353
Breen Office, 336, 374, 401–5 passim, 428n9
Brennan, Walter, 145
Bresson, Robert, 191
Bridge on the River Kwai, The, 37
Brief Encounter (1945), 26, 262, 410–11, 419, 427n2
Bringing Up Baby, 139–43 passim, 145, 146
British Board of Film Censors. *See* BBFC
British Film Institute. *See* BFI
Bronston, Samuel, 183
Brook, Lyndon, 104
Brooks, Ray, 54
Bruce, Sally Jane, 292
Bryden, Sonja, 312, 412
Bulmershe College of Higher Education, 8, 19n9. *See also* Berkshire College of Education
Burton, Richard, 171, 172
Buscombe, Edward, 234

Butler, David, 292
Buttons, Red, 145, 147

Cabot, Bruce, 147
Cagney, James, 167, 171, 172
Cahiers du Cinéma (magazine), 9, 11, 19n7, 45, 49n2, 101n1, 162, 220
Calhoun, Rory, 117
Cameron, Ian, 19nn1–2, 19n6, 19n8, 25–26, 49n1, 160
Can-Can, 102
Capra, Frank, 299n7
Capucine, 103
Carabiniers, Les, 194
Carmen Jones, 193
Carol, Martine, 451, 453
Carradine, John, 360
Casablanca, 218, 350
Case Against Brooklyn, The, 42
Caught (1949), 11, 12, 211–12, 214, 240–43, 248, 250, 251–55
Cavell, Stanley, 239n7, 247, 402, 415, 416
Chabrol, Claude, 29, 32n12, 156
Chaffey, Don, 43, 50n4
Chandler, Jeff, 123
Chandler, Joan, 152
Chanslor, Roy, 361
Chapin, Billy, 292
Chaplin, Charles, 26, 29, 32nn4–5
Chapman Report, The, 61, 62, 63
Charisse, Cyd, 88, 90, 104, 163, 167, 173
Cheyenne Autumn, 184–88
Chien andalou, Un, 29, 33n13
Children's Film Foundation, 80, 83n1
China Gate (1957), 133, 136
Christians, Mady, 312
Ciment, Michel, 232
Cinematograph Films Act, 64
Citizen Kane, 12, 82, 156, 270–77, 284, 289, 337, 338
City of the Dead, The, 43
Clair, René, 27
Clayton, Jack, 38, 39, 40

Clift, Montgomery, 366, 387, 388
Clouzot, Henri-Georges, 44
Cobb, Lee J., 90, 169, 211
Coburn, Charles, 143
Cocteau, Jean, 27
Cohn, Harry, 341
Collier, Constance, 152
Collingwood, R. G., 260–61
Columbia Pictures, 341
Comedians, The (1967), 71
Cooper, Ben, 362
Cooper, Gary, 387
Costello, Dolores, 225
Cottafavi, Vittorio, 180
Cotten, Joseph, 225
Coward, Noël, 410
Crawford, Joan, 165, 304, 350–62 passim
Criminal, The (1960), 41, 43, 44
Crimson Kimono, The, 122, 130, 137
Crosby, Bing, 103
Cukor, George, 27, 35, 139, 151, 163, 167; *Let's Make Love*, 102–5 passim; *Song Without End*, 102–5 passim
Curse of the Werewolf, The, 45
Curtiz, Michael, 218, 350

Dall, John, 152
Dann, Roger, 373
Dano, Royal, 109
Darrieux, Danielle, 444
Da Silva, Howard, 169
Dauphin, Claude, 435
Dead of Night (1945), 429
Dean, James, 88–93 passim, 108, 128, 163–70 passim, 173, 176, 232
Dearden, Basil, 38, 39, 45, 46
Death of a Cyclist, The, 123
Deer Hunter, The, 258
Derek, John, 167, 172
Desert Mice, 42
de Vargas, Valentin, 148
Devil Never Sleeps, The, 3, 37, 53
Diaboliques, Les, 44

Diary of Anne Frank, The, 127
Dick, Douglas, 152
Dickinson, Angie, 133, 145, 148
Dietrich, Marlene, 232
Dillaway, Don, 225
Dirty Dozen, The, 72
Dixon, Jean, 472
Doctor Zhivago, 72
Domarchi, Jean, 45, 99, 151
Don Giovanni (opera), 401
Donnell, Jeff, 340
Donner, Clive, 4; *Some People*, 51–60
Donovan's Reef, 185, 187
Donskoy, Mark, 27
Dorn, Dolores, 133
Douchet, Jean, 90, 99
Douglas, Angela, 54
Downs, Cathy, 229
Dracula (1958), 45
Dreigroschenoper, Die (*The Threepenny Opera*), 29, 32n11
Dreyer, Carl Theodor, 194
Dr. No, 62
Drums Along the Mohawk, 235
Drury, Allen, 132, 134
Dubost, Paulette, 453–58 passim
Dubov, Paul, 131
Duck Soup (1933), 232
Duke of Edinburgh's Award, 51, 52, 54, 60n1
Dyer, Peter John, 46
Dymon, Frankie, 54

Eady money, 79–83 passim
East of Eden, 197, 232
Eaubonne, Jean d', 434
Eisenberg, Emanuel, 184
Eisenstein, Sergei, 27, 29
Eisner, Lotte, 32n3
Ellsworth, Liz, 478
Elmer Gantry, 46
Emhardt, Robert, 131
Encore (1951), 429, 441n1
Entertainer, The, 35, 38, 40, 42
Entr'acte, 33n13

Evanson, Edith, 153
Exodus (1960), 113n1, 114

Face in the Crowd, A, 131
Family Way, The, 79
Father Brown, 43
Ferguson, Frank, 362
Fest, Joachim, 393, 394
55 Days at Peking, 7, 178–83
Film as Film (book), 1, 4, 8, 9, 12, 32n8
Finney, Albert, 41
Fisher, Terence, 45
Fixed Bayonets!, 122
Flaherty, Robert, 41
Flame in the Streets, 42
flauto magico, Il. See *Magic Flute, The*
Fleischer, Richard, 180
Fleming, Victor, 283
Fonda, Henry, 229, 278, 460, 463
Fontaine, Joan, 214, 225, 312–23 passim, 392, 403, 405, 408, 409, 413, 417, 418
Forbidden Planet, 40
Ford, John, 27, 183n1, 227, 233, 341; *Cheyenne Autumn*, 184–88
Ford, Tennessee Ernie, 351
42nd Street, 29
Franju, Georges, 26, 35, 82, 89, 92
Freeman, Howard, 312
Fregonese, Hugo, 3, 37
Frenzy, 238n3
Fuller, Samuel, 6, 202, 233; *Merrill's Marauders*, 122–25; *Underworld U.S.A.*, 130–38
Funny Girl, 258
Fury at Showdown, 42

Gabin, Jean, 445
Gable, Clark, 353
Gainsborough Studios, 259, 263, 429
Galland, Jean, 434
Gardner, Ava, 7, 181, 183, 353
Gargan, William, 278, 472
Garland, Judy, 244

Gates, Larry, 131
Gay, John, 32n11
Gélin, Daniel, 436
Gentlemen Prefer Blondes, 142
Giallelis, Stathis, 197
Giant (1956), 126–29
Gibbs, John, 5, 6, 19nn2–4, 19nn6–8, 31n1
Gilliatt, Penelope, 51, 60n2, 109
Girls, Les, 103
Gish, Lillian, 292–97 passim
Glenville, Peter, 71
Godard, Jean-Luc, 35, 46, 82, 166, 177n2, 433; *Vivre sa vie*, 189–95
Goebbels, Josef, 394
Goethe, Johann Wolfgang von, 399
Goldfinger, 79
Gombrich, E. H., 245
Good, John, 312, 392
GPO Film Unit, 32n5
Grahame, Gloria, 90, 341
Grande Illusion, La, 263
Granger, Farley, 152, 169
Granger, Stewart, 264, 267
Grant, Barry Keith, 485, 487
Grant, Cary, 140, 141, 149, 228, 232
Grapes of Wrath, The, 29, 33n14, 244
Great Dictator, The, 26
Green, Guy, 38, 39
Green, Janet, 38
Gregor, Nora, 212
Grierson, John, 32n5
Griffith, D. W., 27, 29
Gruener, Allan, 131
Grunberger, Richard, 395, 398
Guardino, Harry, 109
Guillermin, John, 43
Guisol, Henri, 453
Gwynne, Michael, 54

Haas, Dolly, 367
Hakim, André, 430
Halliday, Jon, 300n24
Hamer, Robert, 3, 43, 46
Hamilton, Margaret, 463

Hammer Films, 44, 45, 75
Hardin, Ty, 124
Hardwicke, Cedric, 152
Hardy, Oliver. *See* Laurel and Hardy
Harris, Julie, 232–33
Harris, Paul, 39
Harris, Robert H., 199
Harry Black, 3, 37
Hasse, O. E., 366, 391n2
Hatari!, 145–49
Hathaway, Henry, 178, 183n1
Hawks, Howard, 3, 6, 27, 37, 173, 231–35; the comedies, 139–43; *Hatari!*, 145–49
Hayden, Sterling, 90, 350, 353
Hayward, Susan, 163, 166
Hazumi, Tsuneo, 49n2
Heartbreak Kid, The (1972), 220
Hecht, Ben, 370
Heerman, Victor, 308n3
Heflin, Van, 127
Heller in Pink Tights, 37
Helpmann, Robert, 180
Hemmings, David, 54
Hemsley, Estelle, 202
Henry, O., 430
Hepburn, Katharine, 139, 140, 214
Heston, Charlton, 7, 180, 226
High Noon (1952), 351, 376
High School (1968), 15, 19n5, 477–93
Hitchcock, Alfred, 6, 20n15, 27, 39, 46, 88, 126–27, 163, 215, 216, 220, 221, 228, 232, 233, 236, 299n9, 300n16; *I Confess*, 365–91; *Psycho*, 96–101; *Rope*, 151–61
Hitler, Adolf, 14, 275, 393–98, 406
Hobbes, Thomas, 94, 135, 138n1
Hollinger, Karen, 404, 427n2
Holt, Seth, 3, 4, 43, 44, 45, 52
Holt, Tim, 225
Home from the Hill, 37
Hope, Bob, 361, 362
Hot Blood, 89, 92, 162, 168, 169
Houseman, John, 337, 338, 404
House of Bamboo, 122

Index • 499

House of the Angel, The (*La Casa del Ángel*), 35
Houston, Penelope, 32nn2–3, 46
Hoveyda, Fereydoun, 177n1
Howard, Lewis, 340
Howard, Trevor, 410
Howard, William K., 468
How the West Was Won, 178, 183n1
Hudson, Rock, 128
Hughes, Dorothy, 334, 335, 337
Hunter, Jeffrey, 107, 108, 110
Huntley, John, 32n3
Hutchins, Will, 124
Hyams, Joe, 339

I Confess, 238n3, 365–91
I Love, You Love (*Io amo, tu ami*), 130
In a Lonely Place, 14, 90, 163, 215, 334–49
Indiana Jones and the Last Crusade, 269n1
Innocents, The (1961), 39
Intolerance, 28, 32n9, 429
Ireland, John, 90, 172
Israeli Love Story (unrealised film project), 36
It Happened One Night, 263, 299n7
It Should Happen to You, 104
Ives, Burl, 90, 93, 110, 172, 174, 175
Ives, Charles, 179
I Was a Male War Bride (*You Can't Sleep Here*), 140, 143
I Was Happy Here, 77

Jacoby, Alex, 50n2
Jazz Singer, The (1927), 26
Johnny Guitar, 14, 110, 162–69 passim, 173, 176, 210, 304–8, 338, 350–64
Johns, Glynis, 441n1
Johnson, Celia, 410
Joker Is Wild, The, 102
Jourdan, Louis, 312, 408, 418, 419
Journet, Marcel, 313, 412
Jürgens, Curd, 172, 214

Kael, Pauline, 20n12, 222, 231, 478–82 passim, 489, 493n1
Karina, Anna, 189, 190
Kassovitz, Peter, 193
Kay, Beatrice, 137
Kazan, Elia, 8, 131, 167, 232; *America America*, 197–204
Keaton, Buster, 28
Keepers, The (*La Tête contre les murs*), 35
Kelly, Grace, 353
Kennedy, Arthur, 166, 174, 188
Kind Hearts and Coronets, 43
Kind of Loving, A, 3, 34, 38, 40, 44
King and I, The (1956), 102
King Kong (1933), 26
King of Kings (1961), 94, 107–11, 162, 163–64, 167, 168, 175, 176, 185
Koch, Howard, 315, 393, 395, 397, 410, 412, 425, 426, 428n9
Kojève, Alexandre, 20n13
Kracauer, Siegfried, 29
Kramer, Stanley, 177n3
Krasna, Norman, 103, 104
Kruger, Hardy, 36, 145, 146

Labarthe, André S., 193
Ladd, Alan, 127
Lady in the Lake, 280, 294, 300n27
Ladykillers, The (1955), 43
Laine, Frankie, 351
Lambert, Gavin, 31n1, 32n3
Land of the Pharaohs, 3, 37
Lang, Fritz, 13, 20n15, 27, 29, 35, 89, 268, 278–84 passim, 342; *You Only Live Once*, 459–75
Lang, Walter, 102
Lapsley, Robert, 234–35
Last Laugh, The (*Der letzte Mann*), 28
Late Spring (1949), 299n12
Laughton, Charles, 292, 294, 296
Laura (1944), 114
Laurel, Stan. *See* Laurel and Hardy
Laurel and Hardy, 32n5, 145; Oliver Hardy, 299n6; Stan Laurel, 142

Laurents, Arthur, 240
Lean, David, 71, 126, 410
Lee, Peggy, 350, 351
Left Handed Gun, The, 82
Légaré, Ovila, 366
Leigh, Janet, 96, 98, 226
Lejeune, C. A., 261–62, 264
Let's Make Love, 102–5 passim
Letter from an Unknown Woman (1948), 14, 20n15, 210, 214, 225–26, 229, 374, 384, 392–406, 408–28; the Linz sequence, 311–33
Levant, Oscar, 139
Lewis, Ronald, 44
Liebelei, 226, 263
Liliom (1930), 459
Liliom (1934), 459
Lindfors, Viveca, 167, 171
Lindgren, Ernest, 31n3, 221
Lineup, The, 42
Liszt, Franz, 314, 397
Lockwood, Margaret, 264
Lola (1961), 35, 45
Lola Montès, 229, 250, 330, 399, 441n1, 451–58
Long Duel, The, 67
Look at Life (film series), 80–83n2 passim
Look Back in Anger (1959), 35, 38, 40, 45
Losey, Joseph, 35, 36, 41, 43, 147
Loudest Whisper, The (*The Children's Hour*), 126
Love Me or Leave Me, 102
Love Story (1944), 263–68
Low, Rachael, 32n3
Lubitsch, Ernst, 268, 291
lustige Krieg, Der (*The Merry War*) (operetta), 428
Lusty Men, The, 162, 163, 166, 174, 215, 216, 300n15, 338

M (1931), 475
MacCabe, Colin, 20n13
Mackendrick, Alexander, 3, 43, 46
MacLane, Barton, 278, 472

Madonna of the Seven Moons, 262
"Maggie," The (*High and Dry*), 43
Magic Flute, The (*Il flauto magico / Die Zauberflöte*) (opera), 399, 400, 401, 403, 404
Magnificent Ambersons, The (1942), 27, 155, 156, 209–10, 225, 226, 238n4
Mailer, Norman, 134–35, 137
Malden, Karl, 185, 186, 368, 372
Mankiewicz, Herman J., 337, 338
Mann, Paul, 202
Man of the West, 35
Man Upstairs, The (1958), 50n4
Manvell, Roger, 28, 32n8
Man Who Knew Too Much, The (1956), 127, 154, 160
Man Who Shot Liberty Valance, The, 185–86, 187, 197
Man with the Golden Arm, The, 114
Marcel, Gabriel, 189
Marcorelles, Louis, 162, 177n1
Mark, The, 39
Marley, John, 199
Marlowe, Hugh, 140, 142
Marsh, Linda, 200
Marshall, George, 183n1
Martin, Adrian, 20n14
Martin, Dean, 145
Martinelli, Elsa, 145
Marx Brothers, 232
Mary Burns, Fugitive, 459, 468
Mason, James, 105, 108, 165, 166, 167, 168–69, 171, 174, 251, 408
Mason, Sarah Y., 308n3
Massey, Raymond, 233
Matchmaker, The (1958), 97
Maté, Rudolph, 236
Matthews, A. E., 266
Maugham, W. Somerset, 429–31
Maupassant, Guy de, 429–34 passim, 438, 442–45 passim
May, Elaine, 220
Mayersberg, Paul, 19n1, 129n1
McCambridge, Mercedes, 167, 304, 306, 355

McCarey, Leo, 3, 37, 232
McGilligan, Patrick, 459
McKenna, Siobhan, 108
Meet Me in St. Louis, 127
Ménilmontant (1926), 33n13
Merrill's Marauders, 122–25, 131
Methot, Mayo, 338
Metropolis (1927), 28–29
MGM, 66, 67, 71, 245
Michel, André, 429
Miles, Vera, 97, 248
Milestone, Lewis, 210
Miller, David, 352
Milton, Gerald, 131
Mineo, Sal, 90, 91, 93, 168, 176, 185, 186
Minnelli, Vincente, 88, 185, 212, 221, 484–85
Mitchum, Robert, 116, 163, 171, 216, 217, 292
Mizoguchi, Kenji, 36, 42, 49–50n2, 299n12
Molnar, Ferenc, 459
Monkey Business (1952), 140–43 passim, 145, 146, 232
Monopolies Commission, 64, 66, 68, 71
Monroe, Marilyn, 103, 104, 116, 140, 143
Montand, Yves, 103, 105
Montgomery, Robert, 280
Moon, Lynne Sue, 7, 181
More, Kenneth, 51, 54
Morecambe and Wise, 67
Morlay, Gaby, 435
Movie (journal), 2–9 passim, 17, 19nn1–3, 19nn7–8, 20nn12–13; 395
Movie: A Journal of Film Criticism (journal), 49n1
Moxey, John, 43
Mozart, Wolfgang Amadeus, 14, 316, 392, 397–406 passim, 439, 440, 445–46
Mr. Topaze, 43
Museum of Modern Art, 32n9

My Darling Clementine (1946), 229, 235, 238n4

Nanook of the North, 41
Natanson, Jacques, 432, 442
National Film Archive, 2, 26, 28
National Film Finance Corporation (NFFC), 76–79
National Film Theatre, 26, 28
Navigator, The, 28
Nelson, Ricky, 145
NFFC. *See* National Film Finance Corporation
Nightingale, Timothy, 54
Night Mail (1936), 27, 32n5
Night of the Demon (1957), 3, 37
Night of the Hunter, The, 292, 294–97, 299n6
Night We Dropped a Clanger, The, 42
North, Alex, 185
North by Northwest, 37, 45, 157, 370
Notorious (1946), 228, 232, 263, 300n16, 300n21, 369, 370, 378
No Trams to Lime Street, 36
notte, La, 45
Novak, Kim, 114
Nowell-Smith, Geoffrey, 230
Nowhere to Go, 4, 52
Nuit et brouillard (*Night and Fog*), 192

Odeon, 66
O'Donnell, Cathy, 163
O'Grady, Gerald, 49–50n2
O. Henry's Full House, 139, 429, 430, 441n1
O'Laoghaire, Liam, 32n3
On Dangerous Ground (1951), 338
One Man Mutiny (*The Court-Martial of Billy Mitchell*), 114
Only Angels Have Wings, 146
Only Yesterday (1933), 396, 402, 403
Ophuls, Max, 10, 11, 13, 14–15, 20n15, 210, 211, 214, 218, 225–26, 229, 268, 292, 384, 484; *Caught*, 240–43, 251–55; *Letter from an Unknown*

Woman, 311–33, 392–406, 408–28; Lola Montès, 451–58; *Le Plaisir*–"La Maison Tellier," 442–50; *Le Plaisir*–"The Mask" and "The Model," 429–41
Orry-Kelly, 387
Osterloh, Robert, 360
Oswald, Gerd, 42
Owen, Alun, 36
Oxford Opinion (magazine), 1, 2, 4, 5, 6, 19n2, 25, 32n2
Ozu, Yasujirō, 20n15, 294, 299n12

Pabst, G. W., 27
Page, Geneviève, 103
Pajama Game, The, 104
Parain, Brice, 189, 193, 194
Paramount, 67, 96, 351
Parker, Bonnie, 459
Partie de campagne, 453
Party Girl (1958), 37, 44, 88, 89, 93, 108, 127, 162, 163, 167, 169, 172, 173, 176, 177n1, 211
Passion of Joan of Arc, The (*La Passion de Jeanne d'Arc*), 194
Pat and Mike, 104
Pathé Pictorial (film series), 81, 83n3
Pawnshop, The, 32n5
Penn, Arthur, 82
Pepusch, Johann Christoph, 32n11
Perkins, Anthony, 96, 97–98
Philipe, Gérard, 455
Pickpocket, 191
Pickup on South Street, 122, 130, 131, 132, 133, 137
Pierrot le Fou, 193
Plaisir, Le, 451, 453; "La Maison Tellier," 442–50; "The Mask" and "The Model," 429–41
Platt, Edward, 92
Plummer, Christopher, 92, 93, 163, 169, 171, 172, 175
Poe, Edgar Allan, 195
Poor Cow, 80

posto, Il, 45
Preminger, Otto, 6, 58, 112–13, 126, 129nn2–3, 147, 151, 193; *The Man with the Golden Arm*, 114; *River of No Return*, 116–21
Princess Yang Kwei-Fei, 36
Private Property (1960), 63
Production Code Administration, 336, 367, 402
Psycho (1960), 6, 46, 53, 96–101, 157, 220, 221, 245, 248
Pure Hell of St. Trinian's, The, 50n3

Quadflieg, Will, 452
Quartet (1948), 429–30, 433, 441n1
Quatre cents coups, Les (*The 400 Blows*), 92
Quinn, Anthony, 172
Quinn, James, 32n6
Quo Vadis (1951), 62

Rachmaninov, Sergei, 410
Rains, Claude, 228
Raise the Titanic, 259
Ramsbottom Rides Again, 3, 34
Randall, Tony, 103
Randell, Ron, 109
Rank Organisation, 65–70 passim, 80–81, 83n2, 258
Ransom of Red Chief, The, 139–40
Raphaelson, Samuel, 370
Ray, Nicholas, 3, 6–7, 10, 13, 20n15, 26, 35, 37, 82, 87–95, 127, 143, 162–77, 185, 192, 202, 210–18 passim, 300n15, 300n24, 459; *55 Days at Peking*, 178–83; *In a Lonely Place*, 334–49; *Johnny Guitar*, 304–8, 350–64; *King of Kings*, 107–11
Ray, Robert B., 9, 20n13
Reach for the Sky (1956), 51
Reading, University of, 8
Rear Window (1954), 156
Rebbot, Sady, 190
Rebecca (1940), 215, 414

Rebel Without a Cause, 35, 87–94 passim, 108, 162–70 passim, 173–74, 176, 300n24, 338, 346
Reckless Moment, The, 210, 211, 226, 408
Red River (1948), 145, 146, 148
Règle du jeu, La (*The Rules of the Game*), 212, 453
Reid, Carl Benton, 336
Reisz, Karel, 32n3, 39, 40, 41, 44
Renaud, Madeleine, 444
Renoir, Jean, 20n15, 27, 29, 199, 212, 233, 268, 453
Republic Pictures, 352
Resnais, Alain, 29, 82, 192
Rettig, Tommy, 116
Richardson, Tony, 40, 41, 46
Rio Bravo, 37, 53, 145, 146, 148
Ritter, Tex, 351
River of No Return, 116–21, 193, 351
Rivette, Jacques, 141, 146
Road to Morocco, 292
Robertson, Cliff, 132
Robinson, David, 45
Robinson, Edward G., 187
Robson, Flora, 181
Roc, Patricia, 266
Rogers, Ginger, 141, 341
Rohdie, Sam, 9
Rohmer, Eric, 29, 32n12, 151, 156
Roman de Werther, Le (*The Novel of Werther*), 399
Ronde, La (1950), 292, 442, 455
Room at the Top, 3, 34, 38, 40, 44, 123
Rope, 151–61
Rossellini, Roberto, 29
Rotha, Paul, 29, 42, 261, 262
Rothman, William, 239n7, 247, 300n26
Roud, Richard, 238n1
Rozakis, Gregory, 200
Ruggles, Charles, 140
Run for Cover (1955), 162, 167, 170, 171, 172, 182
Run of the Arrow, 124
Russell, Jane, 361, 362

Rust, Richard, 133
Ryan, Robert, 107, 240

Sale, Chic, 263
Sanshô Dayû, 36, 299n12
Sapphire, 38
Sarris, Andrew, 11, 220, 222–24, 232, 238n2
Saturday Night and Sunday Morning, 38, 41, 44
Savage Innocents, The, 3, 6, 37, 92, 94, 162, 168, 172–76 passim, 178
Saxton, Aaron, 211
Scapegoat, The (1959), 43
Scarface (1932), 146
Scarlet Empress, The, 458
Schlesinger, John, 38, 40
Schlumberger, Guylaine, 191
Schnitzler, Arthur, 455
Schubert, Franz, 397
Schumann, Robert, 399
Screen (journal), 9, 20n13
Secret Partner, The, 42, 45
Sellars, Elizabeth, 182
Sellers, Peter, 43
Sequence (journal), 25, 31n1, 38
Servais, Jean, 430, 431, 434, 436
Sevilla, Carmen, 107
Shadow of a Doubt (1943), 370, 375
Shane, 127, 351, 361
Shivas, Mark, 19n1
Sidney, Sylvia, 278, 459, 460, 471
Siegel, Don, 42
Sight and Sound (magazine), 2, 6, 19n4, 25, 26, 31n1, 32n2, 45, 63n2, 101n1, 478
Simon, Neil, 220
Simon, Simone, 436, 441n1
Sinatra, Frank, 114
Sirk, Douglas, 10, 13, 210, 218, 221, 284, 285, 288, 289, 291, 300n24
Sloan, Jane E., 391n2
Smith, Art, 312, 336, 345, 413, 455
Some Came Running, 212
Some People, 4, 51–60

Song to Remember, A, 102
Song Without End, 102–5 passim
Son of Paleface, 361, 362
Sound of Music, The, 79, 258
Spare the Rod (1961), 38
Sperling, Milton, 337
Splendor in the Grass (1961), 197
Spoto, Donald, 391n1
Stagecoach (1939), 187
Stage Fright (1950), 379
Stahl, John, 396, 402
Staiger, Janet, 246
Stanwyck, Barbara, 284, 289, 301, 302, 358
Star Is Born, A (1954), 104, 105
Stars (*Sterne*), 35
Steel Helmet, The, 122
Stella Dallas (1937), 301–4, 308nn1–4, 358
Sternberg, Josef von, 27, 232, 458
Sterne, Lawrence, 26, 300n14
Stevens, George, 361; *Giant*, 126–29
Stevens, Marti, 39
Stewart, James, 152, 188
Storm over Asia (1928), 26
Strangers on a Train, 216, 299n9, 366, 388
Strasberg, Susan, 44, 45
Strauss, Johann, 255, 398
Strauss, Johann II, 398, 428n8
Strauss, Richard, 395
Street of Shame, The (*Akasen chitai*), 42
Strike (*Stachka*), 32n10
Stroheim, Erich von, 27
Sturges, John, 236
Sudden Fear, 352
Sunset Boulevard, 351
Suspicion, 370
Sutherland, Allan T., 478
Sweet Smell of Success, 43

Tales of Manhattan, 429
Talton, Alix, 336
Tango Tangle, 32n4
Tani, Yoko, 174

Tannhäuser (opera), 398–405 passim
Tashlin, Frank, 26
Taste of Fear (*Scream of Fear*), 3–4, 44–45
Taste of Honey, A, 3, 34, 38, 40
Taylor, A. J. P., 393
Taylor, Elizabeth, 127
Taylor, Henry, 470, 471
Taylor, Robert, 93, 108, 163, 172, 173, 176
They Live by Night, 6, 82, 108, 162, 163, 169, 214, 344, 459
Thing, The (*The Thing from Another World*), 147
Thomas, Deborah, 14, 300n25, 391n1
Thompson, J. Lee, 46
Thompson, Kristin, 486
Thomson, David, 250
Thring, Frank, 107
Tierney, Gene, 353
Times Higher Education Supplement (newspaper), 8
Time Without Pity, 43
Tiomkin, Dmitri, 179, 351, 372, 376
Tobacco Road, 235
To Be or Not to Be (1942), 291–92, 300n25
Todd, Ann, 45
Tom Jones (1963), 79
Torch Song, 352, 353
Torn, Rip, 108
Touch of Evil, 19n7, 156, 226–27
Tourneur, Jacques, 3, 35, 37
Toutain, Roland, 212
Towne, Gene, 459
Tracy, Spencer, 214
Trevelyan, John, 4, 61, 62
Trevor-Roper, H. R., 395, 396
Trio, 429, 441n1
Trois Femmes, 429, 433
Trouble with Harry, The, 98
True Story of Jesse James, The (*The James Brothers*), 162, 163, 165, 166
Truffaut, François, 92, 365, 366, 375, 381, 387, 433

Turner, Lana, 353
Twentieth Century Fox, 66, 102, 139, 429, 430, 459
2001: A Space Odyssey, 80
Two Weeks in Another Town, 185

Ugetsu Monogatari, 36, 42
Ulmer, Edgar G., 42
Underworld U.S.A., 61, 130–38
Ustinov, Peter, 454

Valère, Jean, 451–52, 453
Van Fleet, Jo, 202
Vaughan, Frankie, 103, 104
Verboten!, 122, 130, 131
Vertigo, 35, 97, 157, 221, 238n3, 369, 375
Victim (1961), 35, 38
Vidor, Charles, 102
Vidor, King, 180; *Stella Dallas*, 301–4, 308nn1–4
Vikings, The, 178
Violent Playground, 51
Visconti, Luchino, 268
Vivre sa vie, 61, 189–95
Vizzard, Jack, 403

Wagner, Richard, 14, 104, 398–99, 401, 404–6
Wagner, Robert, 163
Walbrook, Anton, 453
Waldis, Otto, 421
Walker, Robert, 366
Walls, Tom, 266
Walsh, Raoul, 35, 127, 173, 202
Walters, Charles, 352
Waltz of the Toreadors, 43
Wanger, Walter, 459
Warner Bros., 66, 185, 365, 377
Warwick, Robert, 340
Warwick, University of, 8, 19n10, 20n11, 20n15, 263
Washington, Ned, 351
Watt, Harry, 32n5
Wayne, John, 145, 148, 149

Welles, Orson, 19n7, 20n15, 27, 29, 82, 88, 154, 156, 202, 209, 210, 225–27, 238n4; *Citizen Kane*, 270–77, 284, 289
Wendkos, Paul, 42
Westlake, Michael, 234–35
What Ever Happened to Baby Jane?, 353
Whirlpool, 193
White, Susan M., 428n8
Who Was That Lady?, 103
Wicked Lady, The (1945), 262
Widmark, Richard, 133, 186, 187
Wilcox, Fred M., 40
Wilde, Cornel, 168
Wilder, Billy, 27, 410
Wild River, 197
Wild Strawberries (*Smultronstället*), 36
Wills, Anneke, 54
Wilson, George M., 239n7, 247, 299n3, 415, 460, 486
Wind Across the Everglades, 89, 92, 93, 110, 162, 163, 164, 169, 172–75 passim
Windell, George G., 398
Winslow, George, 140, 142
Winters, Shelley, 127
Wisdom, Norman, 67
Wiseman, Frederick, 15, 19n5; *High School*, 477–93
Witchfinder General, 79
Wittgenstein, Ludwig, 20n13
Wizard of Oz, The (1939), 11, 244–45, 247, 284, 300n23, 463
Wolfe, Ian, 214
Wolff, Janet, 260
Wolf Trap, The (*Vlčí jáma*), 35, 123
Wollen, Peter, 10, 224–35, 238n6
Woman's Secret, A, 337
Wong Howe, James, 102
Wood, Natalie, 90, 91, 168
Wood, Robin, 49n1, 101n1, 311
Woodfall, 38, 39, 40
Wright, Basil, 32n5, 33nn14–15
Wright, Frank Lloyd, 89

Wright Wexman, Virginia, 404, 427n2, 428n8
Written on the Wind, 46, 210, 221, 300n24
Wrong Man, The (1956), 96, 160, 238n3
Wyler, William, 126, 127, 154

Yordan, Philip, 109, 308n6
Young, Victor, 306, 350, 358

Young Mr. Lincoln, 235
Young Ones, The (1961), 51
You Only Live Once (1937), 13, 278–83, 459–75

Zauberflöte, Die. See *Magic Flute, The*
Ziehrer, Carl Michael, 398, 422
Zinnemann, Fred, 126, 127
Zweig, Stefan, 314–16, 392–96 passim, 401, 403, 413, 416

V. F. Perkins (1936–2016) was Honorary Professor of Film at the University of Warwick. His publications included *Film as Film* (1972) and the volumes on *The Magnificent Ambersons* (1999) and *La Règle du jeu* (2012) in the British Film Institute Film Classics series. He was a founder editor of *Movie*, the journal in which much of his film criticism was published, and a member of the editorial board of its successor, *Movie: A Journal of Film Criticism*.

Douglas Pye is senior visiting research fellow in the Department of Film, Theatre & Television at the University of Reading. His publications include *The Long Take: Critical Approaches* and *Style and Meaning: Studies in the Detailed Analysis of Film* (both co-edited with John Gibbs), *100 Film Musicals* (with Jim Hillier), and *Movies and Tone*. He co-edits the series Palgrave Close Readings in Film and Television and is a member of the editorial board of *Movie: A Journal of Film Criticism*.